Canadian Policing

Second Edition

Canadian Policing

Colin S. Campbell
John Cater
Nahanni Pollard

OXFORD
UNIVERSITY PRESS

Oxford University Press is a department of the University of Oxford.
It furthers the University's objective of excellence in research, scholarship,
and education by publishing worldwide. Oxford is a registered trade mark of
Oxford University Press in the UK and in certain other countries.

Published in Canada by
Oxford University Press
8 Sampson Mews, Suite 204,
Don Mills, Ontario M3C 0H5 Canada

www.oupcanada.com

Library and Archives Canada Cataloguing in Publication
Title: Canadian policing / Colin Campbell, John Cater, Nahanni Pollard.
Names: Campbell, Colin, 1948- author. | Cater, John, 1967- author. | Pollard, Nahanni, 1977- author.
Description: Second edition. | Includes bibliographical references and index.
Identifiers: Canadiana (print) 20200403362 | Canadiana (ebook) 20200403443 | ISBN 9780199036493
(softcover) | ISBN 9780199036523 (EPUB)
Subjects: LCSH: Police—Canada—Textbooks. | LCGFT: Textbooks.
Classification: LCC HV8158.5 .C36 2021 | DDC 363.2/30971—dc23

Cover images: (clockwise from left) © Mariemily Photos/Shutterstock,
© ACHPF/Shutterstock, © Sevenstock Studio/Shutterstock, annedehaas/© iStock.
Cover design: Laurie McGregor
Interior design: Sherill Chapman

Oxford University Press is committed to our environment.
Wherever possible, our books are printed on paper which comes from
responsible sources.

Printed and bound in the United States of America

1 2 3 4 — 24 23 22 21

DEDICATED TO:

Brodie Osborne-Campbell
(1991–2007)
Ne Obliviscaris

Jocelyn Marie and Meaghan Joy

Beatrice and Noah

Contents

Part I • Background and Current Framework of Policing in Canada

7   Performance Measurement   125

Part III • On the Job as an Officer

8   Patrol   146

9   Investigations   168

Part IV • Current Trends and Challenges

Publisher's Preface

Contemporary Coverage of Policing in Canada

Written by an impressive author team with experience from the field, research, and teaching, *Canadian Policing,* second edition, examines the most up-to-date research and theories of policing as well as on-the-ground implementation to give students a well-rounded, realistic understanding of policing in Canada. This down-to-earth introduction incorporates extensive features and material designed to make the text engaging and thought-provoking for students and instructors alike. The following exciting and helpful features make this book one of a kind.

15

National Security Policing in the Twenty-First Century

Learning Objectives
After reading and studying this chapter, students will be able to:

- List and describe the major violent confrontations that challenged police and political authorities in Canada during the twentieth century.
- Review and discuss the history of the RCMP's involvement in security and intelligence.
- Describe and assess the historically controversial national security issues reviewed in this chapter.
- Review and discuss the circumstances of the creation of CSIS in 1984.
- Assess the recent changes to law and policy in regard to policing terrorism in the twenty-first century in Canada.
- Identify and discuss the Canadian agencies sharing responsibility for security and intelligence.
- Apply and discuss the notions of risk and risk society to Canadian perceptions of and responses to terrorist threats.
- Describe and discuss securitization.

Introduction
On 11 September 2001, 19 militants associated with Al-Qaeda, an Islamic extremist group, hijacked four passenger aircraft and crashed them in suicide attacks against several targets in the United States, including the twin towers of the World Trade Center in New York and the Pentagon near Washington, DC. The fourth plane crashed in a field in Pennsylvania. Millions of horrified viewers around the world watched the attacks on the World Trade

Case Study

High-Profile Injustices

The many incidents of inadequate and inequitable treatment of Indigenous Peoples in recent history at the hands of police and other criminal justice officials are too numerous to discuss in detail here. It is, however, instructive to be reminded of the following partial list of events, conflicts, and circumstances:

- the federal Residential School program of forcefully relocating Indigenous children from their homes to boarding schools operated by Christian churches from 1831 to 1996;
- "The Highway of Tears Murders"—since 1970 women, many of whom are Indigenous, have been reported missing and murdered along Highway 16 (the Yellowhead Highway) in Northern British Columbia;
- the wrongful conviction for murder in 1971 of Mi'kmaq First Nations youth Donald Marshall;
- the brutal murder of Indigenous high school student Helen Betty Osborne near The Pas, Manitoba, in 1971 and the inept investigation that followed;
- the Winnipeg police shooting of Indigenous leader J.J. Harper in 1988;
- the Oka Crisis (July to September 1990) land title dispute that resulted in an armed stand-off between Oka Mohawks and the Sûreté du Québec (later replaced by the RCMP and the Canadian army);
- the Ipperwash Provincial Park, Ontario, 1995 land title dispute leading to an armed confrontation between Ojibwa members and the OPP that resulted in the shooting death of Dudley George by an OPP officer;

- the 1998 death of Mi'kmaq First Nations man Frank Joseph Paul as a result of being in police custody in Vancouver;
- the "Starlight Tours" and freezing deaths of Rodney Nastius, Lawrence Wegner, and Neil Stonechild in Saskatoon, Saskatchewan, between 1990 and 2000;
- the "Winnipeg 911 Murders"—in February 2000 two Indigenous sisters were murdered despite five calls to 911 over a six-hour period; the police dispatcher neglected to take the sisters' calls for help seriously;
- "Forsaken"—the missing and murdered women in Vancouver's Downtown Eastside between 1997 and 2002, many of whom are believed to have been victims of convicted serial killer Robert Pickton; and
- the January 2005 shooting of 18-year-old Indigenous youth Matthew Dumas by Winnipeg police.

The above listing is a select cataloguing of the relatively high-profile injustices that Indigenous persons have experienced throughout the twentieth century and into the twenty-first. Citations of specific references to these incidents are intentionally omitted. Readers are encouraged to choose key words and use any internet search engine to locate the numerous studies, official reports, discussions, and media coverage that have been generated in the aftermath of these matters. As a whole, the examples listed above provide vivid representations of the long history of conflict between Indigenous Peoples and Canadian authorities; they also stand as examples of both under-policing and over-policing of Indigenous Peoples within Canada.

Applied Approach

Policing and its challenges are presented in an understandable and practical way, providing insights that students can apply to their future careers in the criminal justice system.

In 2020, protests against systemic racism and the disproportionate number of deaths of Black people at the hands of police took place worldwide, including in several cities in Canada. (Pictured is one of the protests in Edmonton.) How important is it to the functioning of a police department that it have a good relationship with the community it serves?

those living in high-crime areas, and those who are most fearful for their safety tend to hold negative views of the police (Cotter 2015, 15). Public opinion surveys shape police practices and public policies (O'Connor 2008, 578).

In fast-paced life in modern North America, the need to have immediate access to information dominates (see discussion to follow on body-worn cameras). In recent years, largely due to the internet, the speed of modern communications, and the extensive use of mobile cellular devices, police encounters with the public can be recorded and made instantly available to mass audiences. It is all too easy for the public to form immediate opinions based solely on what they see on television or in social media or read in popular tabloid newspapers like the *Calgary Sun*, *Toronto Sun*, or Vancouver's *The Province*. A picture of an event paints a thousand words (particularly when brought to life with a few seconds of amateur video and posted online) and allows many people to reach emotional conclusions about situations even though the complete context is not conveyed. Given the media rule of thumb "if it bleeds, it leads," particularly if police actions are called into question, public reaction can be swift and vitriolic.

Increasingly, much of what the public knows about the police is based on a seemingly limitless barrage of mainstream and social media. Much media coverage focuses on what the police appear to have done wrong as opposed to what they have done right. Coverage

Thought-Provoking Visuals

Carefully chosen photos and captions encourage students to consider how what they are learning will apply to their future careers.

Police officers watch over the harbour district of Vancouver from the water. What unique elements of policing on bodies of water do you think might require special training?

Case Studies and Critical Viewpoints

Provocative chapter-opening case studies, critical perspectives incorporated throughout, Case Study and Challenge Your Assumption feature boxes, and end-of-chapter Critical Thinking questions all work together to encourage readers to adopt a critical viewpoint, and to challenge them to consider not just how the criminal justice system currently functions, but how it can be improved.

Case Study Boxes

Case Study boxes in each chapter highlight real investigations, studies, or hypothetical situations and encourage students to consider the case or situation critically.

Challenge Your Assumptions Boxes

Challenge Your Assumptions boxes in each chapter present students with facts or scenarios that might go against their preconceptions of policing, and that correct any misapprehensions they may hold.

Canadian Policing is part of a comprehensive package of learning and teaching tools that includes resources for both students and instructors.

For Instructors

- An **implementation guide** includes sample course outlines and content mapping to seamlessly integrate the text into your existing course materials.
- A comprehensive **instructor's manual** provides an extensive set of pedagogical tools and suggestions for every chapter, including overviews, debate questions, class assignments and activities, and links to relevant videos and online teaching aids with discussion questions for each resource.
- Classroom-ready **PowerPoint slides** summarize key points from each chapter and incorporate graphics and tables drawn straight from the text.
- An extensive **test bank** offers hundreds of questions in multiple-choice, true–false, and short-answer formats.

For Students

- The **Student Study Guide** includes a summary of key concepts in each chapter, self-grading quizzes, and further recommended readings and websites with annotation to help students further their knowledge on the concepts presented in each chapter.

www.oup.com/he/Campbell2e

Authors' Preface

As was noted in the first edition of this text, the three of us have taught courses on Canadian policing for more years than we care to remember. In our teaching practices, we have brought our distinctive perspectives to the classroom and offered our students an opportunity to learn from our various experiences. Through our discussions and collaborations with each other, we realized that we wished to have an instructional textbook that better fit the direction in which we wanted to take our students. Ultimately, the best way to do that was to write a textbook that represents the aspects of policing in Canada that we have come to view as essential for undergraduate students to understand.

The second edition continues to build on base information with a deeper foray into aspects of modern policing beyond traditional patrol work and into the increasing role and contributions of crime analysis, national security police work, and critical discussions on police–media relations and the economics of policing. The second edition adds an updated discussion of the challenges to policing presented by Canadian diversity. Specifically, considerable attention is directed at the challenges for both the police (and Canadian society as a whole) in responding appropriately to the historical injustices that have characterized the criminal justice system's relationship with Indigenous Peoples in Canada.

As with the first edition, this edition of *Canadian Policing* has been written as a hybrid text that seeks to engage undergraduate students at the introductory level as well as more advanced students in upper-level criminology, policing studies, legal studies, human justice, and sociology of crime and deviance courses. The text is intended to provide a comprehensive cutting-edge overview of practices, perspectives, initiatives, and policies that inform modern Canadian policing. The target audience is primarily undergraduate university and college students, many of whom who will aspire to become police officers or to work elsewhere within the criminal justice system. The text will also be of interest to police practitioners and to policymakers.

The second edition of this textbook is neither an anthology of existing articles nor a product of original research. Rather, *Canadian Policing* relies on existing academic studies and on a range of grey literature sources—that is, literature and studies drawn from in-house policing and other government agency reports. Efforts were made to draw upon Canadian data. The text is both descriptive and analytical, and addresses contemporary policing issues as well as future challenges. Research findings, contemporary practices and, where appropriate, theoretical perspectives are discussed in an analytical yet readable and comprehensible manner. Indeed, the overall strengths of the text lie in the contemporary applied content and the highly readable style that will appeal to undergraduate students.

Perhaps one of the more distinctive features of this textbook is its authorship, as the three co-authors combine a wealth of teaching, research, advisory, and practical experience in policing. Indeed, one of the authors, Staff Sergeant John Cater, had over twenty-seven years of experience as a senior investigator with the Royal Canadian Mounted Police before retiring to become a full-time instructor at Douglas College. He holds an MA in criminology. He is an experienced post-secondary instructor and is highly regarded within the policing community for the many in-service training programs he has taught. The other two authors hold Ph.D.s in criminology; Nahanni Pollard has extensive experience in conducting research on contemporary policing issues and was a member of the Provincial Municipal Policing Transition Committee, chaired by Wally Oppal, tasked with examining the plan to establish the Surrey Municipal Police Department. Colin Campbell had over 30 years of teaching post-secondary courses in criminology before retiring as *Faculty Emeritus* at Douglas College.

Acknowledgements

We would like to extend our gratitude to the reviewers of the previous edition, and of the manuscript stages of the new edition of our book: Mehmet Bastug (Lakehead University); Shafik Bhalloo (Simon Fraser University); Galib Bhayani (Kwantlen Polytechnic University); Nitin Deckha (University of Guelph-Humber); Michael Fleming (St. Thomas University); Carson Fougere (Nipissing University); Doug King (Mount Royal University); Keiron McConnell (Kwantlen Polytechnic University); Julien Pelletier (University of Ottawa); as well as those who chose to remain anonymous.

Additionally, we are particularly appreciative of the efforts and goodwill of our colleagues at Oxford University Press including Acquisitions Editor, Ian Nussbaum, and our conscientious and hard-working Developmental Editor, Amy Gordon. Amy's suggestions and sage advice have added immeasurably to the discussion of diversity presented in Chapter 3. As well, and most certainly, we have benefited from the diligent and skillful copy editing of Susan Bindernagel.

Nahanni Pollard extends her immense appreciation to the numerous police officers she has worked with over the years for expanding her understanding of the profession, and for being such positive ambassadors. In particular, she wishes to thank Deputy Chief Leslie Stevens of the Port Moody Police Department; and, Superintendent Michelle Davey, and Chief Constable Adam Palmer of the Vancouver Police Department. It was, and continues to be, a pleasure and an honour. And to Dr. Curt Griffiths, thank you for being so generous with your wisdom and friendship.

John Cater recognizes his many peers and mentors in the policing and criminal justice community. To serve the public as a police officer is a tough, challenging, but rewarding career. "The key to a successful career in policing is to commit to making other police officers around you better than you ever were." He thanks his family for their unconditional love and support.

Colin Campbell extends his appreciation to former students, now respected friends, for their willingness over many years to join his classes as guest lecturers: S/Sgt. Stuart Jette of the New Westminster Police and Sgt. Mike Wheeler of the Vancouver Police Department.

PART I

Background and
Current Framework
of Policing in Canada

1

The Context of Policing in Canada in the Twenty-First Century

Learning Objectives

After reading and studying this chapter, students will be able to:

- Describe what public policing means.
- Differentiate between policing as an organization and policing as a process.
- Identify and discuss the forces shaping the transformation of policing.
- Describe and discuss what the crime complex entails.
- Describe and discuss how the crime complex affects policing.
- Describe the structure and levels of policing in Canada.
- Identify and discuss First Nations policing arrangements.
- Identify and discuss the concerns about the blurring of lines between private security agencies and the public police.

Introduction

Chapter 1 begins with a discussion of the concept of policing and how it is evolving. Subsequently, this chapter provides an overview of the various forces currently buffeting Canadian policing. As well, a quick overview of two competing perspectives on the roles and functions of law and policing is provided.

Chapter 1 also provides a brief history of Canadian policing before considering the various levels of policing evident in Canada: federal, provincial, regional, municipal, and First Nations. The chapter concludes with a brief consideration of the blurring of the lines between public police and private security personnel.

The Concept of Policing

For most Canadians, policing is taken for granted. It also conjures relatively simple stereo-typical images of armed uniformed officers, wearing trousers with red or blue or yellow stripes, patrolling communities in marked cars decked with emergency equipment for the broad purpose of serving and protecting the public. In reality, however, policing in the early decades of the twenty-first century is increasingly rife with complexity.

Public Policing

This textbook is principally concerned with **public policing**. Notwithstanding the emergence of a series of interrelated transformations that are reshaping modern policing and that have led to what several authors have referred to as a policing identity crisis, this textbook is focused on public police officers who are employed, trained, and paid by the state[i] and whose principal mandate is to enforce state laws (Seagrave 1997, 2). Two key characteristics identify public police. The first of these is that the police are distinct from

Case Study

A Current Canadian Snapshot

In Canada in 2018 there were 68,562 public police officers, representing a ratio of 185 police officers per 100,000 population. Women police officers numbered 14,943 and accounted for 22 per cent of all police officers. In 1986, when data was first collected, women comprised 4 per cent of all police officers. Women also represented 15 per cent of commissioned officers in 2018—the highest proportion on record (Conor, Robson, and Marcellus 2019). Police services also employed 26,851 civilians (Conor, Robson, and Marcellus 2019).

According to Conor, Robson, and Marcellus, in 2018 Indigenous persons made up approximately 5.0 per cent of the Canadian population and made up 4 per cent of police officers.

In 2018, visible minorities (not including Indigenous persons) made up 22 per cent of the Canadian population and represented 8 per cent of all police officers (Conor, Robson, and Marcellus 2019).

Across Canada, total expenditures on police services amounted to $15.1 billion dollars. Salaries, wages, and benefits accounted for 82 per cent or $12.5 billion of this total. In 2018, the average annual police salary was approximately $99,000. (See Chapter 11 for further discussion of policing costs.)

According to Rigakos and Leung (2006), the five largest police agencies in Canada (the Royal Canadian Mounted Police [RCMP], the Toronto Police Service, the Ontario Provincial Police [OPP], the Sûreté du Québec [SQ], and the Montreal Urban Community Police) account for 60 per cent of all Canadian public police.

Do these statistics reflect your expectations of diversity and distribution of police forces? Take a moment to think about why these facts might matter to individual police forces, to policing in Canada, and to different communities.

other government agencies in that they are legally authorized to use coercive force in the course of their duties. The other is that police are non-military, albeit historically embracing a militaristic-bureaucratic hierarchical chain of command.

Jane Seagrave (1997) provides the following definition: "The police can be defined as non-military individuals or organizations who are given the general right by government to use coercive force to enforce the law and whose primary purpose is to respond to problems of individual and group conflict that involves illegal behaviour" (Seagrave 1997, 2).

Police or Policing?

As R.I. Mawby has pointed out, there are significant differences between policing as an "organization" and policing as a "process" (Mawby 2008, 17). Historically, much academic attention was directed toward seeing and understanding policing as an organization—or as a series of collaborating organizations—dedicated to

- protecting the public from criminals;
- providing general assistance in time of need; and
- maintaining order and preserving the peace.

This conception of the police is perhaps best captured in the colourful words of Egon Bittner, who suggested that police organizations are typically called upon to act when situations in which "something-that-ought-not-to-be-happening-and-about-which-someone-had-better-do-something-now" are transpiring (Bittner 1974, 249, cited in Brodeur 2010, 104).

Policing

In the early twenty-first century, however, a multitude of interrelated factors have combined to dramatically alter police organizations. Scholars who have identified these transformations no longer view policing as an organization or as a series of organizations. Rather, they see policing as a process in which a myriad of individuals (including volunteer members of the public and victims), government agencies, organizations, partnerships, and private-sector corporations combine, both domestically and transnationally, to mitigate and prevent threats to security, including those posed by criminals. Ian Loader, for example, has described this change in the conception of policing as "a shift from *police* to *policing*" (Loader 2000, 323, emphasis in original). In many respects, this shift has represented an identity crisis for police as organizations (Bayley and Shearing 1996, 592).

Forces Shaping Early Twenty-First-Century Policing

A range of interrelated forces have shaped and continue to reshape the policing process. A brief description of these forces is in order.

Perhaps foremost of these forces is the general recognition by the public, government, and the police themselves of the limited ability of police and the traditional components of the state criminal justice system (such as the courts and the correctional system) to prevent crime and to ensure security (see Chapter 12). Modern policing is now less "a crime-fighting force than a responsive public service, aiming to reduce fear, disorder and incivility and to take account of community feelings in setting enforcement priorities" (Garland 2001, 18). Relevant here is the overall increase of police selectivity with respect to which calls for service they will respond to. In the not-so-distant past, police would respond to almost all calls for service. However, as part of cost-saving resource allocation measures, alongside the realization that police are unlikely to be able to provide a meaningful intervention anyway, police now routinely select which calls will be attended. For example, in many jurisdictions, car burglaries and other relatively minor property crimes no longer warrant police attendance. Rather, victims and complainants are merely provided with a file number for insurance purposes. No police officers are dispatched.

Accompanying the recognition of the state's inability to prevent crime has been the widespread mobilization of **community policing** (discussed in greater detail in Chapter 12). Since the 1970s, western police agencies have actively solicited and fostered the involvement of communities through the deployment of a range of crime prevention issues such as block watch or neighbourhood watch (Garland 2001, 126). Garland has referred to the development of these initiatives as "responsibilization strategies" that entail extending the reach of state agencies (like the police) and linking them to the community. In short, responsibilization strategies seek to activate a range of non-state actors, including citizens and private interests, in an extended network of informal controls that complement the formal controls of the state (Garland 2001, 124). In simple terms, a partnership of citizens, community groups, and private interests are encouraged by the police to take responsibility for ensuring the safety and security of their communities. In many respects, this has signalled an end to the state monopoly of formal controls exercised primarily through the police and traditional criminal justice systems.

The demise of the state monopoly over crime and public security has also been facilitated by the dramatically increased involvement of for-profit private-sector companies that provide a range of crime prevention services, security functions, and security products (such as closed-circuit TV monitoring systems for homes or businesses) to a host of clients, including individuals, corporations, and government agencies. According to Shearing and Stenning (1987), the emergence of "mass private property"—privately owned properties such as office towers, high-rise apartments, immense shopping centres, sporting stadiums, and other sites routinely inhabited for varying durations by multitudes of persons—has spurred a significant need for security and protection services. Private-sector security personnel and security companies, as a result, have proliferated to provide surveillance and security services on these privately owned and managed properties.

Private security firms are also deeply involved in the manufacture and marketing of security technology. Private-sector security companies make and distribute a diverse array of security products ranging from conducted energy weapons (CEWs; more infamously known as the Taser), to razor wire, to X-ray booths in airports (Brodeur 2010, 278–88). Of course, state agencies, including the police, are the biggest consumers of security technology.

The meaning and impact of the exponential growth of private security will be further addressed later in this chapter. What is to be noted at this point is that private policing agencies are not simply replacing public police but that public police agencies are both divesting responsibilities to the private-sector interests and forging partnerships with them for the purpose of extending surveillance and security (see also Chapter 15).

An additional factor reshaping public policing is the growing concern at municipal, provincial, and federal levels of government of the financial cost of policing services. The economics of policing are given greater consideration in Chapter 11. Certainly Canadian public police are increasingly under pressure to convince government leaders that costs are justifiable in terms of greater protection, security, and overall service. This, in turn, has compelled police administrators to give a new priority to the type of performance management indicators and measures embraced by private-sector corporations. These matters are subsequently considered in Chapter 7. And, of course, the reliance on unpaid volunteers from the public (including the use of unarmed but uniformed police "auxiliaries"), community groups, and comparatively lower-priced private security firms allow for the maintenance of surveillance and protection services without appreciably eroding police budgets.

Another influence responsible for changing the face of policing in the twenty-first century is that of technology, particularly the use of computers and the reliance on massive information data banks. Although technological developments (for example, the advent of automobiles and wireless communication) have always had a profound impact on the nature and delivery of policing services, in the first decades of the twenty-first century public police reliance on a variety of digital technologies is having an even more profound influence on how public police do business (see Chapter 10 for a discussion of digital forensics). As Ericson and Haggerty noted, "Patrol officers now patrol the beat with a keyboard, rather than a nightstick in hand" (Ericson and Haggerty 1997, 10).

Another discernable change affecting police agencies is a general rethinking of the traditional quasi-military hierarchical command structure that characterized policing through the twentieth century. With the increased emphasis on community policing initiatives, front-line police officers have been afforded greater responsibility, autonomy, and discretion in their interactions with members of the public. This development coincides with the recognition that the rigid command-and-control structure of military-style leadership (in which junior ranks are required to follow orders from those in higher ranks), may no longer be compatible with twenty-first century human resource management practices. Indeed, some advocates of community policing have called for a "flattening-out" of the rank structure and for more egalitarian relationships among members.

Although police-reported crime in Canada increased for the fourth consecutive year in 2018, the rate was nevertheless 17 per cent lower than a decade earlier (Moreau 2019), Thus, in a period during which there has been a demonstrable reduction of reported crime, the persistence of high levels of fear of crime held by the general public—particularly the middle class—has constituted a quandary for police. A complete explanation of high levels of fear of crime is complicated, involving a constellation of social, economic, political, and cultural influences that shape public beliefs and anxieties about crime and criminals.

Garland (2001) has pointed out how media representations of sensational, extraordinary, and atypical crimes shape public consciousness about crime in general. Many Canadians are well aware of such high-profile criminal events in Canada as the multiple murders of young women perpetrated by convicted serial killer Robert "Willie" Pickton; the "Surrey Six" executions in British Columbia by organized crime gang members; the killing and dismembering of Greyhound Bus passenger Tim McLean in Manitoba by Vince Li; and the first-degree murder conviction of Luka Magnotta, who killed and dismembered his victim, posted video recordings of the killing to the internet, and mailed body parts through Canada Post. More recently, Canadians were shocked by convicted landscaper Bruce McArthur who, between 2010 and 2017, serially murdered eight men, most of whom had ties to Toronto's gay community. Sensational, emotionally charged cases like these shape Canadian perceptions and attitudes toward crime in general. As a result, Canadian anxieties about crime run high. In turn, political leaders exploit these anxieties in an effort to win votes by demonstrating their responsiveness to public fears and by promising to introduce more punitive measures for all criminal activities, including terrorist activities. (See Chapters 14 and 15.)

David Garland has suggested that the constellation of issues that frame the public's perceptions of high crime rates and consequent fears can be termed the **crime complex** (Garland 2001, 163). The crime complex is characterized by a distinctive cluster of attitudes, beliefs, and assumptions:

i)   high crime rates are regarded as a normal social fact;
ii)   emotional investment in crime is widespread and intense, encompassing elements of fascination as well as fear, anger, and resentment;
iii) crime issues are politicized and regularly represented in emotive terms;
iv)   concerns about victims and public safety dominate public policy;
v)   the criminal justice state is viewed as inadequate or ineffective;
vi)   private, defensive routines are widespread and there is a large market for security;
vii) a crime consciousness is institutionalized in the media, popular culture, and the built environment (Garland 2001, 163).

It is within the context of this crime complex that police find themselves in a quandary, seeking meaningful and acceptable ways to respond to public fears and searching for alternative strategies beyond the now widely discredited reactive response strategy of traditional policing. Today's police have reconsidered the effectiveness of the traditional practice of waiting for crimes to be reported before reacting. Instead, police have turned to community policing and a host of proactive crime prevention initiatives. (See Chapter 12.)

The Origin of Policing in Canada

Not surprisingly, Canadian police institutions—as with the Canadian system of parliamentary democracy that will be reviewed in Chapter 2— reflect those of Great Britain.

The British Model of Policing

According to Brodeur (2010), there are competing accounts of the development of policing in Great Britain. One account holds that the creation of public police was a solution to the property crime and social disorder that prevailed in London in the late eighteenth and early nineteenth centuries. This account also suggests that the development of police was welcomed by all segments of society. Conversely, a competing account holds that there was considerable resistance to the development of a non-militarized civilian police force. A standing force was viewed with considerable suspicion and apprehension by wealthy, propertied classes.

In the nineteenth century, social conditions in major European cities were creating considerable political tension. In London, existing law enforcement was diverse and fragmented among the night watch, constables, and thief-takers—essentially unscrupulous bounty hunters who, for a reward, would aid in the apprehension of thieves and the recovery of stolen property. Brodeur suggests that thief-takers were a "tainted interface" between criminals and law enforcement (Brodeur 2010, 59). However, in a primitive sense, thief-takers also represented a symbiotic relationship between public authorities and private entrepreneurs. Subsequently, thief-takers illustrated the extent to which police depended on informers to detect and apprehend criminals (Brodeur 2010, 59). As will be discussed in Chapter 9, police utilization of confidential informers is an essential component of contemporary policing.

The creation of the London Metropolitan Police in 1829 irrevocably altered the meaning of the word "police" (Brodeur 2010, 62). Similar to the use of the word "police" in France, police had previously referred to governance or regulation of a territory. That is, the word "police" initially referred to a self-contained system that possessed the attributes of government: legislative, regulatory, judicial, and executive powers. In England, the scope of these powers was narrowed to limit the capacity of the police to apprehending offenders and presenting them to the judiciary for a determination of criminal guilt and to addressing matters related to national security and order. In England, therefore, the word "police" became used to refer to a body of men entrusted with policing duties such as providing protection and security, preventing crime, and apprehending criminals (Brodeur 2010, 63).

From its inception, the London Metropolitan Police was, even by today's standards, a police force of some significance.

> . . . [T]he police force created by Sir Robert Peel in 1829 . . . [was] originally led by two commissioners . . . [and consisted of] 17 superintendents, 68 inspectors, 318 sergeants, and 2892 police constables. . . . The men wore the same blue uniform, designed to contrast with that of the military, and were armed with only a wooden truncheon. Cutlasses were available under special circumstances and members with the rank of inspector and above could carry pocket pistols. [Brodeur 2010, 63]

The founding figure of the London Metropolitan Police, in an effort to win broader public support for the inauguration of a standing non-military police agency, articulated a series of nine guiding principles to govern the police–public relationship. The Peelian Principles stand today as guiding principles for most modern western democratic police agencies. (See Challenge Your Assumptions.)

The Canadian Experience

Given the geographic vastness of Canada, the implementation and delivery of policing services posed and continues to pose challenges. The establishment of large populations in Upper and Lower Canada (now Ontario and Quebec respectively) led to the development of

Challenge Your Assumptions

Sir Robert Peel's Principles

Although now almost 200 years old, the nine principles, generally attributed to Sir Robert Peel, stand today as modern axioms for many western democratic police agencies. Police leaders often invoke references to the principles as reminders of what good policing should strive for. See, for example, the website of the Ottawa Police Service: https://www.ottawapolice.ca/en/index.aspx

Peelian Principle 1 — The basic mission for which the police exist is to prevent crime and disorder.

Peelian Principle 2 — The ability of the police to perform their duties is dependent upon public approval of police actions.

Peelian Principle 3 — Police must secure the willing co-operation of the public in voluntary observance of the law to be able to secure and maintain the respect of the public.

Peelian Principle 4 — The degree of co-operation of the public that can be secured diminishes proportionately to the necessity of the use of physical force.

Peelian Principle 5 — Police seek and preserve public favour not by catering to the public opinion but by constantly demonstrating absolute impartial service to the law.

Peelian Principle 6 — Police use physical force to the extent necessary to secure observance of the law or to restore order only when the exercise of persuasion, advice and warning is found to be insufficient.

Peelian Principle 7 — Police, at all times, should maintain a relationship with the public that gives reality to the historic tradition that the police are the public and the public are the police; the police being only members of the public who are paid to give full-time attention to duties which are incumbent on every citizen in the interests of community welfare and existence.

Peelian Principle 8 — Police should always direct their action strictly towards their functions and never appear to usurp the powers of the judiciary.

Peelian Principle 9 — The test of police efficiency is the absence of crime and disorder, not the visible evidence of police action in dealing with it.

Source: Ottawa Police Service, https://www.ottawapolice.ca/en/about-us/Peel-s-Principles-.aspx

Is there anything in Peel's principles that surprises you? Do you feel that these principles have relevance for modern policing? Are any principles outdated given the modern public's expectations of police?

police institutions that most resembled the English model (Brodeur 2010, 75). In 1670, the Hudson's Bay Company had been granted a monopoly by the British Crown over trading rights in the vast northwestern territory known as **Rupert's Land**. In 1870, Rupert's Land was sold by the Hudson's Bay Company to the Government of Canada (Ray, 2009). With the acquisition of this territory, settlement of the Canadian west was actively encouraged

The RCMP is more militaristic and hierarchical than today's municipal police forces. What do you think are the advantages of working in a centralized, hierarchical structure? What might the disadvantages be? Which might suit you better?

by the Canadian government. Subsequently, the Canadian federal government was compelled to provide policing services in order to facilitate settlement and development of its hinterland regions. Settlement was to be assisted by the construction of the transcontinental Canadian Pacific Railroad.

Uprisings by Indigenous persons and Métis, initially in the Red River Valley in 1869 and led by Louis David Riel, forced the federal government to give thought to establishing a military policing presence in Western Canada. To that end, in 1873 the national government established the North-West Mounted Rifles (later to become the Royal Northwest Mounted Police and eventually the Royal Canadian Mounted Police). The North-West Mounted Rifles were established as a military force and modelled not on Sir Robert Peel's London Metropolitan Police but on the Royal Irish Constabulary—a British military unit dispatched to quell revolutionaries seeking Irish independence.

Today, the Royal Canadian Mounted Police (RCMP) remains militaristic in rank and hierarchical structure, and highly centralized, with its headquarters based in Ottawa. Police services operating in the provinces of Ontario and Quebec and in urban centres across Canada are unionized, less militaristic, and relatively decentralized (Brodeur 2010, 78).

While Canadian police officers, like their American counterparts, routinely carry firearms, they are less prone to use lethal force and have not been affected by as many corruption scandals. Brodeur has astutely observed, "Although no two countries share such a long common border as the United States and Canada, and although the ties between the two countries are very close, Canadian criminal justice institutions are vastly different from those of the United States" (Brodeur 2010, 76).

Levels of Policing in Canada

Federal Policing

Federal policing in Canada falls under the jurisdiction and responsibility of the RCMP. Created and regulated under federal legislation, the *Royal Canadian Mounted Police Act*, members of the RCMP are designated as peace officers in every part of Canada, irrespective of where they may be stationed, and have all the powers, authority, protection, and privileges that a peace officer has by law.

Federal duties undertaken by the RCMP encompass those without geographic boundaries or that are outside the scope and expertise of provincial or municipal law enforcement agencies. However, federal policing initiatives may be operated collaboratively with provincial or municipal agencies as integrated units. In some provinces, British Columbia, particularly, integrated units have become common.

Federal areas of policing responsibility may include such areas as

- anti-terrorism enforcement and intelligence;
- immigration and passport enforcement;
- Interpol (international policing);
- National Child Exploitation Coordination Centre;
- National Weapons Enforcement Support Teams (NWEST); and
- International Peace Operations.

The federal arm of the RCMP may also be involved in operations and investigative support through scientific and technological forensic analysis at regional laboratories and similar specialist headquarters. The enforcement of airways, waterways, and borders also falls under the RCMP's federal responsibility, particularly in the following areas:

- border law enforcement;
- Integrated Border Enforcement Teams (IBET);
- cross-border crime;
- marine and ports operations; and
- underwater recovery.

Provincial Policing

Since each province is responsible for the administration of justice within its borders, as will be discussed in Chapter 2, provinces are required to provide policing services for those areas that fall outside federal jurisdiction. This includes every municipality, including towns and villages with populations of 5000 or less, Métis settlements regardless of population, and First Nations communities where other policing arrangements, such as the establishment of a First Nations Policing Program, have not been implemented.

Three provinces in Canada have chosen to establish and maintain independent provincial police forces. These include Newfoundland (the Royal Newfoundland Constabulary or RNC), Ontario (the Ontario Provincial Police or OPP), and Quebec (the Sûreté du Québec, or SQ). Each of these provinces has passed legislation that creates and authorizes these agencies as the designated provincial police. Ontario has passed the *Police Services Act of Ontario* establishing the OPP as the provincial police; Newfoundland, the *Royal Newfoundland Constabulary Act*; and Quebec, the *Police Act of Quebec*.

The RNC is the oldest civil force in North America. Newfoundland had appointed the first police constables in 1729 but in 1844 reconfigured its police structure based on the Royal Irish Constabulary. As of May 2017, the RNC was made up of over 404 officers and 120 civilians. Male officers numbered 284 and female officers numbered 120 (*Royal Newfoundland Constabulary Activity Report 2018*). The RNC delivers policing services to 15 communities including the cities of St. John's, Mount Pearl, and Cornerbrook (*Royal Newfoundland Constabulary Corporate Plan 2018–2021*). Its headquarters are located in St. John's. As well, since 1950, the RCMP provides policing services to other municipalities and in rural Newfoundland and Labrador under agreements between Newfoundland and the federal government.

> The OPP operates out of 162 detachments, five regional headquarters, one divisional headquarters and a general headquarters in Orillia. OPP members are responsible for traffic safety on Ontario's roadways, waterways and trails, policing more than 1 million square kilometres of land and waterways. The OPP provides policing services to 323 of Ontario's 444 municipalities and, under the Ontario First Nations Policing Agreement, provides for the administration of policing services in 20 First Nations. The OPP also works with 22 First Nations that fall outside the First Nations Policing Agreement and provides specialized support to 9 Self-administered First Nation Policing Services. [Ontario Provincial Police 2017]

The OPP has over 8300 employees including more than 5700 uniformed members, 35 per cent of whom are female, and over 2570 civilian members (Ontario Provincial Police 2017).

The Sûreté du Québec (SQ) was established in 1870 and currently employs over 5400 sworn police officers and over 1700 civilian employees. Approximately 24 per cent of the uniformed members are female while almost 71 per cent of civilian members are female. SQ headquarters are located in Montreal. The SQ currently provides police services in over 1200 municipalities divided into 85 regional county municipalities (RCMs) throughout Quebec. The SQ negotiates service agreement contracts with local governments and more than half of SQ police personnel are assigned to the regional county municipalities. SQ officers work out of police stations established in each RCM. Larger RCMs may have auxiliary stations (Sûreté du Québec, n.d.).

Contract Policing

Under the *Constitution Act* (discussed in Chapter 2), provinces and territories have jurisdiction over the establishment and operation of policing within their borders. As is evident in the examples of Newfoundland, Ontario, and Quebec just discussed, provinces can choose to establish and operate their own provincial police agencies.

The RNC, OPP, and SQ provide policing services to municipalities under negotiated contracts under which municipalities pay for the policing services received.

Other provinces in Canada have also passed provincial police acts authorizing the establishment of policing services within their borders, including the establishment of municipal policing agencies. However, most Canadian provinces and territories have implemented provincial policing by contracting with the federal government to have the RCMP serve in the capacity of provincial police. The Canadian provinces of Prince Edward Island, Nova Scotia, New Brunswick, Newfoundland and Labrador, Manitoba, Saskatchewan, Alberta, and British Columbia have all chosen to contract formally with the federal government to have the RCMP serve as the designated provincial police. Provinces pay annual contract fees to the federal government for the RCMP's service. (See Chapter 11.)

Within the provinces that retain the RCMP under contract, each municipality under provincial law also has an option of creating its own municipal police force or of subcontracting the RCMP to serve as municipal police. This is the case in communities ranging from Red Deer, Alberta, to Swift Current, Saskatchewan, to Moncton, New Brunswick, and to Surrey, British Columbia. Indeed, the vast majority of police officers serving in the RCMP do so as municipal police.

While the majority of provinces and the territories today contract with the RCMP to provide provincial/territorial policing, all provinces including British Columbia, Alberta, Saskatchewan, Manitoba, New Brunswick, Prince Edward Island, and Nova Scotia at one time operated their own provincial police forces. The demise of these forces in the late 1920s and 1930s and the absorption of their officers into the RCMP coincided with the end of the Prohibition era and the onset of the Great Depression. At that time the federal government, through the RCMP, sought to exercise greater control at a national level over perceived threats to the Canadian social order, particularly threats from communism (Phyne 1992, 181).

Municipal Policing

In those provinces where the RCMP are contracted to provide provincial policing services, municipalities may opt to subcontract with the RCMP for municipal police services. Compared to other provinces, more urban communities in British Columbia have chosen to retain and deploy the RCMP as their municipal police. As a result of this, about one-third of the entire RCMP force is located in British Columbia.

In Ontario, small communities are billed annually by the OPP. Similar billing arrangements exist in the provinces where the RCMP deliver rural policing services.

Many communities across Canada, though, have chosen to organize and maintain independent municipal police forces. While it may be tempting to think that only large urban centres such as Montreal, Toronto, and Vancouver maintain their own municipal police agencies, population size is not a primary determinant. For example, relatively small communities, such as Nelson, British Columbia, with a population of 10,000, maintain their own municipal police. Yet a city like Richmond, British Columbia, with a population of over 200,000, currently contracts with the RCMP for municipal policing services.

Independent municipal police services are typically authorized and regulated under provincial police acts of the province in which they are located. They have responsibility for enforcing the *Criminal Code*, other federal statutes (such as the *Controlled Drugs and Substances Act* and the *Youth Criminal Justice Act*), provincial laws, and municipal bylaws within the community they serve.

Regional Policing (Including Transit Police)

Most provincial police acts include the option for adjacent municipalities to amalgamate their individual police departments into one large police service. While considerable controversy surrounds amalgamation (or regionalization, as it is also known), a number of regional police forces exist. For example, in southwestern Ontario, there are the Peel Regional Police, York Regional Police, Durham Regional Police, Halton Regional Police, and Niagara Regional Police. In Nova Scotia, there is the Halifax Regional Police.

In Ontario, regionalized police forces were first structured in the 1970s. However, what facilitated the regionalization of policing services was a concurrent political willingness to restructure local governments in an attempt to deliver greater efficiencies and cost savings alongside better levels of protection to taxpaying citizens.

Amalgamation of several municipal police forces can be a controversial and emotive political issue. For example, in the early years of the 2000s, in the aftermath of serious organized crime gang wars over control of the illicit drug trade in British Columbia's lower mainland, much media attention was given to the possibility of ending the RCMP contract to provide policing services to communities in greater Vancouver. Adding fuel to the fire was the additional controversy generated over the inability of police services in the Lower Mainland first to acknowledge that women were missing from Vancouver's Downtown East Side and, subsequently, to come to terms with the possibility that a serial killer was at work.

A host of assertions were made about the benefit to be gained from amalgamating existing forces into one regionalized police service. Since organized crime interests paid no heed to municipal borders, so these claims went, it was time to free the police from the constraints imposed by geographic boundaries. Amalgamation, it was claimed, would facilitate greater criminal intelligence sharing and more effective, more efficient, less costly, harmonized policing strategies in the war against organized crime and against other potential serial criminals. Emotions ran high as citizens and local politicians trumpeted their concerns about the loss of control of existing local police services. Others voiced concerns about the consequences of downsizing the venerable RCMP. Yet others, including prominent past and present chiefs of police, insisted that the existing system was too fragmented to be effective.

In 2013, the RCMP and the Province of British Columbia signed a contract renewing the RCMP as the provincial police until 2033. Under the terms of this contract, municipalities with a population of over 5000 have the option of establishing their own independent police agency. For communities that subcontract the RCMP to serve as their municipal police, the contract also specifies that the RCMP can be replaced with two years prior notice. In November 2018, the City of Surrey with a population of over 400,000 subsequently voted unanimously to replace the RCMP by creating its own municipal police department.

As of summer 2020, a municipal team was working on a transition plan to establish a Surrey Police Department with the intended launch date of April 2021. Nevertheless, the plan to introduce a municipal police agency in Surrey has faced controversy and formidable hurdles, including growing public opposition (Zytaruk 2020).

Historically, two other distinct police services have operated in Canada. Given the historic economic importance of railroads in facilitating and sustaining transnational commerce, the Canadian Pacific and the Canadian National railroads are permitted under federal legislation to institute and maintain police services for the purpose of enforcing the federal *Canada Transportation Act*. The Canadian Pacific Police Service and the Canadian National Police Service are also empowered to enforce any other federal and provincial laws insofar as they relate to protecting the property owned or administered by the railway companies and to protecting people on that property. Members of these police services have all the same powers to detain, arrest, use force, search, and compel people to court. Although they are employed by railway companies, they are deemed to be public servants just as are city police employed by a municipality. In the United States, Canadian railway police are also considered to be fully commissioned police officers and are empowered to enforce laws in those states where Canadian Pacific and Canadian Nation railways operate rail lines (Canadian Pacific Police Service, n.d.).

Finally, consider the Metro Vancouver Transit Police, a distinctive, unique police service in Canada. Formed in 2005 under the *British Columbia Police Act*, the Transit Police is the only police force in Canada dedicated to providing police service on an urban public transit system. Transit Police officers are sworn members with full police powers throughout British Columbia. They work collaboratively with other municipal police agencies including the RCMP to ensure safety aboard the Lower Mainland's public transportation system, known as TransLink.

First Nations

Given the division of powers under the *Constitution Act*, discussed in greater detail in Chapter 2, while provinces have jurisdiction over the "administration of justice," the federal government has authority over "Indians and Lands reserved for the Indians" (Auditor General Canada 2014). In the late 1980s and early 1990s, concerns were raised that First Nations communities did not have access to the same level and quality of policing services as other communities. A variety of concerns were expressed about policing services in Indigenous communities, including

- poor police response times;
- inadequate crime prevention measures;
- high crime rates, particularly for violent crimes; and
- inadequate training for band constables (Auditor General Canada 2014).

Historically, the RCMP provided policing services to Indigenous communities. However, in the 1970s the Supreme Court of Canada ruled that reserves were not exempt from all provincial laws. This meant that provincial legislation with respect to law enforcement would apply to Indigenous communities.

As a result, the federal government introduced the **First Nations Policing Policy** and the **First Nations Policing Program**. The purpose of the policy was "to contribute to the improvement of social order, public security, and personal safety in First Nations communities, including that of women, children, and other vulnerable groups" (Auditor General Canada 2014).

The First Nations Policing Program (FNPP) established funding arrangements between the federal and provincial/territorial governments and Indigenous communities in order to enhance the quality of policing services. Under the FNPP, the federal government, through Public Safety Canada, negotiates cost-sharing agreements with the provinces (Auditor General Canada 2014). The program was intended to ensure national consistency in policing services available to First Nations.

There are two main types of policing agreements under the FNPP:

- Self-administered Agreements, where an Indigenous community manages its own police service pursuant to provincial/territorial policing legislation and regulations; and
- Community Tripartite Agreements, where a dedicated contingent of officers from an existing police service, typically the RCMP, provides policing services to an Indigenous community (Public Safety Canada 2018).

The FNPP is administered under the authority of the Aboriginal Policing Directorate, which provides broad policy advice on Indigenous public safety and justice issues. The directorate also undertakes research and periodic performance measurement to ensure adequacy of services.

In 2015–2016, under the FNPP there were

- 185 policing service agreements;
- policing services to 450 Indigenous communities (serving a total population of 430,000); and
- 1299 police officers (Public Safety Canada 2018).

Under the self-administered agreement provisions, Indigenous communities can develop and administer their own autonomous police services. These services are authorized to enforce a full range of laws, including the *Criminal Code* of Canada, provincial statutes, and band bylaws on reserve lands enacted under the *Indian Act*. More specifically, in 2017, there were 36 Indigenous self-administered police services in Canada employing some 874 officers (Statistics Canada 2018). Under the agreements, Indigenous police agencies are overseen by reserve-based police commissions or by local band councils.

Under the tripartite agreements, Indigenous communities receive policing services from existing local police agencies that are dedicated to serving the policing needs of the community. Where possible and practical, efforts are made to recruit and hire capable Indigenous persons to serve as police officers.

Other Indigenous reserves utilize band constables who are overseen by local band councils. Band constables usually are responsible for administering only band bylaws and do not have police powers.

President of First Nations Chief of Police Association Dwayne Zacharie has been vocal about the need for pay parity and a federal "essential service" designation for the stand-alone First Nations Police Services across Canada. One of the many recommendations from the 2016 Roundtable on Missing and Murdered Indigenous Women and Girls (a precursor to the National Inquiry) was to provide equitable and sustainable resources—funding, training, and human resources—to First Nations Police Services.

According to an analysis of self-administered police services in Canada (Kiedrowkski, Jones, and Ruddell 2017), the motivation to facilitate autonomous professional and culturally appropriate policing services in Indigenous communities was well-intended. In this regard, Canada, when compared to other countries with large Indigenous populations such as Australia, New Zealand, and the United States, has been distinctive. However, since establishing the First Nations Policing Policy, Canada has fallen short of attaining its goals. More specifically, a lack of stable and consistent funding has compromised the FNPP goals and has resulted in high turnover rates, poor performance, inadequate infrastructural support (e.g., police buildings), and a declining number of Indigenous officers (Kiedrowkski, Jones, and Ruddell 2017, 594). In short, the federal government has not lived up to its commitments under its own First Nations Policing Policy.

Private Policing

As has been noted earlier in this chapter, private policing has become a major industry within Canada and globally. It has had a profound effect on policing, and will continue to do so well into the future.

It is difficult to ascertain just how many private police personnel (in the form of security guards or private investigators) there are in Canada. However, a 2008 report by Statistics Canada points out that private security outnumbers public police by a ratio of 3 to 2. The ratio was based on estimates in 2006 of about 102,000 private security personnel and approximately 69,000 public police (Li 2008).

Most provinces maintain a licensing and registration system for regulating security guards and private investigators who typically work for private companies that contract their services to a range of agencies, organizations, and corporations that need security services. For example, Ontario has passed the *Private Security and Investigative Services Act* and British Columbia has passed the *Security Services Act*. Both statutes regulate private security agencies and their personnel.

Increasingly, provincial authorities seek to impose minimal training and performance standards as well as establish formal complaint processes. Such regulatory measures facilitate accurate estimates of the number of personnel involved in licensed security work. However, estimating the strength of private security personnel is difficult because many positions are "in house." That is, a variety of organizations such as colleges and universities have security personnel who undertake a variety of public-safety and risk-management functions. Of course, some public institutions, including universities, have mixed models in which there is a combination of contracted security personnel and in-house personnel. In-house personnel are not licensed or regulated in any way, although a crop of professional associations have sprouted and endeavour to establish professional standards, including accreditation. As well, private companies also employ in-house security personnel who specialize in corporate security and risk management. Although the magnitude is difficult to estimate, many former public police officers migrate into such private-sector security positions.

An ongoing concern with private security is the potential for violations of individual rights. For example, as discussed in Chapter 8, strict constraints are placed on the authority of the public police by the Canadian *Charter of Rights and Freedoms* to search members of the public. However, given that private security personnel are likely to be working on large private properties, they can conduct virtually unfettered searches of persons and their possessions. Anyone who has attended a rock concert or a professional sporting event in Canada will be familiar with being patted down (frisked) and having his or her purse or backpack searched for alcohol. (Of course, the issue is not that alcohol is prohibited inside the stadium. Visitors just have to purchase it from stadium vendors.) Such searches are conducted not on the basis of any legal authority possessed by security guards but rather on the basis of visitors consenting to the search as a condition of entry to the venue.

Another concern regarding the proliferation of private policing alongside the downsizing of policing services is that in many respects security has become a commodity to be purchased (Law Commission Canada 2002). Simply stated, those who are affluent are much more able than the poor to buy protection for themselves. Whether it is in the form of expensive home alarm-monitoring services, living in gated communities, or simply the installation of hardware such as locks for doors and windows, the poor are less able than the wealthy to be able to afford personal security. As the Law Commission of Canada noted, Canadians should be entitled to safety and security irrespective of their class or wealth.

Yet another set of concerns voiced by observers of the growth of private security is the continued blurring of lines between private and public police. Increasingly, private security personnel wear uniforms, carry equipment, and drive patrol vehicles that closely resemble those utilized by the public police. Ordinary Canadians are less and less able to distinguish between a private security officer and a public police officer.

There is also a growing network of policing that involves both private security companies and public law enforcement agencies. Complex networks and relationships can be found in the Canada Border Service Agency's reliance on contracted security guards to secure and maintain detention facilities at Canada's major airports. Persons detained for immigration purposes, including those held for deportation, are routinely guarded and monitored by private security personnel who work for private companies that have been contracted by Canada Border Services. Such arrangements are typically justified as cost-saving measures given that private personnel are paid significantly less than regular members of Canada Border Services. What is problematic is that there is generally little oversight or monitoring of the activities of private personnel.

Since the terrorist attacks of 11 September 2001 in the United States, Canada has enhanced its security measures at airports. Principally, this has entailed the creation of the Canadian Air Transport Security Authority (CATSA), a federal agency. Security staff at Canadian airports wearing CATSA uniforms routinely X-ray carry-on luggage, monitor screening devices, and search passengers. What is not obvious to most passengers is that the personnel wearing CATSA uniforms are not government employees but employees working for private companies who have been contracted to provide personnel. Again, these arrangements are justified on the basis of cost saving but nonetheless blur the lines between public law enforcement and private security.

Last, as a result of continued anxiety regarding the potential of fundamentalist terrorist activity, Canadian surveillance and policing agencies have admitted to engaging in **electronic metadata trawling** of Canadian wireless electronic communications, including cellular telephone calls, text messages, and emails. To what extent metadata trawling is carried out is difficult, if not impossible, to discern given the national security concerns and secrecy that surround such intelligence gathering. Little is publicly known about the relationships that now exist between private-sector internet providers and Canadian security and intelligence apparatuses. In this era of massive utilization of such social media as Facebook and Twitter, it would be naive to assume that diligent, if not hypervigilant, security specialists are not monitoring the millions of daily transmissions in an effort to thwart future terrorist threats. What working relations have evolved formally or informally between government agencies responsible for public safety and the risk-management staff of privately owned social media giants remains relatively unexplored and unknown. These concerns are addressed further in Chapter 15. Suffice it for now to merely acknowledge that the relationships between private policing activity and the public police are intertwined and complex.

Conclusion

Chapter 1 has addressed a range of issues relevant to the context of policing in Canada in the twenty-first century. Foremost of these issues is the suggestion that the concept of policing is evolving and that it is no longer relevant to think of the police as a singular entity working to provide security and safety to the Canadian public. Chapter 1 also sought to consider a series of forces that currently shape policing in Canada and elsewhere.

Important for understanding the delivery of policing service, the chapter also reviewed how Canadian policing is structured on different levels. Finally, Chapter 1 ended with a consideration of the close alliances between private security companies and the public police.

Chapter 2 next examines the structure and operation of the Canadian criminal justice system.

Critical Thinking Questions

1. How does the public police differ from private security companies? Are the lines between the two being blurred?
2. What is the crime complex described by David Garland? Is the crime complex an accurate account of how Canadians feel about crime and policing?
3. What are the major forces shaping early twenty-first-century policing in Canada?
4. Which of the nine Peelian Principles are most relevant to modern-day policing? Justify your answer.
5. Is there a fundamental tension between the values of a democratic society and the authority given to the public police?
6. If you were seeking a career with a Canadian police agency, which one would you choose?

Endnote

i   Throughout this text, the words "government" and "state" are used interchangeably as synonyms. It should be noted, however, that there is a nuanced meaning associated with these terms. More specifically, elected governments come and go (for example, a Conservative party government replaces a Liberal party government or vice versa). The state and the state apparatus (consisting of civil servants, programs and policies, bureaucratic structures, ministry/departmental/agency staff), however, have, if not permanence, at least a constancy.

2

The Canadian Criminal Justice System—An Overview

Learning Objectives

After reading and studying this chapter, students will be able to:

- Compare and contrast the powers and responsibilities of the federal government and the provinces with regard to Canadian criminal law.
- Describe and assess the rights of persons accused of crime in Canada.
- Differentiate among summary conviction offences, indictable offences, and hybrid offences.
- Describe and discuss the structure of Canada's court system.
- Describe and discuss what is meant by "adversarial system."
- Describe and discuss how a criminal case progresses through the criminal justice system.
- Describe the differences between the two phases of a criminal trial.
- Distinguish clearly between probation and parole.

Introduction

Of the many components that comprise the Canadian criminal justice system, the police enjoy the highest public visibility. Since the golden era of early mass media such as widely circulated newspapers, radio broadcasts, and motion pictures, police have been romanticized and glorified in news reports and in fiction as dedicated crime fighters perpetually waging a war on rampant criminality. Police also have vicariously been portrayed as violent and corrupt. Such widely held imagery continues in the modern age of mass electronic social media. In fact, such imagery continues to the extent that "the intertwining of images and reality is so pervasive in the case of policing that . . . fact and fiction become barely distinguishable" (Brodeur 2010, 4). However, when all is said and done, the public police are but one of several components that constitute the modern Canadian criminal justice system. In order to comprehend fully the role that police play in the overall criminal justice system, it is first necessary to understand not only the other components of the justice system but the nature of the Canadian political and legal systems as well.

This chapter also introduces readers to the basic elements of criminal law and the criminal justice process in Canada. The discussion is not intended to train police officers in the technical legal issues necessary for police work. Instead, it is intended to broaden and enrich students' understanding of fundamental issues in an effort to overcome many of the misleading impressions about crime, law, and the police that are fictionalized, sensationalized, and perpetuated in popular media accounts. Notwithstanding the challenges and transitions that are buffeting Canadian policing as discussed in Chapter 1, additional issues deserve consideration in order to understand the role of policing in Canadian society. With that in mind, the discussion now turns to an examination of the role of police in democratic societies.

Police in a Democratic Society

Many textbooks on policing note a fundamental tension between the ideals enshrined in democratic societies and the authority given to police (see Forcese 1999; Seagrave 1997). On the one hand, democratic societies, like Canada, place a high regard on fundamental rights such as freedom and equality. However, societies also create and deploy police to engage in both subtle and obvious forms of social control. For example, the visible presence of a police car in a driver's rearview mirror turns that driver into the most conscientious and attentive driver on the road—until, of course, the police car turns down another street. In this sense, the mere presence of police serves to exert a subtle but real control over behaviour. However, in the more obvious sense of control or coercion, police are granted formal powers such as the legal authority to arrest persons suspected of serious criminal conduct and to use force if necessary. Thus, even in democratic societies, the police represent the ultimate authority that the government has over citizens. There are also competing perspectives regarding the nature of this authority.

Consensus and Critical Perspectives

Two competing perspectives have been used to study the origin and use of criminal law. The **consensus perspective** sees laws as originating out of a democratic society's sense of needs and shared values and beliefs about what is right and what is wrong. In short, laws are seen to grow out of the need to protect society from actions and behaviours that are collectively deemed to be harmful or otherwise unacceptable. From the consensus perspective, it is the role of the police to impartially enforce laws for the purpose of protecting all of society. A second perspective, however, sees laws as originating not out of a concern to protect all of society, but out of a need to protect the interests of specific powerful groups. The **critical perspective** sees society dominated by powerful economic groups who successfully influence government to pass laws that serve their long-term needs and interests. From the

THE CANADIAN PRESS/Graham Hughes

Montreal Police officers watch over a Black Lives Matter protest in Montreal, June 2020. Do you see the police as a force exerting power over citizens or as a service that protects the rights and property of citizens? What is your view on the police as a means for the government to assert authority?

critical perspective, police are seen simply as agents of social control who act to protect the interests of the powerful groups who control both the government and the law.

As Dennis Forcese (1999) has argued, police invariably end up applying laws in ways that reflect social biases. More specifically, street-level crimes committed by socially and economically marginal persons tend to be more conspicuous, are perceived by ordinary citizens as more threatening, are easier to detect, and receive considerable attention from the police. "By being 'forced' to respond to conspicuously deviant or antisocial behaviour, the police are used to control and order society, a society that is inherently class-bound" (Forcese 1999, 51).

Police nevertheless are expected to be politically neutral. In theory, police are not to be used for partisan political interests. That is, police are expected to be free from the influence of any given political party or government—even though, strictly speaking, public police are funded by government and report typically to provincial attorneys general or ministers of justice.

Police and Government

To understand properly where police fit as agents of the state, it is important to consider the three branches of government and how they relate to law and law enforcement. Perhaps the most recognizable feature of democratic governments is the **legislative branch** of government. In this branch, elected representatives make the laws that police are required to enforce. A second branch is the **executive branch**. This branch consists of such government leaders as the prime minister (or at the provincial level, the premier) and the Cabinet (a group of senior elected officials chosen by the prime minister or premier to head various government departments called ministries.) Formally, the executive branch leads the government and establishes its goals and priorities. Police are formally considered to be part of the executive branch but, as stated above, are also formally expected to remain neutral and free of political interference. The third branch of government, independent in its own right, is the **judiciary**. This branch consists of judges and courts appointed at both federal and provincial levels. The role of the judiciary is simply to interpret and adjudicate the law.

Despite the expectation that the police remain politically neutral, Canadian history reveals a number of occasions in which police political neutrality has been breached. As reviewed in Chapter 15, the partisan involvement of Canadian police in a variety of political issues was evident throughout the twentieth century. However, especially with the reverberations throughout the security apparatus of western democracies in the wake of the 2001 attack on the World Trade Center (see Chapter 15), there has been an evident willingness to permit police, including Canadian police, to engage in what Brodeur has described as **high policing for national security**. As Brodeur has noted, high policing is and has always been an essential activity even in democratic societies. However, it has the potential to conflict with the taken-for-granted freedoms enjoyed in democracies (Brodeur 2010).

Making Criminal Law: An Exclusive Federal Responsibility

Under the terms of the *Constitution Act*, the federal Parliament has exclusive jurisdiction over enactment of criminal law. The *Constitution Act* in sections 91(27) and 92(14) delineates responsibilities over criminal justice issues. More specifically, section 91(27) empowers the federal government alone to enact legislation in regard to criminal law and to establish legal procedures for dealing with criminal matters (Ismaili, Sprott, and Varma 2012, xvii).

Efforts by provincial governments to pass criminal law have been ruled *ultra vires*, that is, outside their constitutional powers. As Judith Osborne (1995) has pointed out, one of the most distinctive features of the *Criminal Code* of Canada is that it is uniform in all provinces and territories. This is in marked contrast to the United States and Australia where criminal laws vary from state to state. For example, in the United States, Washington and Colorado have legalized certain aspects of the use and distribution of marijuana. These state laws, however, are in direct conflict with federal law that continues to prohibit the sale and possession of controlled substances including marijuana.

Osborne has also noted that, historically, it was the intent of the Fathers of Confederation to allocate jurisdiction over criminal law to the federal government not only to ensure uniformity and consistency across the country, but to serve as "a tool to draw the country together" (Osborne 1995, 275). While the federal government in Canada has absolute jurisdiction over passing criminal laws, the federal government typically consults carefully with provincial governments before introducing new criminal prohibitions or amending existing ones. However, this is not to say that such consultations result in unanimity and mutually satisfactory agreements over proposed amendments. For example, in 2011, the province of Quebec openly clashed with the federal government over provisions of Bill C-10 that were intended to deal with young offenders. Quebec favoured pursuing a more lenient and rehabilitative strategy over the federal government's preference to invoke tougher sentences for young offenders (Seguin and Mackrael 2011).

The *Constitution Act* also spells out a special set of responsibilities for provincial governments. That is, the *Constitution* grants provinces legal powers to provide for the administration of justice, including the creation, maintenance, and operation of provincial civil and criminal courts. These legal powers also enable provinces to establish provincial police services to enforce the federal criminal law and to oversee the creation and administration of municipal police agencies (Ismaili, Sprott, and Varma 2010, xvii).

Jurisdiction over correctional facilities such as penitentiaries and prisons is split between the two levels of government. As the result of a negotiated agreement between the federal and provincial governments, the federal government funds and operates **penitentiaries**, which incarcerate convicted offenders who are serving sentences for two or more years. **Prisons**, on the other hand, are funded and operated by provincial and territorial governments and hold inmates who are sentenced to periods of confinement of less than two years. This division of jurisdiction for inmates is informally known as the two-year rule.

In sum, although it is enacted by the federal government, the criminal law in Canada is actually "enforced by the provinces; and the decision to investigate, charge and prosecute offences are therefore matters of provincial policy which will no doubt be framed in response to local conditions and sentiments" (Hogg 1985, 398, cited in Ismaili, Sprott, and Varma 2012, xvii–xviii).

The *Charter of Rights and Freedoms*

The *Charter of Rights and Freedoms* and the *Constitution Act* are regarded as entrenched legislation. In other words, both the *Charter* and the *Constitution*, while properly falling under federal jurisdiction, cannot be amended or repealed unilaterally by the federal government. Rather, provinces and the federal government are required to reach a considerable degree of agreement before either the *Charter* or the *Constitution* can be changed. (For a more detailed discussion of how these pieces of federal legislation can be amended, see Boyd 2002, Chapter 4.)

Together the *Charter* and the *Constitution* put limits on what federal, provincial, and territorial legislatures and government officials—including the police—can do. The *Charter* specifically defines the rights of Canadian citizens and has been extended to protect the rights of immigrants and refugees as well. When an individual believes that his or her guaranteed freedoms have been violated, he or she has the right to ask the courts for help. In such a case, the courts may declare a particular law or action of a government official to be invalid or illegal to the extent that it conflicts with the *Charter*. Additionally, courts may order other appropriate remedies to individuals whose rights have been infringed (Department of Justice 2005, 11).

Even in a democracy like Canada, rights and freedoms are not absolute. For example, even though the right to freedom of speech and expression is protected by the *Charter*, no one has the right to stand up in a crowded theatre and shout "fire" when there is none, to slander someone, or to spread hate literature (Department of Justice 2005, 11–12).

> . . . Parliament or a provincial legislature can limit fundamental rights, but only if that government can show that the limit is reasonable, is prescribed by law and can be justified in a free and democratic society. The interests of society must be balanced against the interests of individuals to see if limits on individual rights can be justified. [Department of Justice 2005, 12]

The *Charter* also protects fundamental freedoms such as the right to practise any religion; democratic rights such as the right to vote or to run for office; mobility rights such as the right to live and work anywhere within Canada; equality rights such that everyone regardless of race, ethnicity, colour, gender, age, religion, or mental or physical disability is equal before the law; and language rights such that both English and French are granted status as Canada's two official languages.

Additionally, the *Charter* also specifically protects the rights of Indigenous peoples (Indian, Inuit, and Métis; see also Chapter 3). In this regard, the *Charter* provisions

- recognize and protect the Aboriginal and treaty rights of Aboriginal peoples and
- help Aboriginal peoples preserve their cultures, identities, customs, traditions and languages (Department of Justice 2005, 15).

With specific regard to legal rights, particularly in matters involving the criminal law, sections 7 through 14 of the *Charter* protect individuals and ensure fairness during legal proceedings. Such rights as *habeas corpus* (the right to challenge being detained or held in custody) and to be presumed innocent until proven guilty—both long recognized in legal custom—are formally guaranteed by the *Charter* (Department of Justice 2005, 13).

Canadians are also protected against unreasonable searches and seizures; Canadians cannot be deprived of their rights to liberty and security of their person without proper procedures. It is to be noted that in the vast majority of searches and seizures conducted by the police in Canada, "force" is typically not required as the need to control someone or secure a place is most often completed before a search and related seizure are carried out. As well, police officers must have reasonable grounds *to suspect* that a crime may have been committed by an individual before detaining that individual. Consistent with authorities granted under the *Criminal Code* s. 495 dealing with arrests, police must have reasonable grounds *to believe* that an individual has acted unlawfully before initiating an arrest by taking that individual into custody. (See also Chapter 8.) In the 2004 case of *R. v. Mann*, the Supreme Court of Canada (SCC) held that while the police had the right to detain Mann for investigative purposes since he matched a description of the suspect in a reported burglary, and had a right to search him for protective purposes, they had no grounds for conducting a more intrusive search of the contents of his pockets. In the course of patting down Mann for possible weapons, the police felt a soft bulge in his pocket. Police extracted the contents and found it to consist of a package of marijuana

Case Study

The Feeney Case

In 1991, Michael Feeney was arrested for the murder of 85-year-old Frank Boyle, whose body had been discovered in his mobile home in the interior of British Columbia. Boyle had died following a fierce beating involving blows to the head with a blunt instrument.

On the basis of information provided by Boyle's neighbours, police learned that Feeney had been seen leaving Boyle's truck, which had been driven into a ditch, and entering a nearby trailer where Feeney lived.

RCMP police officers arrived at Feeney's trailer, knocked on the door, and shouted "Police!" Hearing no response and without a warrant, police officers entered, found Feeney sleeping, and woke him up by shaking his leg. Feeney's shirt and shoes were covered in blood, and money stolen from Boyle was discovered in Feeney's mattress. Feeney was arrested, cautioned about his rights, and taken to the detachment where he was allowed to telephone a lawyer. However, before he was actually able to consult a lawyer, investigators interviewed him. During the interview Feeney admitted to beating Boyle; stealing cigarettes, beer, and cash; and placing the cash in the mattress. The police then obtained a search warrant authorizing them to seize the shoes, the stolen cigarettes, and the money found in the mattress. Feeney was again interviewed and fingerprinted. He still had not seen a lawyer.

Feeney was charged and subsequently convicted of second-degree murder in a British Columbia Supreme Court jury trial.

Feeney's conviction was appealed to the British Columbia Court of Appeal, which unanimously upheld the conviction. The conviction was appealed to the Supreme Court of Canada in 1996 where Feeney's legal counsel argued that his *Charter* rights had been violated. More specifically, his legal counsel argued that (a) the police officers should have obtained a search warrant before entering his residence; (b) the police did not have reasonable grounds to arrest him; and (c) the police had not given him sufficient opportunity to consult a lawyer.

In a split decision, five of the Supreme Court judges held that Feeney's fingerprints and incriminating statements should be excluded as evidence because the police had violated his *Charter* rights, and voted to overturn the conviction. Four of the judges disagreed and voted to uphold the conviction, believing that the police had acted appropriately. However, the majority vote carried and the Supreme Court of Canada ordered a new trial, ruling that the bloody shirt and shoes and the seized money were inadmissible as evidence.

The Feeney case is well known to most police officers and has had significant consequences for police investigation procedures. (See Chapter 9.) However, what is not so well known is that at the retrial, Michael Feeney was eventually convicted of second-degree murder by a jury in 1999 and sentenced to life in prison. He was convicted on the basis of other legally obtained evidence; specifically, Feeney's fingerprints had been found on beer cans in Boyle's truck and refrigerator, and his saliva had been found on cigarette butts in Boyle's mobile home. An attempt to appeal the conviction was rejected by the British Columbia Court of Appeal.

(See *R. v. Feeney* [1997] 2 S.C.R. 13.)

and several baggies. Mann was subsequently charged with possession for the purpose of trafficking. The SCC determined that the search of the contents of his pockets exceeded a search for protective purposes and therefore violated Mann's rights against unreasonable search. His conviction of possession for the purpose of trafficking was overturned. Out of the Mann decision, investigation detentions are required to be short in duration and only if necessary. Furthermore, the person being detained is under no legal obligation to respond to police officer questions and must be advised of this. Yet other Supreme Court of Canada decisions have added to the requirements that police must adhere to in order to conduct legal and reasonable searches. (See, for example, *R. v. Stillman* [1997]; *R. v. Golden* [2001]; *R. v. Saeed* [2016]; and *R. v. Le* [2019].)

In addition, the *Charter* ensures

- that citizens are protected against arbitrary actions by police agencies;
- that accused persons have the right to know why they are being arrested or detained;
- that accused persons have the right to consult a lawyer without delay and to have a court quickly determine whether a detention is lawful;
- that accused persons have the right to be presumed innocent until proven guilty beyond a reasonable doubt by an independent and impartial tribunal; and
- the right not to be denied bail without cause (Department of Justice 2005, 13).

As Paul McKenna has noted, police exercise considerable discretion. (See Chapter 5 for an elaborated discussion of police discretion in Canada.) In the execution of their duties, police have considerable power to curtail the liberty of individual citizens. Indeed, "no other public organization can directly impact the rights and freedoms of individual citizens to the extent of the police" (McKenna 2002, 4). For this reason, the *Charter* has a profound influence on the way police officers in Canada carry out their duties. In short, the *Charter* is the overarching legislation that holds police officers—as agents of the state—accountable for their exercise of authority.

There are, however, certain critics, including some police officers, who believe the *Charter* gives too much of an advantage to criminals. Critics of the *Charter*'s protection of basic legal rights often phrase their criticisms in simplistic terms, claiming that cases are decided on the basis of "legalistic technicalities" or that the *Charter* "ties the hands of police behind their backs in their war on crime." Others, though, argue that it is the *Charter*'s protection of fundamental rights, including the legal rights summarized above, that clearly distinguishes democracies like Canada from totalitarian dictatorships where no such rights exist or are completely ignored. Indeed, in dictatorships the police and military are under no obligation to respect the rights of persons suspected of wrongdoing or of expressing dissenting political opinions. In many respects the legal protections enshrined in democracies and, in particular, in the Canadian *Charter of Rights and Freedoms* are not created simply to protect the rights of criminals. Rather, such rights are there for the purpose of protecting innocent persons from the sometimes powerful over-reach of the state. And, without a doubt, the *Charter* did not create new legal rights for persons accused of crimes but, for the first time in Canadian history, simply codified a series of long-standing common-law principles.

To this point, the discussion has sought to provide an overview of the structure and operation of the Canadian political system, particularly the division of powers between federal and provincial governments under the Canadian *Constitution*. The preceding discussion has also sought to demonstrate the supremacy of the *Charter* to the extent that all government laws and actions—especially the actions of the police—must comply with its provisions. The discussion now turns to a more specific discussion of Canada's criminal law, or, as it is formally known, the *Criminal Code* of Canada.

The *Criminal Code* of Canada

Criminal law may be generally understood as legal rules that are imposed by the federal government that prohibit certain behaviour that society considers to be either harmful or inappropriate and for which specific punishments may be applied. Criminal law thus stands distinct from other forms of law, such as the civil law, to the extent that penal aspects are attached to it. Breaches of the criminal law hold the potential to result in court-ordered punishments such as fines or imprisonment. This section provides a skeletal overview of key features of Canadian criminal law, and is not intended to teach law to police officers. Practical knowledge of Canadian criminal law for enforcement purposes is taught to police recruits in all police training programs across the country. The discussion here is simply intended to introduce and foster a foundational understanding of key criminal law issues.

The *Criminal Code* of Canada, first enacted in 1892, is the principal source of criminal law in Canada. It has been amended many times since the nineteenth century. Other federal laws also contain penalties and are properly considered to be criminal law. For example, the *Controlled Drug and Substances Act*, the *Youth Criminal Justice Act*, and the *Anti-Terrorism Act* are all forms of criminal law in which punishments are specified for particular breaches.

As discussed above, jurisdiction to make and revise criminal law rests solely with the federal government. Provinces have no authority to enact criminal laws. However, provinces may create laws regarding particular areas that do fall within provincial jurisdiction. For example, provinces have authority to regulate motor vehicles and their operation on provincial roadways. Provinces also have jurisdiction over the sale and consumption of alcoholic beverages. In British Columbia, for example, the *Motor Vehicle Act* creates offences and penalties for the unsafe operation of motor vehicles, and the *Liquor Control and Licensing Act* prohibits the illegal sale and consumption of alcohol to and by minors. Both *Act*s specify penalties for the violation of their provisions. These statutes, however, are not regarded as criminal laws, per se. Rather, these provincial laws are considered **quasi-criminal laws**. Typically, violations of quasi-criminal laws result in relatively minor penalties such as fines or limited incarceration.

The *Criminal Code* sets out a system for classifying criminal offences. How a crime is classified in the *Criminal Code* has consequences for

- the type of arrest that may be used (i.e., arrest with or without warrant);
- the level of court that will adjudicate the case;
- whether or not a jury will try the case;
- the nature of punishment that will be applied in the case of a conviction; and
- the nature of the appeal process (Griffiths and Verdun Jones 1994, 216).

Summary Conviction, Indictable, and Hybrid Offences

Summary Conviction Offences

Summary conviction offences are less serious and are subject to lesser forms of punishment. They are sometimes referred to as petty crimes. The maximum sentence for a summary conviction offence generally carries a penalty of no more than six months in prison or a $5000 fine or both (Jones 2015, 52–3), unless otherwise proscribed. Examples of summary conviction offences include causing a disturbance; public nudity; fraudulently obtaining food, beverages, or accommodation; and theft valued under $5000.

Given the provisions of the *Criminal Code*, authorities must lay charges for summary conviction offences within six months of the offence. As well, summary conviction offences are dealt with summarily, that is, are heard by a provincial court judge without a jury.

Indictable Offences

In comparison to summary conviction offences, indictable offences are more serious and consequently may result in much severer punishments. There are no time limits as to when charges can be laid. Examples of indictable offences include first- and second-degree murder, manslaughter, and aggravated assault.

AntonioGuillem/iStock/Thinkstock

Theft under $5000 is a summary conviction offence. What do you think a fair or just punishment for the theft of a $900 phone should be?

Depending on the nature and seriousness of the crime, indictable offences may be tried in different ways. Some indictable offences fall within the absolute jurisdiction of provincial courts. For example, such offences as theft, false pretenses, or keeping a common bawdy house are indictable offences, but also are criminal offences that are tried only in provincial court. More serious offences such as murder are tried in Superior Court and, depending on the choice of the accused, may be tried either by a judge alone or by a judge and a jury.

Certain other offences entail a range of choices for the accused person. Having a range of choice entails the accused person electing the mode of trial. Such crimes include robbery, dangerous driving, break and enter, and attempted murder. Persons facing prosecution for these crimes may choose to be tried by a (a) provincial court judge; (b) superior court judge; or (c) superior court judge and a jury.

Hybrid (or Dual) Offences

Hybrid or dual offences lie somewhere between summary convictions and indictable offences. In this category of offence, Crown prosecutors have the authority to determine whether or not to proceed to trial either by summary conviction or by indictment. With regard to assault, for example, depending on the seriousness of the particulars of the offence, the prosecution has a choice of proceeding by either summary conviction or indictment. This choice allows the prosecution to influence such matters as what level of court will try the case, the type of trial (either by judge alone or by judge and jury), and the severity of the penalty to be faced if the accused is convicted.

Typically, until a prosecutor formally elects the method of proceeding in regard to a hybrid offence, the criminal matter is presumed to be an indictable offence. This has the consequence of allowing police officers additional powers of investigation that exist in regard to indictable offences. More specifically, with respect to indictable offences, police can demand that the accused undergo photographing and fingerprinting under the terms of the *Identification of Criminals Act*. Such matters are not required of persons charged with summary conviction offences.

The Structure of the Canadian Court System

Historically, Canadian police work has always been influenced by court rulings. Even prior to the *Charter*, Canadian police agencies had been legally obliged to adhere to particular court decisions. Given Canada's historical legacies from Great Britain with regard to both law and policing practices, a ruling in the early twentieth century in Great Britain (*Ibrahim v. R.* [1914] AC 599) established the rules for police when conducting interrogations. Under what is referred to as the Ibrahim Rule stemming from this case in 1914, it has long been a legal principle that statements made to police during interrogations are inadmissible unless the prosecution can clearly demonstrate that they were given voluntarily. Police therefore are unable to extract confessions from suspects by making threats, offering promises, or in any way engaging in oppressive behaviour during interrogations.

The manner and extent to which court interpretations of the law have significant consequences for the police are illustrated by the Ibrahim Rule. While law is most often specified in **statutes** (or formal codified legislation passed by governments), law is also found in judicial **precedents** such as the Ibrahim case. Precedents (or the decisions made by judges in previous similar cases) constitute **common** or **case law**. Decisions made by judges in earlier cases serve to guide the decisions to be made by other judges who may be adjudicating similar cases. That previous decisions of judges influence the interpretation of the law by other judges occurs on the basis of the legal principle called *stare decisis*. *Stare decisis*—a Latin phrase that means to stand by decided matters—ensures consistency in the interpretation and application of the law by the courts. Court systems are typically structured in a hierarchy (see Figure 2.1) with superior courts setting precedents that lower courts must adhere to in their decision making. In this sense, decisions made by the higher courts become part of the law and become binding on other courts and on other criminal justice officials, including the police.

In Canada, decisions made by provincial superior courts or by provincial courts of appeal have legal force only in the province in which the decision was rendered. For example, courts in Ontario are not bound to adhere to decisions reached by courts in Alberta. So said, courts in other provinces may be swayed by compelling legal reasoning in the cases, but they are not formally bound by them. However, in any case decided by the Supreme Court of Canada—the highest court in the land—the decision becomes binding across the entire country. In this sense, Supreme Court of Canada decisions become Canadian law. Of course, give the supremacy of Parliament, Parliament has the ultimate authority to amend or repeal existing laws and implement new ones.

Case Progression: From Offence to Incarceration

Since criminal offences are considered offences against society, the state usually assumes responsibility for initiating charges and prosecuting someone who has been accused of a crime. As noted above, this responsibility rests with provincial authorities.

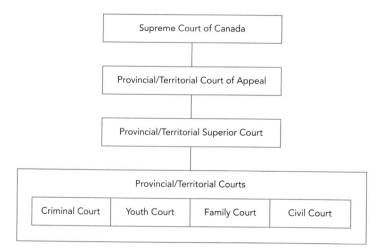

Figure 2.1   Structure of Canada's Court System

Adversarial System

Our justice system, inherited largely from the United Kingdom, has adopted many of the practices that evolved there. One such practice is that of the adversarial system, characterized as a battle between two adversaries—the prosecution and the defence. Following the British system, prosecutions are conducted symbolically in the name of the Queen. Thus prosecutors are known as Crown counsel. In the United States, prosecutions are done in the name of "the People" and are conducted by district, state, or federal attorneys.

Theoretically, the idea underpinning the adversarial system is that an equal and fair competition occurs in which the defence is pitted against the prosecution. The legal battle is conducted before an independent and impartial judge or jury. Justice is seen to prevail when one of the sides succeeds in persuading a judge or jury that its argument is correct.

The adversarial system is a marked contrast to the inquisitorial system used in some European and Islamic nations. Inquisitorial systems often entail very limited rights for persons accused of offences and often begin with the assumption that the accused is guilty. There is also little distinction between prosecution, defence, and judges. The goal of inquisitorial systems is to seek truth rather than establish the legal guilt of the accused person.

Offence

Criminal cases typically begin when a victim or witness draws the matter to the attention of the police. If the matter is serious enough, the police will respond by initiating an investigation. Investigations can vary in complexity from relatively simple and straightforward to extremely complex and time-consuming. A relatively simple and straightforward case might be a theft charge where an employee is caught on closed-circuit television camera stealing from his or her workplace. A simple questioning by police might produce an admission of guilt by the suspect, a charge would be laid, and the accused would plead guilty in a provincial court and receive a sentence.

A more complex and time-consuming criminal case is perhaps best illustrated by the terrorist bombing of Air India Flight 182 in June 1985 that killed 329 people. The subsequent investigation and prosecution lasted almost twenty years and was the most expensive trial in Canadian history, costing in the range of $130 million. Despite the belief that many others were involved in the conspiracy to bomb the plane, only one person was convicted (see Major 2010; note also Chapter 15).

Of course, while police respond to alleged criminal events and carry out investigations, police are not always responsible for laying charges. Responsibility for laying charges varies from province to province. In New Brunswick, Quebec, and British Columbia, police carry out investigations and make recommendations to Crown counsel. Subsequently, Crown counsel have the ultimate authority as to whether or not charges are laid and eventual prosecution occurs. Two considerations underpin Crown counsel decisions to proceed with charges: (a) is there a likelihood of winning a conviction based on the available evidence, and (b) is prosecution in the public interest?

In the rest of Canada, police have the authority to lay charges directly. However, as Crown counsel prepare cases for prosecution, charges laid by police are screened by Crown counsel and may still be amended or dropped before proceeding to trial.

Challenge Your Assumptions

Most Common Offences in Criminal Court

Five offence types made up nearly half of all completed cases in adult criminal and youth courts.

In adult criminal court cases, the five most common offences in 2016/17 were theft, impaired driving, failure to comply with a court order, common assault, and breach of probation, which represented 47 per cent of all completed cases. These same five offences were the most common in 2015/16, and made up 48 per cent of all completed cases then.

In youth court cases, the five most common offences in 2016/17 were theft, offences under the YCJA, common assault, break and enter, and major assault, which represented 44 per cent of all completed cases in that year. This is similar to the previous year, when the five most common offences of theft, offences under

the YCJA, common assault, break and enter, and failure to comply with a court order also made up 44 per cent of all completed cases (Figure 2.2).

What do the graphs below tell you about crime in Canada? Is there anything about these crime statistics that surprises you? How would you generally characterize these crimes?

Take a moment to think about what doesn't appear on the graphs below.

Why is murder not shown on the pie graphs? If you were to try to determine the incidence of murder in Canada for the same time period (2016/17), what would be a reputable source?

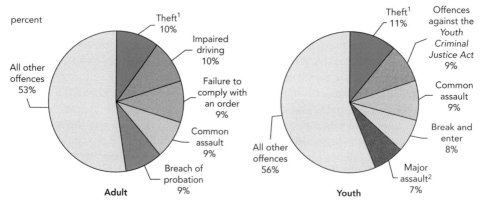

1. Theft includes, for example, theft over $5,000, theft $5,000 or under, as well as motor vehicle theft.
2. Major assault includes, for example, assault with a weapon (level 2), and aggravated assault (level 3).
Note: Note: Cases that involve more than one charge are represented by the most serious offence. A case is one or more charges against an accused person or company that were processed by the courts at the same time and received final decision. Data exclude information from superior courts in PEI, ON, MB, and SK as well as municipal courts in QC due to the unavailability of data.

Figure 2.2   Five Most Common Offences for Cases Completed in Adult Criminal and Youth Courts, Canada, 2016–17

Source: To come; https://www150.statcan.gc.ca/n1/pub/85-002-x/2019001/article/00002-eng.htm Chart 3

Judicial Interim Release

If the accused person has been arrested, that person is entitled to be brought before a judge or justice of the peace at the earliest opportunity—usually within 24 hours, unless released sooner by the police. In most cases, unless there are good grounds for keeping the accused in custody, the accused will be released. This is referred to as **judicial interim release**. If there are concerns about the accused's possible behaviour while on release, a show-cause hearing will be held during which a prosecutor must demonstrate why the person should not be released. If the judge decides to release, the accused person may be granted **bail** with or without conditions. Breaching the conditions may result in re-arrest and a continuation of custody pending trial. Judicial interim release will be refused only if there are very strong reasons for doing so (Department of Justice 2005, 22).

Role of Prosecution

If an accused is charged with a summary conviction offence, he or she will appear before a provincial court judge. The overwhelming majority of all criminal charges are dealt with in provincial court. Of these, over 80 per cent of all charges dealt with in provincial court result in guilty pleas (Martin 1993, 25, cited in Manarin 2004, 151). No more than 5 per cent to 10 per cent of criminal charges proceed to trial (Burstein 2004, 159). Contrary to lay impressions, criminal trials are relatively rare in the Canadian criminal justice system.

Role of Defence Counsel

After a person has been arrested, received preliminary legal advice, and been granted bail, the individual may qualify for a legal aid lawyer or be able to retain a lawyer privately. The principal role of a defence counsel is to be able to mount a defence on behalf of his or her client. As Burstein (2004) has pointed out, there are essentially two categories of a legal defence that a lawyer may prepare. The first is a factual defence that entails mounting a challenge to police-generated evidence—such as demonstrating that a witness is lying or is just mistaken in what he or she recalls. The second defence described by Burstein is that of a legal defence. A legal defence might entail developing an argument that the accused is not guilty by reason of insanity. Examples of other legal defences that may be argued include that an accused was acting in self-defence or that the accused may have acted out of provocation (Burstein 2004, 161).

Criminal Trial Process

As is pointed out in *Canada's System of Justice*, although relatively rare, a "criminal trial is a particularly serious matter because liberty, as well as the stigma of a criminal conviction, is at stake for the accused" (Department of Justice 2005, 22).

In an actual criminal trial, when the accused has entered a plea of not guilty, the obligation is entirely on the prosecution to prove that the accused is **guilty beyond a reasonable doubt**. If, after hearing the evidence, a judge or jury holds a reasonable doubt about the accused person's guilt, Canadian law stipulates that the accused person must be acquitted. This requirement is referred to as the prosecution's **burden of proof** in a criminal case. In this regard the accused person has no requirement to prove his or her innocence. Nor can the accused person be required to give evidence, although he or she may choose to do so.

The burden of proof in a criminal trial is significantly different from the burden of proof in civil trials. In civil trials that occur typically between private parties (individuals, companies, or both) a **plaintiff** seeks damages from **respondents**. Civil law requires that cases be determined on the **balance of probabilities**—a matter of weighing the preponderance of evidence that has been entered. The balance of proof in civil law is thus significantly less rigorous than that required in criminal law. An American example that best illustrates the differences in the burden of proof in criminal and civil law is the case of former professional football player O.J. Simpson. Simpson was acquitted by a jury on the criminal charges of murdering his wife, Nicole, and her friend Ronald Goldman. In civil proceedings brought by Ronald Goldman's father, Simpson was held civilly liable for the deaths and ordered to pay damages. The different outcomes in the two separate and distinct trials hinged largely on the different burdens of proof.

Criminal Trial Phases

There are two principal phases to a criminal trial: adjudication and disposition. During the **adjudication phase**, the prosecution will introduce evidence in an effort to demonstrate the guilt of the accused person. This phase will entail the prosecution's introduction of sworn testimony from witnesses, police officers and, if necessary, experts in relevant fields. After the prosecution has examined the witnesses, the accused, through his or her defence lawyer, is entitled to cross-examine these witnesses in an effort to call their testimony into question. Subsequently, when the prosecution has called all its evidence, the accused's defence lawyer may call witnesses or introduce other evidence in an effort to establish doubt about the prosecution's case. In turn, the prosecution then is allowed to cross-examine any witnesses called by the defence.

As the adjudication phase comes to a close, both the prosecution and the defence are given the opportunity to summarize their arguments. The defence always presents its summary last. If the case is being heard by a judge and jury, the judge will typically summarize the evidence presented and send the jury to deliberate on a verdict. If the trial is being conducted by a judge alone, he or she may similarly take time to weigh the evidence in order to reach a verdict.

If there is a finding of not guilty, the accused person is said to have been **acquitted** and is free to go. It is to be noted that courts in Canada do not find accused persons "innocent." Simply stated, persons are found "not guilty."

Upon a determination of a guilty verdict, the criminal trial enters the **disposition phase**. In this second phase, also called the "sentencing phase," both the prosecution and the defence are entitled to make submissions to the court regarding what each considers to be an appropriate sentence given the particulars of the offence. This means taking into account the seriousness of the offence, the range of sentences spelled out in the *Criminal Code* or other relevant statutes, prevention or deterrence of the offender or others from similar crimes in the future, and the prospects for the accused's rehabilitation. During this phase, details of the accused's past criminal record, if any, can be disclosed to the judge for consideration in reaching an appropriate disposition. During the adjudication phase, however, the accused's past record cannot be disclosed to the judge or jury. This would be seen as **prejudicial** and might bias the decision regarding his or her guilt with respect to the charges faced. As noted in *Canada's System of Justice*, judges may impose different kinds of sentences or a combination of penalties that may include the following:

- a fine (payment of a sum of money to the government);
- restitution (compensation for injuries or damages to a victims);
- probation (release of the offender under court-ordered conditions);
- community service (hours of volunteer work);
- imprisonment in a prison or penitentiary (depending on whether period of incarceration is lesser or greater than two years);
- a conditional sentence; or
- a combination of the above (Department of Justice 2005, 23).

Depending on the circumstances of the case, judges have the option of awarding an absolute or conditional discharge. Under a conditional discharge, a judge will impose certain conditions on the offender. Breach of the conditions can lead to a more severe sentence. However, offenders who are given discharges will not get a criminal record for their offence. Discharges are usually given only to first-time offenders who have committed relatively minor offences.

Appeals

Given the possibility that errors may be made in a criminal trial, the right to appeal is an important safeguard in the criminal justice system. A decision reached at one level of the court system can be appealed to a higher level.

Either the prosecution or the defence can file for an appeal of a court decision and either side can appeal the adjudication (guilty or not guilty), the disposition (sentence), or both. Depending on the offence, there may be an automatic right of appeal. In some cases, however, permission or "leave" to appeal must be sought. The higher level of court may refuse leave to appeal, affirm, or overturn the original decision. In some cases, a new trial may be ordered. Of course, decisions reached by the Supreme Court of Canada are final. It is the court of last appeal (Department of Justice 2005, 23–4).

Incarceration

As noted previously, the federal government assumes responsibility for funding and operating federal penitentiaries, which incarcerate convicted offenders who are serving sentences of two or more years. Offenders are not sentenced by the court to a particular institution. Rather, if their sentence is two years or longer, they are turned over to Correctional Services Canada, a division of the Ministry of Public Safety, for assessment. The assessment process entails an evaluation of the offender's offence, medical and mental history including substance abuse issues, and his or her past record before determining the level of security under which the inmate should be placed. Accordingly, a decision will be made as to at which institution and level of security the offender will be confined.

Offenders sentenced to less than two years are turned over to provincially or territorially authorities. Provincially sentenced offenders are similarly assessed and sent to appropriate custodial facilities.

Parole

When offenders have completed a portion of their sentence, they become eligible for parole. Not to be confused with **probation** (a court-ordered sentence under which an offender is supervised in the community), **parole** is a conditional release from incarceration. The National Parole Board assumes responsibility for the supervision of both federal and provincial offenders who have earned a conditional release from their incarceration.

Conclusion

This chapter has reviewed the constitutional division of powers between the federal government and the provinces with respect to making and administering criminal laws in Canada. As well, the chapter has sought to provide an overview of the major provisions of the Canadian *Charter of Rights and Freedoms,* particularly as they pertain to policing and criminal law in Canada. A brief review of the types of criminal offences was presented prior to an overview of the structure and operation of the Canadian court system. Last, a descriptive overview of how criminal cases proceed through the criminal justice system was provided.

Critical Thinking Questions

1. What are the advantages and disadvantages of having a *Criminal Code* that is national in scope?
2. Which of the two competing perspectives that have been used to explain the origin and use of criminal law and actions of the police do you agree with? Explain your reasons.
3. Does the *Charter of Rights and Freedoms* go too far in protecting the rights of persons accused of crimes?
4. What are the advantages and disadvantages of making Canadian provincial governments responsible for the administration of justice?
5. Should police officers be able to lay charges directly or should they be subject to approval by Crown counsel? Justify your answer.

3

Canadian Diversity and Policing

Learning Objectives

After reading and studying this chapter, students will be able to:

- Describe and discuss diversity and multiculturalism in Canada today.
- Describe and explain the overrepresentation of Indigenous people in the Canadian criminal justice system.
- Define and explain what is meant by "the colonial problem."
- Describe and discuss diversification as it relates to Canadian police agencies.
- Distinguish between racialized policing and racial profiling.
- Explain the police practice of carding and why it is controversial.
- Distinguish between under-policing and over-policing.
- Describe the challenges in policing for visible minorities, women, and LGBTQ+ persons.

Brief but Important Disclosures

In keeping with current ethical practices regarding the disclosure of the backgrounds of researchers, and for the purpose of situating ourselves,[i] it is fitting that the authors of this book, self-reflectively, divulge that we are three white, heterosexual, nominally Christian, college instructors of relatively advantaged social and economic backgrounds who are of Anglo-European heritage. One of us is female, one of us is an immigrant, and one of us served twenty-seven years as a member of the Royal Canadian Mounted Police. As self-reflective researchers, it therefore behooves us to strive to be aware of how our backgrounds may have shaped our biases, perspectives, and understanding of diversity issues and minority rights in Canada. We concede that we possess an incomplete knowledge of the lived experiences of Indigenous Peoples, of persons of colour, and of members of the lesbian, gay, bisexual, transgendered, questioning/queer, and related (LGBTQ+) communities. Nonetheless, we share personal and professional commitments to the egalitarian and just treatment of all persons. We also hold a genuine interest in challenging discrimination, oppression, and injustice irrespective of their forms. We are thus acutely aware of the egregious injustices that have been perpetrated historically in Canada and elsewhere against Indigenous persons, women, members of LGBTQ+ communities, and other minorities. Unfortunately, many of these injustices persist today.

It is also important that we respectfully acknowledge that the Douglas College campuses where the three of us work and learn are located on the unceded traditional territories of the Coast Salish peoples of the Qiqéyt (Qayqayt) and Kwikwetlem Nations.

In the discussion presented in this chapter, we have endeavoured to consider how the diversity of Canadian society poses challenges for Canadian police agencies. To that end, the chapter considers such issues as Indigenous Peoples, gender, and LGBTQ+ communities and their relationships to Canadian police.

Introduction

This chapter first provides an overview of the nature of diversity within Canada. Subsequently, the chapter examines the challenges that diversity poses for Canadian police agencies. Special attention is given to the overrepresentation of Indigenous people in the Canadian criminal justice system. Issues related to gender and to lesbian, gay, bisexual, transgendered, and questioning/queer communities are also examined.

Multiculturalism and Diversity

According to a national poll of Canadians conducted in 2005 that asked the question "What makes Canada unique?" the dominant response was "our diverse, multicultural nature" (Evans 2005 in Graham and Phillips 2007, 1).

The concept of diversity refers to differences among groups. Typically, considerations of diversity involve such matters as ethnicity, culture, race,[ii] gender, sexual orientation, religious beliefs, and age. Multiculturalism is a closely allied concept and is used to refer to a society that is characterized by a high degree of ethnic or cultural heterogeneity. In 1971, Canada became the first country in the world to adopt multiculturalism as an official policy. This was enshrined in federal law in 1988 when Canada enacted the *Canadian Multiculturalism Act*, which declares that multiculturalism is "the policy of the Government of Canada" and that it is the government's policy "to ensure that all individuals receive equal treatment and equal protection under the law, while respecting and valuing their diversity."

Canadian laws, including the *Charter of Rights and Freedoms*, "recognize Canada's diversity by race, cultural heritage, ethnicity, religion, ancestry and place of origin and guarantees complete freedom of conscience, of thought, belief, opinion, expression, and peaceful assembly" (Citizenship and Immigration Canada, n.d.). In fact, section 15 of the *Charter of Rights and Freedoms* explicitly addresses equality rights:

> s15. (1) Every individual is equal before and under the law and has the right to the equal protection and equal benefit of the law without discrimination and, in particular, without discrimination based on race, national or ethnic origin, colour, religion, sex, age or mental or physical disability. [*Charter of Rights and Freedoms*, s15]

In 1995, the federal government passed the *Employment Equity Act*, which required employers to proactively seek out minority candidates (women, people with disabilities, visible minorities, and Indigenous persons) in order to increase workplace representation (Szeto 2014, 2). This legislation had an impact on the hiring priorities of federal government agencies, including the RCMP. It also had a ripple effect in that it set an example for provinces to follow. In turn, diversity hiring was given higher priority within provincial and municipal police agencies (Szeto 2014, 43).

Even with formal commitments in both law and public policy to ensuring equality, in Canada, as in the United States, policing as an occupation remains dominated by white, Christian, heterosexual males. This remains true after years of progressive leaders calling for police agencies to diversify in terms of race, ethnicity, gender, and more recently, sexual orientation (Hassell and Brandl 2009, 409; Roberg, Novak, and Cordner 2005).

Indigenous Peoples within Canada at a Glance

> Aboriginal people are not just another "minority group" or "ethnic group" and characterizing them that way fails to take into account the special place they occupy in the nation's history as the original people of the land. [Comack 2012, 65]

Canadian diversity, however, is not merely attributable to immigrants. Urban diversity grew more complex in western Canadian cities with the migration of Indigenous people, particularly youth, from rural to urban settings. Around half of Indigenous people within Canada now live in urban centres. In 2016, there were 1,673,785 Indigenous people in Canada, accounting for 4.9 per cent of the total population (Statistics Canada, 2017(b)). Since 2006, the Indigenous population has grown by 42.5 per cent—more than four times the growth of the non-Indigenous population. The largest urban Indigenous populations are found in the cities of Winnipeg (92,810), Edmonton (76,205), Vancouver (61,460) and Toronto (46,315). According to Statistics Canada, by 2037 the total Indigenous population in Canada will likely exceed 2.5 million persons (Statistics Canada, 2017(b)).

From 2006 until 2016, Indigenous youth aged 15 to 34 increased by 39 per cent. This compares to an increase of just over 6 per cent for non-Indigenous youth (Statistics Canada, 2018). While the Indigenous population is relatively young and growing in size, it is also relatively poor. According to Beedie, Macdonald, and Wilson (2019), child poverty on reserves has remained almost unchanged since 2006. Indigenous children (53 per cent of those living on reserves and 41 per cent of those living off reserves) rank among the most impoverished groups within Canada. These rates are significantly higher than the national average of 17.6 per cent (or nearly one in five) of all Canadian children living in poverty (Beedie et al. 2019).

By comparative standards, living conditions on some reserves are dire. In 2016, one in five Indigenous people lived in a home that was in need of major repairs. This stands in contrast to 6 per cent of non-Indigenous persons who live in homes in need of major repairs (Statistics Canada, 2018). As Elizabeth Comack (2012) points out, most Canadians take such things as clean water, adequate sanitation, and waste disposal for granted. In 2015, there were 105 long-term drinking water advisories on reserves in place; however, as of October 2019, this had been reduced to 57 drinking water advisories on reserves. With continued progress toward rectifying on-reserve conditions, it is projected that there will be zero long-term drinking advisories on reserves by March of 2021 (Government of Canada 2019).

The social and economic conditions and the lack of opportunity have led many Indigenous people to migrate to urban centres. Sadly, conditions in urban settings for Indigenous persons are often no better. As has been pointed out by Beedie, Macdonald, and Wilson (2019), Indigenous "parents desire nothing less for their children than do other parents in Canada: to provide them with good health and the best opportunity for success" (np). Toward this end, it is noteworthy that from 2006 to 2016, the number of Indigenous persons who had completed high school increased by approximately 10 per cent (Statistics Canada, 2018). In 2016, all Indigenous groups in Canada had also made gains in post-secondary educational achievement. In turn, higher educational qualifications have led to significantly better chances of employment and in 2016, employment rates were above 80 per cent for Indigenous persons who held degrees. However, between 2006 and 2016, in spite of the gains in educational qualifications, the overall employment rates of Indigenous people did not increase (Beedie, Macdonald, and Wilson 2019).

There is no easy explanation for the cause of the persistent poverty for Indigenous Peoples. It is a complex issue without an easy solution. In some cases, Indigenous communities have worked successfully with non-Indigenous partners to foster programs and policies that have reduced poverty. However, given that poverty, and especially child poverty, are most severe on reserves for which responsibility rests exclusively with the federal government, the need for solutions to the chronic underfunding of on-reserve public infrastructure and services rests clearly in the hands of the Canadian federal government (Beedie, Macdonald, and Wilson 2019).

Indigenous Overrepresentation at a Glance

A fair and thorough discussion of Indigenous Peoples' historical relationship with the police and the Canadian criminal justice system deserves more space than can be provided here. Suffice it to say that most Canadians, and especially new Canadians, remain blissfully ignorant of the historic reasons underpinning the continued social, political, and economic exclusion of Indigenous Peoples.

Targets of British colonialism, traditional cultural practices disrupted and then banned, located to postage-stamp–size federal reserves under the *Indian Act* of 1876, and over-policed first by the North-West Mounted Police and then its successor, the RCMP, the history of Canada's treatment of Indigenous Peoples has been dreadful by any measure of decency. As sociologist Rick Ponting (1998, 270) has commented in reference to the

Challenge Your Assumptions

Words Matter: Indigenous, Aboriginal, First Nations, Native, or Indian?

As Lisa Monchalin has pointed out ". . . the word Indigenous is used to describe a large and diverse group of people in Canada" and is inherently problematic to the extent that its usage encompasses a wide variety of cultural groups, traditions, languages, and identities and misleadingly portrays them as homogenous (2016, 1). Nonetheless, it is a term that is increasingly preferred to that of "Aboriginal." "Aboriginal" is used in the *Constitution Act, 1982* and is defined therein as referring to ". . . the Indian, Inuit and Métis peoples of Canada." Also increasingly viewed as derogatory is the word "Indian"—though it is still used within Canadian laws such as the *Indian Act*. Likewise, the word "Native" is now similarly regarded as somewhat disparaging. Also, the term "First Nations" is frequently used incorrectly. As a term, First Nations "is not synonymous with 'Indigenous Peoples' as it does not include the Inuit or Métis" (Monchalin 2016, 5).

For scholars like Monchalin, such terminology taken together constitutes "pan-Indian" expressions that lump distinctive groups together and therefore inaccurately represents diverse peoples, nations, and cultures. The use of such terminology serves to define original inhabitants in relationship to their colonizers. Cognizant of the shortcomings thus embedded in the use of the nomenclature and following Monchalin's lead, the discussion that follows nevertheless relies upon the term "Indigenous Peoples" to refer to the First Nations, Inuit, and Métis. It is also to be noted that the term "Aboriginal" may nevertheless occasionally appear throughout this textbook, such as when it is used within the quoted words of other authors or accords with the legislation being discussed.

As noted in the discussion above, words do matter. Why is it therefore important to be aware of the use of particular terminologies that have been used historically to refer to Indigenous Peoples within Canada? What are "pan-Indian" expressions and why are they regarded as inappropriate ways to describe Indigenous people?

treatment of Indigenous Peoples within Canada, "Like the tap root of the common dandelion, racism's roots extend deep below the surface of Canadian society."

It has long been recognized that Indigenous people are grossly overrepresented in the Canadian criminal justice system. The following summarizes the basics of Indigenous incarceration rates in Canadian correctional facilities:

- Indigenous persons are overrepresented in segregation and maximum-security populations;
- Indigenous offenders are disproportionately involved in self-injurious behaviour, accounting for 48.3 per cent of all self-injurious incidents; and
- Indigenous persons have lower rates of release on parole, and are more likely to be returned to prison for parole revocation (Zinger 2018).

In his *2017–2018 Annual Report* to the Minster of Public Safety, federal correctional investigator Ivan Zinger stated,

> In the ten-year period between March 2009 and March 2018, the Indigenous inmate population increased by 42.8% compared to a less than 1% overall growth during the same period. As of March 31, 2018, Indigenous inmates represented 28% of the total federal in-custody population while comprising just 4.3% of the Canadian population. The situation continues to worsen for Indigenous women. Over the last ten years, the number of Indigenous federally sentenced women increased by 60%, growing from 168 in March 2009 to 270 in March 2018. At the end of the reporting period, 40% of incarcerated women in Canada were of Indigenous ancestry. These numbers are distressing. [Zinger 2018, 61]

Research has confirmed that the overrepresentation of Indigenous people in the Canadian criminal justice system is largely due to their disadvantaged living conditions. According to La Prairie and Stenning (2003), Indigenous Peoples disproportionately experience circumstances and conditions that give rise to the greater likelihood of becoming embroiled in the criminal justice system. That is, younger, single, less educated, unemployed males living in poverty with substance abuse problems are more likely to come to the attention of the criminal justice authorities. And research conducted by Fitzgerald and Carrington in Winnipeg showed that Indigenous persons are highly overrepresented as offenders in police-reported crime data and are nearly seven times as likely to be identified by police as offenders than non-Indigenous people (Fitzgerald and Carrington 2008, 547). Their research also confirmed that Indigenous people are more likely to live in neighbourhoods characterized by levels of social disorganization and social disadvantage. In order to make complete sense of Indigenous overrepresentation, Fitzgerald and Carrington argue that what is needed is an exploration of how the social conditions of neighbourhoods influence police decisions regarding patrol and response priorities and their inclination to use formal measures (such as arrest and prosecution) as opposed to informal social controls (such as warnings, diversion to non-criminal justice social agencies, or referral to restorative justice programs) (Fitzgerald and Carrington 2008).

The Colonial Problem

Traditional explanations (both academic and in popular media) have tended to frame the gross overrepresentation of Indigenous people in the Canadian criminal justice system as "an Indian problem." Framed this way, "the Indian problem" places the blame for the overall social and economic plight of Indigenous Peoples and for their overrepresentation in the justice system clearly on the individuals or groups who are experiencing the overrepresentation (Reasons, Hassan, Ma, Monchalin, Bige, Paras, & Arora, 2016, 89). Most certainly, casting overrepresentation as an "Indian problem" facilitates the perception that Indigenous persons and their communities are to blame for their own circumstances. What is ignored is the ". . . impact of colonization resulting in economic and social marginalization, high rates of incarceration, and the generational transmission of trauma related to the experience of residential schools. . ." (Reasons et al. 2016, 92).

Lisa Monchalin (2016), however, has stood this conceptualization on its head and has made the claim that the historical and continuing injustices perpetrated against Indigenous Peoples within Canada (and other countries) are not "an Indian problem"; rather, they are the direct result of colonialism and its vestiges that persist today. Thus, Monchalin (2016) characterizes the modern circumstances of Indigenous Peoples within Canada not as "an Indian problem" but rather as "the colonial problem." Framed this, way, the colonial problem offers a structural understanding of both macro- and micro-level issues that have influenced and continue to influence the lives of Indigenous persons and their communities (Monchalin 2016; Reason et al. 2016).

From the late 1400s through the mid-1900s, European countries such as Great Britain, France, Spain, and Portugal, functioning on policies of colonialism, took political and economic control of people and resources in North and South America, Africa, Asia, and Australia (FemNorthNet 2016). In what is now Canada, Europeans signed (in bad faith) treaties for lands and resources with Indigenous Peoples in a quest for wealth that could be wrought initially from furs and fish, and subsequently from agricultural, timber, mineral, and oil resources.

The history of the colonization and the exploitation of Indigenous Peoples and their lands is both nuanced and complex; however, the most obvious example of colonization is evident in the passage of the *Indian Act* in 1876 and its continued existence today. The *Act*, which has been amended many times over the years, establishes the formal relationship between the Government of Canada and Indigenous Peoples. Broad in scope, the *Act* covers such matters as governance, land use, health care, and education. It also defines in legal terms who is considered "Indian" and spells out conditions under which reserve lands and bands are to be governed. Critics of the *Act* maintain that its continued existence undermines the cultural, social, economic, and political distinctiveness of Indigenous Peoples and that it implicitly exists to achieve an objective of absorbing Indigenous Peoples into mainstream Canadian life (Alfred 2009; FemNetNorth 2016, 4).

For over 150 years, the Canadian government sought to "civilize" and Christianize Indigenous children by forcing them to attend residential schools run by churches. Although the residential school program was initiated in the 1830s, it was in 1933 under the *Indian Act* that RCMP officers were legally appointed as "truant officers" to enforce the program and return truant children to residential schools. The role that the RCMP came to play in literally forcing children to attend residential schools—where atrocities against children were perpetrated—has historically generated profound and lasting resentment among Indigenous groups toward the RCMP. The ill-will between Indigenous groups and the RCMP has been sufficiently severe that two Commissioners (Giuliano Zaccardelli in 2004 and Bob Paulson in 2014) deemed it necessary to formally and publicly apologize for their agency's role in maintaining the residential school program (RCMP, n.d.).

As has been noted by FemNetNorth,

Children's pain of being away from family was often worsened by disease, hunger, and physical and sexual abuse. This attempt to strip Indigenous children of their culture and language lasted for generations, with the last residential school closing in 1996. Many former students are alive today and are living with the effects of the trauma they endured in these schools. Residential schools had impacts on the physical and social health of children who attended them, and on the generations that followed. These impacts have included:

- Medical conditions
- Mental health issues
- Post-traumatic stress disorder
- Changes to spiritual practices
- Loss of languages and traditional knowledge
- Violence
- Suicide, and
- Effects on gender roles, childrearing and family relationships. [FemNetNorth 2016, 5]

The effects of the residential schools are still felt today. At its core, the residential school program was intended to force the assimilation of Indigenous children by inculcating Christian beliefs and values and by destroying Indigenous languages and cultural practices. Discussions today of the history of residential schools frequently invoke comparisons to **genocide**. Genocide is the destruction, not necessarily the mass killing, of all members of a nation, religion, or cultural group, and was evident in the goals of the Canadian federal government's residential school programs.

THE CANADIAN PRESS/Ben Nelms

Cindy Tom-Lindley, a residential school survivor, speaks during the opening of the Indian Residential School History and Dialogue Centre at UBC in Vancouver in April 2018. The Centre works to amplify conversations around the legacies of the Indian Residential School System and the on-going impacts of colonialism in Canada.

Case Study

High-Profile Injustices

The many incidents of inadequate and inequitable treatment of Indigenous Peoples in recent history at the hands of police and other criminal justice officials are too numerous to discuss in detail here. It is, however, instructive to be reminded of the following partial list of events, conflicts, and circumstances:

- the federal Residential School program of forcefully relocating Indigenous children from their homes to boarding schools operated by Christian churches from 1831 to 1996;
- "The Highway of Tears Murders"—since 1970 women, many of whom are Indigenous, have been reported missing and murdered along Highway 16 (the Yellowhead Highway) in Northern British Columbia;
- the wrongful conviction for murder in 1971 of Mi'Kmaq First Nations youth Donald Marshall;
- the brutal murder of Indigenous high school student Helen Betty Osborne near The Pas, Manitoba, in 1971 and the inept investigation that followed;
- the Winnipeg police shooting of Indigenous leader J.J. Harper in 1988;
- the Oka Crisis (July to September 1990) land title dispute that resulted in an armed stand-off between Oka Mohawks and the Sûreté du Québec (later replaced by the RCMP and the Canadian army);
- the Ipperwash Provincial Park, Ontario, 1995 land title dispute leading to an armed confrontation between Ojibwa members and the OPP that resulted in the shooting death of Dudley George by an OPP officer;

- the 1998 death of Mi'kmaq First Nations man Frank Joseph Paul as a result of being in police custody in Vancouver;
- the "Starlight Tours" and freezing deaths of Rodney Nastius, Lawrence Wegner, and Neil Stonechild in Saskatoon, Saskatchewan, between 1990 and 2000;
- the "Winnipeg 911 Murders"—in February 2000 two Indigenous sisters were murdered despite five calls to 911 over a six-hour period; the police dispatcher neglected to take the sisters' calls for help seriously;
- "Forsaken"—the missing and murdered women in Vancouver's Downtown Eastside between 1997 and 2002, many of whom are believed to have been victims of convicted serial killer Robert Pickton; and
- the January 2005 shooting of 18-year-old Indigenous youth Matthew Dumas by Winnipeg police.

The above listing is a select cataloguing of the relatively high-profile injustices that Indigenous persons have experienced throughout the twentieth century and into the twenty-first. Citations of specific references to these incidents are intentionally omitted. Readers are encouraged to choose key words and use any internet search engine to locate the numerous studies, official reports, discussions, and media coverage that have been generated in the aftermath of these matters. As a whole, the examples listed above provide vivid representations of the long history of conflict between Indigenous Peoples and Canadian authorities; they also stand as examples of both under-policing and over-policing of Indigenous Peoples within Canada.

Going Forward

Most scholars would agree that Indigenous Peoples within Canada have systematically been politically, economically, and socially excluded from the benefits and advantages of mainstream society. However, Indigenous Peoples have not been passive victims of colonial-instigated oppression, racism, and systemic poverty, and there have been significant positive developments within Indigenous communities due to the continuous work of Indigenous people within those communities.

Monchalin (2016) has pointed to a number of generally positive legal and political developments, all resulting from Indigenous activism and campaigning. For example, in 1996 the report of the Royal Commission on Aboriginal Peoples was released. The five-volume report was the culmination of over five years of public consultation and research and constituted the most comprehensive report ever done about Indigenous Peoples within Canada. Costing over $58 million to produce, the final report is over 4000 pages long and has 440 recommendations. The report calls for a new relationship between Indigenous Peoples and non-Indigenous Canadians based on mutual respect. The recommendations point to the need to address critical issues facing Indigenous persons and their communities: child welfare, crime, education, and health care. The report also recommended restoration of self-government, the return and control of adequate land bases, and a restructuring of institutions according to Indigenous cultural values and organizing principles (Monchalin 2016, 290).

In 1996, the Canadian federal government amended the *Criminal Code* of Canada in an effort to address the high rates of incarceration of Indigenous persons. More specifically, section 718.2(e) was amended to read: "All available sanctions other than imprisonment that are reasonable in the circumstances, should be considered for all offenders, with particular attention to the circumstances of Aboriginal Offenders." In 1999, a decision of the Supreme Court of Canada extended the impact of the 1996 amendment by concluding that "the jail term of an Aboriginal offender *may* [italics added] in some circumstances be less than the term imposed on a non-Aboriginal offender for the same offence" and that "Aboriginals must always be sentenced in a manner which gives greatest weight to the principles of restorative justice, and less weight to goals such as deterrence, denunciation and separation" (*R v. Gladue* [1999] cited in Monchalin 2016, 268). Subsequently, in another Supreme Court of Canada decision, *R v. Ipeelee* [2012], the direction given to the courts by the Gladue decision was strengthened such that "When sentencing an Aboriginal offender, courts *must* [italics added] take judicial notice of such matters as the history of colonialism, displacement and residential schools and how that history continues to translate into lower educational attainment, lower incomes, higher unemployment, higher rates of substance abuse and suicide, and of course higher levels of incarceration for Aboriginal peoples" (*R. v. Ipeelee* [2012] cited in Monchalin 2016, 269).

In 2008, the United Nations General Assembly adopted the United Nations Declaration on the Rights of Indigenous Peoples. The declaration set international standards for Indigenous rights, including ". . . the right to determine their own identity or membership in accordance with their customs and traditions . . ." as well as ". . . to maintain, control, protect, and develop their . . . cultural heritage, traditional knowledge and traditional cultural expressions" (Monchalin 2016, 291; United Nations 2008). The declaration was ultimately endorsed by all members of the United Nations and demonstrates the commitments of all governments to work in cooperation with all Indigenous groups and acknowledges Indigenous rights around the world (Monchalin 2016, 291).

In a promising development with regard to the UN Declaration on the Rights of Indigenous Peoples, in November 2019 the province of British Columbia passed Bill 41 into law. The new law, passed unanimously by the Legislative Assembly of British Columbia, will ensure that all provincial laws and policies will align with the United Nations Declaration on the Rights of Indigenous Persons. Drafted in consultation with Indigenous leaders, the legal commitment is the first of its kind in Canada (Hunter 2019).

In 2015, the Truth and Reconciliation Commission of Canada released its Calls to Action, which include a section on justice reforms such as more support for Indigenous programming, eliminating the overrepresentation of Indigenous people and in particular Indigenous youth in custody, and the implementation of Indigenous justice systems (Truth and Reconciliation Commission of Canada, 2015).

While these developments represent major achievements in recognizing the needs of Indigenous persons and their communities, taken together they represent not only an important recognition and acknowledgement of Indigenous rights but also of the social dislocation resulting from colonialism. However, in all fairness and despite the importance of these developments, it must be conceded that some Indigenous writers are cynical about how slowly recommendations and changes are being implemented (see Younging 2013).

Beyond these political–legal developments with respect to Indigenous rights, other progressive initiatives and developments are apparent. For example, in opposition to the Conservative federal government led by Prime Minister Stephen Harper, an Indigenous grassroots movement coalesced in late 2012 to resist a series of sweeping changes to environmental law and Indigenous rights. The movement known as Idle No More spontaneously grew out of responses to an omnibus bill (Bill C-45) introduced by the federal government. The bill was perceived to have a negative impact on Indigenous rights by drastically revising the *Indian Act*, the *Fisheries Act*, the *Canadian Environmental Protection Act*, and the *Navigable Waters Protection Act*. Passage of the bill sparked a series of protest rallies across the country. Using a variety of social media, activists in the movement were able to mobilize considerable interest and opposition among both Indigenous people and environmentalists. Initially directed at Bill C-45, Idle No More quickly grew into a global movement advocating for Indigenous human rights, equal treatment of Indigenous Peoples, and recognition of treaty rights.

The formation of Idle No More thus demonstrated the potential for effective mobilization of Indigenous Peoples and their supporters to strive for Indigenous sovereignty and for the resurgence of their cultural traditions. As Lisa Monchalin has commented:

> . . . the Idle No More movement united long-time Indigenous advocates with new generations of justice advocates. It brought Indigenous peoples together under a common vision. Using Twitter and other social media, such as Facebook, Indigenous peoples rallied, assembled flash mobs, and engage in peaceful protests, some of which garnered over 1,000 participants. This grassroots movement of the people has gone global—attracting supporters in the United States as well as in various other countries . . . [Monchalin 2016, 230]

Additionally, a broad spectrum of other Indigenous-specific initiatives has been initiated to further the well-being of Indigenous persons and their communities:

Indigenous specific prevention programs:
- That target risk factors related to health and well-being; crime.
- Aboriginal Justice Strategy—that has established community-based programs as an alternative to the criminal justice system.

Indigenous specific education programs:
- Establishment of support systems for Indigenous students attending universities and colleges in Canada.

Indigenous community-based organizations:
- National Association of Friendship Centres—provide social programming for children, youth and families, including sports, recreation, cultural education, teen parenting workshops, family violence intervention, family support programs, substance abuse interventions, and job skills training.
- Special programs to address risk factors associated with crime and victimization. [Monchalin 2016, 306–21].

Additional measures toward ensuring improved relationships between Indigenous Peoples and the Canadian criminal justice system can be found in the recommendations offered in June 2019 in the *Final Report of the National Inquiry into Missing and Murdered Women and Girls* (MMIWG). The report was submitted to the Canadian federal government and was based on more than three years of work, dozens of community hearings, and testimony from over 2000 people. Within its 1200 pages, 231 recommendations or "calls for justice" were directed primarily at ending the cycle of endemic violence that has claimed unknown numbers of Indigenous women and girls. The calls for justice also included calls for social and economic reforms, including that official language status be granted to Indigenous languages, a guaranteed annual livable income for all Canadians, sweeping reforms to the justice system and policing, and harsher penalties for those convicted of spousal or partner abuse.

The report's recommendations were directed at all levels of government—federal, provincial, territorial. and Indigenous—and included the following:

- training for police officers with regard to violence against women, cultural sensitivity, including sensitivity training for dealing with grieving family members and traumatized individuals, as well as the unique circumstances of protests on reserves;
- improved community policing, including developing relationships with vulnerable persons and others most at risk of being treated unequally by public services;
- collaborative relationships between police and Indigenous communities;
- creation of more independent Indigenous police agencies with funding equal to that of non-Indigenous police agencies; and
- increased recruitment of Indigenous police officers (MMIWG 2019).

It is apparent that many of the recommendations tendered in the *Final Report* have been brought forward by a host of other federal and provincial public inquiries, provincial coroner's inquest reports, Indigenous women's groups, Amnesty International, and other international agencies. However, what is also apparent is the lack of resources (and political will) to improve the living conditions for Indigenous Peoples and, in turn, to reduce the social factors that make people more likely to become involved with the criminal justice system. Greater investment in policing resources, in police inter-cultural training, and in active police outreach programs in order to strengthen positive relations between Indigenous communities and the police that serve them are the obvious ways forward. Initiatives in these directions, however, are often stymied by inadequate resources.

Indigenous Recruitment Issues in Policing
To be certain, as noted in Chapter 1, concerted efforts have been made over many years to foster and develop greater self-policing in and for Indigenous communities, albeit not without problems with regard to the allocation of adequate resources and funding. Although Indigenous people in Canada account for 5 per cent of the total population, of the total number of police officers in Canada, 4 per cent (or 2829 officers) self-identified in 2016 as Indigenous. Within First Nations police services, 62 per cent of police officers self-identified as Indigenous. The proportion of Indigenous officers in municipal departments, the OPP, RCMP, and the SQ ranged from 1 to 8 per cent (Conor, Robson, and Marcellus 2019).

In a prescient examination of systemic injustices toward Indigenous Peoples, the 1991 *Report of the Aboriginal Justice Inquiry of Manitoba* (Hamilton and Sinclair 1991) concluded with recommendations intended to increase the representativeness of Indigenous people working within the justice system, including within policing services in Manitoba. The recommendations were directed at both the RCMP and at municipal police services.

Prominent among the recommendations was that the province of Manitoba should increase the number of Indigenous police officers (of all genders) and the number of Indigenous civilian employees. To that end, the inquiry called for police departments to review their hiring practices for the purpose of eliminating formal recruiting criteria or processes that had adverse impacts on Indigenous recruiting (Hamilton and Sinclair 1991, 645). The report specifically pointed to such barriers to equity hiring as the formal qualification requirements, many of which discriminated against potential Indigenous applicants. For example, formal requirements such as high school completion or some level of university/college education meant that relatively few Indigenous persons stood a chance of being considered (Hamilton and Sinclair 1991, 666). Instead, recruitment of all applicants should be based more on specific skills, knowledge, and life experiences required to do the job. The report furthermore argued that a minimum target level for Indigenous representation in the criminal justice system, including policing, should be equivalent to the Indigenous proportion in the general population.

Since 1991, however, gains toward greater Indigenous representation have been modest despite efforts by all levels of policing to redress inequities in hiring. A review of official websites of select municipal police departments (Halifax, Regina, Winnipeg, Toronto, and Vancouver) and their respective strategic plans revealed prominent public commitments to diversity and to the inclusiveness of minorities, Indigenous persons, women, and LGBTQ+ persons. Most of the websites and strategic plans that were reviewed prominently displayed women and visible minorities in photographs as evidence of their commitment to inclusiveness and equity. However, other than occasional messages pointing to positive relationships and communication with Indigenous leaders and their communities, very little information conveys just how greater levels of Indigenous inclusion will be achieved through recruitment plans. The Toronto Police Service and the Vancouver Police Department were exceptions. Official websites of both these agencies provided information regarding Police Cadet Training programs (Toronto) and an Indigenous Cadet Program (Vancouver). Information pertaining to these programs explicitly reveals efforts to prepare potential Indigenous recruits to achieve a "pre-recruitment readiness" that will enhance their prospects for success once they commence the formal application process.

As Hamilton and Sinclair (1991) pointed out, the matter of greater Indigenous representation within policing is important because many Indigenous persons simply associate the police with authority and prosecution. For many Indigenous persons, the police (and the laws they enforce) are also highly visible reminders of colonial oppression, as discussed above.

Decolonization and Resurgence

Beyond the developments reviewed above, other positive measures are being are found in the strategies of **decolonization** and **resurgence** (Monchalin 2016, 297). For Lisa Monchalin, decolonization is both a process and a goal. However, for the process to work and for the goal to be attainable, both Indigenous and non-Indigenous people must "decolonize." As Alfred has noted ". . . decolonization starts becoming a reality when people collectively and consciously reject colonial identities and institutions that are the context of violence, dependency and discord in Indigenous communities" (Alfred 2009, 44 in Monchalin 2016, 293).

Allied to the notion of decolonization and the resistance to dominant colonial practices and belief systems is the need to stimulate and foster the resurgence of Indigenous culture through the restoration of traditional teachings, practices, ceremonies, and lifestyles. For Taiaiake Alfred, the political and economic domination of Indigenous Peoples within Canada has had profound consequences for ". . . the cultural integrity and mental and physical health of the people who make up these nations" (Alfred 2009, 43). However, Alfred is also of the view that economic and political aspects of decolonization are less important than efforts toward "spiritual revitalization and cultural regeneration" (Alfred 2009, 45).

Monchalin has pointed to contemporary Canadian Indigenous musicians, performers, and artists who are creatively debunking colonial misrepresentations of Indigenous lifestyles and who, through their original performances, art, and music, are reestablishing positive connections to Indigenous cultures. Specifically, Monchalin provides an overview of the work of A Tribe Called Red—an Indigenous DJ group who earned a Juno Award in 2014 as the Breakthrough Group of the Year. The group has been lauded for its reworking of racist- and stereo-typifications in existing visual and musical representations in such a way that undoes negative colonial images. A Tribe Called Red resists and debunks colonial representations of Indigenous Peoples and cultures. Their music reaches out to both Indigenous and non-Indigenous audiences.

Of the several Indigenous artists and performers lauded by Monchalin as stimulating a cultural resurgence, the anti-colonial themed work of artist Kent Monkman is notable, especially his graphic depictions of colonial authorities enforcing mandatory residential school attendance.

More recently, tenor-pianist Jeremy Dutcher has been acclaimed for his creative renderings of traditional Indigenous songs performed with symphonic orchestral backing. Indeed, Dutcher won a Juno Award in 2019 for his debut album, *Wolastoqiyik Lintuwakonawa,* which presents songs in his Indigenous language, Wolastoqey. Dutcher's artistry intentionally seeks to keep the Wolastoqey language alive (Martin 2019).

In British Columbia, non-Indigenous school teacher and graphic artist Ilonka Kuhl-Harris has endeavoured to keep Indigenous languages alive through the medium of illustrated comic books. Using self-created avatars and Photoshop software, Kuhl-Harris has created realistic illustrations as aids to her storytelling. Her first book, *Nighthawk and Little Elk*, follows the lives of two children who are being raised by an evil foster mother, *Thoxweya*. While it reads like a children's book, the evil foster mother stands as a symbolic representation of the residential school experience and the "Sixties Scoop," in which Indigenous children were taken from their homes to be adopted by Canadian families, often on tenuous and racist assumptions about Indigenous parenting. Her work has been published in English, German, syllabic Cree, Romanized Cree, Arabic, and Inuktituk (Kennedy 2019).

Such artistic cultural expressions represent small but vital steps toward overturning and replacing existing racist stereotypes in order to undo persisting colonial imagery of "Indians." Individually and collectively, the artists just reviewed and the work that they present seek not only to resist but to debunk colonial representations and colonial thinking about Indigenous Peoples and cultures. At the same time, they offer a new, rich, and relevant celebration of Indigenous cultures.

Canadian Diversity

Diversity in its settlers is a defining feature of Canada's major cities. Graham and Phillips (2007) have pointed out that by international standards Canada's largest cities have highly diverse populations. The metropolitan areas of Toronto, Vancouver, and Montreal are the place of residence for over half of all immigrants (61.4 per cent) and recent immigrants (56.0 per cent) to Canada. In 2016, immigrants represented 46.1 per cent of Toronto's population, 40.8 per cent of Vancouver's, and 23.4 per cent of Montreal's (Statistics Canada 2017(a)).

According to the 2016 Census, over 7.5 million foreign-born individuals came to Canada through immigration. This represents just over one-fifth (21.9 per cent) of Canada's total population. The proportion of foreign-born individuals was much lower from 1951 to 1991, when it ranged from 14.7 per cent to 16.1 per cent. Since 1991, the proportion has continued to rise due to the large number of immigrants admitted into Canada each year, the gradual rise in the number of deaths, and the relatively low fertility rates in Canada (Statistics Canada 2017(a)).

In the early years of the twentieth century, immigrants to Canada were predominantly European. In 1961, almost 97 per cent of Canada's population was European; nearly half of these were of British origin (Stenning 2003, 14). By the close of the twentieth century, this had shifted dramatically. By 2016, Asia (including the Middle East) was the top source of recent immigrants. The majority (61.8 per cent) of newcomers to Canada from 2011 to 2016 were born in Asia (Statistics Canada 2017(a)). In 2016, 13.4 per cent of recent immigrants were born in Africa, which ranked second behind Asia but ahead of Europe as source continents of recent immigrants to Canada (Statistics Canada, 2017(a)). Increasingly, Canadian cities have thus become more multiethnic and multiracial.

Multiculturalism and Policing

In a 2003 article, Phillip Stenning documented the difficulties that Canadian police agencies faced in delivering effective services to multicultural communities. Problems during the 1970s, 1980s, and 1990s had resulted in numerous public inquiries, coroners' inquests, and political protests, all of them addressing dissatisfaction with the organization and delivery of policing service (Stenning 2003). Canadian police were criticized for discrimination, stereotyping, insensitivity, alienation from the community, and their overly military-style police subculture and chain of command. Even the events following the 9/11 terrorist attacks were a reminder of the need for Canadian police to adapt to diversity. In the intensification of security measures in the aftermath of the attacks, Muslim communities complained of harassment. At the same time, police recognized their inability to engage meaningfully with Canadian Muslim communities (Ben-Porat 2008, 416–17).

As Ben-Porat has argued, alienation of large sectors of the Canadian population (minorities, women, LGBTQ+) from the police is often perceived as discrimination. Discrimination undermines the effectiveness of police to serve the community. At the same time, it prevents minority groups from receiving the fair and equitable policing services and protections to which they are entitled. In relatively simple terms, problems of poor police–minority relations manifest themselves in two ways: over-policing and under-policing (Ben-Porat 2003).

Over-policing entails "mistreatment of minorities by the police either by excessive use of force towards minorities or by discriminatory practice against them that includes excessive use of routine 'stop and search' and disproportionate arrest rates" (Ben-Porat 2008, 415). **Under-policing**, on the other hand, "is largely about police neglect in minority communities with high crime rates" (Ben-Porat 2008, 415). For example, under-policing can result from police unresponsiveness to domestic assaults in ethnic enclaves in some communities. Police sometimes come to see (and stereotype) domestic violence as typical of some ethnic groups and therefore are less willing to initiate criminal charges (Ben-Porat 2008).

Out of the concerns that had resulted in public inquiries and coroners' inquests, the principal means by which Canadian police agencies sought to address problems associated with a lack of representatives was by diversifying the workforce.

Diversification of the Police Workforce

Police recruiting programs have made sincere efforts to solicit recruits who are more reflective of Canada's multicultural society. Police agencies in the United States are also generally acknowledged to have made remarkable progress in their efforts to diversify, albeit with variations among departments (Sklansky 2006). As Sklansky observes in his discussion of the demographics of American public policing,

[t]he virtually all-white, virtually all-male departments of the 1950s and 1960s have given way to departments with large numbers of female and minority officers, often led by female or minority chiefs. Openly gay and lesbian officers, too, are increasingly commonplace. [Sklanksy 2006, 1210]

Diversification of the police in the United States, in sharp contrast to Canada, has been forced by court-ordered affirmative action initiatives and hiring quotas. Lawsuits brought by minorities, particularly African-Americans, and by women have produced court decisions that have forced American police departments to open their ranks (Roberg, Novak, and Cordner 2005; Sklansky 2006).

In Canada, while police agencies have been criticized by public inquiries and have often been subject to negative media coverage, senior police administrators have generally been both more aware of and responsive to the need for their agencies to reflect the broader communities that they serve. In part, this may be due to the fact that Canadians are not as litigious (that is, less likely to launch lawsuits) as Americans, but may also mean that Canadians and their police leaders are generally more sympathetic to inclusiveness.

Despite the willingness of Canadian police agencies to actively recruit minority and women candidates, pre-existing limitations hamper success. For example, immigrants, similar to Indigenous candidates as discussed above, may lack formal educational requirements. Immigrants may also not see policing as a desirable career given their perceptions of police in their home countries. Similarly, some immigrant communities resent the police and will see members of their community who become police officers as "selling out" or being co-opted.

In response to such recruiting challenges, the Toronto Police Service has adapted by portraying itself as a desirable occupation for immigrants and minorities and has set targets to increase applications from women, visible minorities, Indigenous people, LGBTQ+ people, and persons who speak more than one language (Ben-Porat 2008, 419). Other agencies, including the RCMP, set recruitment targets as well.

Despite genuine efforts to better reflect the cultural and gender composition of communities, police services have had only limited success in reaching targets. For example, legal scholar and criminologist Phillip Stenning, writing in 2003, states,

In Toronto, the Canadian city with the largest municipal police service and a very substantial ethnic/visibility minority population (estimated now to be close to half the population), ethnic/visible minority representation among sworn officers in the police service increased from less than 6 per cent in 1991 to 10 per cent (508 of its 5089 sworn officers) in 2000. . . . In Montreal, Canada's second largest city, the visible minority population constituted 12 per cent of the total population in 1996, but by the year 2000, [after] 10 years of aggressive recruitment efforts, visible minority members still constituted only 3.7 per cent of the sworn officers in the Montreal Urban Community (MUC). [Stenning 2003, 19]

Stenning's point is simple enough: Even with the best of intentions, changing the face of policing is a slow process. Although his data and observations are now 17 years old, the slow pace and challenges of diversification continue today. This is underscored in recent work by Justin Szeto (2014).

In his 2014 study of minority police officers' perceptions of diversity, Justin Szeto acknowledges that impressive steps have been taken by Canadian police agencies to embrace diversity. However, the impressive steps hide some blemishes.

In a compilation of descriptive statistics for the years 1999 to 2012, obtained with the cooperation of an anonymous Canadian police academy, Szeto calculated a series of averages pertaining to the 15,716 recruits trained over this time frame. He found that

- males on average comprised 81 per cent of new recruits, females 19 per cent;
- non-minorities comprised 83 per cent, visible minorities (including Indigenous people) 17 per cent;
- English was the first language for 82 per cent of recruits; 9 per cent had a first language other than English or French; 4 per cent had English and French; 3.6 per cent had English and another language; 1.3 per cent had French as a first language; and
- 33 per cent had completed university education; 48 per cent had completed college; 11 per cent had some college or university; and 8.2 per cent had no college or university (Szeto 2014, 35–45).

While Szeto's analysis makes no claim that his data are representative of recruiting patterns in other jurisdictions throughout Canada, white, English-speaking males made up the majority of recruits entering policing over this time span. His data indicate that in real numbers there has been significant progress in recruiting women and minorities to Canadian police agencies. However, as much as recruiting patterns are changing, the increased representation of women and minorities is not keeping pace with the increasing diversity in the communities being served. Furthermore, while the progress to date is impressive with respect to greater inclusiveness of women and minorities, the progress may be slowing (Szeto 2014, 44).

The problems police organizations face in correcting the historic underrepresentation of women and visible minorities is evident in a report by the Human Rights and Youth Rights Commission in the province of Quebec. Released in 2015, the report points out that women are still woefully underrepresented in the upper ranks of the Sûreté du Québec (SQ). However, since 2015, of the 50 municipal police services in Canada serving populations of 100,000 or more, the highest proportion of female officers was found in Quebec. Langueuil had the highest proportion, with 34 per cent of officers being female, followed by Montreal with 33 per cent—both higher than the SQ with 23 per cent (Conor, Robson, and Marcellus 2019).

As Szeto acknowledges, the slowing of diversification of Canadian police agencies echoes the pattern of the successful integration of police departments in the United States. That is, initial progress in recruiting women, African-Americans, and gay officers in the United States appears to have stalled (Sklansky 2006, 1243). In the United States, the stalling is partly attributable to the expiry of time frames that had been imposed by court-ordered affirmative action. It is also partly attributable to the growing **civilianization** of policing (see Chapters 11 and 13). Rather than seeking work as uniformed officers, women in particular opt for work with police departments as civilians in clerical jobs that pay significantly less (Sklansky 2006).

Szeto's research also offers distinctive observations on the perceptions and experiences of visible minority officers. Relying on a small sample of twelve minority police personnel composed of officers having varying years of experience and varying non-commissioned ranks, Szeto argues that police organization commitments to diversity are perceived by minority officers as rhetorical. He claims that police diversity policies create "a rationalized institutional myth" that serves to "window dress" barriers and challenges within police services (Szeto 2014, 3) and that the internal dynamics of police organizations remain unchanged. This, according to his sample, creates problems for visible minority officers.

Drawing on studies of organizational behaviour in private corporations, Szeto suggests that progressive diversity policies are used as a sign of good performance and as an expression of commitment to being open to equal opportunity. In short, it is good public relations to appear to be actively diversifying the work force. However, for Szeto and his research participants, adoption of a commitment to diversity may not reflect the actual inner workings of the organization.

While Szeto agrees that there have been significant objective indications of progress in hiring women and minorities in Canadian police agencies, there is still massive underrepresentation in police organizations, which is masked by the public campaigns, advertisements, and recruiting drives (Szeto 2014, 64).

Rationalized institutional myths also create tensions for minority officers and obscure the problems they experience within the police organization. For example, it is a widely held belief that minority officers bring culturally sensitive attitudes to their work. This is generally seen as beneficial to the police organization but is often ignored in policing practices (Szeto 2014, 68). As well, language barriers between police and ethnic communities have a negative impact on community relations. Police agencies have therefore recognized the advantage of having multilingual visible minority officers, not only in regard to fostering good community relations, but also in regard to intelligence gathering and undercover work in ethnic criminal activities. However, the participants in Szeto's research reported that there is not enough formal recognition of these contributions and in this light drew attention to what they perceived as an underrepresentation of minorities in the upper ranks (Szeto 2014, 70). Szeto points out that the culture of policing, despite marked progress in recruitment of women and minorities, is still very much a white-male–dominated occupational culture.

Police Occupational Culture

As has been noted by many authors, police agencies in Canada (as well as in the United States, the United Kingdom, and Australia) have exhibited an occupational culture that has been characterized as overly male, heterosexual, conservative, and white. The concept of an occupational culture is not distinct to policing. Other occupational groups, including lawyers and medical doctors, have similarly fostered widely shared occupational norms, standards, beliefs, and practices.

While many components of police culture are thought to be transmitted to police recruits in the course of the occupational socialization that occurs in formal training programs and in on-the-job interactions with other police officers, scholars like Janet Chan

(1997) give additional weight to how individual officers experience, interpret, and react to the circumstances they encounter in the course of police work (O'Neill 2016, 477).

As Colin Goff has noted, the notion of a police occupational culture is "an important concept in terms of understanding a large number of issues surrounding policing, including how new members of the police organization 'learn the ropes' of policing, the success or failure of attempts to reform the police, and how the police function on a day-to-day basis" (Goff 2017, 169). Such historical and problematic matters as racism, sexism, and homophobia within policing, along with police resistance to change and to greater levels of public accountability, have been attributed to the persistence of an entrenched police culture. The existence of a police culture has also led to what commentators have referred to as the "blue wall of silence"—a term used to describe such matters as police solidarity, police emphasis on secrecy, and a general mistrust of the outside world.

As Goff (2017) has noted, an understanding of police culture is an important consideration for explaining police practices in the community. It is also vital for understanding police resistance to change, for example, initial police resistance to greater civilian oversight.

Notwithstanding the public imagery of actively seeking to diversify, much work is needed to improve the intra-organizational legitimacy of diversity. In other words, despite the public face of efforts of police agencies to diversify in order to reflect the community, persistence of the traditional male, white culture internal to most police departments presents barriers to minorities, women, and LGBTQ+ who are recruited.

Racial Profiling or Racialized Policing?

In an important study of race and policing titled *Racialized Policing: Aboriginal People's Encounters with the Police*, published in 2012, sociologist Elizabeth Comack seeks to make sense of the relationship between police agencies and persons of colour. Her work deserves consideration in the context of diversity and Canadian policing.

Comack's analysis of how race and racism invade police work is primarily focused on the relationship that police have with Indigenous Peoples within Canada. The book develops insights into three high-profile instances of systemic racism at work in Canada toward Indigenous Peoples: the 1988 killing of J.J. Harper, the 1990s Starlight Tours in Saskatchewan, and the 2005 shooting death of Matthew Dumas. Her work, however, is also informed by the experiences of Black Canadians and particularly by the controversies that erupted in Ontario in 2002 and 2010 over the police use of discretionary stops to query Black people in instances of what is colloquially referred to as "driving while Black."

The *Toronto Star* newspaper had filed freedom-of-information requests and had obtained access to the Toronto Police Service Criminal Information Processing Systems (CIPS). An analysis of the data revealed that Black residents were routinely subjected to ticketing by Toronto police for "out-of-sight-offences" (offences that cannot be detected without stopping the driver, for example expired insurance or lacking a current driver's licence). In short, in both 2002 and 2010, in a series of articles focused on crime and race, the *Toronto Star* alleged that police were consistently singling out drivers on the basis of skin colour or, in other words, systematically engaging in the practice of racial profiling. (See Challenge Your Assumptions: Carding and the Toronto Police Service.)

Challenge Your Assumptions

Carding and the Toronto Police Service

The 2002 and 2010 series of articles published by the *Toronto Star* newspaper pointed out that the practice of carding (in which police officers routinely stop, question, and record encounters with members of the public who are not immediately or necessarily suspected of involvement in criminal activity) was racist. The series pointed out the practice was disproportionately used by Toronto police against young Black men.

The articles also generated considerable public and academic debate (see Comack 2012; note also Chapter 14 in this text).

In late 2014 and early 2015, with the reverberations from the wave of shootings of young African-Americans by white police officers in the United States, the mayor of Toronto, supported by members of the Toronto Police Services Board, called for the end of carding. As a result, Ontario's Minister of Community Safety and Correctional Services announced that new provincial regulations would ensure that people in Ontario would no longer be stopped simply based on the way they look or the neighbourhood they live in.

According to the *Toronto Star*, with the new regulations people who are subsequently street-checked by the police will be

- told they have the right to walk away;
- advised they do not have to provide information;

- advised why they are being stopped and questioned;
- provided with a written record of the interaction;
- given information about the police officer; and
- informed about the police complaints system (Gillis, Ranking, and Winsa 2015).

Some police officers in Canada defend the practice of carding, believing it to be an invaluable tool vital to police efforts to protect the broader community. Former Toronto Police Chief Mark Saunders, himself a person of visible minority status, supported the continuation of carding as long as it is carried out in an acceptable and unbiased manner. As of January 1, 2017, Ontario implemented a series of regulations requiring that police advise people who are about to be "street-checked" that they have a right not to talk with them. Refusal cannot be used by police as a basis to compel further information. Since this has been implemented, the number of people who have been stopped on the street has been significantly reduced, and there are calls to end carding in other cities and provinces (*CBC News* 2016).

Should police officers be able to card anyone they wish? What benefits are gained from the practices of carding? What are the negative consequences of carding? Will making carding voluntary impact the effectiveness of the tool?

In a more serious vein and given the lack of Canadian national statistics regarding fatal encounters with the police, CBC journalists Jacques Marcoux and Katie Nicholson pulled together data on 461 fatal police encounters between 2000 and 2017 (Marcoux and Nicholson 2017). Even when adjusted for population growth over the 17-year period, the number of people dying in police encounters has risen steadily. More than 70 per cent of victims suffered from mental health and substance abuse problems. When racial and ethnic composition is taken into account, overrepresentation of minorities in fatal encounters with police is also problematic. Black people in Toronto, for example, made up approximately 8.3 per cent of the population but represented nearly 37 per cent of victims. In Winnipeg, Indigenous people represented on average 10.6 per cent of the population but accounted for almost 66 per cent of the fatalities (Marcoux and Nicholson 2017).

Acknowledging that policing is a difficult and challenging job done admirably by the vast majority of men and women who work as police officers, Comack argues that to characterize the inordinate police attention directed at Indigenous Peoples and Black Canadians as racial profiling is simplistic. Defining **racial profiling** as "relying on racial stereotypes to single out certain individuals and groups in society as being more suspect and therefore subject to increased scrutiny and harsher treatment," Comack takes exception to the term, arguing that its use individualizes the problem (Comack 2012, 14). That is, use of the term "racial profiling" facilitates overly convenient and easy explanations that "police are racist bigots" or that it is "a few bad (racist) apples" that are the cause of problems (Comack 2012, 23). Racial profiling is more than the exercise of discretion by individual police officers and is too narrow to explain the complex ways in which race and racialization interact with policing.

Comack argues that in order to understand police interactions with visible minority groups, it is necessary to understand the wider social contexts in which police carry out their work. In a process called **racialization**, societies construct race and come to believe races are "real, different and unequal in ways that matter to economic, political and social life" (Cole and Gittens 1995, 30). For Comack, "racialization involves the production of differences; it is the process of constructing racial categories, identities, and meanings" (2012, 17). Part of the process of racialization of society entails the absorption of often subtle but real beliefs about the superiority of white people and the inferiority of others into a variety of social systems, including the criminal justice system. In short, Comack's thesis is that Canadian society has always been racialized and that, in turn, Canadian policing has been shaped by it historically.

The term **racialized policing** therefore points to a much wider context that shapes the interactions between police as an institution and racialized groups. Racialized policing underpins the construction of the "usual suspects" and the heightened sensitivity to particular persons and situations (which many officers jokingly refer to as a "Spidey sense" about persons and places). In the United States, as Comack points out, scholar Jerome Skolnick has unreservedly argued that racialized police have come to associate the Black man with danger (Skolnick 1975 in Comack 2012, 62).

For Comack, the concept of racialized policing thus allows for a richer understanding of the ways in which police encounter racialized groups. As a concept, it also serves to make greater sense of the persistence of the subtle but real systemic racism within policing and the criminal justice system.

Gender and Policing

According to the 2016 Census data available from Statistics Canada, almost 17.9 million of the total Canadian population of 35.5 million, or approximately 51 per cent of the total population, was female (Statistics Canada, 2017(c)). In police work, women accounted for

22 per cent of sworn officers and numbered 14,943. As discussed in Chapter 1, women also represented 15 per cent of senior officers in 2018—the highest proportion on record (Conor, Robson, and Marcellus 2019).

The proportion of women working as police officers has consistently risen over the years from 4 per cent in 1986, when data collection began, to 9.1 per cent in 1994, to 16.5 per cent in 2004, and to 22 per cent in 2018 (Conor, Robson, and Marcellus 2019). As noted earlier in this chapter, despite an increase in the actual number of women recruits, the rate at which they are being hired appears to have slowed.

Two factors may account for the slowing rate of recruitment. First, police work is still viewed by many as a male (and dangerous) occupation and the potential pool of women who are prepared to enter police work may be dwindling. Second, those women who do aspire to police work may be opting to join police agencies as civilian employees, as the number of civilians in police work continues to grow. In 2018, police services in Canada employed 26,851 civilians, which entailed a 7 per cent increase over the previous year. Women accounted for 71 per cent of civilian personnel and held a variety of positions: clerical, reception and front desk services, court services, finances, human resources, legal services, and operational communications (Conor, Robson, and Marcellus 2019). Civilians are doing routine work once done by more highly paid police officers. (See Chapter 11.)

Challenges for Women and Policing

Contrary to the myth that women do not have the natural physical abilities to engage in the sometimes physically demanding aspects of police work, overall physical ability has not been shown to be a strong predictor of success in law enforcement. Other factors contribute to the relatively small pool of women who aspire to policing as a career: recruitment and retention practices of police departments, family and work–life balance issues, and gender-based harassment and violence within policing organizations (Province of Manitoba 2014, 2).

Many police departments have now developed recruiting programs that target and fast-track women applicants. Police recruiting teams are also themselves intentionally composed to reflect diversity—visible minorities and women play active and prominent roles in promoting their agencies. Increasingly, police agencies actively participate at career days and recruitment fairs at colleges and universities in the hope of encouraging a diverse range of applicants. As well, some police agencies have amended physical testing practices unrelated to job requirements so that height, weight, and strength standards do not discriminate against women recruits (Province of Manitoba 2014, 2).

Police departments have also come to realize that it is not just with respect to the intake of new recruits that diversity goals are to be achieved, but that retention of serving officers is equally as important. Women leave police work for a variety of reasons including perceived lack of promotional opportunity, inflexible working arrangements, and the perceived lack of support from male peers and superiors (Hassell and Brandl 2009; Province of Manitoba 2014, 3).

Work–life balance is also a factor in retention of women officers. Many female officers have children and are the principal caregivers. Women too take greater responsibility for aging parents. Female officers have also been found to experience overall higher levels of stress than their male counterparts, especially as their rank increases. In large police agencies, such as the OPP, SQ, and RCMP, promotions often require relocation. Women are less likely to accept such promotions due to concerns about disrupting their partners' careers and/or their children's lives.

Finally, as widely reported in popular media, gender-based discrimination and sexual harassment in Canadian police agencies create an inhospitable work environment for women. While many police agencies have developed aggressive zero-tolerance anti-discrimination and anti-harassment policies and procedures, negative perceptions and experiences abound. Nowhere is this more evident than in the class-action sexual harassment lawsuit brought against the RCMP by some 362 women in 2015 (see Macdonald and Gillis 2015).

LGBTQ+ Communities and Policing

Canada's major cities are home to important populations of gay, lesbian, bisexual, transgender, queer, and questioning persons. According to Statistics Canada, there were 72,880 same-sex couples in Canada in 2016; this represented just under 1 per cent of all couples. Half of Canada's same-sex couples lived in Canada's four largest metropolitan areas: Toronto, Montreal, Vancouver, and Ottawa-Gatineau. About one-eighth (12 per cent) of all same-sex couples had children living with them compared with about half (51.4 per cent) of opposite-sex couples (Statistics Canada 2017(d)).

In order to properly meet the needs of increasingly diverse communities, police agencies have come to appreciate the need to be more representative of the communities they serve. As a result, otherwise conservative police departments have had to adapt by actively recruiting members from LBGTQ+ communities. However, the history of the relationship between police and those who are not exclusively cisgender and heterosexual has had its controversy and conflict.

While it is beyond the scope of this discussion to trace the history of homophobia and transphobia within the policing subculture, a passing review of some examples of police persecution of homosexuality will illustrate the extent of overt discrimination that has existed and the resistance that has had to be overcome.

In the post–World War II period in Canada, the RCMP turned their attention to what was then termed "moral lapses or character defects" (Whitaker, Kealey, and Parnaby 2012, 189). These lapses or defects were simply euphemisms for homosexuality, which was viewed as "an abominable perversion, the sexual counterpart to the political deviancy of Communism—and inexorably linked to it" (Whitaker, Kealey, and Parnaby 2012, 190). In short, during the Cold War (see Chapter 15), the RCMP zealously investigated civil servants and military personnel to purge sexual deviants who were perceived to be vulnerable to blackmail by Communist spymasters. Persons who were discovered to be homosexual were deemed to be potential threats to national security and were forced to resign. This homosexual witch hunt continued into the 1960s and by then at least 113 individuals had been dismissed or forced to resign (Whitaker, Kealey, and Parnaby 2012, 191).

During this time, the RCMP security services also added the threat of "outing" suspected homosexuals to their intelligence-gathering techniques. That is, if the RCMP could discover that someone was homosexual, they would coerce the individual into becoming an informer under the threat of being publicly disclosed. The RCMP used this technique to coerce information from staff members at foreign embassies, from union activists, and from others involved in left-wing political action groups.

From the vantage point of modern sensibilities, much of the activity directed at homosexuality seems absurd. Nevertheless, by the 1960s, alongside the rise of the civil rights and peace movements that sought equality for African-Americans in the United States and for women generally, and sought an end to the war in Vietnam, gay, lesbian, and transgender people found a space to push back on discrimination against their communities.

In June 1969 at the Stonewall Inn, a popular gay bar in Greenwich Village, New York, trans women and gay men resisted harassment by the police. In an angry confrontation with the police that evolved into a riot that lasted hours, other gay men and women joined the initial protesters by hurling objects at the police and taunting them with chants of "Gay Power!" Police reinforcements arrived to subdue the crowd. However, the crowd of protesters returned the following night, this time numbering over 1000. Again, a riot squad dispersed the crowd. For days, various demonstrations and protests erupted spontaneously throughout New York City, marking the birth of the gay liberation movement (Leadership Conference on Civil and Human Rights, n.d.).

In Canada, during this time, the federal government under Liberal Prime Minister Pierre Trudeau recognized that the "government has no business in the bedrooms of the nation" and amended the *Criminal Code* of Canada in 1969 by removing some of the prohibitions against homosexual acts in private by consenting adults. However, acceptance of the law and of homosexuality was slower to develop.

Frank Lennon/Toronto Star via Getty Image

A photo from the 1981 bathhouse raids in Toronto. How might this kind of institutional history prevent certain community members from trusting, cooperating with, or joining police services in Canada?

In 1981, 12 years after the amendment, the Toronto police raided a series of gay steam rooms in a highly controversial crackdown on homosexual behaviour. On the evening of Thursday, 5 February 1981, using crowbars, sledgehammers, and flashlights, the Metropolitan Toronto police smashed their way into four downtown bathhouses. As result of the raid, 250 men were charged with being "found-ins" in common bawdy houses. Doors were broken, windows and glass were smashed, and pictures were ripped off the walls. The chief of police justified the raid on the grounds that police had reasonable and probable grounds to believe that the bathhouses were being used for prostitution and "indecent acts."

As Augustine Brannigan observed, "Clearly on this raid the police were out fishing for a certain kind of offender. No one casually rounds up 250 homosexuals on regular patrol. In fact, it was the greatest mass arrest in Canada since the declaration of the *War Measures Act* in 1970" (Brannigan 1984, 99). As Brannigan points out, 250 men successfully challenged the charges, 19 pleaded guilty, 18 were found guilty at trial, and the remaining cases were not pursued. In other words, the charges were unfounded in 87 per cent of these arrests (Brannigan 1984, 99).

Speaking generally, academic studies of serving police members who are LGBTQ+ are rare. While police departments are increasingly open to hiring persons who are LGBTQ+, personal sexual preference is still a sensitive and private issue and thus difficult to research. Police officers may simply choose to not disclose their sexual orientation. Statistics Canada's annual report *Police Resources in Canada* does not report data related to the sexual orientation of Canadian police officers. Ultimately, sexual orientation should be of little significance other than to ensure that homophobic and transphobic attitudes do not lead to overt or covert discrimination in hiring or promotional practices or otherwise affect the working environment.

In what is believed to be the first Canadian study to examine the workplace and career experiences of lesbian, gay, bisexual, and transgender (LGBT) police officers, Joe Couto conducted interviews with a sample of 21 police officers with varying sexual orientations and gender expressions (Couto 2014; 2018).

Participants in the study reported that while they believed the police culture is still dominated by conservative, male, heterosexual outlooks, a shift toward greater inclusivity of women, racialized groups, and LGBTQ+ persons is evident (Couto 2014, 36). It is a shift that has been driven by legislative changes rather than a wholesale progressive move in traditional police culture. In part the shift is also attributable to the transition of police departments toward the community policing model. In order to be successful, community policing must be more responsive to and reflective of the community it serves. (See Chapter 12.) The shift in attitudes, however, is occurring "in an evolutionary, not revolutionary manner" (Couto 2014, 37).

Couto's participants demonstrated a strong commitment to the overall law enforcement goals of maintaining order and fighting crime. However, in a manner that supports the findings of Szeto (2014) discussed earlier in regard to visible minorities in policing, Couto's LGBT participants also identified a gap between the formal rhetoric of their police departments and "how things really are" (Couto 2014, 38). That is, while there is a public face to police agency commitment to inclusivity, the internal organizational features that support it are often lacking. Specifically, Couto's sample noted that the most common frustration of LGBTQ+ officers was the lack of support and influence in the workplace. As noted above, this rings true for the experience of women officers and racialized officers as well.

Conclusion

This chapter began with an overview of diversity and multiculturalism in Canada.

Special consideration was given to the under-policing and over-policing of Indigenous Peoples within Canada, keeping in mind that they are not just another minority/ethnic group. The social, economic, and political exclusion of Indigenous Peoples presents serious challenges for Canadian police and even bigger ones for Canadian society as a whole.

It also briefly considered the ways in which relatively recent immigration patterns have changed and are changing the face of Canada, particularly in major cities. These demographic shifts have forced police agencies to adapt in order to meet the needs of increasingly diverse communities. Police have thus sought to recruit visible minorities, women, and LGBTQ+ persons to reflect this diversity.

Finally, the chapter considered policing challenges associated with the recruitment of women and LGBTQ+ persons.

Critical Thinking Questions

1. Is diversity important in policing? Should police agencies reflect the diversity of the communities they police? Explain your answer.
2. Despite a general acceptance of diversity in sexual orientations in Canada, many faiths, including some Christian and Muslim faiths, still denounce homosexuality. Is it appropriate for police officers to threaten to disclose the sexual orientation of persons suspected of crimes to their colleagues, families, and peers in order to elicit information? Explain your answer.
3. What is the colonial problem? How does this concept account for the gross overrepresentation of Indigenous people in the criminal justice system?
4. What is "decolonialization"? What is "resurgence"? How do these concepts relate to the future of Indigenous Peoples within Canada?
5. Does the term "racialized policing" account for the over- and under-policing of Indigenous Peoples within Canada? Explain your answer.
6. Some people believe that the pool of available women motivated to become police officers is getting smaller. In what ways might more women be encouraged to apply to join a police department?

Endnotes

i   In situating ourselves in our roles as instructors, as researchers, and as authors of this textbook, we have been guided by the discussion provided by Lisa Monchalin (2016, see pages xvii–iv).

ii   Despite the use of the term "race" in official documents (including statutes), the concept of "race" is itself controversial. Scholars increasingly have come to view the concept of "race" as a socially constructed myth. Assigning human beings into distinct groups based on perceived distinctive features lacks empirical objectivity. Variations such as skin colour, hair type, nose or eye shape, or height do not form regular patterns and do not represent objective criteria by which people can be assigned into groups (see Cole and Gittens 2005; Comack 2012, 14).

PART II

Becoming a Police Officer

4

Recruitment and Training

Learning Objectives

After reading and studying this chapter, students will be able to:

- Describe and discuss future challenges facing Canadian police agencies.
- Identify and discuss the qualities of a desirable candidate for recruitment.
- Describe and discuss Canadian police training programs.
- Explain the concept of continuous learning as it applies to a policing career.
- Identify and discuss the challenges of police work as a career.

Introduction

As in most occupations, the major challenge of police recruitment is securing the right person. The questions thus arise: Who is the right person? What qualities are essential for a police officer to think and act decisively in stressful situations? What type of person is the right person to mediate a myriad of conflicts that arise in situations to which police respond? The job of policing is nuanced, variable, and complex. It is important to hire **recruits** who are best able to meet the complex demands of modern police work (Iacobucci 2014, 129).

Fundamentally, police agencies in Canada try to address these questions as they compete with each other to identify, screen, train, and hire **recruits** who will develop into competent police officers. What screening tools are available to measure such key attributes as honesty, integrity, propriety, maturity, and the ability to respond appropriately in diverse circumstances? While there is consistency among municipal, provincial, and federal police in the preferred qualities of potential recruits, there is also variance. "The selection of the right people is crucial to any agency's survival and success in a world where police are more visible and police discretion is more scrutinized than ever before" (Cohen McCullough and Spence 2014, 1).

Why do people seek a career in policing? Popular media of all kinds certainly highlight the perceived excitement of a police career. In 2019, and in preceding decades, police and/or criminal justice has been a significant focus of many television dramas and movies. Shows such as *Criminal Minds*, *Law and Order*, *Blue Bloods* and the *CSI* series have dominated North American television for many years. One might ask whether the influence of such shows is a factor as viewers see non-stop excitement, challenging mysteries to solve, and the battle of good versus evil.

Other people who take an interest in policing may feel they would like to contribute something important to their communities. Still others may be drawn by the sense of prestige attached to a career in policing, despite the often-negative public perceptions of dramatic situations where the actions of the police are questioned and openly criticized. Finally, the belief that police work is based upon integrity, diligence, commitment, effort, and responsibility is also a draw to the occupation.

Police work is forever changing, trying hard to match the pace at which Canadian society evolves. For example, Duxbury (2015, 6) observed that over the past 25 years, external changes including social media, technology, new legislation, community police collaboration, and the downloading of services, particularly in relation to individuals dealing with mental health issues, have shaped the policing environment.

The population is multicultural and aging—for example, in 2016, among the working-age population, 49.9 per cent were in the age group 45 to 64, a record-high proportion (Statistics Canada 2017(a)). Advances in technology have changed how people communicate and go about their lives. Policing must adapt in order to understand not only the changing social demographics but crime trends and criminal justice priorities established by governments, the judiciary, and the Canadian public. In short, as society changes, policing adjusts; as policing changes, training shifts (Chappell, Lanza-Kaduce, and Johnston, cited in Dunham 2010, 53). As much as police agencies try to be proactive and understand their communities, it is often the case that police have to contend with competing expectations of what they should focus on and how they should best serve the community. An additional challenge is that there are often smaller enclaves within any given police jurisdiction where immigrants or people with common backgrounds tend to live. Expectations of the police can therefore literally vary from block to block in some cases.

Without question, all police agencies in Canada try to recruit police officers who are representative of their communities and of the whole country more generally. Chief Charles Bordeleau of the Ottawa Police Service "underscored the importance of a diverse workforce in order to improve police services' effectiveness in an ever-diverse and technologically oriented society" (Bordeleau 2015, 15) Potential recruits who have the basic qualifications will enhance their chances at getting serious consideration in the recruiting and hiring process if they have multiple language skills and broad life experience. Life experience may include such things as job stability, specific job responsibilities (such as supervising others), working with the public, higher education, and travelling abroad

Recruitment standards are similar within most Canadian police agencies, as is the priority given to hiring visible minorities and women. As defined by Statistics Canada, "visible minorities are those persons (other than Indigenous persons[i]) who are non-Caucasian in race or non-white in colour" (Statistics Canada, n.d.). However, Canadian police have struggled with attracting potential recruits who are visible minorities. There may be many reasons for this, but Cao (2011, 1) found that "visible minorities in Canada had lower levels of confidence in the police than non-members of visible minorities," and reported that "equal race confidence in the police is yet to be achieved and continued reform measures are needed if the police force is to win the hearts and minds of visible minorities in Canada." (See Chapter 3 for further discussion.)

Recruitment

Recruitment can be defined as the "development of a pool of sufficiently qualified applicants from which to select officers" (Gaines and Miller 2013, 290). It is a long-held belief that a progressive police service must evolve to reflect the communities it serves.

Recruiting is an important function to ensure that police forces deal with **attrition** from retirement, and the ability to respond to population growth, crime trends, and other factors that may necessitate growth in authorized strength. One cannot overemphasize the importance of recruitment, selection, and training for the overall health of a police department (Alpert, Dunham, and Stroshine 2006, 36). A lot of time, effort, and money go into trying to attract a variety of people who could become assets to the police agency. Police agencies attend career fairs at universities, colleges, and high schools as well as use print, television, and radio advertising to actively solicit qualified applicants. The importance of social media is recognized as an excellent tool to complement other recruiting efforts and to target younger candidates and to encourage them to consider a career in policing.

Law enforcement chiefs and organizations are in continual pursuit of the ideal police officer candidate. A desirable candidate is one who is assertive and decisive, yet compassionate and empathic. This individual is level-headed, an effective communicator, emotionally stable, courageous under pressure, and, most importantly, is one whose ethics are beyond reproach (LePard and Davey 2014, 1). Recruiting can build legitimacy (Cohen McCullough and Spence 2014, 1), as being able to attract candidates with impressive backgrounds, such as former elite athletes, speaks to the reputation of the police agency. Trust and confidence in the police are fundamental to the effectiveness of any police agency. Reputation, trust, and credibility are vital.

The Five Cs

Arnold (2014) referred to the **five Cs** of law enforcement leadership desirable in recruits: courage, character, commitment, compassion, and communication. From the uniformed patrol officer to police officers working in specialized units, considerable weight is given to the five Cs. Patrol policing is an activity in which police never know what is around the corner. Every call for service is different and circumstances may become instantly dynamic. Courage to face unknown situations and deal with them within both departmental policy and the law is fundamental. First-responder patrol officers have no choice but to address the immediate circumstances that unfold before them. They are required by law and by departmental policy to stop or prevent the crime, solve the problem, or otherwise assure public safety.

Since the patrol officer often deals with difficult and tragic situations, character (or integrity) and commitment are essential. Compassion and well-developed communication skills are often key to defusing situations as safely as possible. The five Cs are also relevant to the plainclothes investigator, albeit in a slightly different context. For example, plainclothes investigators must have the courage to take investigative risks on short- and longer-term strategies, such as prioritizing suspects when the offender is yet to be identified and the offences are continuing. Investigators must have the character and commitment to work hard and maintain focus for months and sometimes years at a time, demonstrate genuine compassion for victims of crime and their families, and communicate effectively both orally and in writing. For certain, to be a well-regarded, successful police officer, one must possess and make significant efforts to develop and refine the five Cs throughout one's career.

In the recruiting stage, police agencies screen potential candidates on the basis of character and communication abilities. These are assessed through employment history and personal reference checks, database checks, a formal interview, and, in many police agencies, polygraph testing. Character is a difficult thing to identify and assess, but it would appear that integrity is a close equivalent. Integrity can be loosely defined as having the qualities of truthfulness, honesty, and respect. It is widely recognized that a police officer should possess a higher moral character. It is also the case that public expectations of the conduct of police officers are high, irrespective of whether the police officer is on or off duty. It could be argued that the remaining qualities of courage, commitment, and compassion can only be observed and meaningfully assessed once a candidate has started training and, subsequently, based on how he or she ultimately performs as a police officer in the field.

The Numbers

Recruiting is an important function and has taken on an even greater significance in the twenty-first century as increasing numbers of experienced, long-serving, "baby-boomer" generation police officers reach retirement age. In 2019, Statistics Canada reported that, as of May 2018, there were 68,562 police officers in Canada. This represented a rate of police strength of 185 officers per 100,000 and a decline of 2 per cent from 2017 (Conor, Robson, and Marcellus 2019, 1).

The primary reason police officers leave their police agency is retirement. In 2017/18, 11 per cent of police officers were eligible to retire (Conor, Robson, and Marcellus 2019, 12). The attrition rate for police officers due to retirement will not decrease in the coming years. Consequently, recruiting qualified replacement officers has become a real challenge (Christmas 2013, 101). Like any business, police agencies are constrained by budgets. Increasingly, police departments must analyze their staffing needs according to a business model. This is no easy calculation and, as a result, police agencies in Canada often state that they are always running short of capable police officers for operational duties.

The police must balance their patrol and specialized unit responses and strategies to deal with ever-changing crime trends in order to forecast and justify hiring a particular number of recruits. Further to these challenges, the actual strength of any police force is always fluid since no one can predict such unexpected developments as officers going off duty due to illness. In addition, it is often difficult to cope with the scheduling of mandatory and advanced training programs, vacations, and other developments such as parental leave that take police officers away from their regular duties. Thus, a series of considerations affect the numbers of officers who can be on duty at any given time.

From a review of the available literature, it is difficult to confirm the total costs of training a police officer in Canada from the recruitment stage through the academy to the street because there are so many factors to consider. To break down all costs and then simply add them together is too simplistic. When police agencies report on what is spent on training generally, the costs associated with training recruits are often blended with the costs related to ongoing training of all members of the force. For example, some police agencies hire recruits before training begins and start paying them a salary. Other police agencies, including the RCMP, bring in recruits to be trained, but individuals must first successfully complete basic training before being officially hired and paid an annual wage. The reality is that the cost of police training in Canada is poorly understood and is not tracked consistently across policing services (Public Safety Canada 2013, 4).

All police agencies in Canada advertise **core values**, principles that they believe are representative of their police force and its officers. These core values are consistent but there is variance. For example, the core values of the Toronto Police Service are stated as service at our core, do the right thing, connect with compassion, and reflect and grow (Toronto Police Service, n.d.(a)). The core values of the Saint John Police Force in New Brunswick include leadership, integrity, constant improvement, openness and partnerships, trust and respect, and investing in our people (Saint John Police Force, n.d.).

Challenge Your Assumptions

Core Competencies

Information from the Discover Policing website (IACP, n.d.) identified the following as **core competencies** for law enforcement officers:

- ability to use good judgment and solve problems;
- capacity for empathy and compassion;
- capacity for multitasking;
- ability to demonstrate courage and to take responsibility;
- ability to be resourceful and show initiative;
- demonstration of assertiveness;
- possession and demonstration of integrity; and

- capacity for engaging in teamwork and ability to collaborate.

Canadian police forces consider many criteria—personality traits, depth of knowledge, skills, and abilities—desirable for a potential recruit.

Do you agree with each attribute and capability? Can you think of others that should be added to this list? Are you surprised by any of the identified attributes and capabilities?

Recruiting Basics

The process of recruiting, selecting, and training police officers is complex (Alpert, Dunham, and Stroshine 2006, 63). The hiring process for police officers across all police agencies in Canada is similar not only in terms of the type of person they are looking for, but in terms of the process itself. The first steps most often include a general aptitude test and an assessment of physical ability.

Aptitude Test

General comprehension tests for Canadian police agencies vary in name and content, but all focus on writing ability and comprehension, problem solving, and understanding basic police scenarios. For example, at stage one of the screening process facilitated through the Ontario Association of Chiefs of Police (OACP), Ontario police agencies require applicants to write a paper and pencil aptitude test focused on deductive, inductive, and quantitative reasoning. At stage two, applicants write a communication test that requires reading a scenario and then organizing important facts to reconstruct what happened (OACP, n.d.)

Physical Abilities

There is variance in the physical testing that has been adopted by police agencies across Canada. For example, the RCMP version of an assessment of physical ability is called the Physical Abilities Requirement Evaluation (PARE), while the equivalents for municipal and provincial police forces vary. The Justice Institute of British Columbia test for the province's municipal police officers is called the Police Officer Physical Abilities Test (POPAT). These assessment tools are similar and comprise an agility run, push/pull station, vault station, and weight-carry station. The standards are time to complete the test in addition to a pass/fail in the push/pull and weight-carry stations. Of interest, the RCMP no longer require recruits to have a valid PARE score as part of their application; rather, it is expected that the candidate will successfully complete the test (within 5 minutes and 30 seconds) within the first two weeks of arriving at Depot. If the cadet fails the PARE twice within three days of their first try, they are sent home (RCMP, n.d.(b)).

Consistent with the standards of the OACP, Ontario police forces including the Ontario Provincial Police and Toronto Police Service rely on the Physical Readiness Evaluation for Police (PREP) test, which is made up of two main components. The first part is the pursuit restraint circuit (PRC) that mimics a foot pursuit and rescue. The second part is a 20-metre aerobic shuttle run. Although the PREP test is still part of the applicant screening process, in 2018, the Ontario Police College advised that they would no longer have PREP as a component of the "Basic Constable Training Program" (DeClerq 2018). The PARE, POPAT, PREP, and others are designed to simulate the basic physical demands of patrol duties.

Tara Walton/Toronto Star via Getty Images

Constable Kenneth Ishmael watches as 24-year-old Erin Chamberlain is put through the force's physical fitness test during a recruiting session.

Background Checks

Police agencies require that candidates provide a great deal of initial information about their work history and personal lives prior to further consideration as a candidate. Information to be provided includes addresses lived at over many years, names and occupations of immediate family members, basic medical history, and other information such as education history. The curriculum vitae of the candidate will be scrutinized and all information contained therein will be confirmed.

References/Work/Character

After the prospective candidate has filled out multiple forms providing detailed personal information, the police agency will undertake closed police database searches and other checks to confirm the information provided. Public internet sources and social media will be reviewed. Assuming there is no adverse information (for example, having a criminal record, prior contact with law enforcement in circumstances deemed to be negative, or indication of an association with known criminals), the police agency will verify an applicant's job history and conduct interviews with references. A thorough review of an applicant's job history is important to establish the accuracy of the information provided and to determine how the individual performed while employed. It is also an opportunity to explore the circumstances under which the person left previous employment.

The candidate will provide references who have known them personally for many years; however, such references may not be relatives. The police agency will contact each of the references and conduct an interview that seeks to understand the character of the candidate. Interviews of others not provided by the candidate, particularly previous employers or neighbours, may be carried out without the knowledge of the candidate.

Formal Interview

At least one detailed interview will take place with the candidate and recruiting staff. The interviewer will use and refer to the information provided by the candidate in the forms and documentation. The main purpose of the interview is to clarify information and seek out more details about possible criminal activity, associates, drug and alcohol use, and lifestyle. The interviewer will also try to ensure that information that has been given is accurate.

Polygraph

The polygraph is considered an effective tool by most police agencies in Canada and is used to complement all other aspects of the recruit screening process. The polygraph is simply another tool used to test the veracity of information already disclosed to police from the other recruiting steps. The pre-employment polygraph is different from the forensic polygraph that is used in criminal investigations; it is considered general-issue testing as opposed to specific-issue testing. In part, the pre-employment polygraph is a test related to integrity, and the candidate is asked about information already disclosed to make sure that she or he has been forthright and not left anything out. For example, the Edmonton Police Service uses the polygraph at stage six of their eight-stage recruitment process, and their website states that "the purpose of the polygraph examination is to verify that applicants are the person they claim to be and that they have been truthful throughout the entire application process" (EPS, n.d.). Similarly, the Regina Police Service and Victoria (British Columbia) Police Department use the polygraph test at stages nine and ten respectively, of their recruit screening process (Regina Police Service, n.d.; Victoria Police Department, n.d.). Ontario police forces do not use the polygraph as a screening tool as in Ontario it is against the law "for an employer or anyone on behalf of an employer to directly or indirectly require, request, enable or influence an employee to take a lie detector test" (Ontario Ministry of Labour, n.d.).

Psychology

Psychological testing for potential recruits varies among police agencies but is often premised on academic testing that may be followed up with an interview from a psychologist. For example, the RCMP and Toronto Police Service (Toronto Police Service, n.d.(c)) rely in part on the Minnesota Multiphasic Personality Inventory (MMPI-2) and, depending on the result, may require a follow-up interview with a psychologist to review and discuss the results. For insight into the purposes of psychological testing to screen prospective recruits, it is helpful to turn to the Iacobucci report (2014) on the Toronto Police Service, which found that "an important part of the constable selection process is psychological testing and a psychological interview" (p. 130). Further, the report said that

> [t]he psychologists screen for the following traits, among others: problem-solving abilities, self-confidence, communication, flexibility, stress tolerance, self-control, ability to build relationships, emotional insight, empathy, tolerance of diversity, and patience. Psychologists also screen for measures of past and present psycho-pathology, and other undesirable psychological traits that may interfere with the safe and effective discharge of the duties of a police constable. [pp. 130, 131]

Medical Assessment and Clearance

While candidates will complete forms disclosing their full medical history and the police agency will follow up on that information, when the candidate gets closer to the end of the whole process, the police agency will arrange for independent laboratory tests (for example, fluid tests). Comprehensive physical examination by a physician will follow in order to establish any pre-existing medical conditions that would be concerning and to determine overall medical fitness for duty. The medical assessment and clearance are premised on the fact that police work can be physically, mentally, and emotionally demanding.

Specific Criteria for Potential Recruits

Specific criteria stated to be **preferred qualifications** are similar among Canadian police agencies and yet there are differences, for example, in minimum academic qualifications and other factors that are attributed to the type of policing in which the police agency is engaged. See Table 4.1 for a few specific examples.

Women in Policing

Conor, Robson, and Marcellus (2019) reported that the trend of seeing increased numbers of women in policing careers has continued through 2018, with women accounting for 22 per cent of all sworn officers. Canada's police agencies are working toward having 30 per cent women officers as a realistic goal. Several Canadian police agencies focus on recruiting women through the use of information sessions that are for women only (see RCMP, n.d.(c); Niagara Regional Police Service, n.d.; York Regional Police, n.d.). One key indication of the commitment to change has been the noticeable increase of women occupying the higher ranks in Canadian police forces. In 2018, women represented 15 per cent of commissioned officers, the highest proportion ever recorded since data collection began in 1986 (Conor, Robson, and Marcellus 2019, 11).

One notable example was the 2018 swearing in of Brenda Lucki as the first permanent female Commissioner of the RCMP. (Beverly Busson served as interim Commissioner from 2006 to 2007.) Of interest was the fact that Prime Minister Justin Trudeau and Ralph Goodale, the minister of public safety, tasked Commissioner Lucki with changing the "culture" of the RCMP (Aiello 2018). It is widely recognized that there continue to

Table 4.1 Examples of Criteria for Recruitment			
Police Force	**Education Criteria**	**Other Skills/Knowledge**	**Other Requirements**
Service de police de la Ville de Montréal (SPVM)	Have a pre-university Diploma of College Studies (2 years) and 30 university credits; or a Technical Diploma of College Studies (3 years, other than Police Technology); or hold a Bachelor's degree	Interpersonal communication (teamwork and self-affirmation); analytical mind; customer orientation; commitment and a sense of responsibility	Canadian citizen; be of Aboriginal origin or belong to a visible minority or ethnic minority
Edmonton Police Service	Grade 12 or equivalent high school diploma, certificate in standard first aid, a current "level C" certificate in cardiopulmonary resuscitation	Excellent physical condition, pass vision and hearing standards; a valid Alberta class 5 driver's licence and good driving record; good writing skills	Canadian citizen or legal permanent residence; of "good moral character" defined in part by not having been involved in detected or undetected criminal activity within the 3 years preceding the application
RCMP	Canadian high school diploma	Proficient in English or French; possess a valid unrestricted Canadian driver's licence; meet the medical, psychological and vision standards; meet the necessary physical abilities	Canadian citizen or permanent resident status for the last 10 consecutive years; of good character; at least 19 years of age at the time of application; be prepared to carry a firearm and use it or any other necessary force; be willing and able to relocate anywhere in Canada; be aware of expectations with regard to tattoos and piercings; and be willing to pledge allegiance to Canada

Sources: Service de police de la Ville de Montréal (SPVM). "Admission Criteria for Employment Equity Police Officers." https://spvm.qc.ca/en/Pages/Careers/Police-Officers/Admission-criteria-for-employment-equity-police-officers-without-police-training (accessed March 3, 2019); Edmonton Police Service. "Join EPS." http://www.joineps.ca/ (accessed 3 March 2019); Royal Canadian Mounted Police (RCMP). "Qualifications and Standards to Become an RCMP Officer." http://www.rcmp-grc.gc.ca/en/qualifications-and-requirements (accessed 3 March 2019).

be serious concerns related to workplace harassment, sexual harassment, bullying, and intimidation in the RCMP (CRCC 2017, 41).

Relative to their efforts to attract women recruits, there is little doubt that aspects of the RCMP culture as highlighted by the 2016 $100-million-dollar Merlo-Davidson settlement have discouraged women from joining. Merlo-Davidson was the result of two class-action lawsuits alleging that female members of the RCMP were or had been victims of discrimination based upon gender and sexual orientation, intimidation, and harassment in their workplace (Merlo-Davidson, n.d.). On October 6, 2016, then Commissioner Bob Paulson publicly apologized to female members of the RCMP by saying, "You came to the RCMP wanting to personally contribute to your community and we failed you. We hurt you. For that, I'm truly sorry" (Harris 2016).

The Recruitment of Experienced Police Officers

In 2016/17, 14 per cent of all new police officers (2917) hired by police services were experienced police officers, with the remainder being new recruit graduates (Conor 2018, 13). The competition for attracting experienced police officers through **lateral transfer** between police forces remains an important way to address attrition due to retirements and other resignations. The loss of trained and seasoned officers constitutes a brain or experience drain. In police work, life and work experience and training indicate how effective a police officer will be. In policing, it is difficult to replace sound investigative, supervisory, or leadership experience. There is obvious organizational benefit in having a police officer with a proven track record of success deal with challenging, high-risk, complex, and often high-profile investigations. The benefits, beyond the experience that these police officers bring, include the reduced cost of training and an ability to hit the road running. The acquisition of seasoned police officers often has an immediate positive impact not only on daily operations but on the mentoring and training of other officers. In every police agency, there are officers who have transferred from other agencies.

Though the recruitment of experienced police officers may seem preferable, cost effective, and simple, each candidate is carefully screened and assessed in a process not unlike the initial recruiting process for new police officers. It is critical to understand why the candidate wants to leave her or his present employment. It is possible that the candidate has had conflicts in the workplace, did not perform duties to a high standard, and/or has lacked a sound work ethic over time. Sometimes police officers have reached a pension limit and then want to work another five or ten years to "double dip," that is, to qualify for a second pension. In these circumstances, the new police force has to have a level of confidence in the work ethic of the individual and his or her capacity to perform consistently at a high level. Whatever the motivation for the transfer, extensive checks are carried out, including interviews with references, examinations of annual performance assessments, a review of performance in providing testimony in court cases over the years, and other measures to ensure that the police agency is indeed acquiring a desirable officer.

Training Facilities in Canada

Police training in Canada is recognized internationally as being of a high standard. This is perhaps best illustrated by the number of police officers who come from other countries to receive training at the Aylmer Police College, Atlantic Police Academy, Canadian Police College, RCMP academy, Justice Institute of British Columbia, and other training centres. Each of these facilities is known for supporting other countries around the world in ongoing training initiatives and for sharing best practices in policing by sending serving police officers and trainers to those countries to provide training and operational guidance. Such initiatives have taken place in several South and Central American countries, in the Middle East, and in Africa.

At the Academy

A number of police training facilities within Canada serve municipal agencies, the three provincial agencies, and Canada's federal police agency, the RCMP. Good training early in a career sets officers on a path for success in a challenging and dynamic profession (Christmas 2013, 108). There is some variance in training structure, format, and cost. For example, the Toronto Police Service requires 24 weeks of Monday-to-Friday training at two different police colleges (Toronto Police College and Ontario Police College). The fees for the Ontario Police College were $11,065 in 2019 (Toronto Police Service, n.d.(b)). In contrast, the Police Science Program in Halifax is 38 weeks long, requires some evening and weekend training as well as on-the-job training on patrol, and fees were listed at $10,000 in 2019. The recruits are responsible for paying those tuition costs. In contrast, the RCMP training academy, referred to as Depot Division, located in Regina, Saskatchewan, does not charge for tuition. During the 26-week-long training, the RCMP covers room and board, uniform, training insurance, and travel, and pays recruits an allowance of $525 per week (RCMP, n.d.(a)).

Both the curricula and instructional methods are similar within all Canadian police training centres. Operational skills such as police driving, **police defensive techniques (PDT)**, arrest techniques, and firearms training are combined with general fitness training. The academic side of police work, such as legal studies, is taught in applied police sciences. **Scenario-based training** is widely used and involves both facilitator and peer review feedback. Based on video- and audio-recorded interactions of recruit performance during simulated calls to such scenarios as domestic disputes, inebriated persons in a public place, and traffic stop situations, the learning techniques are dynamic and stressful. The purpose is to assess how recruits will react; how well they apply mature and logical reasoning; and how well they demonstrate knowledge of criminal laws, policies, and the *Charter*. Of course, all of this is combined with an emphasis on alertness and responsiveness to both police officer and public safety as it might arise in each scenario.

There are important aspects of police training that condition the ways in which recruits think act and react. For example, in police defensive techniques, seven tactical principles are studied:

1. Use of Cover—take cover and/or conceal yourself from the threat;
2. One Plus One—always assume another threat may be present, either another person or weapon;
3. Verbalization—clear direction in simple language;
4. Threat Cues—body language, motions, voice tones, verbal threats, "the thousand-metre stare" (when an individual is "looking right through you" with no apparent focus);
5. Tactical Repositioning—take a defensive position, find method of concealment if necessary;
6. Time–Distance Ratio—the time it takes for the person posing the threat to close the distance between himself or herself and the police officer(s); and
7. Survival Mentality—never, ever give up.

The seven tactical principles are studied and drilled into recruits as they come to realize that policing can be dangerous and significantly different from what they may have learned from movies and television. Recruits learn that policing is teamwork, that they are only as strong as the weakest link, and that they must learn to trust other recruits because one day a colleague could save their life in the field. There are a number of training challenges in basic training for recruits in all police academies. Training police officers requires hundreds of hours of intense classroom work and fieldwork (Alpert, Dunham, and Stroshine 2006, 63). Beyond the more glamorous operational skills, police training has to teach practical skills such as report writing, law, warrant applications, interpersonal communication, drug and alcohol effects, cultural sensitivity, and mental illness awareness (Chappell, Lanza-Kaduce, and Johnston cited in Dunham 2010, 55). Most police academies have integrated mental health awareness and building resiliency into basic training. Recruits are taught about what to expect from a career in policing from a work/life balance perspective and to understand that they will often see people at their worst, whether it be violent acts, accidents, or events related to the most tragic circumstances (Nemetz, G., 2019; see Chapter 9 for further discussion).

Formal and Informal Socialization

Not surprisingly, new police officers quickly come to appreciate that there is a significant difference between the classroom and the street. Nonetheless, formal classroom learning experience establishes the extent to which recruits are receptive to applying what they are being taught, to situations they encounter on the street. The process of socialization at training academies will have an impact on the how the recruits see themselves and will enhance confidence and change perceptions of people and situations. For example, if recruits did not know about or have exposure to people with mental health challenges or addictions, their preconceived notions of people with those issues will change. Being sensitized to cultural conflicts and stereotyped ideas about why people commit crime, and better understanding victims of crime are similarly powerful learning experiences.

All of this training, combined with the strengths and weaknesses of individual personalities, will dictate how well recruits perform and deal with people and situations in the real world. Despite the importance of police training at the academy, there is no question that the learning is enhanced for first-response patrol police officers once they hit the streets. There is no replacement for dealing with people in the real world. Only after the academy does the new police officer really start to understand his or her role, and test and refine communication, problem-solving, and basic skills learned in training academies.

Field Training

Once a recruit has graduated from the academy, field training is the next step in the process. Each recruit is assigned a **field trainer**, a senior experienced police officer who is responsible for mentoring and assessing the recruit as he or she applies the basic skills learned at the academy to the street. Dealing with the public for the first time, especially in adverse situations, is stressful and it may take weeks or even months for the new police officer to gain sufficient proficiency such that the field trainer believes the recruit has the

Case Study

What Is a Policing Problem?

You recently graduated from the police training academy and you have successfully completed field training with a senior police officer. You are a uniformed patrol police officer in a suburb of one of Canada's larger cities. Your shifts are set out in blocks of four eleven-hour shifts, two days and two nights. The area you patrol is densely populated and is made up of retail businesses, restaurants, hotels, office towers, and high-rise residences. There are parks and green spaces with playgrounds and walking trails. The crime rate in the area is considered moderate but your shifts are always busy. The common types of calls for service that the police here receive include shoplifting, robberies, assaults, fraud, and thefts of and from automobiles. Street-level drug trafficking is present in the area and there are known criminals who frequent the area to facilitate drug trafficking and crimes related to the trade. Within your patrol district, many homeless people live their lives. You have been working this area for six months and you have come to know many people who live and work in the area. Your duties include investigating crimes and gathering evidence to support prosecutions. When required, you arrest those engaged in criminal activity. However, your job is also about safe communities, public safety generally, and problem solving through diverse community policing strategies.

Charles is a 42-year-old homeless man with documented mental health and addiction issues. You met Charles on your first shift on patrol in this district six months ago. Within the last six months, there have been 85 calls for service from the public about Charles's activities. The majority of calls are concerns related to his well-being as he sleeps where he can; however, others are related to him using drugs or drinking beer in public places. Reports are received about Charles "acting strange" or

"appearing threatening" toward others, at times suddenly yelling out in apparent anger. When it is cold, Charles favours sleeping in sheltered areas accessible to the public such as just inside the doors of financial institutions where bank ATMs are located. Sometimes, people call 911 because they fear that Charles is going to rob them.

Charles has received sporadic assistance for his health issues and been through drug and alcohol detox more than 10 times over the last three years. Charles has been arrested and charged 40 times in the past three years for thefts he committed related to his need to buy drugs and alcohol for his addictions. He has been arrested 10 times under the provincial *Mental Health Act* out of concern for his well-being. Charles panhandles at times and people have called police about him being too aggressive. Charles has a criminal record related to minor property crimes and two assault convictions from more than 10 years ago. The majority of the time, there are few beds and services in the area for people like Charles but he calls it home and does not want to go anywhere else. He has no known family. The police are always the ones to be called in the first instance to deal with Charles. Your supervisor has asked you to take Charles on as a project to see if you can help him and, at the same time, reduce the number of calls from the public about his lifestyle.

Is dealing with Charles a "policing" problem? What short- and long-term strategies would you take to be successful in the task that your supervisor has assigned you? Are there other partners outside of the resources of your police force that you could engage, and, if so, which ones?

competency to take the lead on most calls for service. As calls for service are attended and dealt with, and as interpersonal skills are refined and experience gained, a policing "style" is developed. In short, the new police officer learns from his or her field training how to interact with the public and how to deal with the multifaceted situations that arise in the course of street work.

Generational Differences

Of some interest is the perception held by senior police officers that today's recruits in North America are different than they were 10, 15, or 20 years ago. Specifically, the perception exists that modern police officers have a different work ethic and are more concerned about work–life balance than about putting in the overtime and additional substantial effort that police work often demands. As Christmas (2013) has observed, the new breed of police officer does not respond well to the rigid, autocratic, "just follow orders" management style of the stereotyped, tough, post–Second World War veteran desk sergeant. This observation underscores that police agencies should consider whether a strict paramilitary framework is best suited to developing and managing police officers. Deputy Chief Adam Palmer of the Vancouver Police Department (appointed to Chief Constable in 2015) stated that the current hiring pool is a generation that has grown up with technology, is well educated, and is in many ways different than the preceding generation of recruits (2015, 16). One of the key challenges for police agencies, units, and teams is to effectively manage intergenerational differences among and between the police officers themselves.

Responding to Losing Experienced Police Officers to Retirement

Many police agencies in Canada have made a practice of rehiring, on a contractual basis, retired but experienced police officers who possess distinctive expertise. This fact has led to some concerns that these contract workers are being paid while drawing their pension from their years of service as an active police officer and often working in the same office they were in on the day they retired. However, most of these retired contract workers do not have full operational police powers and are limited to specific jobs for which they were contracted. These specific jobs may include such tasks as reviewing unsolved homicide case files or assisting larger police investigations by vetting materials for disclosure in upcoming court proceedings. One exception is the RCMP "reservist" program, which is made up of retired officers who have chosen to return and perform operational policing duties as and where they are required. For example, reservists are often asked to cover shifts in smaller northern detachment areas so that the members posted there can take holidays (RCMP, n.d.(c)).

The justification for hiring retired police officers is that the police agency is buying experience to make sure the work is completed to the high standards expected in court. For this reason, the argument that these contract workers may be displacing new recruits is moot. That is, not that many serving police officers in any given police agency have the collective knowledge, skills, experience, or ability to fully and completely review an unsolved homicide investigation. Not every police officer possesses the ability to creatively review a multitude of investigative files and documents in order to develop a viable innovative strategy to move an otherwise stalled investigation forward. Such skills take years to develop and police agencies frequently struggle to find adequate replacements when senior officers retire.

In-Service Training/Continuous Learning

All Canadian police agencies recognize that while there are best practices in policing, there are always better practices. This fact confirms that continuous learning through training initiatives is among the most important challenges to police agencies in Canada. There is a saying in policing that once you start to think you know everything about policing, you had better give your head a shake. Continuous learning throughout one's career is a vital aspect of becoming a seasoned police officer. And indeed, while there are many competent and experienced police officers with expertise in given fields, the best ones will admit that they look to sharing their knowledge, skills, and abilities and to learning from others in order to make themselves even more proficient at what they do.

Conventional wisdom in policing holds that many risks can be reduced through effective training. Baker (2011, 128) states that well-trained officers are likely to more successfully operate under stress and perform duties. They develop a winning attitude and are more confident when performing tasks and objectives. In fact, inadequate training impedes the development of officers who lack confidence and are not mission-oriented (Baker 2011, 123).

Police agencies ensure that active duty police officers maintain a minimum proficiency in such areas as first aid, CPR, and firearms, most commonly by having annual mandatory testing. For example, RCMP officers qualify in firearms on an annual basis and also must attend operational skills training (OST) every three years, which is a week-long course that includes refresher training in the use of the collapsible baton, handcuffing, carotid artery, OC pepper spray, and other defensive techniques; firearms; first aid; and CPR. Like recruit training, OST involves scenarios with facilitators to test decision-making skills, use-of-force techniques, and other competencies necessary for modern police work.

Advanced Investigative Training

While police officers can acquire diverse skill sets over their years of service, it is impossible to master them all and most police officers develop an area of expertise for which they have a keen affinity. Through personal interest, an unexpected assignment arising out of an operational need, or simply by chance, police officers have opportunities to learn on the job as an investigation unfolds. Police officers may also simply have a personal interest in taking courses or further training to gain expertise and experience in specific areas. Baker (2011, 127) stated that "police training is one of the most significant management functions. Training supports the mission, at the same time cultivating motivation and morale." Continuous learning is so important that several police agencies across the country link course completion with pay raises. Training that adds to or updates any police officer's knowledge, skills, and abilities is always in addition to maintaining currency in legal authorities and procedures impacted by new case law decisions.

For years, police agencies have cross-trained with each other, sharing training and experience in the search for better practices. It is routine to have municipal police officers on RCMP or OPP training courses and vice versa. One example of consistent formal training among police agencies is that offered by the Canadian Police College (CPC). The CPC runs courses on a national basis at its headquarters in Ottawa and in major cities across the country. Courses offered by CPC include Major Case Management, Major Case Management (specific) for Team Commanders, Organized Crime Investigations, Drug Investigative Techniques, and Major Crime Investigative Techniques. These courses are developed and maintained by CPC with input from police agencies across Canada.

The efficiency and effectiveness of an organization are directly related to the amount and quality of training conducted within that agency (Baker 2011, 129). Training in all areas of policing is a career-long effort. For example, training in legal applications can vary from basic introductory courses to the detailed two-week-long National Interception of Private Communications (wiretap) course. Over the past decades, it has been common for police officers with a demonstrated expertise in areas of **high-risk policing** such as legal applications to help in the development and delivery of new courses. Often, skilled police officers cooperate with Crown counsel and defence counsel to ensure that the course content is appropriate, current, and factually correct. Joint training with Crown counsel also occurs.

Interviewing is another critical area of ongoing training for all police. There are different levels of training related to intense, fact-driven, well-planned interviews. Some interview training courses are content specific, for example those that specialize in interviewing children. Generally, the courses are progressively more detailed and sophisticated, such as interviewing suspects with the assistance of a polygraph. Interview and interrogation courses are most often developed and delivered by police officers with significant operational experience and skills in the subject area. Examples of other advanced courses include internet crime investigations, forensic crime scene investigation, sex crimes, national security, and management of confidential informers.

Unfortunately, training is expensive and budgets are increasingly limited. To reduce the overhead costs associated with training, police agencies often partner with other agencies to share knowledge and reduce costs. Conducting training in house, that is, having the training brought to the local police office or unit, is becoming common in an effort to reduce travel and other costs associated with attendance. There are other benefits of multi-jurisdictional cross-training, such as making new contacts, sharing experiences, and learning from each other's mistakes and successes.

Specialized Training

Depending on the size of the police agency and its operational needs, specialized units may be developed. For example, police agencies that are located near larger bodies of water may require a marine unit with watercraft and specially trained officers for patrol work and to deal with emergencies. For example, the Toronto Police Service, Vancouver Police Department, Halifax Police Service, and several RCMP and OPP detachments across Canada have marine operational capability. Police officers assigned to such duties are specially trained and are posted to the respective units on a full-time basis.

Emergency response teams (ERTs) are an important component of urban police agencies and often have the capacity and resources to assist smaller police agencies in rural areas. RCMP ERT have protocols to maintain the capacity to deploy anywhere in Canada within a relatively short period of time. ERT members are highly trained police officers who have advanced expertise in the use of force, use of special weapons and explosives, high-risk tactical entries to homes or buildings, vehicle stops, extractions, and other skills. ERT members must maintain an exceptional level of fitness and shooting proficiency that far exceeds that required by most other police officers. Emergency response teams commonly log more time in training than in time deployed to calls for service.

ERT members wear heavy body armour and helmets and are trained in specialized weapons. ER teams are often supported by police dog handlers and armoured vehicles. In recent years, ER teams in Canada have been required to add specialized training in **active shooter** situations to their training curriculum, sadly precipitated by school shootings such as the École Polytechnique de Montréal; Columbine high school; Virginia Tech; La Loche, Saskatchewan; and similar critical incidents. These tragedies have forced police agencies to cooperate in sharing tactical strategies and responses in their efforts to best respond to such dire emergencies.

There are a number of other specialized operational support units where training is fundamental to acquiring and maintaining the required skills. Examples of other units include underwater search and recovery teams, tactical squads to deal with unruly crowd behaviour including riots, air services such as helicopter and fixed-wing patrols, and

THE CANADIAN PRESS/John Lehmann/The Globe and Mail

Members of the emergency response team (ERT) from the Vancouver police department at the ready during a large emergency-responders exercise on the grounds of the University of British Columbia in Vancouver.

various investigative support units such as integrated technological crime teams. It often takes many years of policing experience before a police officer can move into specialty units; however, it is possible that skills acquired prior to joining the police agency, for example having a pilot licence, may expedite the process.

Online Training

Online training has emerged and expanded in order for police agencies to ensure that officers remain up to date. Given budgetary constraints and the logistics of police officers leaving their duties to attend training sessions, it has made sense to develop online training in a number of areas. For example, online training courses on harassment, respectful workplace practices, domestic violence, and Indigenous awareness are core components of ongoing mandatory training that police officers must complete. Where such training is mandatory, online learning platforms record that the training is complete and automatically credit a police officer's personnel file. Online training is also an effective way to ensure that officers are made aware of any changes in law (case law), internal policies, and procedures.

Online training is most often made up of video scenarios with questions to be answered, followed by a pass/fail multiple choice exam. The effectiveness of online training may be in question, especially as concerns retention of the information; however, there are few alternatives to distributing information in a condensed, cost-effective manner that can be tracked to confirm completion of the training curriculum.

Conclusion

This chapter has identified challenges in meeting the complex and diverse requirements of the future training needs of policing in Canada. The chapter also outlined the recruiting process and basic training before reviewing examples of advanced and specialized training. As police agencies seek to find the best combination of programs and strategies to better serve and protect Canadians, the quest to identify, train, and hire the best available people remains key to maintaining public safety. In the face of tighter budgets, changing technology and crime trends, increasing public scrutiny, and other pressures such as changes in the criminal law due to case law decisions, it could nonetheless be argued that finding the right people is the most important challenge facing modern police agencies.

Critical Thinking Questions

1. What do you think are the key attributes of a police officer recruit? How would you screen candidates or test for those attributes?
2. Does the training described reflect the current state of policing in Canada as described in Chapters 2 and 3? Why or why not?
3. Why do you think individuals with police experience are valued over new recruits in certain cases?

4. Why do you think life experience (for example job stability, supervisory responsibilities at work, and travelling abroad) is considered a strength in being considered as a police recruit?
5. What are your reasons for wanting to join a police agency?
6. What factors will you take into consideration when deciding which police agency to apply to?

Endnote

i   The *Employment Equity Act* separately defines (Aboriginal) person(s) as a "North American Indian or a member of a First Nations, Métis or Inuit. North American Indians or members of a First Nation include treaty, status or registered Indians, as well as non-status and non-registered Indians."

5

Ethics and Discretion

Learning Objectives

After reading and studying this chapter, students will be able to:

- Identify and discuss how discretion runs through all aspects of police work.
- Describe and discuss ethics and ethical decision making as it relates to the role of the police in Canada.
- Review and discuss how ethics and discretion are integral components of successful police officers.
- Describe and assess police decision making and discretion in real-life situations.
- Describe and discuss the role of police policies, the law, and the *Charter* in police discretion.

Introduction

What does being an ethical police officer really mean? Would it be a police officer who is empathetic to others regardless of their situation? Is it a police officer who treats everyone fairly in all circumstances or one who lets strict legal parameters guide their decisions? **Ethics** is a grey word like reasonable, justifiable, or discretionary. The *Oxford English Dictionary* defines ethics as "moral principles that govern a person's behaviour or the conducting of an activity." **Morals**, in turn, are defined as "concerned with the principles of right and wrong behaviour" and "concerned with or derived from the code of behaviour that is considered right or acceptable in a particular society." This chapter will review the extent to which ethics are instrumental in guiding the vast discretionary powers that permeate all aspects of policing.

A definition for discretion depends on the context in which it is used. Everyone uses discretion in some way throughout their daily lives, for example, when deciding just what personal information to tell others; determining what television shows their children will not be allowed to watch; or whether or not to call the police when the neighbours are hosting a noisy party. Police use discretion when deciding whether to respond quickly to a call for service, how to prioritize call types (see also Chapters 9 and 10) and whether to detain, arrest, charge, or release a suspect. They also use discretion when they defuse a situation by facilitating an informal resolution without engaging the criminal law. Discretion dictates the level of force to be employed. It underpins decisions about whether to issue a warning or a ticket for a traffic violation or which unsolved homicide investigation receives priority over others. Decisions are guided by a case-by-case analysis of morals, ethics, and law. Discretion in policing is about having the authority and the ability to make decisions that suit the circumstances.

Discretion in the Field

Knowledge, education, training, and experience are the cornerstones of being able to make ethical, practical, lawful decisions. Virtually everything in a patrol officer's shift is subject to some degree of discretion. Call response and prioritization (attending one call over another, often based upon minimal information); use of force (anticipated by the reported nature of the call and dependent on circumstances at the scene of the incident); decisions about how to defuse a situation, whether to detain or arrest, whether to charge or release; and determining the type of evidence to be gathered (interviews, neighbourhood

Photo by Roberto Machado Noa/LightRocket via Getty Images

In 2018, the impaired driving laws were changed to grant police officers more discretion with regard to demanding a breath test. Previously, officers required reasonable suspicion of a driver's impairment to demand a breath test, but under the change an officer can demand a breath test of any driver who has been legally stopped, without reasonable suspicion. What are the implications of increased discretion for officers to demand a breath test?

canvassing) and which evidence is related to the elements of the offence being investigated are all examples of decisions relevant to nearly every call a police officer responds to.

Police work by its very nature is discretionary in the sense that it involves the exercise of choice or judgment on a routine basis (Bronitt and Stenning 2011, 320). In a situation where two calls are received at the same time, which call to attend first, how quickly to respond (i.e., emergency driving), to attend with backup or without, and a multitude of other decisions must be made quickly. When two cars are seen to be speeding on the same roadway, the police officer must decide which car to pull over. While on routine patrol in a high-crime area, a police officer may decide to street check a person in the area in the early morning hours. Police officers routinely decide why or when to criminalize someone's actions through arrest and charge, or to provide a person with guidance or an informal warning. Sunahara (2004) observed that operational police work is characterized by the potential conflict inherent in attempting to control the behaviour of others.

Police must use discretion in their day-to-day jobs when deciding how to operate their motor vehicle in the case of emergencies. Every provincial *Motor Vehicle Act* has exemptions for emergency vehicles that allow those vehicles to drive contrary to legislated restrictions such as speed limits, often referred to as **code driving**. **Code 3** is police language describing a police vehicle operating with full emergency lights and siren. **Code 2** describes a police vehicle operating with full emergency lights, but no siren. An example of driving Code 2 may be attending an armed robbery call where the siren may cause the suspects to flee or further act out against the public (e.g., take a hostage). The police officer remains accountable for driving as safely as possible in the circumstances.

Goldstein (1977) described police discretion as applying to the following areas: (1) choosing objectives, (2) choosing methods of intervention, (3) choosing how to dispose of cases, (4) choosing investigative avenues, (5) choosing field procedures, and (6) issuing permits and licences.

Discretion is not usually criticized when a person is "given a break" by a police officer. However, it most certainly can become contentious when a police officer is seen as acting unfairly. When the public perceives that the law is unfairly or arbitrarily applied, police discretion is called into question. For example, it is entirely possible that people in similar situations such as being drunk in a public place are treated differently. One person is arrested while the other person has a taxi called for them; alternatively, the driver of one speeding vehicle gets a warning while another gets a fine. If police officers consistently make decisions that are moral, ethical, legal, and appropriate in the circumstances, more often than not, they will be beyond reproach.

La Fave (1969 cited in Bronitt and Stenning 2011, 323) identified four main reasons why discretion is both a necessary and legitimate aspect of police work. He noted that

1. no legislature has succeeded in formulating laws that encompass all conduct intended to be made criminal and that clearly exclude all other conduct;
2. failure to eliminate poorly drafted and obsolete legislation renders the continued existence of discretion necessary for fairness;
3. discretion is necessary because limited resources make it impossible to enforce all laws against all offenders; and
4. the strict enforcement of the law would have harsh and intolerable results.

Situational Variables

Several variables influence a police officer's decision making during most encounters with the public. Most important of these variables is the overall safety of the public followed closely by the seriousness of the criminal offence or action. Other variables include

- age (for example, whether the suspect is under 12 years old and cannot be charged, or is a young offender; adult offenders are treated differently in law);
- gender of offender (for example, females are generally perceived to be less confrontational than males and therefore their cooperativeness may influence police discretion);
- social class (for example, an economically disadvantaged person who has shoplifted food because he or she was hungry may not be formally charged);
- relationship of the suspect to the victim (for example, an unprovoked attack on a stranger is a threat to the public at large; however, that victim is unlikely to be attacked again by the same suspect. On the other hand, whether a suspect is known to the victim and the type of relationship—a domestic situation, family member—may be factors. If the victim is known by the suspect, the chances of re-victimization are higher and the victim must be protected by taking appropriate steps in the circumstances);
- seriousness of the offence in all the circumstances (generally, when an offence is more serious, for example, a physical or sexual assault or robbery, the police officer will have much less discretion);
- concern about continuation of the offence (for example, in any situation where continuation of the offence is a concern, appropriate steps to prevent ongoing threats to public safety must be taken such as arresting the suspect; see also Chapter 8); and
- the amount of evidence (for example, compelling evidence identifying a suspect may become known where the suspect is "found committing," such as the offence being directly observed by police officers and independently corroborated by having been captured on a security video camera; there are many other instances where a crime has been committed but sufficient evidence is absent, with no suspects and no witnesses identified; where there is no forensic information available; and no other leads to follow up on pending new information received from another source).

Jurisdictional Variables

Any community may want their police to focus on specific crimes and priorities, and these will differ from community to community. For example, in an urban environment, panhandling and open drug use may be a concern and the police will focus on appropriate enforcement or other strategies to reduce the effects of those issues. The street sex trade may be a problem in another area and the police may initiate community policing partnerships and ideas to effectively mitigate the concerns reported by the community. In school zones or intersections where vehicle collisions are more frequent, selective traffic

GerryRousseau/Alamy Stock Photo

An officer provides directions to a woman on the street in Vancouver. A police officer's day can fluctuate between these relatively mundane moments and intense life-threatening circumstances with no warning. What are some strategies you might use to cope with this strain?

enforcement measures may be taken, including zero tolerance for traffic violations and increased presence.

While discretion is a necessary aspect of policing, a multitude of factors influence any individual officer's decision making. For example, a career in policing entails a personal and lifelong commitment to a particular lifestyle. What happens at work will invariably affect a police officer's view of the world. In turn, this will affect spouses, significant others, family, and friends. There are some calls for service that police officers will attend that are so tragic that the images of the scene and memories of dealing with the people involved will never leave them. (See also Chapters 8 and 9.) In reality, a police officer gets to see people at their worst far more often than at their best. The reason is simple: In most cases, police are called because something is wrong. Someone is not having their best day. Life experience and job experience thus have an enormous impact on discretion exercised by individual police officers.

The ability of police officers to exercise sound discretion is fluid not only in specific situations but throughout their career and is affected by their knowledge of the law; their age, experience, maturity; and other factors. The foundation of a competent police officer entails having a strong moral character and an almost innate ability to make sound ethical decisions. Sunahara (2004) believed that ethical behaviour is learned and shaped by experience. That police work deals with people in a variety of situations, often traumatic, begs the question of how police officers positively enhance their ethical standards and view of the world as they move through their careers.

Competent, seasoned police officers come to know how best to deal with the positive and negative aspects of their careers. Such officers realize that their on-the-job experiences are evolutionary and learn to put unpleasant and stressful circumstances in perspective. There is little doubt that a career in policing changes a person, yet a majority of officers find their careers to be exceptionally rewarding. Officers who are able to find a sense of purpose and pride in policing tend to develop and draw upon a sound ethical foundation that evolves and matures in positive ways throughout the course of their careers. Most certainly, police work involves not only making sound professional ethical decisions but also living one's personal life according to high standards of integrity. This is true across the spectrum of police duties and assignments but is perhaps most critical for officers engaged in the everyday reality of routine patrol work.

Indeed, it is in patrol work that ethical decisions are never black or white. Rather, patrol work is inevitably shaded in different tones of grey (Alain and Gregoire 2008, 170). As Sunahara (2004) has observed, acting ethically comes easily when temptations and threats are few; however, in street police work, hostile environments, temptations, insults, and threats are routine and acting both ethically and with integrity becomes a challenge and a constant dilemma for police officers.

Broadwell, McCarthy, and McCarthy (2002) identified three ethical dilemmas officers face:

1. a situation in which the officer did not know the right course of action;
2. a situation in which the course of action the officer considered right was difficult; or
3. a situation in which the wrong course of action was very tempting.

Integrity and the ability to make consistently sound ethical decisions are expected to comprise the character of individual police officers. In reality, people come from different backgrounds, have vastly different life experiences, and possess a range of personality traits. The question thus arises: How do police agencies achieve and maintain a consistent, effective, and fair service to the public? Wilson (2011) believes that there are no easy solutions to the problem of ensuring consistent police integrity, but the solution requires recruiting, training, and supervising police officers in a way that increases the chances of appropriate behaviour.

If a community is going to regard its police as having legitimate authority, police must be respected and be seen to be fair. Fairness is usually defined as the equal treatment of people in similar circumstances (Gleason 2006, 60). In an era in which news and social media can quickly portray police actions in extremely negative ways, police have been forced to realize that their best response is to be as open, fair, and transparent as possible. (See Chapter 14 for further discussion.)

An important area of law in which police must regularly exercise discretion is in the situationally dependent **reasonable grounds**. This is a subjective and objective test that is applied in consideration of the totality of the circumstances: what the "average person, dispassionate of the situation" would believe to be reasonable. For example, if a vehicle is observed to be driving erratically, moving slowly across lanes, and disobeying road signs, a reasonable person would have reasonable grounds to suspect that the driver of that vehicle may be impaired by drugs or alcohol, or be engaged in distracted driving such as texting or talking on the phone.

Commonly, there are two legal tests that police officers must consider in their duty: **reasonable grounds to suspect** and **reasonable grounds to believe**. Reasonable grounds to believe is a higher standard based upon the facts of the situation. Relevant to the example given, if the vehicle were subsequently pulled over by the police officer and the police officer could smell liquor emanating from the driver's breath and make observations that the driver had glassy, bloodshot eyes, spoke slowly, and slurred his or her words, it would support reasonable grounds to believe that the driver was operating the vehicle while impaired by alcohol and therefore trigger a lawful arrest and investigation.

Do I have sufficient factual information to accurately assess the situation?

Do the current facts of the situation constitute reasonable grounds to suspect? Reasonable grounds to believe?

Will engaging the criminal justice system solve the problem? Improve overall public safety?

Is arresting and laying charges against the individual in that person's best interest? Is it also in the public's best interest?

Figure 5.1   Flow Chart of Questions Police Consider when Making Decisions

Challenge Your Assumptions

Ethical/Discretion Decision Maker

You are a uniformed police officer on foot patrol in a small geographic area known for high levels of criminal activity (a **hot spot**), all of which revolves around the drug market. There is a large homeless population, an active street sex trade, and open drug use is common. A critical part of your everyday job is to ensure that people feel safe in their communities, victims of crime are treated respectfully, and those who engage in criminal activity are dealt with fairly and proportionately. Part of that job is to know the people in your patrol area and understand the real and perceived concerns that they have in their community. By walking around, you are in fact "flying the flag," as your presence is generally intended to make people feel safer and to act as a deterrent to those who may engage in criminal activity.

You see a lone male who appears confused and under the influence of either alcohol or drugs. You hear him yelling at no one in particular. You see him stumble and nearly fall off the sidewalk into traffic several times.

You decide to initiate a street check out of concern for his safety and a reasonable belief that he may be intoxicated in a public place. The male is polite and respectful and, when asked, provides you with a government-issued identification card with the first name Robert. You ask Robert a few questions and learn that he is a 50-year-old homeless person who most often lives on the street but will take shelter in community-supported rooms when the weather is poor. Robert tells you that he has an addiction to alcohol and crack cocaine. He has tried going to detox when beds were available; however, it has never worked out for him. Robert is on welfare but when that money runs out, as it does every month, he often turns to crime including selling small quantities of drugs to support his own habit. You ask Robert if he has any weapons or anything illegal on his person and he admits that he has two $15 "crack rocks" in his front pocket, along with medication for depression. He tells you that this is for personal use and that he consumes two rocks a day to keep him functioning, otherwise he gets "drug sick."

Pursuant to the law of investigative detention (see *R. v. Mann*, 2004 SCC; see also Chapter 2 of this text) and combined with Robert's admission of having an illicit drug, you conduct a cursory search of Robert's person, emptying his pockets. You look up his information in the **Canadian Police Information Centre (CPIC)**, a police database maintained by the RCMP in which information about criminal records and information for police use is housed. (Information for police use might include, for example, information about a gang member known to carry firearms that justifies a "caution armed and dangerous" entry. Outstanding warrants for arrest, probation, and parole conditions linked to those offenders are also available on CPIC. CPIC is interfaced with records from each provincial motor vehicle branch and can link to the National Crime Information Center hosted by the Federal Bureau of Investigation in the United States.) Your CPIC check informs you that Robert has a lengthy criminal record dating back 20 years for property crimes and several convictions for drug possession. You note that he has been arrested a few times for concerns about his mental health. He does not have any outstanding warrants. Robert assures you that he has a safe place to stay and he is safe. You tell Robert your concerns about his behaviour and that you wanted to make sure he was not inebriated to the point where he could hurt himself or someone else. You are satisfied that Robert is fine. You tell Robert to take care of himself and to stay out of trouble. Robert tells you to stay safe and have a good shift.

You decide not to seize the two crack rocks or to arrest Robert and charge him with possession. Your decision is based upon your experience, which tells you that Robert is a victim of drug addiction and has no legitimate source of income. If you seize the crack rocks as a "no-case seizure" you know that Robert likely will be forced to commit crimes such as breaking into cars to replace those crack rocks. Your experience tells you that it is not in the public interest for you to seize the rocks or arrest Robert and charge him with possession, and that if you did, he would quickly be back on the street again and in the same situation.

What assumptions did you make when you first encountered Robert? Is Robert a criminal or a victim of drug addiction? Would the average Canadian think that the decision not to seize the crack cocaine or to arrest and charge Robert is an appropriate use of discretion? Or did you not do your job?

The Supreme Court of Canada has confirmed that "the integrity of our legal system depends in large measure on the integrity of those charged with its administration and enforcement" (*R. v. Beaudry* 2009, SSC at line 113). Discretion is an integral aspect of policing and flows through everything a police officer does. The question therefore arises as to how it is possible to ensure an acceptable level of consistency among officers in their exercise of discretion.

Bronitt and Stenning (2011, 320) observed that a distinction is to be made between discretion and interpretive judgment. Specifically, the former almost always involves some of the latter. That is, a police officer must interpret a situation before he or she can exercise appropriate discretion with respect to it. However, interpretive judgment does not itself necessarily constitute discretion. Interpretive judgment is the subjective analysis of the entirety of each interaction as independently verified by the objective facts available at the time. Discretion entails finding an appropriate and dispassionate balance given the particular facts, circumstances, and persons involved in any given situation.

The Application of the Law Is Far from Black and White

Three principal factors influence police in their discretionary decision making. Crime type and the facts of the case are the most important. Serious crimes will limit the range of options open to the police. These options range from warning and releasing a suspect, to detaining the suspect for further investigation, to arresting and releasing, to arresting and charging. A second important factor is how the suspect or accused behaves during the encounter with police. Belligerence, combativeness, or disrespect will almost always invite an elevated response from the police. A third important factor (and often related to the seriousness of the alleged offence) is the existence of formal departmental policies that dictate how particular offences are to be addressed. For example, many departments have zero-tolerance policies with respect to domestic violence. That is, if police have evidence that an assault has occurred independent of the victim's willingness to proceed with charges, police are required under departmental policies to initiate charges.

Case Study

Discretion

You are a uniformed patrol police officer working a double overtime shift on a roadblock initiative to detect and reduce impaired driving. You are standing in a line of police officers, each of whom has a role in efficiently checking many vehicles. A vehicle stops with the driver side window down. You note that the middle-aged female driver has slightly glassy, bloodshot eyes. She is wearing a formal dress. You detect a mild odour of liquor on her breath. You ask whether the driver has had any alcohol, and she answers that she has had two beers and two glasses of wine over the last eight hours. Her name is Pamela and she is on her way home from her only daughter's wedding.

You have grounds to suspect that Pamela may be impaired and you read her the formal demand to provide a breath sample for a roadside screening device. Pamela assures you she is fine, but is polite and respectful and complies with your request. The roadside screening

device shows that Pamela "blew a fail" or "over .08" blood alcohol content (BAC). You ask Pamela for another breath sample and it confirms a "fail, over .08". You advise Pamela of the results and she is upset, cannot believe it: she thought she had eaten enough and spaced out her alcoholic drinks appropriately. Pamela was the emcee at the wedding and led toasts throughout the evening. You take Pamela's driver's licence and conduct police checks that show that there is no adverse information at all on her, no contact with police, and no driving infractions. You ask Pamela what she does for a living and she replies she has been a school teacher for over 25 years. Pamela tells you that if she loses her licence, it will have a devastating effect on her life and her ability to get to work as there is no suitable public transit where she lives.

Within the law, you have reasonable grounds to believe that Pamela was operating a motor vehicle while impaired by alcohol contrary to Section 253 of the *Criminal Code of Canada*. You may arrest her, bring her back to the office, and perform a breath test on a proper breath analyzer. If Pamela blows over .08 BAC on a proper breath analyzer, you may initiate charges to engage the court process. However, if Pamela's BAC is found to be between .05 and .079, the "warn" range, a police officer may issue Pamela an immediate roadside prohibition (IRP), tow her car to prevent continuation of the offence, and have a taxi safely drive her home. If you choose this option, Pamela will have her licence immediately suspended, the incident will be documented on her driving record and a police file generated, but she will not face the prospect of having a criminal record (provincial *Motor Vehicle Act* provisions vary as to when an IRP may be issued, the length of licence suspension, and any associated fines).

Are the circumstances of this offence such that the exercise of discretion is reasonable?

If you were the police officer, what would you do?

Limits to Police Discretion

Domestic Violence

Domestic violence has been identified as a serious problem. Sustained efforts have been made by Canadian police agencies to raise awareness and sensitivity of both recruits and experienced officers with respect to domestic violence. Serious efforts have also been made to develop formal policies to address domestic violence. It is widely accepted by criminologists and by policing personnel that domestic violence is grossly underreported to authorities. As a result, many departments have embraced zero-tolerance policies regarding domestic violence. That is, at calls where domestic violence is evident, the required response is that if there is evidence independent of the victim (for example, obvious bruising, black eyes, cuts, bleeding nose), police must arrest and charge, or forward charges to Crown for consideration. In these circumstances, police discretion is severely curtailed. Gone are the days where police would defer to the wishes of the victim and where victims would, all too frequently, withdraw their complaints, change their original statements, and/or refuse to testify, thus resulting in a stay of the criminal proceedings.

Indeed, Fraehlich (2014, 507) found that many police departments across North America have adopted pro-arrest policies in intimate partner violence cases with the intent of constraining police discretion and providing better protection for victims of interpersonal violence. Years earlier, Ursel and Farough (1986) found that pro-arrest policies for domestic violence reflected a decreased public tolerance for this type of criminal behaviour. Legislative reforms and changes in law enforcement practices thus reflect a decrease in societal tolerance of violent crimes against family members (Stephens and Sinden 2000, 535). It is clear that restricting discretion by police officers does result in higher arrest rates (Ursel and Farough 1986). What are the effects of substantive changes in law and policy that limit police discretion? Research conducted by Rowe (2007, 293) found that police officers were often concerned that limits on their discretion undermined their professional autonomy and limited their ability to find an informal but workable balance in particular situations.

Youth Criminal Justice Act

Often changes in the law can affect police discretion. For example, the *Youth Criminal Justice Act* (YCJA) enacted in 2003 has had an impact on police autonomy to make decisions. Carrington and Schulenberg (2008) evaluated the extent to which the YCJA achieved the objective of reducing formal action by police—such as referrals to youth court—during the first three years after its implementation. Carrington and Schulenberg (2008) noted that the YCJA makes clear that measures other than laying a charge—also known as **extrajudicial measures**—such as taking no action, giving an informal warning or a formal caution, or diverting to a community-based program, are entirely appropriate forms of law enforcement for young offenders.

The spirit and intent of the YCJA demonstrates that

Canadian society should have a youth criminal justice system that commands respect, takes into account the interests of victims, fosters responsibility and ensures accountability through meaningful consequences and effective rehabilitation and reintegration, and that reserves its most serious intervention for the most serious crimes and reduces the over-reliance on incarceration for non-violent young persons. [*Youth Criminal Justice Act* 2002]

Carrington and Schulenberg (2008, 349) did find that the *Youth Criminal Justice Act* was successful in achieving its objective of reducing youth court referrals by facilitating an increase in police discretion. It caused a substantial change to the ability of the police to exercise discretion with respect to apprehended youth. In turn, this has led to a substantial decrease in the use of charges and a corresponding increase in the use of alternatives to charging. Allen and Superle (2014) reported that the rate at which youth were charged by police dropped considerably with the introduction of the *Youth Criminal Justice Act* in 2003. They also noted a gradual decline in the proportion of youth who are sentenced to custody.

Use of Force and Discretion

Routinely, police officers make decisions and act quickly to balance competing and conflicting values and interests, frequently with incomplete or inaccurate information, often in highly emotional and dynamic circumstances, and typically under pressure (Gleason 2007). There are situations in policing where two police officers in attendance at the same call, having been provided with the same information and seeing exactly the same situation unfolding, react differently. One police officer draws and readies her firearm while her partner does not. What accounts for the difference in the decision to use a particular level of force? Is one officer wrong, while the other is right?

The easy answer is that the decision to unholster your firearm is an individual decision, an entirely subjective interpretation of otherwise objective criteria of both law and policy surrounding the use of force. It all depends on how an officer perceives the entirety of the situation. The primary variables that influence an officer's perception include training, level of fitness, competence in the use-of-force options (see Chapters 4 and 8 respectively), and breadth of experience. Secondary variables include an understanding of the applicable laws and policy. Every time a police officer draws and points a firearm at someone, the questions that arise revolve around how and why the officer perceived that there was a threat of grievous bodily harm or death to either him- or herself or any other person at the scene.

Gleason (2006, 58) suggested that a police response to any particular situation has two components: reaction (emotions and thought) and action (behaviour). The subjective assessment by the police officer and independent (objective) verification of the facts are key to concluding whether a police officer acted properly within the scope of Section 25 of the *Criminal Code*.

As discussed in Chapter 8, the use-of-force models that police have adopted across Canada are designed to help police officers have a frame of reference in encounters with suspects. They are designed to help police officers describe and explain their actions, particularly when some level of force has been deployed. There is no definitive guideline specifying what level of force is called for in any particular situation. Both laws and policies seek to establish broad parameters for police officer actions. However, the reality is that each action a police officer takes is entirely contingent on an assessment of the totality of the circumstances he or she faces.

Discretion and the Charter

As this text addressed earlier, certain sections of the Canadian *Charter of Rights and Freedoms* provide a basic framework for everything that a police officer does. The Supreme Court of Canada (SCC) has addressed police discretion in a number of rulings that consistently revolve around the principle that "discretion is an essential, judicially recognized feature of the criminal justice system" (*R. v. Beare* 1988, 389). In *R. v. Beare* (1988, 410) the Court went further to say that "a system that attempted to eliminate discretion would be unworkably complex and rigid."

With respect to police specifically, the SCC said ". . . police necessarily exercise discretion in deciding when to lay charges, to arrest and to conduct incidental searches, as prosecutors do in deciding whether or not to withdraw a charge, enter a stay, consent to an adjournment, proceed by way of indictment or summary conviction, launch an appeal and so on. The *Criminal Code* provides no guidelines for the exercise of discretion in any of these areas. The day-to-day operation of law enforcement and the criminal justice system nonetheless depends upon the exercise of that discretion" (*R. v. Beare* 1988, SCC, 410).

In *R. v. Beaudry* (2007), the Supreme Court of Canada addressed police discretion in saying,

> A police officer who has reasonable grounds to believe that an offence has been, is currently being, or is about to be committed, or that a more thorough investigation might produce evidence that could form the basis of a criminal charge, may exercise his or her discretion to decide not to engage the judicial process. But this

discretion is not absolute. The exercise of the discretion must be justified subjectively, that is, the discretion must have been exercised honestly and transparently, and on the basis of valid and reasonable grounds; it must also be justified on the basis of objective factors. In determining whether a decision resulting from an exercise of police discretion is proper, it is therefore important to consider the material circumstances in which the discretion was exercised. The justification offered must be proportionate to the seriousness of the conduct and it must be clear that the discretion was exercised in the public interest. [*R. v. Beaudry*, 2007 1 S.C.R. 190, 2007 SCC 5]

Ethics Training

Recognizing that ethical standards evolve over time, Canadian police agencies have developed training in ethics for their officers. Gleason (2006, 60) has stated that ethics training should encourage police professionals to be persons of integrity, since "excellent qualities of character must become integral to a police officer's public and private lives."

Ethics training should openly acknowledge and provide guidelines for exercising discretion. To deny that police professionals routinely exercise discretion is simply inaccurate; police officers must exercise discretion: "Police discretion is absolutely essential. It cannot be eliminated. Any effort to eliminate it would be ridiculous. Discretion is the essence of police work" (Kenneth Culp Davis 1975 cited in Gleason 2006, 60).

> Indeed, police officer discretion is "far from having *carte blanche*, police officers must justify their decisions rationally" (*R. v. Beaudry*, 2007 1 S.C.R. 190, 2007 SCC 5). Ethics training must provide not only broad guidelines and parameters to follow when exercising discretion, but also a vocabulary, a "logical thought process," and acceptable boundaries within which to exercise it. Discretion, properly exercised, makes the law more just. As much as equity can soften the impact of the law, so too can the wise exercise of discretion soften the law's application.
>
> An officer develops his or her moral compass, character, or ethical base from interacting with other individuals and studying ethics. Ethics training for police professionals helps them do the following:
> * readily recognize an ethical problem or dilemma;
> * identify various options to address the particular issue;
> * make a rational and ethically sound choice of which option to choose;
> * take prompt action based upon that choice;
> * accept responsibility for the outcome. [Gleason 2006]

Police officers cannot simply think ethically; they must also act ethically. Ethics training provides tools for addressing ethical problems, but individual officers must have the courage to act. Papenfuhs (2011) stated that learning is not a one-time event in police work; rather, it is a continuous process of review and reinforcement and therefore ethics training should continue throughout an officer's career. Canadian police agencies have recognized the importance of ethics to competent police work and to their ability to ensure and maintain public trust. Maintaining high ethical standards that in part guide discretionary response and decisions is thus increasingly paramount for police agencies in western democratic nations.

Unethical Behaviour by Police Officers

Lundman (1980) stated that ever since the first police forces were formed, police misconduct and the abuse of police powers have always been a concern. In fact, the police discretion issue is the predominant source of allegations of police misconduct in the United States (Albrecht 2011, 2). While police discretion is seen as inevitable and essential, there remains an underlying fear that its exercise may lead to arbitrary, corrupt, or unethical behaviour (Bronitt and Stenning 2011, 324).

Gilmartin (Gilmartin 2002 in Sunahara 2004) has argued that the frequent and harsh criticism of police causes police officers to see themselves as victims. In turn, they develop a sense of entitlement, believing that they deserve special compensation for the onerous duties they perform. It is thus suggested that unethical behaviour arises when officers' expectations of compensation override their public duty. Gleason (2006), however, believes that a consideration of ethical conduct must assess not only the behaviour but the motivation for the behaviour. For example, doing the right thing for the wrong reason is not ethical, such as a supervisor encouraging an officer to seek psychological support, not because the supervisor cares about the person but to look good in the eyes of their supervisors. Police administrators and trainers striving to instill a sense of ethical excellence must consider motives behind behaviour, in addition to the behaviour itself.

Off-Duty Conduct

Being a police officer, at least in most western democratic nations, carries with it a **master status**. That is, police officers are viewed on the basis of one key attribute—their legal authority to enforce the law. Whatever other personal or social qualities police officers as individuals may possess, they are judged primarily by this one attribute (Linden 2012, 416). However, as sociologist Everett Hughes (1945) pointed out many years ago, a master status invariably also entails a number of auxiliary traits. For example, with regard to police officers, when friends, neighbours, or members of the public learn that someone is a police officer, they make assumptions about the type of person the police officer is. They have expectations about how police officers should conduct themselves in both their professional and private lives. It is expected that a police officer is a particular type of person who is to be trusted and who will help others in need. It is also expected that police officers will have high moral standards, possess leadership abilities, and be able to solve problems in the course of their duties.

It is generally accepted that police officers are expected to carry themselves to a higher standard throughout their working lives. The police are influenced and constrained by the broader ethical standards and expectations of their societies (O'Donnell 2011). Police officers are thus held to a higher standard of behaviour because they are stewards of the public trust and have the authority to use force and infringe upon constitutional (*Charter*) rights when lawfully justified. Police officers are also expected to comply with professional codes of ethics and, in addition to obeying the laws, are subject to various policies, rules, and regulations (Gleason 2006, 58).

Off-duty misconduct reflects negatively on the police organization and has the potential to undermine organizational legitimacy and public confidence in the police (Stinson, Liederbach, and Freiburger 2012, 141). On most occasions, in major urban centres, it is not newsworthy to publish the names of those arrested and charged for impaired driving. However, should the arrested person be an off-duty police officer, the circumstances are likely to make the news. When unprofessional conduct or a criminal offence is attributed publicly to a police officer, all police officers are affected. Policing is subject to such scrutiny that when police officers are alleged to have breached public expectations, the effects are immediate and widespread.

There are a number of reasons why off-duty police officers may make poor decisions; however, the hope is that police officers will make fewer poor decisions than the average person. While there is no valid excuse for a police officer not to consistently conduct him- or herself to the expected standard, police officers are nonetheless subject to the same pressures as anyone else. For example, police officers have financial problems, relationship problems, family stresses, worries about children, and health issues, and experience the general ups and downs of everyday life. In addition, police work itself is stressful. On any given shift, a police officer may attend a traumatic car accident, be first to the scene of a homicide, interview a child victim of a sexual assault, save someone's life, or conduct a next-of-kin notification—having to tell someone that a loved one has been killed. For certain, what happens on the job affects police officers long after the shift ends. (See Chapters 8 and 9 for further discussion.)

What are the common misbehaviours that off-duty police officers get involved in? Stinson, Liederbach, and Freiburger (2012, 154) have found, perhaps not surprisingly, that problems associated with off-duty alcohol abuse appear to be pervasive. Driving while intoxicated, domestic violence, and other assaults committed by off-duty police officers constitute the principal challenges to senior police executives responsible for disciplining and deterring misbehaviour (Stinson, Liederbach, and Freiburger 2012, 156). Whether there is a definitive connection between the demands of police work and alcohol or marijuana abuse in Canada has yet to be determined.

When faced with conflict with partners or family members, police officers are expected to walk away before a situation escalates to any physical confrontation. When socializing with friends at a pub or restaurant, police officers are to be vigilant and mindful of alcohol intake if driving. With certainty, police officers are expected to make better decisions more often than not.

Conclusion

This chapter introduced and discussed the concepts of ethical decision making and highlighted how decision making and discretion flow directly through all aspects of police work, both on and off duty. Using real-life scenarios and guided by critical-thinking questions, it is easy to see that policing is a challenging occupation and you never know what you are going to face, in what circumstance. It is often impossible to predict how any call for service is going to play out in the end. To achieve and maintain public trust, police officers have to be right more often than not, while operating within the law, the *Charter*, and best practices. With significant consistency, polls and studies (Angus Reid 2014; Department of Justice 2015; Seglins 2010) confirm that a significant majority of Canadians have considerable faith and trust in their police.

The police provide service, protection, and public safety and are the agency of last resort. Police officers are admired by most and despised by some, but are nonetheless expected to respond to virtually all calls for service. Police in most western democracies are often held to be the foundation on which just, fair, and decent societies are built. When police act with predictability, restraint, and fealty to the rule of law, ordinary people gain faith in their government (O'Donnell 2011).

Critical Thinking Questions

1. Discretion is required in virtually everything the police do in carrying out their duties. What are the effects on the criminal justice system when legislation or policy acts to limit police discretion?
2. Do you think that ethics can be taught or refined in police officers, or are ethics guided by individual personality traits that were developed long before the individual ever thought of becoming a police officer?
3. Would you expect that a career in policing negatively or positively impacts police officers' moral character and ethical thinking as they move through their careers?
4. What do you anticipate would be the effects on the public if police began taking a consistent zero-tolerance approach to all minor traffic violations and drug offences? Consider the examples of driving 52 km/h in a designated 50 km/h zone and being issued a violation ticket rather than a warning, or being arrested for causing a minor public disturbance and charges being forwarded to trigger a court process.
5. Do you believe that a police officer with fifteen years of experience generally makes better ethical decisions than a police officer with two years of on-the-job experience?

6

Accountability and Oversight

Learning Objectives

After reading and studying this chapter, students will be able to:

- Identify and discuss issues of accountability within policing.
- Describe and discuss accountability of police officers on and off duty.
- Review and discuss how police are accountable to Crown counsel and the court process.
- Identify and discuss public oversight mechanisms for Canadian police.
- Review and discuss identify the factors that affect accountability and police.

Introduction

The previous chapter introduced and discussed a range of issues related to the accountability of police in Canada. Starting with an overview of Canada's status on a world scale, Chapter 6 considers accountability factors for individual police officers and police agencies as a whole. Accountability in policing and public oversight mechanisms are defined and discussed. Professional standards and anti-corruption units are reviewed as areas where the police still investigate themselves. Subsequently, civilian-led investigative bodies and public inquiries are considered as mechanisms by which police are held accountable. In other words, this chapter addresses how police officers are held accountable for their conduct not only while on active patrol duty but through to their testimony in court.

Oversight and Accountability

Police are agents of the state and, like any other government agency, are ultimately accountable to the public. The *Oxford English Dictionary* defines **accountability** as "the fact or condition of being accountable; responsibility," and in democracies like Canada, accountability is a core principle (Behn 2001). Accountability is important to all public organizations. By being accountable, government agencies demonstrate their legitimacy (Schillemans, Van Twist, and Vanhommerig 2013, 408). The fundamental function of police is to assure the safety of the public. This occurs through proper and efficient execution of duties while maintaining public trust (Lamboo 2010, 617). Along with ensuring public safety and trust comes the ongoing challenge of providing police services as openly and transparently as possible.

Globally, many governments face problems of corruption. This is true for their police agencies as well. Of 180 nations studied by Transparency International (TI), an organization that tracks corruption and related concerns around the world, unacceptably high levels of corruption were identified in more than two-thirds of those countries. More specifically, abuse of power, secret dealings, and bribery were common (Transparency International, n.d.). In 2018, Canada scored 81/100 on the Corruption Perception Index, which is based upon how corrupt a country's public sector is believed to be, with 100 being considered "very clean." In Canada, public confidence in the police historically has always been high, with a significant majority of Canadians having a great deal of trust in and respect for their police forces (Tinsley 2009, 2). Clark et al. (2017, 102) stated that "Canadian policing is very well respected and often envied around the world, and in this regard, Canada is doing many things right."

For most countries, the manner in which police conduct themselves, their level of trust, and how they are regarded both domestically and internationally reveal important insights into how that society operates. This assessment is largely based upon how open and accountable the police and other government agencies are. Trust in law enforcement is essential for belief in the legitimacy of law enforcement, or feeling obliged to obey the law and defer to decisions made by legal authorities (Friedman 2014). The maintenance of law and order is critical to how safe people feel in their communities and directly influences how free they are to go about their daily lives.

The police are at the front end of most systems of justice. That is, without actions from the police, the rest of the criminal justice system is not engaged. Policing is an important element in most societies. As The Honourable Mr. Justice Peter Cory has pointed out, "No (democratic) society can exist without a police force" (Cory 2001, 47). In fact, the law enforcement duties carried out by police officers are vital to the very survival of society (Van Allen 2009, 6).

In the context of policing in Canada, the word "accountability" is raised with some regularity. However, there is often little real understanding of the context in which it is applied. For example, what does accountability really mean with respect to police officers? Unfortunately, with every suggestion that the police are abusing their powers, public confidence in the integrity of the criminal justice system is weakened. Media and sometimes subsequent judicial scrutiny of police and their investigative practices have resulted in unprecedented attention directed toward the police in general (Van Allen 2009, 9). **Public confidence**, so fundamental to successful policing and to the operation of the criminal justice system in general, is often undermined (Roberts 2007, 154).

Accountability involves a range of related issues, including integrity, ethics, and morals. These issues play an important role in the assessment of both individual officers and of the departments in which they serve. Van Allen (2009, 1) noted that peace officers are granted extraordinary powers that are entrusted to no other professions within our society. It is therefore reasonable to expect that when a decision is made by police officers to use force, search and seizure, or arrest, these powers will be used in compliance with law, policy, and public expectations. While it is easy to state that the police should only exercise these powers when legally justified, the reality is that the law is never black and white, especially not at the street level of enforcement, nor in complex investigations (see also Chapters 2, 4, 5 and 9 in this text). The best police officers come to understand that the law is grey and that the application of the law during an encounter (whether it be for arrest, use of force, or other discretionary actions) must be understood taking into account the totality of the circumstances.

Goff (2014, 197) identified two foundational streams of accountability: Police must conform to the appropriate legal standards of **due process**; and police must be responsive to the citizens they serve. These often conflict and therefore the key is how best to achieve the correct balance such that the people feel safe in their communities yet maintain confidence in the criminal justice process. Roberts (2007, 153) observed that promoting and engaging public confidence in criminal justice processes have emerged as important issues in most western nations. Based on data gathered in 2013, Cotter reported that three in four Canadians had either "a great deal or some confidence" in the police while the remaining components of justice system and the courts were found to have the confidence of just over half of Canadians (2015, 2).

Public Perception

Perhaps the most important consideration is the public perception of police. Police have both a significant legal authority and a duty to uphold the law and protect citizens. The issue is not that the police have such responsibilities, but rather the level of **discretion** that police exercise when fulfilling their duties. It is accepted that police work frequently requires decisive action, often under circumstances in which information is minimal. Frequently, decisions and actions undertaken by the police are later scrutinized by the media and other social commentators who often are not in possession of all the facts related to the circumstances. It is then up to the police to respond as quickly as possible to explain the actions of their officers, often in adverse situations. The challenge for the police is to inform the public without breaching individual privacy rights and without saying or doing anything that might impede an ongoing investigation or prejudice any future court process. All of these factors underscore the importance of accountability and public trust (Lamboo 2010, 613).

In the Canadian **multicultural mosaic**, the perception of police is influenced, in part, by immigrants from countries in which corruption, including that of the police, is a way of life. Negative and often fearful perceptions of the police are often brought to Canada. From the perspective of Canadian police, this is challenging to the extent that the lack of trust toward the police creates barriers to cooperation between the police and new arrivals (as discussed in Chapter 3). Canadian police agencies are aware of this and many have developed initiatives or programs to reach out to ethnic communities in the hope of fostering greater respect and trust.

Public opinions of the police are important indicators of how well the police are performing their duties (see Chapter 7). Young people, visible minorities, victims of crime,

Carol Provins/Shutterstock

In 2020, protests against systemic racism and the disproportionate number of deaths of Black people at the hands of police took place worldwide, including in several cities in Canada. (Pictured is one of the protests in Edmonton.) How important is it to the functioning of a police department that it have a good relationship with the community it serves?

those living in high-crime areas, and those who are most fearful for their safety tend to hold negative views of the police (Cotter 2015, 15). Public opinion surveys shape police practices and public policies (O'Connor 2008, 578).

In fast-paced life in modern North America, the need to have immediate access to information dominates (see discussion to follow on body-worn cameras). In recent years, largely due to the internet, the speed of modern communications, and the extensive use of mobile cellular devices, police encounters with the public can be recorded and made instantly available to mass audiences. It is all too easy for the public to form immediate opinions based solely on what they see on television or in social media or read in popular tabloid newspapers like the *Calgary Sun*, *Toronto Sun*, or Vancouver's *The Province*. A picture of an event paints a thousand words (particularly when brought to life with a few seconds of amateur video and posted online) and allows many people to reach emotional conclusions about situations even though the complete context is not conveyed. Given the media rule of thumb "if it bleeds, it leads," particularly if police actions are called into question, public reaction can be swift and vitriolic.

Increasingly, much of what the public knows about the police is based on a seemingly limitless barrage of mainstream and social media. Much media coverage focuses on what the police appear to have done wrong as opposed to what they have done right. Coverage of such police successes as rescuing or helping persons at accident scenes, defusing violent domestic situations, arresting and charging a dangerous sex offender, or solving a homicide is relatively rare. Kaufman (1998, 8) suggests that the public are often most interested in the findings of misconduct made against individuals or organizations.

The Influence of the United States

What the average Canadian knows and understands about police work and about the broader criminal justice system is most often gleaned from American news and entertainment media. Perhaps the main concern with the shaping of Canadian opinions or perceptions of police by American news and entertainment media is that it is all too easy for Canadian viewers to remain unaware that there are significant differences between both countries with respect to laws and the operations of the police.

Statistically, it is much more dangerous to be a police officer in the United States than in Canada. This, in part, is due to the wide availability of firearms, particularly handguns, in the United States. There are also significant cultural and legal differences between Canada and the United States. For example, in the United States, once an arrested suspect has contacted a lawyer, police officers can no longer speak to the suspect until the lawyer is present. In Canada, once the right of a suspect to contact legal counsel has been satisfied, police may still conduct a warned interview. A **warned interview** is one in which detained persons have been read their Section 10 *Charter* rights, advised that they do not have to provide any information, and have spoken to legal counsel. Once this is satisfied, it is up to the individual to invoke his or her right to silence or to speak to the police. While the constitutional right to silence is similar in both countries, there are nonetheless differences in the degree to which police can continue to interact with suspects (see Chapter 9).

In Canada

Canadian police are subject to a number of oversight mechanisms, all of which are designed to maintain accountability. From this, it may be said that the police are more accountable than at any other time in history. Certain sections of the Canadian *Charter of Rights and Freedoms* have a specific impact on policing. As well, other federal statutes such as the *Criminal Code*, the *Youth Criminal Justice Act*, and the *Controlled Drugs and Substances Act* provide the primary legal framework under which the police carry out their duties. Beyond these formal legal frameworks are internal mechanisms that are the foundation of any police force.

As confirmed by **case law**, the totality of the circumstances is critically important when considering the actions of the police from an objective standpoint. Yet it is also critical to take into account the subjective view of the police officer who was engaged in the situation at the time. The significance of the subjective view of the police officer is integral to police work. For example, within the past few years, training on the use of force has been updated to include an enhanced focus on teaching police officers to articulate what they were thinking at the time of the incident and what they felt emotionally (i.e., afraid, anxious, threatened, and so on) in addition to their perception of the entirety of the situation (see also Chapters 5 and 8).

This relatively recent addition to the training curriculum seeks to have police officers improve their ability to articulate what they did and why they did it. This arises out of the experiences of police giving testimony in court but being unable to articulate their legal authority to have acted as they did. For example, it was often difficult under cross-examination for officers to articulate their justification for using a particular level of force. Police officers who may have acted appropriately and legally were often unable to properly express themselves while attempting to describe their definition of the situation, and in accounting for their consequent actions arising from the decisions that they made at the time.

Formal Structures

Current research has shown that the management and culture of a department are the most important factors influencing police behaviour (Fridell et al. 2001). A report prepared for the Toronto Police Service stated that the continuing challenge to maintain ethical standards and professional integrity will be won or lost depending on the performance of its management (Ferguson, 2003). Traditionally, Canadian police forces have been structured on the **paramilitary model** or, as Murphy and McKenna (2007, 8) have called it, the military bureaucratic model of police organization that can be traced historically to the influence of Sir Robert Peel. In 1829, Peel declared that the London Metropolitan Police "must be stable and efficient and organized along military lines."

More accurately, modern Canadian police agencies may be considered paramilitary in structure. While private-sector companies have presidents and vice presidents and police have chiefs and deputy chiefs, both have rank-ordered reporting lines. This combination of military and bureaucratic organizational principles comprises the basic model of conventional modern police organizations. While some variance exists, all police agencies in Canada remain similarly structured with the following organizational characteristics:

- rank-based authority structure;
- highly centralized administration—all important decisions are made at the top;
- command-and-control management philosophy;
- formalized—heavy reliance on formal written communication, rules, procedures, and policies;
- specialization of many police administrative and operational functions;
- emphasis on technology and technique—generally rigid and inflexible organizational structure; resistant to change; and
- insular and closed—organization typically resistant to outside influences (Murphy and McKenna 2007, 7).

Police agencies are constantly trying to refine policing models to suit not only their needs but those that best serve their communities. In fact, the two key areas with the greatest variance among police forces are "rigid and inflexible organizational structure; resistant to change" and "organization typically resistant to outside influences." All police agencies work hard to evolve in these areas, some with more observable results. However, the foundational paramilitary structure is not likely to change radically in the near future.

The Individual, or the Structure of the Police Force?

Fundamental matters such as integrity and accountability start with rigorous recruiting and training standards. These standards are subsequently reinforced by the swearing of oaths of duty, formalized processes for promotions, and ongoing expectations regarding professional and personal conduct both on and off duty. Police officers in Canada are fully expected to conduct their professional and personal lives with integrity and according to the highest ethical and moral standards.

An interesting question to consider is whether performance and integrity are more affected by the structure of police forces or by the individual officers. Sherman (1974) considered that it is far easier to point to the moral failings of individual officers by labelling them disciplinary problems than it is to acknowledge that management may be systematically turning its officers into behaviour problems by treating them unfairly. For example, if police officers feel they are not being compensated fairly for their work, a police officer may be tempted to right the imbalance by claiming expenses or overtime that he or she is not entitled to. Whatever the reason for integrity concerns, poor conduct, or corruption issues within policing, police forces treat these issues seriously, as even one bad cop or situation paints everyone else in policing in a poor light. The empirical reality is that in many police services, a small group of police officers account for a large number of citizen complaints (Goff 2014, 196).

Three Levels of Accountability

Sutton (2009) believed that accountability in law enforcement has three equally important components that must work together to be effective. The first is **self-accountability**. Each police officer has an important role within the framework of his or her police organization. Self-accountability refers to officers being accountable to themselves and to each other, whether on or off duty.

Supervisory accountability is the second component. It is critical that the right police officers are promoted into supervisory roles based on a proven track record of performing duties at a high level, but also on having a demonstrated ability to provide leadership and manage people effectively.

Administrative accountability is the third component. All police agencies in Canada have similar hierarchical structures based on a paramilitary foundation. The top of the hierarchy is the Chief Constable in most municipal police agencies, the Director-Général of the Sûreté du Québec, and Commissioners in the OPP and the RCMP. No matter who the individual is at the highest rank in the police agency, there is no doubt that the entire ethical personality of an agency is determined by the head of that organization (Sutton 2009).

Individual or Self-Accountability

Concern about integrity is perhaps the most important issue facing the profession of policing. As Klockars et al. (2000, 1) point out, "policing is an occupation that is rife with opportunities for misconduct. Policing is a highly discretionary, coercive activity that routinely takes place in private settings, out of the sight of supervisors, and in the presence of witnesses who are often regarded as unreliable." Cases of police misconduct can seriously harm years of work to establish trust and confidence between the police and members of their community (McDevitt et al. 2011, 1).

Individual accountability as a police officer starts after successful completion of police training, formal swearing-in ceremonies, and oaths of allegiance to the police agency that has hired the officer. The oaths relate to what they represent and stand for, and pledge allegiance to serve the country and the public. From that point, the police officer has chosen a career in which one must carry oneself to the highest moral, ethical, and legal standards at all times.

Case Study

The "Surrey Six"

On the afternoon of October 19, 2007, six men were executed in suite 1505 at the Balmoral Tower, an apartment building in Surrey, British Columbia. They were shot to death while lying defencelessly on the floor. The victims were Corey Lal, Michael Lal, Edward Narong, Ryan Bartolomeo, Edward Schellenberg, and Christopher Mohan. The murders have become known as the "Surrey Six" in reference to the six victims (*R. v. Haevischer* 2014 BCSC 1863 p6).

Ed Schellenberg was servicing gas fireplaces in the building and happened to be in the suite when the killers arrived. Chris Mohan, age 22, was entering his neighbouring residence when the killers forced him into suite 1505, for the purpose of eliminating a witness. Both Schellenberg and Mohan were victims of circumstance. The other four men were drug dealers known to police.

The Lower Mainland joint forces Integrated Homicide Investigative Team (IHIT), was immediately tasked with a massive investigation.

Several men (Cody Rae Haevischer, Matthew Johnston, Michael Le, and Persons X and Y [who cannot be named due to a court order]) connected to a criminal group known as the Red Scorpions were eventually convicted of various offences. On October 2, 2014, Haevischer and Johnston were found guilty of six counts of first-degree murder (*R. v. Haevischer* 2014 BCSC 1863 p6).

In the course of the criminal investigation, it became evident that RCMP members of IHIT had engaged in highly inappropriate conduct. As a result, the Ontario Provincial Police were tasked with investigating allegations related to fraudulent claims for overtime and expenses. It was also alleged that certain RCMP officers had acted inappropriately with key witnesses. Following the OPP investigation, members of the RCMP faced a number of criminal charges.

On 18 January 2019, Derek Brassington (an RCMP Sergeant with IHIT) pled guilty in the BC Supreme Court to a criminal breach of trust related to his involvement with a witness and to "having wilfully attempted to obstruct, pervert or defeat the course of justice by compromising the integrity and safety of a witness." The facts showed that Brassington had engaged in a long-term sexual relationship with a female witness and that they took trips within Canada together and shared hotel rooms that were paid for by the government (*R. v. Brassington*, 2019 BCSC 265 p3).

Azpiri and Little (2019) reported that during the Court proceeding, a tearful Brassington said ". . . instead of restoring public trust and faith in the RCMP, I killed it. I made it 1000 times worse by what I did. I'm sorry to everyone in this country that loves the police. As a dad, I shouldn't have done this. As a husband, I shouldn't have done this. As a cop, I shouldn't have done this".

Is a Police Officer Ever Off Duty?

The easy answer to whether a police officer is ever really off duty is no. Police officers are expected to apply sound judgment and common sense to everyday life situations in both their occupational and personal lives. For example, police officers are expected to act responsibly in their personal lives with regard to such matters as drinking and driving and avoiding domestic conflicts. Whether on or off duty, police officers are often relied on to intervene and/or provide assistance when anyone needs it. Police officers are fully aware that when they join a police agency, they are agreeing to conduct themselves with the highest levels of propriety whether on or off duty.

On occasion however, police officers do make poor decisions and exercise bad judgment in their personal lives. Lamboo (2010, 613) observed that next to misuse of force and neglect of duty, misconduct in a police officer's private life is a major form of discreditable behaviour, although it is often neglected in academic discussions of police wrongdoing. While it is difficult to know the full extent to which police officers engage in off-duty misconduct—for example, conduct unreported or undetected—when it does occur and is identified, police agencies in Canada are quick to address it. Public trust in the police depends on it. Police agencies are keenly aware that trust is directly related to transparency and having truthful answers to "what did you know, when did you know it, and what did you do about it?" Depending on the situation, investigating and appropriately dealing with off-duty misconduct cases can consume substantial time and resources and cost the police agency (and taxpayers) thousands of dollars.

The **code of silence** is a powerful occupational norm governing how colleagues act to protect each other and their organization from outside criticism. This has been especially true of the police (Lamboo 2010, 615). However, within the police community, there is often little tolerance of fellow police officers who engage in discreditable conduct. Contrary to lay misconceptions, police officers who turn a blind eye to such discreditable conduct potentially put their own careers at risk. For example, amendments to the *Royal Canadian Mounted Police Act* that came into effect in 2015 mandate that officers are to report anyone in the RCMP for acting in a manner that would discredit themselves or the force. Should they fail to report such behaviour or activity, members may face disciplinary measures following an internal code-of-conduct investigation. It is impossible to measure the extent and impact of any "code of silence" within policing. However, it is reasonable to assume that improved training, awareness, and stricter policies with swift and certain remedies will improve the culture within policing.

If an off-duty police officer is found committing a traffic violation or a criminal offence, that officer will be treated like any other citizen. Tickets will be issued, charges will be laid and, if deemed necessary, arrests will occur. In addition, when such an incident occurs, the police officer's agency will be notified immediately. This, in turn, will trigger additional measures such as a separate internal investigation of the circumstances. Depending on the nature of the circumstances, different investigative units will be assigned responsibility for follow-up.

Accountability Mechanisms within Police Agencies

Lamboo (2010, 614) identified four aspects of internal investigations: (1) external oversight and control, (2) internally or externally initiated investigations, (3) relevant procedures, and (4) reactive and proactive investigations. With internal investigations, the police themselves investigate allegations of wrongdoing by police officers. Many observers are critical of this approach, arguing that it is inherently biased in favour of the police and that when an officer is found guilty of wrongdoing, the resulting penalties are too lenient (Goff 2014, 198). However, often based upon the seriousness and complexity of the situation, there remain several different ways in which police forces investigate themselves.

Professional Standards Units

All police agencies in Canada have a mechanism to deal with adverse on- and off-duty conduct of their officers. Investigators assigned to these units approach investigations (most often internal) much like they would any criminal investigation. Steps include interviewing witnesses, including other police officers, and collecting any other available evidence to corroborate or refute the allegation(s) against the officer. If the allegations are founded, sanctions exist relative to the seriousness of the offence. For example, sanctions may range from a formal written reprimand, completion of a refresher or additional training course, or suspension with or without pay. While not that common, the police officer may be dismissed in the most serious of matters. Another remedy not immediately apparent to the Canadian public is the fact that individual police officers can be found civilly liable for their misconduct (including motor vehicle incidents, use of force incidents, execution of warrants or actions arising from warrantless searches, and so on) (Goff 2014, 201).

While professional standards units deal with a vast array of misconduct, when police officers derive a personal benefit (most often financial gain) by taking advantage of their activities, this is considered corruption.

Anti-Corruption Units

Anti-corruption units generally operate internally, but depending on all the circumstances of the situation, other police forces may be engaged. This is done in the spirit of transparency and to ensure unbiased objectivity throughout the investigative process. Corruption may be defined as "dishonest or fraudulent conduct by those in power, typically involving bribery" (*Oxford English Dictionary*). All major police forces in Canada have an internal unit responsible for investigating allegations of corruption. This often falls within the purview of professional standards units, while others have a separate unit. For example, the E Division RCMP in British Columbia operates the two units separately. The anti-corruption unit operates within the major crime unit. Names for these internal units vary from agency to agency.

Corruption investigations are often complex, as the task of gathering evidence of corruption can be challenging. In part, this is because police officers themselves are trained to conduct investigations. This may mean that a corrupt officer has the know-how to cover his or her tracks. Given the difficulties associated with investigating trained police officers, corruption investigations are typically assigned only to experienced investigators with a proven track record in complex investigations. Anti-corruption investigations may require various investigative strategies ranging from routine interviews to those reserved for the most serious criminal offences, including undercover operations and wiretaps.

Police Oversight Models

There are three main categories of police oversight models: (1) dependent, (2) interdependent, and (3) independent.

The **dependent model** essentially represents more traditional police investigation of police. There is no civilian involvement in the criminal investigation and, therefore, there is a total dependence on the police for the handling of criminal investigations. There are two subcategories to this model: **police investigating police** and **police investigating another police force**.

Case Study

Civilian Oversight Models: Examples

The Special Investigations Unit (SIU) in Ontario was created in 1990 and was the first of its kind in Canada. The SIU is an independent civilian agency that has a mandate to investigate when police officers are involved in incidents where someone has been seriously injured, dies, or alleges sexual assault. The SIU is mandated by law to conduct independent investigations to determine whether a criminal offence took place (SIU, n.d.).

The Independent Investigations Office (IIO) of British Columbia evolved in part from a recommendation of the Braidwood Commission of Inquiry that dealt with the Vancouver airport Tasering death of Robert Dziekański in 2007. The IIO was formed in 2012 and is a civilian entity under the Ministry of Justice. Under the direction of the Chief Civilian Director, the IIO conducts investigations into incidents of death or serious harm that may have been the result of the actions of a police officer, whether on or off duty (IIOBC, n.d.).

In 2019, the federal government formed the civilian-led RCMP External Review Committee (ERC). The mandate of the ERC is to conduct impartial case reviews when an RCMP member wishes to appeal decisions made by RCMP managers, including

- to dismiss or to demote an RCMP member, or to impose a financial penalty of more than one day's pay, for contravention of the RCMP *Code of Conduct*;
- in a harassment complaint investigation;
- to discharge or to demote a member for being absent from duty; and
- to stop a member's pay and allowances when the member has been suspended from duty. [Government of Canada, 2020]

The ERC provides findings and recommendations for a final decision in the matter to the Commissioner of the RCMP. The Chair of the ERC reports annually to Parliament. [RCMP External Review Committee, n.d.]

In the police-investigating-police subcategory, the police service is fully responsible for the criminal investigation and administration of public complaints alleging criminal offences. The oversight body does not conduct criminal investigations, but it may recognize complaints regarding service, internal discipline, or public trust.

The second subcategory involves police investigating *another* police agency in specific cases so that the police service does not investigate its own members in instances of serious injury or death. In selected Canadian provinces, memoranda of agreement exist between the local police and the RCMP that allow an outside police agency to handle the investigations of RCMP members.

The **interdependent model** introduces into the criminal investigation civilian involvement to varying degrees. There are also two subtypes to this model: **civilian observation** and **hybrid investigation**. Examples of civilian observation include the Public Complaints Commission in Saskatchewan (Province of Saskatchewan, n.d.), the Office of the Police Complaints Commissioner in Nova Scotia (Province of Nova Scotia, n.d.), and the Police Ethics Commissioner in Quebec (Gouvernement du Québec, n.d.).

The Globe and Mail/The Canadian Press/Tibor Kolley

A member of the Special Investigations Unit examines a crime scene alongside a forensic officer in Oshawa, Ontario. During a domestic dispute, one person was murdered, children were injured, and the attacker was shot by police. Why are independent civilian investigative units important for police–community relations?

In the first subtype of the interdependent model, a civilian observer is assigned to the police investigation to ensure that the investigation is conducted with impartiality.

The hybrid investigation comprises a civilian oversight body whose involvement in the investigation goes beyond the role of mere overseer. In this model, the police agency may be engaged in some form of collaboration with the oversight body, although the latter may have the ability to conduct the investigation entirely on its own.

The independent model is embodied by a totally independent investigation. There is no police involvement in the investigation. The oversight body, composed of civilians, undertakes independent criminal investigations that cannot be referred to the police force, and may have the authority to make binding findings and lay charges (adapted from the Civilian Review and Complaints Commission for the RCMP, n.d.).

Should the Police Investigate Themselves?

There is great public support establishing independent oversight mechanisms, which provides the public's answer to the question of whether police should investigate themselves. In Canada, all policing jurisdictions have established some form of civilian oversight designed to regulate police conduct (Randall and Ramirez 2011, 4). Civilian review agencies act to make police truly accountable to the public (Goff 2014, 198). The Canadian Civil Liberties Association states that "[Police] powers demand great scrutiny and oversight from the public in order to ensure that individuals and communities are treated with respect and dignity."

Police are judged with a wary eye and the job they are asked to do is often challenging. Years ago, police officers in Canada would shudder at the thought of having anyone other than a police officer investigate police actions. Police officers believed that only a police officer could understand the job, reasons for decisions, and action in context. While a few old-school police officers may still hold such views, overall it is fair to say that independent oversight is now generally accepted with a considerable degree of cooperation. It is also recognized as a necessary aspect of police professionalism and as enhancing overall community confidence (Tinsley 2009, 2). In fact, Canadian police are much more receptive, in fact relieved at times, to have independent investigations into accusations of wrongdoing.

Many civil libertarians believe that current Canadian police powers are too wide-reaching and excessive. As Van Allen (2009, 6) notes, one of society's basic rights is to effective law enforcement to ensure order and crime control. However, the challenge in any free and democratic society is to ensure safety and security while balancing individual rights against society's right to protect itself.

Public Inquiries

Historically, Canada has relied extensively on public inquiries, which have played an important role in resolving problems and in enhancing the public's confidence in the justice system. Fulfillment of a particular judicial inquiry's mandate rests, in large measure, upon the openness of the inquiry (Kaufman 1998, 10).

Essentially, there are two types of public inquiries: those with a mandate to find and report on facts, and those with a mandate to make recommendations for the development of public policy. **Policy-based inquiries** are mandated to examine a particular area or issue of public policy and to make recommendations for future policy direction. Some inquiries have a fact-finding mandate as well as a policy-based mandate. It is important to distinguish that inquiries are not trials; rather, they are investigations that result in findings of fact and/or recommendations (O'Connor, Kristjanson, and Gervais 2007, 1).

Over the past few years in British Columbia there has been a spotlight on the police and notably on the RCMP. This has been due in part to several high-profile cases where the accountability of police has been severely criticized by both local and national media. More specifically, both the October 2007 death of Robert Dziekański and the circumstances surrounding the investigation of convicted serial killer Robert William Pickton led the province of British Columbia to convene provincial Commissions of Inquiry. These Commissions were asked to address concerns regarding (a) how police carry out their duties, (b) possible training deficiencies, (c) the apparent absence of cooperation among police agencies, and (d) public skepticism regarding police ability to investigate themselves in an objective fashion.

The Pickton inquiry (also referenced as the Missing Women Commission of Inquiry overseen by Wally Oppal, the results of which led to *Forsaken: The Report of the Missing Women Commission of Inquiry* [Oppal 2012]) was established to review the actions of police into the investigation of the missing women from the Downtown Eastside of Vancouver. Many marginalized women had gone missing over a period of years from this small geographic area. Convicted serial killer Robert William Pickton is believed to be responsible for the murders of 33 of these women and is suspected of having murdered up to 49 women. The Pickton inquiry recommended establishing a new regionalized police agency in the greater Vancouver area to replace the combination of municipal police departments and RCMP detachments that have been in place for decades. The justification, in part, for a regionalized police agency arose from the Oppal inquiry finding that identified long-standing problems with respect to the lack of cooperation between police agencies. More specifically, it was particularly problematic that police agencies were not sharing vital investigation information with each other. This, in turn, meant that police were unable to identify and apprehend an offender who committed offences in different municipal jurisdictions. The recommendation for regionalization is one of the few that has not been implemented.

Accountability on the Street

Since patrol officers most frequently deal with the public, patrol or general-duty police officers are more likely to be involved in controversies related to the use of force in making arrests. Patrol officers are also more likely to be the subject of citizen complaints. Many factors, such as the number of cars and officers attending a call, the priority given to the call, the time that elapses before police arrive, and the tone of voice and language used by attending officers shape individual and public perceptions of police actions. The general public is generally unaware of how little background information is available to the police responding to a call for service.

Police actions, in contrast to calls for service, are frequently based upon prior information known only to the police through having previously dealt with a person, through being advised of alerts on the computerized database maintained by the Canadian Police

Information Centre (CPIC), and through information shared at briefings. If a casual observer were to witness a seemingly routine traffic stop but observed the police officer approach the vehicle with her hand on her gun, such an observer might think the officer was overreacting. However, what the casual observer would not know is that the police officer had been advised by her dispatcher that the registered owner of the vehicle is a known gang member with outstanding warrants for his arrest and is flagged as "caution armed and dangerous."

Tracking and Documenting the Activities of the Police

In contrast to historical policing, today's attitudes and technology enable and support increased surveillance and accountability. GPS systems, which are standard equipment in patrol police vehicles in Canada, allow dispatchers to know where every police officer is at all times. Body-worn cameras, currently being tested by police agencies across Canada, increases both surveillance and accountability of police officers.

Wain and Ariel (2014, 279) note that, in police culture, the constructs of surveillance and accountability appear to clash. However, the RCMP has stated that "with today's mobile technology, police are being recorded by the public during many interactions. Police are routinely called to resolve difficult situations involving emotionally charged individuals. Body-worn cameras would provide additional evidence to support the work of front-line officers." The British Columbia Civil Liberties Association says the key consideration is when to use them and how to use them. "We are in favour of police accountability . . . [W]e are always concerned about privacy, including the privacy of officers." It will be interesting to see what the future looks like as oversight of police actions evolves (*The Province* 2014).

Crown Counsel Relationship with Police

The many ways in which police and Crown counsel work together may be considered an important accountability mechanism related to police oversight. A professional, mutually respectful, and productive Crown–police relationship is often key to the evidence-gathering process, and is essential both to Crown case preparation and to the overall criminal court process. However, the role of the Crown is to be separate and distinct, or at "arm's length," from the police. The Supreme Court of Canada has described the police and Crown roles as being interdependent and "while both have separate responsibilities in the criminal justice system, they must inevitably work in cooperation to administer and enforce criminal laws effectively" (*R. v. Beaudry*, 2007).

In the majority of investigations, direct Crown involvement with police is initiated shortly after an individual has been charged (recall that in Quebec, New Brunswick, and British Columbia, the Crown holds the responsibility for charge approval). In more complex investigations where the nature of the criminal offence, volume of evidence, use of advanced investigative strategies, or even the number of persons to be charged are complicating factors, Crown are more often involved at the earlier stages to provide advice and guidance on an ongoing basis.

In serious investigations where, for example, a judicial authorization to intercept private communications (or "wiretap") may be sought by the police, the law states that a Crown counsel, specially designated in writing by the respective Attorney General, is to "bring the application" and acts as the "gatekeeper" to the Supreme Court. This additional requirement is related to protecting the *Charter* right to "be free from unreasonable search and seizure" for the most intrusive judicial authorization that the police may pursue.

Accountability to the Court Process

One of the primary investigative skills honed during police training is the ability to gather admissible evidence to support viable prosecutions. In this way, accountability to the law and the court process starts in training. It continues at the beginning of every police officer's shift and is ideally maintained until each investigation and any related prosecution is complete. When responding to calls for service that range from the most mundane to the most serious of matters, officers must consider admissible evidence, carefully gathered within the appropriate law, including the *Charter*. Accountability to the Court process entails not only making every effort to gather admissible evidence, but recording competent notes, disclosing all investigative material, and being well prepared to testify at trial.

Challenge Your Assumptions

Body-Worn Cameras (BWCs) and Accountability

By February 2019, the New York Police Department had issued body-worn cameras to all uniformed patrol officers in New York City. Approximately 20,000 cameras were distributed to police officers, detectives performing patrol functions, supervisors, and others. Another 4000 cameras will be distributed to specialty units (NYPD, n.d.).

Police forces in jurisdictions across the United States and Canada continue to assess the utility and viability of BWCs. Key concerns about the widespread deployment of BWCs relate to privacy, technology, and cost.

A 2015 report from the Office of the Privacy Commissioner in Canada highlighted the fact that BWCs have significant privacy implications that need to be weighed against the anticipated benefits. Arising from the results of a pilot project, in 2019, the Service de Police de la Ville de Montréal (SPVM) concluded that the cost of BWCs was not worth the results (Valiante 2019). Having conducted various studies, as of 2016, the RCMP has said that they were "delaying any widespread roll-out of BWCs" (RCMP 2016). The Bureau of Justice Statistics in the United States found that economic costs are the primary reason police agencies give for not acquiring BWCs (cited in Malm 2019, 8). As Malm (2019) has noted, BWC research has produced ambiguous results and that [BWCs] are "far from a panacea for all that ails contemporary policing." See Table 6.1 for a summary of findings in two Canadian pilot studies of body-worn cameras.

continued

Table 6.1	Canadian Body-Worn Camera Pilot Study Findings, 2015–16	
	Findings	
Issue	**Toronto Police Service Pilot Project**	**Edmonton Police Service Pilot Study**
Officer Safety	Officers were divided on this issue. Some officers wearing BWCs felt safer and more confident while dealing with the public. They observed the cameras to have a calming effect on people—specifically that people tended to be less confrontational and more respectful; it was also noted that during interactions with people who were emotionally disturbed or drunk, the cameras sometimes aggravated the situation. Other officers did not feel the BWCs made any difference in how members of the public interacted with them.	Observations from the pilot study included that deciding when to record is complex: no simple rule applies for all scenarios; the decision can be affected by technical issues, priorities during sudden dynamic events, concern for the protection of sources (confidential informers), and dealing with sensitive situations.
Public Complaints	BWCs tended to give some officers a sense of confidence as they felt any potential complaints would be more easily resolved. All or almost all of the officers testing the BWCs agreed at the end of the pilot that BWCs would help with the response to public complaints; however, officers were less certain that BWCs would reduce the actual number of complaints made.	The pilot found no quantitative evidence that BWC had an impact on the number of complaints made.
Use of Force	There was an insufficient number of occurrences during the pilot to make a meaningful assessment. Whether an officer wearing a BWC hesitates to use force even when it may be appropriate, and whether the presence of the camera actually aggravates people were two important considerations moving forward.	There was no statistically significant evidence that the presence of BWC reduced use of force; BWC presence may cause EPS members to hesitate to use appropriate levels of force.
Officer Perceptions of/ Experience with the Cameras	Officers felt that the cameras limited their ability to use discretion; technical problems and an increased administrative workload were particular challenges; officers felt that people were less willing to provide them with information; officers felt that there needed to be clearer direction about when the BWCs should be on and when they should be off.	Training must be a major component in any successful BWC program, requiring substantial investment of resources for planning and delivery.
Cost	If fully implemented, the costs were estimated to be $20 million in year one with a total five-year estimated cost of roughly $51 million, not including costs of integrating the Service's (TPS) current records management and video asset management systems with a BWC system. The most expensive component of wider adoption of BWCs is the storage of the video recordings.	n/a
Investigations and Court	A majority of officers involved in the pilot said they believed that videos from the BWCs would be valuable in court, for example, to back up evidence or to resolve complaints.	The pilot produced no evidence that BWC has significant prosecutorial value.

	Findings	
Community Feedback	There is considerable public interest in the use of BWCs by the Toronto Police Service and community expectations for BWCs are high; people in the community did say they would feel comfortable talking to an officer with a BWC, particularly as a victim of a crime, though they thought they would be less comfortable in investigative or enforcement situations; relatively few people showed concern for possible negative aspects of the BWCs, including privacy issues and the associated costs.	The effect of BWC on citizens varies with the situation and is highly nuanced; it is as likely to be negative as positive.

Sources: Modified from Toronto Police Service (TPS) Body Worn Cameras: A report on the findings of the pilot project to test the value and feasibility of body-worn cameras for police officers in Toronto. June 2016; and Edmonton Police Service Body Worn Video: Considering the Evidence. Final report of the Edmonton Police Service Body Worn Video Pilot Project. June 2015.

Police Officer Notes

An important accountability mechanism for police officers is documenting their actions, usually in notebooks and later followed up with formal electronic reports. Note taking is an important and basic function for all police officers, particularly given that the time between initial police contact and any court proceeding may be months and possibly years. The police officer's notebook is a fundamental investigative tool. It is essential that notebooks be legible, detailed, complete, and accurate in order to document investigations, corroborate evidence, and support the credibility of testimony for the Court. Notes may also be invaluable to other investigations years after the initial investigation. It is not uncommon for a police officer to deal with a certain person in a given situation only to learn years later that the facts and circumstances of that interaction were important to another investigation.

There are a number of court decisions where the reliability of a police officer's testimony was questioned based upon his or her lack of notes about significant observations and decisions made or actions taken. In the case of *The Queen v. Mercer* (2006), the Court stated: "It is not the position of the Court that the absence of detail in an officer's notes always reflects negatively on the reliability of the officer's observations; however, I would generally expect that to be useful as an *aide memoire* all significant observations that directly relate to the offence should be referred to in an officer's notes. If evidence is given by an officer that is not corroborated by other reliable evidence and not referred to in his, or her, notes, reliability, in my view, will become an issue." It is therefore imperative that police officers involved in an investigation take early and meaningful notes of their observations and actions.

Disclosure

The principles of innocent until proven guilty and open and fair judicial process were underscored by the landmark Supreme Court of Canada decision in *R. v. Stinchcombe* (1991), where the *Charter* right of the accused to be able to make **full answer and defence** was established. The principles of this case forced major changes in how police, from the patrol officer to the major crime investigator, carried out his or her duties. The **Stinchcombe decision** upholds the duty of the Crown to "disclose to the defence all material evidence whether favourable to the accused or not." The ruling clarified that there is discretion for the Crown to withhold information or to delay timing of when certain disclosure is made; however, all such decisions are ultimately up for review by the trial judge. The vast majority of information gathered by police in the course of an investigation will be subject to disclosure.

As earlier stated, the law is rarely black and white and a perfect example of this can be found in the guidelines that govern how the Crown discloses information and evidence to defence counsel. Although the Crown does not have to disclose material that is "clearly irrelevant, one measure of relevance is its usefulness to the defence and if it is of some use, it is relevant and should be disclosed." In *R. v. Dixon* (1998), the Supreme Court of Canada stated that "the right of disclosure of all relevant material has a broad scope and includes material that may have only marginal value to the issues at trial."

Police officers are trained to understand that the role of Crown counsel in Canada is to remain at arm's length from the investigation and to act as a sober second look in assessing evidence gathered by the police to support any prosecution. However, the fact remains that the police and Crown, to a certain degree, must still work collaboratively. In the simplest of terms, if the police know it (facts of the case that support or refute evidence related to the accused person), the Crown must know it.

Arising from *R. v. Stinchcombe*, disclosure is a **constitutional obligation** and the role of the police is to help the Crown counsel meet that obligation. From the police perspective, Crown counsel are often consulted early in the process of preparing materials for disclosure and police should ensure that Crown counsel is aware of the method and structure of disclosure material that will be provided. For example, Adobe PDF documents using the **redaction** feature for **vetting** are common, as are standard audio and video formats.

In the spirit of *Stinchcombe* and guided by Sections 7 and 11(b) of the *Charter*, the Supreme Court of Canada in *R. v. Jordan* (2016) ruled on the accused's right to be tried within a reasonable time. Immediately following an individual being charged with an offence, the "clock starts ticking" for the Crown counsel to complete Stinchcombe disclosures and initiate the court process. The Jordan framework is such that Provincial Court trials must be completed within eighteen months and Supreme Court trials must be completed within thirty months, unless there are extraordinary circumstances. Thus, there is now enormous pressure on the police, Crown and defence counsel, and the judiciary to expedite all processes related to criminal trials.

Disclosure of Police Disciplinary Records

Another Supreme Court of Canada judgment that had a major impact on police across the country was in the case of *R. v. McNeil* (2009). McNeil created an obligation for the Crown to disclose the disciplinary records of investigating police officers, where those records are based on serious police misconduct and where those records could reasonably impact the case against the accused. In the past, defence counsel in seeking production of such records, would have to do so via an O'Connor application (*R. v. O'Connor* 1995). The McNeil decision now makes disclosure of those records a first-party disclosure obligation. The types of records stated in the McNeil decision that would be subject to disclosure include the following:

a) any conviction or finding of guilt under the Canadian *Criminal Code* or the *Controlled Drugs and Substances Act* for which a pardon has not been granted;
b) any outstanding charges under the Canadian *Criminal Code* or the *Controlled Drugs and Substances Act*;
c) any conviction or finding of guilt under any other federal or provincial statute;
d) any finding of guilt for misconduct after a hearing under the *Police Services Act* or its predecessor *Act*; and
e) any current charge of misconduct under the *Police Services Act* for which a Notice of Hearing has been issued.

The impact of the McNeil ruling has potentially serious effects on a police officer's career, such as being excluded from involvement in a specific investigation and the negative impact on credibility in court proceedings that is maintained throughout the officer's career.

The *Globe and Mail* Test

Within the police community, the informal litmus test for police conduct has been referred to as the *Globe and Mail* test. The *Globe and Mail* **test** helps establish what an average Canadian would think of any action or investigative strategy, assuming they were armed with the same information and understanding of the situation at the time. More specifically, if the details of a situation were printed on the front page of a major newspaper, would it shock the public or otherwise portray the police in a negative light? This hypothetical test covers all aspects of police work from the actions (or inaction) of patrol officers to the decisions of detectives in specialized investigative units working sex crimes, robbery, arson, and matters of national security.

Conclusion

This chapter introduced the importance of accountability in policing and the internal and external infrastructure designed to provide ongoing oversight of police operations. Accountability was highlighted from the perspective of individual police officers to themselves, to their police agency, the courts, the *Charter*, and the public at large. It will be interesting to see where Canadian police agencies are headed with regard to oversight and accountability over the next ten years. What will be the effects on police work of various additional surveillance mechanisms? What will the public demand and police officers tolerate? For certain, public perception is everything and police in Canada can always be expected to work hard to gain and maintain public trust.

Critical Thinking Questions

1. Do you believe that the police in Canada should investigate themselves?
2. In your opinion, are systems such as GPS in patrol cars and body-worn cameras designed to enhance accountability? How do they achieve that? If they serve some other purpose, what is it and why and how do these systems support that purpose?
3. Identify and discuss the pros and cons of police officers wearing video cameras capturing their actions. What is your opinion on whether body-worn cameras should be mandatory for police?
4. What is your opinion of police in Canada and how well they perform their duties? What, if anything, could be improved?
5. Discuss the constitutional pillar that assures the right of the accused to make full answer and defence.

7

Performance Measurement

Learning Objectives

After reading and studying this chapter, students will be able to:

- Describe and explain what classic performance measures are and how they are calculated.
- Explain the benefits and criticisms of classic performance measures.
- Discuss the differences between quantitative and alternate and qualitative performance measures.
- Describe and explain new approaches in performance measurement.

Introduction

Many organizations, including police, often have to assess whether they are providing good service. In policing, this has become a significant issue in the face of rising costs and increased pressure from local and national governments to account for those costs. Police departments are therefore faced with having to show they are providing cost-effective and efficient policing in their jurisdictions. Over the years, performance measurements using various metrics have been instituted in police departments to varying degrees.

Police performance management entails efforts to both measure and improve performance through ongoing feedback processes. The system requires setting goals, desired outcomes, and performance standards followed by systematic observation and analysis used to modify current practices. Performance management models are now prominent across the United States, the United Kingdom, and Canada, particularly since the inception of CompStat (see page 237 and Chapter 12) in New York.

The decision of what and how to measure police performance is often led by the dominant model or guiding principles of policing at the time. During the period highlighted by the traditional (or professional) model of policing (see Chapter 11), classic measures such as crime rates and arrest rates were relied upon to measure how good a job the police were doing. Modern movements and a return to a community policing approach, along with the proliferation of police research, have brought new measures and clarified what the classical measures can and should be used to show.

This chapter focuses on describing classic quantitative performance measures, such as crime rates, and discusses the benefits and pitfalls associated with their use. The chapter will next familiarize the reader with some alternate measurements used for police departments, as well as newer paradigms and innovations that seek to legitimize and provide more relevant measurements from which to assess performance. The chapter concludes with a discussion about some of the foreseeable problems with trying to measure police performance.

Inputs, Outputs, and Outcomes

An important aspect of identifying and collecting performance metrics is to be clear on the difference between inputs, outputs, and outcomes. **Input measures** are used to gauge the human and capital resources used to produce outputs and outcomes. These may include reports filed in a particular area or jurisdiction, calls received by dispatch, or community opinion surveys. These inputs, once counted and measured, can form **output measures**. Therefore, output measures reflect the product of a particular activity, such as the number of reports filed, the number of calls dispatched, the number of police complaints, etc. Output measures in and of themselves do not depict performance until standards, baselines, and targets have been set according to the goals and objectives laid out in the performance management plan. **Outcome measures**, therefore, focus on the actual results from activities: Was there a reduction in reported crimes, an increase in conviction rates, a decrease in officer complaints, and so on? Outcome measures, utilizing outputs, can then inform the police executive on how well the agency is meeting its goals (Geerken 2008; Roberts 2006).

As outcomes occur farther down the chain of causation than outputs, outputs are generally easier to acquire and measure. An important implication of this is that outcomes are often shaped by many factors that lie outside of the control of the organization, whereas outputs are more often under direct control of the police department (Moore and Braga 2003a, 2003b). Due to this control, outputs often become the main focus; however, although it is more difficult to ascertain the exact influence police activities have on outcomes, outcomes are the factors that should be used to indicate the performance toward specific goals (Cockcroft and Beattie 2009). The danger in this is apparent, as the temptation is to continue measuring what the police department does, and not necessarily what it achieves or accomplishes (Garland 2001).

Classic Quantitative Performance Measures

Although **performance measurements** are now being used throughout many police departments, there are no universally accepted standard means of evaluating police functions, and no legislative requirements for their use or standards in Canada. In 1997, Alpert and Moore (in Verma and Gavirneni 2006) re-emphasized the relevance of using "reported crime rates, arrests, clearance rates and response times" as measures of productivity and performance of police efficiency (265). These classical measures have become some of the most commonly used metrics, despite some significant drawbacks and misapplications. These measures also reflect a particular outlook on policing—that which sees the primary purpose of police being to reduce crime by responding quickly to calls and arresting offenders (Moore and Braga 2003a, 2003b). Today, however, attention has turned to the development of more all-inclusive measures of police performance (Milligan, Fridell, and Taylor 2006) that go beyond the crime-control function to acknowledge the multifaceted nature of the police role. This does not, however, necessitate discarding classical measures for monitoring performance in the police department. Rather, today's performance measurement systems must be acutely aware of the limitations of such methods, and devise the proper way to incorporate these into a comprehensive system of department performance evaluation.

In recognition of the lack of objective and universal police performance metrics, in 2014 " . . . Statistics Canada, in collaboration with Public Safety Canada and Police Information and Statistics (POLIS) committee of the Canadian Association of Chiefs of Police (CACP) undertook a review of current performance measures being used by police services in Canada" (Mazowita and Rotenberg 2019, 3) Their review noted that not only was there a lack of consistent measures being used, but there was a need for the establishment of metrics that go beyond the traditional methods. The report further acknowledged that while these traditional methods (discussed below) may bring some necessary information into the evaluation of police performance, they "do not reflect the complexity and scope of contemporary policing responsibilities" (Mazowita and Rotenberg 2019, 12).

Crime Rate

Use and Benefits

Crime rates are perhaps the most easily attainable, publicly available, and understandable measure of police performance. They also represent, to most individuals both inside and outside the criminal justice realm, the primary mission of a police force (i.e., to lower crime) (Moore and Braga 2003a, 2003b). The **crime rate** is measured by taking the number of reported offences (the numerator), and dividing by the total population (the denominator), then normalizing by some figure—usually 1000 or 100,000 population. This allows for comparison of fluctuations over time, as well as between areas with different population levels.

$$CR = (\text{Reported Offences/Population}) \times 100,000$$

In Canada, the crime rate has been generally on the decline since the mid-1990s, although this trend is more or less pronounced in various jurisdictions across the country. (See Figure 7.1.)

Often police services use the crime rate as a measure of how they are doing year after year. They may also use the crime rate to establish performance targets, such as specific

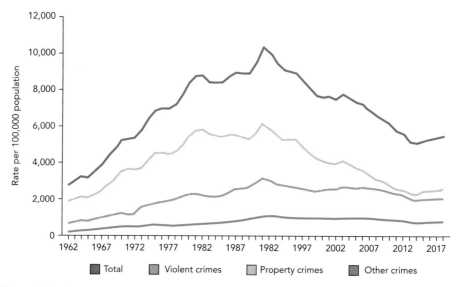

Figure 7.1　Police-Reported Crime Rate, Canada, 1962–2018

Source: Statistics Canada. *Police-Reported Crime Statistics, 2018. The Daily:* Ottawa: Statistics Canada, 2019.

reductions in overall or certain types of crime. For instance, police departments might set a 5 per cent reduction in property crime for the following year. This would be measured by calculating the property crime rate in the first year, and comparing that to the property crime rate in the second year.

Despite some limitations, crime rates have some value in monitoring performance, if collected and reported carefully and properly. For instance, if the police institute a targeted crime-reduction program in a small geographic area, crime rates may be useful to assess changes in reporting activity, overall crime (if used in conjunction with victimization surveys that measure the amount of reported and unreported crime), and any possible **displacement** (Stephens 1999). In this way, crime rates may be a better indication of how the city or geographic area is doing as a whole, and not simply how the police are performing (Municipal Research and Services Center 1994).

Police can influence the crime rate with what they do, but many other forces exert a much stronger influence over it. Therefore, relying on the overall crime rate as the sole indicator of how well a police agency is performing can be problematic.

External Impacts

The most prominently featured caveat in the literature is the recognition that police activities are not the only factor that influences crime rates. Rather, crime rates are a function of countless forces, many of which (such as economic and political pressures) are outside the control of police agencies (Maguire 2003; Stephens 1999; Verma and Gavirneni 2006). For instance, the increase or decrease of different age cohorts or international drug market movement can significantly impact crime rates, regardless of local police efforts (Blumstein 1999).

In addition, spontaneous crimes of violence appear to be largely unresponsive to police action, but other aggressive or targeted tactics (perhaps against organized violent or gang crime) may have a more noticeable impact (Blumstein 1999). In this scenario, police action may not reduce random acts of violence, but may cut down on planned and targeted attacks. By simply using the violent crime rate as a measure of effectiveness, the two may cancel each other out, which could theoretically result in absolutely no overall change, leaving the department to conclude that it has failed.

Reported Crime

In addition to the external impacts comes the well-known reality that not all crime is reported to police. In most cases, the percentage of crimes that goes unreported is significant. In 2009 in Canada, approximately 69 per cent of violent victimizations and 62 per cent of household victimizations were not reported to the police (Perreault and Brennan 2010). If police are learning about only a fraction of all the crimes that occur, are the increases and decreases of the crime rate a function of police behaviour or reporting behaviour? If it is the latter, then reporting simply on the crime rate may be detrimental to measuring success, as fluctuations in citizens' willingness to report can severely impact the crime rate. If citizens become more trusting of the police (Verma and Gavirneni 2006) and become far more apt to believe their cases will be solved, reporting will understandably increase. If that happens, the crime rate may increase, leading many to panic as they perceive increasing danger in society. However, it should be obvious that this is an artificial fluctuation—there really is no more crime, just more reported crime. While it may be possible to explain this to the general population, the damage will already be done by those who view this "rise" as the sole responsibility (and possibly fault) of police departments. Therefore, it becomes problematic to compare very different police jurisdictions using crime rates only. For instance, if there are more sexual assaults in one jurisdiction over another, does that indicate that the jurisdiction with the lower rate is doing a better job at curbing sexual violence, or does that number actually signify how much distrust exists between victims of sexual assault and police (Kelling 1999)?

A second consideration is the amount of crime that may be reported *by* police (rather than *to* police). Some official counts of crimes are often solely at the discretion of police reporting activity. Rates of minor drug use, prostitution, and drinking and driving are almost exclusively a function of the amount of police activity dedicated toward enforcement, rather than the actual rise and fall of these types of incidents (Klockars 1999). For instance, during times of active drinking and driving enforcement, the number of impaired drivers who are caught may increase substantially. However, if police were to cancel or cut back on roadblocks or other tactics, the number of impaired drivers who get caught would likely decrease substantially. Therefore, while police activity may result in higher crime counts if enforcement is increased, it does not necessarily mean the actual crime rate is higher.

Without the ability to understand and report on what factors are shaping the crime rate and why, police may bear the brunt of changes outside of their control. Therefore,

Gian-Paolo Mendoza/CBC

The Vancouver Police Department runs Counterattack approximately twice per year to check for drunk or impaired driving. How would these blitz checks affect the statistics on impaired driving in Vancouver?

simply using the upward or downward fluctuation of the crime rate as a sole measure of police success can be detrimental to the public's perception and faith in the department's ability.

Crime Severity Index

In the mid-2000s, Statistics Canada introduced a new variation metric on the traditional crime rate, called the **Crime Severity Index**. This index measures not only the volume of crime, but the relative severity of crime as well. As many crime categories in the traditional crime rate were dominated by less serious offences within their respective categories, such as Level 1 Assaults (relatively minor assaults involving little bodily harm) in the violent crime category, the crime rate was felt to misrepresent the severity of offences occurring in Canada. The Crime Severity Index assigns weights to particular crimes. More serious crimes receive higher weights, while less serious crimes receive lower weights. In this way, the Index could be used to track both volume and the relative seriousness of the crimes occurring over time.

As seen in Figure 7.2, the Crime Severity Index in Canada has been steadily decreasing since the late 1990s. This closely matches the overall police-reported crime rates, although there are often regional or local differences that more micro-level analysis would highlight.

The Index is now regularly reported by Statistics Canada, and many police jurisdictions have started to use it as a performance management and tracking tool alongside their traditional crime-rate change reporting.

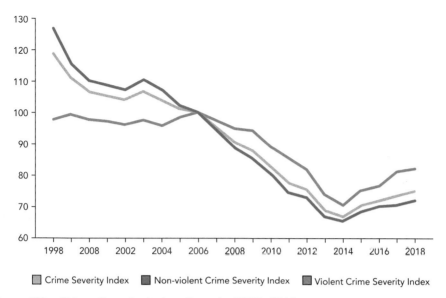

Figure 7.2   Crime Severity Index, Canada, 1998–2018

Note: The base index was set at 100 for 2006 for Canada.

Source: Statistics Canada. (2019). Police-reported crime statistics in Canada, 2018. Ottawa: Juristat. https://www150.statcan.gc.ca/n1/daily-quotidien/190722/cg-a001-eng.htm

Arrest Rates

Use and Benefits

Police arrests are perhaps one of the most visible measures of police output; however, the definition of what constitutes an arrest may differ among jurisdictions (Geerken 2008). Generally, an arrest can be said to occur when an offender is apprehended for a particular offence, regardless of whether the offender continues on in the justice process following the arrest. This type of output is often tied strongly to clearance rates (discussed below) as well as the police impact on crime rates (discussed above). Some may consider an offender released on his own recognizance to count as an arrest, as the officer has ensured the offender will subsequently appear in in court to face charges. However, as it is defined, arrests are simply outputs. They do not connote any sort of outcome, positive or negative, on their own. Arrests, however, may be used as a demonstration of how many suspects have been "rounded up" that participated in a particular activity that held significant public importance. For instance, the Vancouver Police Department reported on the number of arrests (or more specifically, the number of recommended charges) for suspects identified to have participated in the 2011 Stanley Cup riots (Integrated Riot Investigation Team 2013). By showing a constant tally of their arrests, the police department could demonstrate they were being both responsive and effective.

While gathering and reporting on metrics of **arrest rates** for specific offences or specific offenders may be useful to show activity and success, there are limitations to broader use of arrest rates.

Discretion

The focus on arresting offenders stems from the belief that once offenders are caught and brought to justice, the process is a success and crime reduction is immediate (Moore and Poethig 1999). However, using arrest rates to indicate positive police performance becomes problematic when departments set quotas or commend those who make numerous "classical" arrests. In some situations, not arresting an individual and using discretion (see Chapter 5 and Chapter 6 for a full discussion on discretion) to divert them away from the formal judicial system is more effective or efficient. Requiring or preferring an arrest in these situations may not only limit police discretion, but may place undue burdens on other ends of the system as more individuals are formally processed. There is no commentary on whether a particular arrest was valuable to the police department's goals or to community safety, and thus, on their own, arrest rates represent little in terms of quantifiable accomplishments for justice.

Political Influence

The political arena also influences arrest rates. This may work both ways by either increasing or decreasing arrest rates. In this way, arresting an individual becomes detached from any desire to deal with a crime phenomenon (Verma and Gavirneni 2006) and, therefore, becomes a false indicator of effectiveness. For example, police may know that it is more effective to practise restraint during public demonstrations or large-scale protests. However, it may become a political issue to ensure the safety of public officials at such demonstrations, and politicians may pressure police to arrest protesters despite officers' better judgment. Again, there is nothing to indicate how effective these arrests are; they are simply a response to political pressure.

Response Times

Use and Benefits
With the advent of 911 call centres and dispatch systems (see Chapter 10), police activity became focused on providing quicker service to those requesting assistance. Due to this, **response times** are used to show how well a police department is serving the public. In the simplest of terms, response times represent the time between when a call is dispatched (i.e., assigned to an officer) and the time the officer arrives on the scene of that call. Other methods may also track the time between when the call was received by the operator, and when police arrived, which would better correspond to the service, not officer, response time. This data is often taken from the police **computer-aided dispatch (CAD)** system, which automatically time stamps a call at various points along the service delivery.

$$RT = \text{On Scene Time} - \text{Dispatched Time}$$

Generally, departments will track and report the average response time utilizing some variation of the method above. However, simply taking the average time can be problematic as some minor calls may be stacked (see **call stacking** in the glossary) for hours or days, inflating the average response time. Other problems may arise if the time an officer arrives on scene is not captured accurately, thereby falsely inflating their response time to that particular call. There are several options for getting a clearer picture of response times. These may include removing extreme cases if using the mean or average, or utilizing the median instead. Some departments have avoided some of the mathematical limitations by setting target response times, and the percentage of calls they aim to achieve within that time. This way of presenting response times assists the agency in guarding against some of the external factors beyond police control. The underlying message, however, is that response times cannot and should not be the sole demonstration of a department's ability to service its community.

Workload Indicators

Response times may, however, indicate police workload or officer scheduling issues within the department and, as such, can be used to spot problems with workload and staffing. The basic premise is that a properly staffed, properly shifted police department should be able to respond to emergency situations within a pre-defined period of time. If a department is not able to reach that target most of the time, it could be that not enough resources are assigned at a particular time or in a particular area. In this way, properly calculated response times can show a department where they may need to make adjustments. For instance, if certain hours of the day are seeing an inability to reach best practice standards, then adjusting shifts to over-lap during busy times of the day could alleviate workload pressure and should allow officers to reach response targets. The limitations of response times in terms of police effectiveness or necessity does not suggest that response times should not be monitored, but each department should be aware of why it is monitoring response times and what measures actually mean.

Clearance Rates

Clearance rates most commonly represent the ratio of solved crimes to the total number of crimes. The rate comes from dividing the number of crimes that are determined to be cleared from police responsibility, either by identification of a suspect or charge being laid with Crown counsel, by the total number of reported crimes. This is usually expressed in a percentage, such as an 80 per cent clearance rate for homicide, which indicates that the police have cleared 8 of the 10 cases that came before them.

$$\text{Clearance rate} = \frac{n_{\text{solved crimes}}}{N_{\text{all crimes}}}$$

Nearly every police department reports on some aspect of their solve rate or clearance rate. While this reporting is generally widespread, it is often not touted by police agencies as a prominent performance measure. This may be due to a number of factors, not the least of which is the disappointingly low rates of clearance, thereby giving the impression that the police are vastly ineffective at their job (Moore and Braga 2003a, 2003b). It is this reality that perhaps impedes departments from making full use of this statistic. There are two primary reasons for this: The first is that the clearance status of a particular offence is often recorded differently from jurisdiction to jurisdiction, and the second is that it is arguable whether clearance rates are calculated consistently enough to be used as an indicator of police effectiveness.

Challenge Your Assumptions

Is a Fast Response Necessary?

Many cite the necessity of fast police response to emergency situations as a justification for monitoring response times and using them as a measure of performance. While few would argue with the underlying logic that in the case of a true emergency it is imperative that police respond as fast as possible, the reality is that, contrary to misconceptions, very few police calls are truly emergencies that require an immediate response (Kelling 1999; Maguire 2003). Often there is a significant delay in the time between when a citizen witnesses or is victimized in a crime and when they actually call the police (Municipal Research and Services Center 1994). Add to that the time it takes an officer to arrive, and the chance of finding the perpetrator still at the scene drops to almost nothing. Despite the classical thinking that rapid response would result in a significant impact on crime, many studies have found that rapid response to serious crimes resulted in an arrest only 5 per cent of the time (Maguire 2003).

Quickly responding to every call not only eats up vast amounts of resources, but does little to solve underlying problems (Johnson et al. 1999). As police departments attempt to satisfy the expectations of the community to have the police respond promptly, officers are unable to commit time to proactive problem solving. The longstanding belief that citizens will only be satisfied with rapid police attention may also be misguided. Surveys have found that, if informed of delays or the inability of officers to respond to a particular call that has no witnesses, no offender on scene, and a lack of violence or damage, many citizens are satisfied to either have their report taken over the phone or have an appointment made for a police officer to visit them at a later date (Maguire 2003).

Response times are also exceedingly difficult to compare across geographic areas and time periods. External realities such as topography, distance, road construction, traffic, and even special events may impair the ability of police to respond quickly, thereby degrading the performance of their average response times through no fault of their own (Maguire 2003).

For many jurisdictions, noting a case as cleared indicates that enough evidence has been gathered for a particular offence to say it is solved. However, there are discrepancies in how departments record this status, making comparisons among jurisdictions difficult. For many departments, a case is cleared when charges are laid. However, in British Columbia, police do not lay charges; rather, incidents are recommended to Crown counsel for consideration. From the police perspective, the case is solved because enough evidence has been gathered to warrant the recommendation of charges and the commencement of the official legal process. However, depending on workload, the strength of the case, internal pressures, and other issues, Crown counsel may decide not to proceed with charges. Using the original definition then, the question arises: Is this case still solved?

If clearance rates are truly to be used as a measure of police performance, then their calculation must be considered more deeply. Often the clearance rate is simply presented as a proportion—for example, a clearance rate of 10 per cent for break and enters indicates that in 90 per cent of incidents, no charges were recommended or laid (depending on the department's definition of "cleared"). However, the reality of investigating these types of offences should come into play if these numbers are to be used to assess who is doing a good job.

For many offences, particularly property offences, by the time the offence is reported, the offender is long gone. These cases often have no witnesses, may be devoid of any forensic evidence, and may be classified as nearly impossible to solve. Some cases may have witnesses, or have partial forensic evidence, or may be part of a pattern of serial offences. It may be possible to clear these types of cases, but it does take effort, ingenuity, and skill. Then there are the "smoking gun" offences. When police arrive, they may find the offender on the scene with property in his possession and a full confession proffered once confronted. Few people, however, would commend officers for their ingenious investigative skills in cases like this; they would be easy to clear. Canada's current clearance rates, however, do not take into account these nuances with offences. Rather, they treat all offences as having the same "solvability." If a department truly wants to assess the skill and ingenuity of its investigative officers, then it would make sense to use only those offences in the middle category to assess performance. Officers should not be seen negatively if their cases fall into the "whodunnit" category, and on the flip side, should not necessarily be seen as a complete success if all of their cases fall into the "smoking gun" category. (See Figure 7.3.)

In a broader sense, a police department with a mix of crime that is relatively difficult to solve may be at a significant disadvantage when clearance rates are compared with those of a jurisdiction that sees a greater mix of simple cases (Pare and Ouimet 2003). For instance, police jurisdictions with larger populations may have a more difficult time solving crimes due to the increased anonymity of offenders within the population (Pare and Ouimet 2003).

Other Quantitative Measures

Police departments publish statistical reports that tally certain activities and measure specific initiatives. For instance, many departments have been challenged by the increasing number of interactions with persons with mental illness (PWMI). This has resulted in further scrutiny of the number and nature of these interactions. Similarly, departments in urban areas may have traffic safety as a central focus. These departments may track traffic collisions and/or fatalities to measure how their actions may be affecting the number of people involved in motor vehicle accidents or fatal collisions.

Figure 7.3   Case Complexity

Often, tracking these activities and outcomes relies simply on counting the number of events. While it may be useful to watch changes in activities over time, there is little context to assess effectiveness when counting is the only measure. Simply counting the activity, such as encounters with PWMI, may not reflect any impact the police are having. The preponderance of PWMI in the general population may have much more to do with public health policies and services in the community than police actions.

Alternate and Qualitative Measures of Performance

Quantitative measures of performance described above do not always provide a complete representation of how the police are viewed or how effective they are. Alternate measures, such as surveys, and **qualitative measures** such as focus groups and/or interviews may be more effective for assessing perspectives on policing of those in the community or those who come into contact with the police.

Surveys can be very helpful to gauge public attitudes toward police or safety initiatives; however, the helpfulness of the survey depends on how it is constructed and deployed. Additionally, as their cost can be considerable, police departments should be aware of their limitations. The objective of a survey should be very clear from the outset, and should focus on one primary purpose or group.

All surveys tend to suffer from some similar deficiencies, such as low response rates and **generalizability** issues. The current relationship with police will often influence who is willing to participate in these surveys and what response the police department is likely to receive. For instance, in areas where satisfaction with police is low, citizens may be less apt to participate in police-conducted victimization surveys, but more than willing to voice all their negative concerns in general satisfaction surveys.

Coverage of the target audience is also an ongoing challenge. As most surveys are conducted either by mail or over the phone, these exclude individuals who are not reachable via these methods. This may be particularly relevant for policing, particularly with vulnerable populations, as the only avenue for connection is through meeting face to face. This reality is beyond many departments' capacity to address. New technologies such as web-based surveys may be easier to deploy and analyze with a large segment of the service population, but again, they exclude anyone without access to the internet or a computer. However, if designed and deployed effectively with limitations and coverage issues in mind, these surveys can provide valuable information to be used in tandem with official statistics and other measures.

Surveys

Community surveys are often employed to assess a community's victimization levels, its fear of crime levels, and/or its general satisfaction with police. Although these surveys can be very informative to police, they are often extremely costly (Moore and Braga 2003a, 2003b), and, if put together poorly, may not engage the issues that the police department wanted to address. If done with care and thought, however, they may provide valuable insight into the community.

Halifax Regional Police Constable Marshall Williams, right, hands out reflective armbands to passing pedestrians as part of a police effort to reduce vehicle–pedestrian accidents. In what ways could the outcomes of this interaction be measured quantitatively, and what outcomes might require an alternative measure to better capture the effect of this kind of interaction?

Community satisfaction surveys are often used by police departments to assess whether the community is satisfied with the police and the level of service it is receiving. Through these surveys, police can learn about the community's experience with the police, whether its members have been victimized by crime, and whether they are fearful in different scenarios or geographic areas. Surveys may also be devised to target specific questions or issues, such as the existence of public disorder issues or other community concerns that may not be adequately captured by official crime statistics (Maguire 2003; Stephens 1999). Surveys may often be quantified, as shown in Figure 7.4, to clearly show respondents' sentiments or attitudes toward specific questions.

The wording and structure of surveys is directly connected to how useful they are and what they are actually able to show. For instance, research has found that community satisfaction surveys that contain many general questions often show a high degree of satisfaction with police. While this may seem positive, this does little to assist police in identifying areas for improvement, and may make comparisons to other jurisdictions difficult, if not impossible (Maguire 2003). Although more specific questionnaires may show a decrease in citizens' levels of satisfaction with police, the usefulness of those responses is often much higher.

Another major drawback to simply using general community surveys is that they run the risk of having a large sample of respondents who have never had any direct

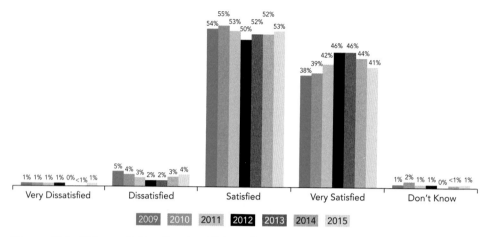

Figure 7.4   Calgary Police Service Citizen Perception Survey 2015

Source: Calgary Police Service 2015 Citizen Survey. Calgary: Illumina Research Partners for Calgary Police Commission, 2013.

contact with police. Rather than from direct experience, impressions of police will come from media reports, second-hand information from friends or acquaintances, or from experience with a police department in another region (Maguire 2003). If these individuals have focused on negative media stories and have had bad experiences in the past with completely different police agencies, their impressions may bias the survey results.

Unlike general community surveys, contact surveys are conducted with those who have had recent contact with police to assess their impressions of that contact. These surveys can be conducted with victims, offenders, witnesses, or arrestees (Maguire 2003). Victimization surveys can highlight where the police department may need to be more responsive to victims' needs to enhance their feelings of safety and security. On the flip side, surveys of arrestees can be useful to assess a department's overall adherence to procedural justice when dealing with offenders, and highlight areas where the police may need to increase professionalism and observance of use-of-force limitations.

Despite the expectation that a survey of offenders or arrestees will always be negative, that has not been found to be the case. People are willing to accept negative outcomes for their actions as long as they perceive their treatment and outcome to be fair and unbiased (Maguire 2003). These surveys must be conducted carefully, however, as much like victimization surveys (discussed below), they must be bound by time restraints to protect against double-counting or **telescoping** problems. For instance, the British Crime Survey asks community residents about their perceptions of police encounters for the previous six months. Because the surveys ask about recent events, those responding recollect experiences in greater detail. Careful selection of the responding group, which might include those who contacted the police themselves, were stopped by police, or were contacted during the course of an investigation (Skogan 1999), ensures useful answers.

Victimization surveys ask respondents whether they have been a victim of crime in a predetermined time period in the past and whether they reported that crime or not. These surveys can be very helpful to see the actual level of crime in a particular jurisdiction and the reasons why individuals may or may not have reported a crime to the police. When individuals do not report a crime, that event is not counted in the official statistics and does not become part of the crime rate. Having accurate knowledge about the realities of crime can enable police departments to assess their effectiveness more reliably. Due to the cost and time involved, conducting victimization surveys is not useful unless the senior police managers are prepared to act on the results (Moore and Braga 2003a, 2003b). If the department is committed to being responsive to such surveys, then their cost may be an efficient use of resources, and continuous victimization surveys may greatly assist in identifying issues that have remained outside of the realm of official statistics.

While alternative and qualitative performance tools have certain drawbacks and limitations, they can provide valuable information to police departments on how they are doing, and where they should be focusing their resources to maintain community satisfaction, safety, and overall well-being.

Unintended Consequences of Performance Metrics

The reality is that police work's impact on communities is difficult to measure (Carmona and Gronlund 2003) due in part to the nuanced nature of the police role and the ever-changing focus on efficiency and value for money. Due to this, more often than not, police departments focus on aspects of police work that are relatively easy to measure, such as the quantitative metrics described above. These provide only a snapshot of the police role and ignore other important aspects of the policing service, particularly services related to getting to know the community, generating tips, and establishing relationships. As these functions are essential to the current movement toward a more holistic community-policing approach, traditional metrics may actually impede growth by narrowing the focus of performance to very traditional models of policing (Carmona and Gronlund 2003; Carter and McGoldrick 1994).

Heavy emphasis on static metrics and traditional performance measures may also open up the possibility of manipulation by those being measured (Blumstein 1999). As the top executive places pressure on street-level officers to deliver in terms of arrests, clearance rates, and other outputs, responses may produce counter-productive results. Rivalry between police teams may result in the withholding of suspect details from another team in order to win "points," and officers may also avoid using alternative measures and focus on making arrests in order to bolster numbers. Heavy reliance on these accountability structures may be demoralizing, insofar as they ignore the nuances of police work, de-emphasize creative approaches to reducing crime and disorder, and have been seen to result in officers cutting corners in some instances to adhere to the standards of what is being measured (Cockcroft and Beattie 2009). This reality was asserted by the former Chief Constable of Gloucestershire, who commented that

> … performance indicators may have a limited impact on real increases in performance, they can have a range of influences on the behaviour of staff, and some of these influences may be perverse. (Butler 2000 in Cockcroft and Beattie 2009, 537)

At best, the sole emphasis on output measures can result in soft manipulation of the statistics or a change in police practice to more countable actions. This was well documented in Chicago, as police were found to be manipulating their statistics by recording numerous offences as "unfounded" without the due course of investigation. This necessitated keeping two sets of books—one public that displayed an ongoing reduction in crime, and one private that showed the true reality (Skogan 1999). At worst, some studies have found that pressure to adhere to classical performance outputs can result in sacrificing legal mandates and due process rights. This reality was evident in some United Kingdom police agencies, with the ongoing pressure to increase productivity and lower expenditures resulting in increased citizen complaints (Police Complaints Authority 1999 in Shane 2010).

Newer Innovations

In nearly all police departments, the emphasis is slowly changing toward problem solving and crime prevention, rather than simply reacting to calls for service. This in turn has prompted changed definitions of success (Mazerolle, Rombouts, and McBroom 2007) beyond crime rates and response times. Many new approaches have attempted to deal with this issue of demonstrating legitimacy and effectiveness. That is not to imply that new monitoring methods do not use traditional measures; rather, each has used various metrics in many ways.

CompStat

CompStat (also see Chapter 12), short for computer statistics, is perhaps the best-known and most well-documented contemporary example of the power of performance measurement in law enforcement management. CompStat is based on four key principles:

1. timely and accurate intelligence;
2. effective tactics;
3. rapid deployment of personnel and resources; and
4. relentless follow-up and assessment to ensure that the problem has been solved (Roberts 2006).

The core function at the heart of CompStat is accountability, as those responsible for particular geographic areas must demonstrate and justify their actions in response to changing levels of crime and disorder in their area. Best practices and successes are shared among other precincts, and tactics are closely related to up-to-the-minute intelligence and data analysis (Bratton 1999).

Although CompStat has been touted as instrumental to the significant reductions in crime and improvements of quality of life (particularly in New York during the 1990s), it has its critics. Some see CompStat as a way to justify zero-tolerance tactics within problem-oriented policing (see Chapter 12) (Silverman and O'Connell 1997 in Mazerolle, Rombouts, and McBroom 2007); others argue it has done little more than reinforce the traditional models of policing without showing that it actually reduces crime (Weisburd et al. 2003 in Shane 2010). Despite this, many agree that CompStat has contributed to the overall professionalization of policing by placing an emphasis on problem-solving strategies and objective analysis of those strategies and their success (Shane 2010). By holding managers and commanders to account, CompStat also ensures that bad practices do not continue, allowing departments to focus on what works. Fundamentally, CompStat is focused on short-term realities and the rapid deployment of intensive police resources in particular areas (Plant and Scott 2009).

Balanced Scorecard Approaches

The **balanced scorecard** was developed as a performance management tool to be used by managers to get a concise and timely view of an organization's performance. The scorecard's approach allows managers to develop indicators of performance that are visibly linked to the overall goals and mission of the organization (Carmona and Gronlund 2003; Cockcroft and Beattie 2009). The scorecard integrates four interrelated perspectives:

1. Financial—How do we look to stakeholders?
2. Customer—How well do we satisfy our internal and external customers' needs?
3. Internal Business Process—How well do we perform at key internal business processes?
4. Learning and Growth—Are we able to sustain innovation, change, and continuous improvement? (Roberts 2006, 28)

Public Safety Canada recently applied Moore and Braga's (2003a, 2003b) balanced scorecard approach for Canadian policing agencies and included numerous quantitative and qualitative measures of performance that could be utilized to address each of the seven dimensions. (See Table 7.1.)

Using a balanced scorecard, the performance measures can be aligned with key community stakeholders, public opinion, and internal police processes (Carmona and Gronlund 2003; Greasley 2004). The balanced scorecard, however, suffered from many of the same deficiencies of traditional performance measurements when first deployed, most notably the absence of the measurement of crucial activities linked to community policing and crime prevention. At its heart, the balanced scorecard reflects the movement away from simply reporting on the volume of crime, to the need to balance multiple measures of police activity and performance that reflect the complex array of the responsibilities of law enforcement (Roberts 2006).

In their review of police performance measures, Mazowita and Rotenberg (2019) developed a pillared approach that somewhat resembles the balanced scorecard approach. In their report, they outline the Canadian Police Performance Metrics Framework (CPPMF) as gathering and reporting on statistics that fall within four pillars of objective and universal performance measurement:

1. Crime and victimization—Measures of the incidence of crime, victimization, and bringing offenders to account, including traditional metrics, linked court data, and re-contact data
2. Police activities and deployment—Measures of police functions and activities that contribute to public safety, including non-crime related policing responsibilities
3. Police resources—Measures of police personnel and operating expenditures
4. Trust and confidence in police—Measures of Canadians' trust and confidence in police, and perceptions of police legitimacy (Mazowita and Rotenberg 2019, 5–6)

Each of these pillars comprises several areas of inquiry that include many of the metrics that were discussed above, utilized in several ways. It is hoped that this framework will outline

Table 7.1 Seven Dimensions of Balanced Scorecard and Selected Key Performance Indicators

Seven Dimensions of Balanced Scorecard	Common Performance Indicators
Reduce criminal victimization	Police-reported crime rates (rates per 100,000 population) Victimization rates Crime Severity Index Police-reported violent crime rates Non-violent Crime Severity Index
Call adult and youth offenders to account in appropriate ways	Clearance rates (e.g., violent crime, *Controlled Drug and Substances Act*) Conviction rates Number of youths diverted Number of outstanding arrest warrants Number of times special courts (e.g., drug, mental health, domestic violence) are used
Reduce fear of crime and enhance personal security	Reported changes in level of fear (from victim surveys) Reported decrease in community concern about drugs/crime in their neighbourhood Reported changes in self-protection measures
Increase safety in public spaces	Reported changes in traffic fatalities, injuries, and property damages Reported changes in use of parks and public spaces Reported changes in property values Reported proportion of community members who feel safe in public areas
Use financial resources fairly, efficiently, and effectively	Data on cost of policing, per citizen Data on the efficiency and fairness of deployment and scheduling of police officers Number and proportion of civilian employees Percentage of working hours lost to sickness for police officers or civilian employees Data on budget compliance Data on amounts of overtime expenditures
Use force and authority legitimately, fairly, and effectively	Number of citizen complaints Number of external police reviews regarding alleged police misconduct Settlements in liability issues Number of police shootings Number of times different kinds of force (lethal and non-lethal) are used
Satisfy citizen demands for prompt, effective, and fair service	Data on average police response time to calls for service, by priority level Survey data on citizen satisfaction with police services and citizen perceptions of the fairness of such services

Source: Kiedrowski, J., Petrunik, M., et al. (2013). Canadian Police Board Views on the Use of Police Performance Metrics. Compliance Strategy Group prepared for Law Enforcement and Policing Branch Public Safety Canada. Report No. 31, 2013. Reproduced with the permission of the Minister of Public Safety and Emergency Preparedness Canada, 2016.

Case Study

Innovations with Statistics in Police Agencies

Police agencies are furthering their ability to analyze their performance by integrating numerous data systems and accessing up-to-the-minute crime statistics and workload measurements. Waterloo Regional Police Force has been working to establish more responsive and intelligence-driven deployment models in order to better deploy resources and respond to crime. Another aspect of this data-driven approach is the implementation of CopLogic, which is an online reporting tool for citizens to report minor crimes and avoid waiting in a telephone queue or waiting for an officer to respond to their call. This will increase reporting and increase the accuracy of the police agency's crime statistics. Other departments have also begun to integrate online reporting to gather statistics without the need for police follow-up. The Vancouver Police Department operates an online system for reporting theft under $5000, fraud under $5000, and some other minor offences. Peel Police, Durham Police, and York Regional Police all operate similar online reporting systems for several minor property offences. York Regional Police have also added the ability for citizens to report historical sexual assaults online; however, this service is intended as a pathway for survivors to initiate contact with the police privately, as officers will follow up and commence investigations on these types of reports. (See Chapter 10 for more on online reporting.)

This move toward data- and intelligence-driven deployment and operations is anticipated to increase the success of numerous measures of performance such as response times, overall community satisfaction, clearance rates, and overall crime rates. However, with so many departments expanding their online and non-emergency reporting mechanisms, the consideration of these data must include a critical examination of errors, omissions, or false reporting.

to police services how they can use performance metrics effectively and appropriately, while also giving them the framework with which to gather the data required and evaluate the results against a backdrop of police effectiveness. As this report has only recently been released, time will tell how it is embraced and adopted by agencies throughout Canada.

Why Performance Measures Fail

Performance management has many challenges and it fails for internal and external reasons. Some of the internal failures come from the police culture itself and the unwillingness to embrace performance management and accountability measures. Within the organization, police officers throughout all ranks may be resistant to change or may view the scrutiny of their performance as intrusive and biased.

Other challenges come from the public, as their priorities often compete with priorities within the police service. While many citizens may express the desire for police to be better problem solvers and community participants, they continue to insist on traditional reactive measures such as fast response times, which inherently limit the police's ability to focus on problem solving.

The sustainability of the performance management process must also be considered. Simply viewing it as a one-time activity will certainly ensure its failure. To be successful over the long term, the strategic planning, goal setting, data collection, analysis, and reporting structures have to be entrenched within the organization and must be able to be maintained, even through budget cuts or other organizational challenges. Organizations must consider the logistics of collecting and producing performance measurement data and reports. A proper performance management system may require securing additional funding for data collection, as well as ensuring that technical competency and analytical capacity either exist within the agency or can be brought into the agency. Managers must also be realistic about their performance management process. Some of the biggest pitfalls in performance management come from incomplete specifications of goals, objectives, and criteria; unclear objectives; unrealistic time frames for success; and initially establishing far too many measures rather than selecting core measures (Roberts 2006). Weighting also comes into play in the success and failure of these schemes, as the objective, mission, and goal-setting process should identify whether measures should be treated equally, or whether they should be weighted toward goals that the agency deems more important than others (Maguire 2003).

If a police department can develop meaningful performance measures and targets that are linked to the strategic plan and are adaptable to community needs, then the department should be able to accurately assess whether they are doing a good job over the long term.

Conclusion

This chapter has discussed how performance measurements can provide valuable insight into the efficiency and effectiveness of the police department and allow the department to audit its actions and move in directions that can ensure citizens are being provided with adequate service while balancing reasonable limits on financial and human resources. However, many classic measurement tools have become problematic and antiquated, or are used in ways that do not lend themselves to an accurate or useful picture of the police agency. Newer methods for measuring success in a department consider the nuances present in policing and try to balance quantitative metrics with qualitative approaches. Many quantitative measurement tools continue to be used today, and with the proper understanding of what they are actually telling the reader, they may be useful as one piece in a larger toolbox for understanding and conveying police performance.

Critical Thinking Questions

1. Why should police departments measure their performance? What are some of the benefits and challenges associated with performance measurement?
2. If police departments are not meeting performance targets, what should be done?
3. Should police be held accountable for changes in crime rates? Why or why not?
4. Why would a victimization survey produce different data than official crime statistics? Should we be concerned with the "dark figure of crime," that is, the large percentage of crime that goes unreported?

PART III

On the Job as an Officer

8

Patrol

Learning Objectives

After reading and studying this chapter, students will be able to:

- Identify and discuss the role of general-duty patrol officers.
- Review and discuss the relationship between patrol officers and detectives.
- Identify and explain the various types of patrols and their strengths.
- Review and discuss the three fundamental authorities given to the police by the *Criminal Code* of Canada.
- Describe and assess the purpose and function of the National Use-of-Force Framework.

Introduction

Chapter 8 examines the core of modern policing—uniformed patrol work. It reviews the principal forms of patrol and how patrol resources are allocated in major urban police agencies. As well, Chapter 8 identifies and discusses the three principal authorities granted to police officers under the Canadian *Criminal Code*: the authority to search and seize, the authority to arrest, and the authority to use force. In the context of using force, the chapter also reviews the Canadian National Use-of-Force Framework endorsed by the Canadian Association of Chiefs of Police. Subsequently, the chapter concludes with a consideration of issues related to high-speed police pursuits.

Uniformed Patrol Officers

It is now a cliché to state that patrol work is the backbone of modern policing; however, it is also true. Police patrol work is highly visible and it is the area of police activity that historically has been most studied and written about.

Regardless of the model of policing (see Chapter 12 for a discussion of the two principal models of policing) that is implemented in a particular community, the vast majority of police officers are engaged in general-duty patrol work. According to David Bayley, in the "United States 65 per cent of police officers are assigned to general duty patrol work, 64 per cent in Canada, 56 per cent in England and Wales, 54 per cent in Australia, and 40 per cent in Japan" (Bayley 1994, 574; Forcese 1999, 87). Indeed, it is widely accepted that it is in the course of learning general-duty patrol work that new officers learn what policing really is and where they hone real policing skills. Furthermore, it is also widely accepted among veteran police officers that being on the street engaging in general patrol work ranks among the best years of their careers. Nevertheless, as several commentators have noted, patrol work is placed at the bottom of the rank structure, has the least prestige of all assignments, and is typically carried out by very junior ranks or by "dead-end older constables" (Dantzker and Mitchell 1998, 42; Forcese 1999, 89).

Generally not realized by the lay public, patrol officers are often shuttled back and forth between patrol and specialized units. That is, they are often transferred back and forth from uniformed patrol work to plainclothes investigation (see Chapter 9). For example, particularly in larger agencies, seasoned patrol officers often receive in-house specialized training and acquire considerable investigative expertise in specific crimes. Depending on openings, these officers may be seconded to a specialized unit but at some later time return to routine patrol. Thus, not only do some patrol officers garner considerable training and expertise in specialized investigations but their assignments are often fluid within their agency. This is particularly the case in urban areas where police agencies partner in integrated police units and officers are seconded for varying durations.

In Canada it is commonly recognized that patrol officers are generalists who engage in a wide variety of policing activities. These activities range from routine patrol and responding to calls for service to carrying out investigations. While patrol activities vary according to the size of the police agency and concomitantly with the degree of specialization within that agency, in most Canadian police agencies patrol officers can expect to be involved in widely divergent policing matters. So said, patrol work is composed of three main functions:

- maintaining order;
- providing service; and
- law enforcement.

As noted briefly in Chapter 1, police work generally and patrol work specifically are principally concerned with maintaining order (for example, directing vehicular and pedestrian traffic at major sporting events or rock concerts) and with providing service (for example, responding to traffic accidents and rendering first aid). Actions by police that entail enforcement of the law constitute a small component of police work. To be certain, overlap between these functions often exists. For example, in seeking to maintain order at a loud party, police may have to engage in law enforcement by arresting an intoxicated and uncooperative partier for disturbing the peace. Nevertheless, within these broad police functions, police patrol work, particularly in agencies committed to the community-policing model (see Chapter 12), also entails a series of broad interrelated objectives:

- crime prevention and deterrence;
- apprehending offenders;
- enhancing public sense of safety and satisfaction;
- providing non-crime–related public services;
- traffic control; and
- problem-solving (Roberg, Novak, and Cordner 2005).

Patrol Methods

Patrol Car

Despite the loss of face-to-face contact with members of the public, the automobile remains the principal means by which patrol is conducted. Much of patrol work, regardless of the model of policing, is characterized by uniformed officers driving around in marked vehicles waiting for dispatchers to relay calls for service that typically come in through designated emergency call numbers such as 911. In fact, according to Bayley, over 90 per cent of patrol work is generated by dispatch (2009, 574). Relatively few calls are related to crime—less than 7 per cent to 10 per cent (Bayley 1994, 574)—and these involve relatively minor crimes. Violent crime in Canada is reported to be about 9 per cent (Bayley 1994, 575). In Canada, patrol officers make one criminal arrest a month and encounter a recordable criminal offence only once a week (Ericson 1982).

Although much of patrol work is non-criminal and routine, it is also often filled with considerable uncertainty. Complacency can be problematic in that officers may inadvertently let their guards down only to have situations suddenly spin out of control.

Patrol officers become familiar with the locations of particular calls. Addresses of regular domestic disputes, bars where rowdy drunks cause disturbances, automotive repair businesses that are known to deal in stolen auto parts, and warehouses that are regularly burglarized become all too familiar to seasoned patrol officers. As well, patrol officers routinely deal with persons on society's margins—uneducated, poor, unemployed, and unemployable—who are both victimizers and victims (Bayley 1994, 576). Often police can do little other than listen and appear supportive.

Automobile patrol offers the greatest coverage and, in most circumstances, provides the most rapid means of responding to calls for service. In the early days of motorized patrol, two officers were typically assigned to a single car. However, with the increased dependence on and reliability of wireless communication, many departments now use single-person cars. This has generated considerable controversy in regard to officer safety and to overall effectiveness.

One- or Two-Officer Cars

Most cities in Canada mix deployment of one- and two-officer patrol cars. Many, however, require two-officer cars during high-crime hours. The RCMP, on the other hand, utilizes only one-officer patrol vehicles even in large urban communities where they serve in the capacity of municipal police.

Throughout North America, policies vary from jurisdiction to jurisdiction. Police unions typically advocate for two-person cars as a matter of officer safety. It is not uncommon for the matter to be negotiated and stipulated in collective bargaining agreements.

Many Canadian city police services have policies that dictate that two officers must be deployed to Priority 1 calls (domestic disputes, robberies in progress, weapons-related calls) regardless of whether they are in the same or separate vehicles (Frontier Centre 2001). Some municipal departments require that only two-person patrol units be on duty during specified hours, for example, between 7:00 p.m. and 7:00 a.m. Other departments maintain fixed ratios of two-person to one-person patrol cars. The City of Vancouver, for example, maintains a ratio of 60 to 40 at all times, with two-person cars being in the majority (Frontier Centre 2001).

Those who advocate for two-officer vehicles claim that officers who are alone are at greater risk of injury or death. The presence of a second officer lessens the risk. Two-person cars are also claimed to facilitate better observations in the course of routine patrol. A second officer is said to be more able to observe and assess the surroundings without having to divert attention from driving. It is also believed that two-person cars are more efficient and able to address situations more effectively. Furthermore, proponents of two-officer cars contend that single officers may be hesitant to assume control of situations but that the presence of two officers increases the likelihood that responders will act more decisively.

Those who favour one-officer vehicles claim that two one-officer patrol cars can provide twice the patrol coverage as two officers in one car. The argument is then made that one-officer cars provide faster responses to calls for service. Proponents of one-officer cars also claim that driving keeps officers alert and more observant. Two-officer teams engage in conversation and thus are likely to divert each other from taking in what may be transpiring around them.

The matter of one- or two-officer patrol units was addressed in the 1970s in a study conducted in San Diego, California. The study found that "one-person units produced more arrests, filed more formal crime reports, received fewer citizen complaints and were clearly less expensive" (Boydstun, Sherry, and Moelter 1977; see also Frontier Centre 2001). The study also found that officers in one-person cars were at least as safe as those in two-person cars.

A study of patrol in Kansas City, which sought to replicate the San Diego study, found that two one-officer cars were able to respond more quickly than one two-officer car and that one-officer cars had a safety advantage (Kessler 1985).

Weighed against officer safety and overall effectiveness is the inevitable matter of cost. In an era in which police agencies are increasingly faced with budgetary constraints, the economics of single-officer cars suggests that there is much greater return for investment in terms of overall police patrol productivity than from two-officer patrol units (Frontier Centre 2001).

Foot/Bike Patrol

With the rise in popularity of the community-policing model and with the corresponding recognition of the loss of contact with the broader community, both foot patrols and bicycle patrols have enjoyed a resurrection. Foot patrols (also referred to as "walking a beat") have proven to be relatively successful and popular in downtown areas of larger municipalities, in large shopping centres, in urban parks, and in other urban areas where there is considerable pedestrian traffic. With the reliability of mobile communication, foot patrol officers are able to maintain contact not only with headquarters, but with other officers in patrol cars. While obviously limited in regard to mobility, foot patrol officers may often be teamed with bike patrols. Studies have revealed that deployment of officers on foot patrol increases the level of positive contacts with ordinary citizens and generates considerable goodwill between the public and the police. Studies have shown that citizen awareness of foot patrol in their neighbourhoods has contributed in significant ways to a decrease in the level of the public's general fear of crime (see Roberg, Novak, and Cordner 2005).

Bicycle patrol has similarly produced positive outcomes in terms of generating goodwill with the public and has shown itself remarkably effective in terms of apprehending street criminals in some inner-city neighbourhoods. Compared to foot and vehicle patrol,

Officers patrolling on foot in downtown Windsor. What are the benefits of patrolling on foot compared to patrolling by car or bicycle? What are the detriments?

Material republished with the express permission of *Windsor Star*, a division of Postmedia Network Inc.

bicycle patrols have been able to bring certain tactical advantages in responding to calls for service. Not only are bicycle patrol officers able to respond quickly within designated areas but they can respond with considerable stealth (Menton 2008, 102).

> The issue of stealth is an important one. . . . There is clearly less drama of bicycles rolling up without a sound. Bicycle patrol officers can quickly situate themselves into the context of a situation. This allows for more effective response. The dynamics of not having to park the car, get out of it, adjust a gun-belt and walk over to the situation create a whole different set of circumstances. There is no time to hide the joint or the open container, and further, the police may be in a better position to address other issues ranging from quality of life to serious crimes. (Menton 2008, 102)

Other Modes of Patrol

Depending on the size and geography of a police jurisdiction, several other types of patrol are deployed: horse, motorcycle, marine, and helicopter (see also Chapter 12). Not every community or jurisdiction will need such specialized patrol units. Nor will all communities be able to afford to maintain such relatively expensive forms of patrol.

Horse patrols, often deployed for the purpose of crowd control or for responding to various service calls in larger urban parks, are effective means of accessing terrain that may be inaccessible to other forms of transportation. They, like foot and bicycle patrols, are particularly popular with ordinary citizens.

Motorcycle patrols, however, have tended to fall into disfavour. Their utility is perhaps limited to responding quickly to motor vehicle accidents on gridlocked roadways. Motorcycles have also proven to be exceptionally dangerous. Few mishaps on a motorcycle are without a serious consequence for the patrol officer. Inclement weather also restricts their overall utility.

Marine patrols are often maintained and utilized in communities such as coastal cities that are in proximity to larger bodies of water. The principal use of marine patrols has less to do with a law enforcement function and more to do with fulfilling a search-and-rescue or a public service mandate.

Last, helicopter patrol (sometimes known as an "Eye in the Sky") with spotlights and infrared cameras has proven invaluable in those jurisdictions large enough to afford it. Helicopters have demonstrated their worth in a range of policing activities. Perhaps the most familiar use of police helicopters has been their utility in pursuits. The capacity of helicopter patrols to maintain visual surveillance of fleeing cars, motorcycles, and even suspects on foot (who have crashed and abandoned their vehicle) is a much-valued tool in agencies fortunate enough to have them. Ongoing surveillance from the relative safety of the sky greatly reduces the need for high-speed pursuit by officers in patrol cars. Helicopter patrol involved in pursuits can direct vehicle patrol units to the location of the fleeing suspects while maintaining surveillance and capturing video images of their activity. Similarly, the search-and-rescue capacity of aerial patrol equipped with heat-sensing technology has proven effective in locating missing persons lost, for example, in regional parks.

Patrol Allocation

Traditionally, officers have been assigned to patrol areas on the basis of police experience and intuition; however, increasingly police administrators have had to become much more adept at recognizing community needs and establishing priorities. The first factors taken into account by administrators involve such demographic variables such as the size of the area to be patrolled and its composition economically, socially, and culturally. An area that is too large poses challenges in terms of being able to adequately respond to its needs and to calls for service.

Urban areas that are known to face economic, social, and cultural challenges such as Winnipeg's inner city and North End and Vancouver's Downtown Eastside are prone to high levels of crime and warrant higher levels of policing. These areas are relatively impoverished and are plagued by substandard housing, few services, substance abuse, domestic violence, and high levels of other interpersonal crimes. Such areas inevitably require more patrol officers than more affluent suburban communities. While police shift or watch scheduling varies from jurisdiction to jurisdiction, it is generally recognized that the evening shift, particularly on weekends, is the busiest patrol shift (Dantzker and Mitchell 1998, 47).

Since the mid-1990s, most major metropolitan police departments have implemented CompStat—or "computer statistics"—in combination with computerized crime mapping as modern methods of assigning patrol resources. (CompStat is addressed in detail in Chapter 13.)

Patrol Officer Relationships with Plainclothes Detectives

After patrol, criminal investigation occupies the next-largest segment of police personnel. In Canada, about 14 per cent of police personnel are tasked with criminal investigation work (Bayley 1994, 576). Although it is contingent on the size of the police agency, investigation of serious crime is often given over by patrol officers to specialized units such as sex crimes, homicide, narcotics, gangs, and burglary. Investigation work typically undertaken by plainclothes detectives is overwhelmingly reactive (Bayley 1994, 578). As Richard Ericson (1981) documented in his classic study of detectives in a major Canadian metropolitan police department, detective work is largely occupied with screening reports initially prepared by uniformed patrol officers and selecting those crimes that are solvable. From the perspective of detectives, solvable crimes are those in which suspects are clearly identified either through eyewitness or victim accounts and/or through the initial investigative efforts of uniformed patrol officers. Not unlike emergency medical personnel, detectives engage in triage—prioritizing those cases that are either serious or sufficiently high profile to warrant public attention and that are solvable; that is, the perpetrators have already been identified in initial reports prepared by responding patrol officers (Bayley 1994, 577). It then becomes the responsibility of plainclothes detectives to secure additional evidence to sustain charges.

General patrol officers are responsible for investigative follow-up for most crimes. As earlier noted, most crimes, contrary to dramatized accounts in the news and entertainment media, are petty nuisance crimes. For that reason, crimes of this nature remain the responsibility of uniformed police officers who follow investigative leads as best they can. As with plainclothes detective work, the success of patrol investigation is dependent on the early identification of offenders.

Although also not depicted in dramatized versions of police work, uniformed patrol officers may often liaise directly with Crown prosecutors in preparing cases for trial. Crown counsel may ask patrol officers who have prepared reports to gather additional evidence necessary to strengthen a particular case. Likewise, Crown prosecutors, attentive to not offending their police counterparts, often consult the investigative officers (either patrol or plainclothes detectives) as they undertake plea negotiations with accused persons and their legal counsel (Ericson 1981; 1982).

To be sure, while it varies among police agencies, there is often a degree of resentment on the part of patrol officers who do the "grunt work" on investigations and who are subsequently made to give over their investigative work to plainclothes detectives who are often viewed as "hot shots" who get credit for the work done by lowly patrol officers. Despite such resentment, it is also true that plainclothes detective investigation is critically dependent on the information provided by uniformed patrol officers who are first on the scene, often taking suspects into custody and gathering essential evidence from victims and witnesses.

Police Officer Authorities

In the normal course of duties, uniformed police officers are involved in daily encounters with a diverse array of people. On a routine shift, police officers will have pleasant exchanges with ordinary law-abiding members of the public. They may also engage with upset and angry victims and witnesses. Alternatively, they may also deal with uncooperative and resentful victims and witnesses. As well, they may deal with uncooperative and aggressive suspects. In all encounters, however, the police carry with them the full authority of the law. In most circumstances, police do not use the criminal law in the course of responding to calls for service. Many of the relatively minor offences are pacified through informal negotiation. Patrol officers mediate resolutions in many situations without invoking the formal authority of the law. Nonetheless, the formal authority of the law is, figuratively speaking, kept in the sleeve of the responding police officer as a trump card. It is a card that may be played (that is, threatened) if the subject of their attention is obdurate or otherwise noncompliant. For example, the power to arrest is a potent tool available to the police in all encounters—the threat of arrest is what makes police intervention authoritative (Bayley 1994, 575). Patrol officers, through both training and experience, thus develop extensive knowledge of and familiarity with the formal authorities given to them under the law, such as the *Criminal Code* of Canada.

Criminal Code Authorities for the Police

The *Criminal Code* of Canada establishes the legal parameters within which police officers are authorized to exercise fundamental powers deemed necessary to enforce the law effectively. Although other federal statutes (such as the *Canada Evidence Act*) and other provincial legislation (such as the *Ontario Police Act* for police in Ontario) empower police officers to act in particular ways, three basic powers—arrest and detention, search and seizure, and the use of force—are granted to all police officers by virtue of specific provisions in the *Criminal Code.*

Arrest and Detention

Perhaps one of the first images the ordinary person has of police powers is an image of the police handcuffing someone and taking them into custody. Beyond this, few people have a complete understanding of the legal authority or of the legal grounds on which police officers may arrest someone. Nor do most people properly understand the purposes to be served when police officers do make an arrest. Powers to detain and arrest with regard to criminal offences are set out principally in the *Criminal Code.* Although it varies from province to province, police officers also have additional powers of detention and arrest granted them under such provincial legislation as *Motor Vehicle Acts* or *Liquor Control Acts.* Depending on the recruit training program and the province in which it is delivered, police officers will be trained in the appropriate powers granted under specific provincial statutes. Nevertheless, given its national scope, all police training programs will give due emphasis to the detention and arrest provisions spelled out in the *Code.*

If a person has been accused of a criminal offence, before that person can be prosecuted he or she must first appear in court. As McKenna has documented, there are two ways in which this occurs: (1) an appearance notice is issued by a police officer[i] or a summons is issued by a provincial court judge; or (2) an arrest is made with or without a warrant (McKenna 2002, 15).

In reality, and contrary to entertainment media–fostered stereotypes, relatively few persons suspected of crimes are arrested when they are charged. Most suspects in a crime will be issued an **appearance notice** or a **promise to appear** (see Forms 9 and 10 respectively in the *Criminal Code*) without being taken into police custody. Indeed, police officers must judge each case on an individual basis and, unless they have reasonable grounds to believe it is in the public interest to take someone into custody, are under an obligation to release the suspect (McKenna 2002, 16). Section 495(2) specifies three considerations that police must take into account in determining if it is in the public interest to arrest a suspect:

1. confirmation of the person's identity;
2. securing or preserving evidence; and
3. preventing the continuation or repetition of the offence or the commission of another offence.

As McKenna has pointed out, "unless an officer has reasonable grounds to believe either that it is not in the 'public interest' to release the suspect or that the suspect will fail to show up for trial, the officer's duty is *not* to arrest the suspect" (McKenna 2002, 16; italics in original).

In some instances where a suspect is no longer at the crime scene or as a result of an ongoing investigation or both, police officers may apply to a court official such as a provincial court judge for an **arrest warrant**—a court-issued document that grants police officers legal authority to arrest a person when there are reasonable grounds to believe that the person has committed a criminal offence. In order to obtain an arrest warrant, a police officer will typically appear before a court official and swear an **information** that the officer has reasonable grounds to believe that a particular person has committed a specific offence. In rural areas or at irregular times such as late night or early morning hours or weekends, appearing before an official of the court such as a justice of the peace (JP) or a judicial justice in person may be impractical. Most provinces, in accord with provisions in the *Criminal Code*, have therefore instituted a tele-warrant system whereby warrants may be applied for and received via fax or telephone.

On some occasions, police officers may have to intervene quickly and therefore can arrest without a warrant under section 495(1) of the *Code* if they have apprehended a person in the act of committing an offence, they have reasonable grounds to believe that a suspect has committed an indictable offence, or they believe on reasonable grounds that a suspect is about to commit an indictable offence.

Arrest is not a form of punishment. Nor is it intended teach the suspect a lesson. As noted in the preceding discussion, the primary purpose of arrest is to ensure that an accused person will appear in court to face charges. According to Bill Van Allen, although taking someone into custody seems relatively simple to the lay person, the process of arrest entails six important steps (Van Allen 2009, 69):

1. Police officers must identify themselves as police officers.
2. The individual must be informed that he or she is under arrest.
3. Police officers take physical control of the individual. Often this is achieved symbolically by the police officer touching or slightly grasping the suspect's arm. Alternatively, if a suspect is resistant, an appropriate use of force may be involved—but no more than that which is reasonable given the circumstances. Coincidental to the arrest, the suspect may be searched for evidence, weapons, or possible escape tools.
4. The suspect is informed of the reason for his or her arrest, including being informed of the existence of any outstanding arrest warrants.
5. The suspect is then informed of the right to retain counsel, the availability of legal aid, and given the standard caution regarding self-incrimination: "You need not say anything, but anything you do say may be used as evidence."
6. Finally, police officers endeavour to ensure that the suspect comprehends not only the reason for the arrest but his or her rights as well.

Closely associated with arrest, **detention** is a distinct issue in its own right. As McKenna (2002, 20) has pointed out, "detention implies something less than an arrest." However, detention may indeed be a precursor to arrest. For example, a person may be legally detained on the grounds of reasonable suspicion for the purpose of conducting further investigation, such as when police officers ask a suspect to provide a breath sample during a roadside check stop for the purpose of assessing blood alcohol level. According to McKenna, the Supreme Court of Canada has recognized that while routine checks of motor vehicles under provincial highway legislation are arbitrary and technically infringe "s. 9 of the *Charter*, the infringement is one that is reasonable and demonstrably justified in a free and democratic society" (Ladouceur ([1990], 56 CCC (3d) 22 (SCC)).

The Supreme Court of Canada has declared that a detention occurs when a police officer "assumes control over the movement of a person by a demand or direction that has significant legal consequences" (*R. v. Schmautz* [1990] 2 SCR 398). For that reason, the *Charter* specifically addresses the matter of detention in conjunction with arrest. Section 10 of the *Charter* holds that anyone who has been arrested or detained has the right to be informed of the reasons therefore, to retain and instruct counsel without delay and to be informed of that right, to have the validity of the detention determined by way of *habeas corpus*, and to be released if the detention is not lawful.

Upon arrest or detention, suspects will be afforded the opportunity to receive initial preliminary legal advice, typically via a telephone consultation with a duty-counsel or a legal aid lawyer. However, beyond this the right to retain counsel for adult offenders is not absolute. That is, the *Charter* does not stipulate that free legal counsel will be provided to all persons as the case proceeds to court. The right to retain and instruct counsel is not an absolute right (as it is for youth charged under the *Youth Criminal Justice Act*). Adults who can afford legal representation indeed have a right to retain and instruct legal counsel of their choosing. For those who cannot afford representation, those accused of a serious criminal offence may apply for legal aid. Legal aid, however, is provided by provincial authorities and varies significantly across Canada. Generally, not all persons qualify for legal aid representation and typically persons seeking assistance must demonstrate a financial inability to retain their own counsel privately. Legal aid similarly is granted only in criminal cases where the accused stands a distinct possibility of extended incarceration. In some instances where an accused person is not eligible for legal aid or has exhausted his or her entitlement to legal aid, a Rowbotham Application may be made to the court for sufficient funding to secure competent legal representation at the government's expense (Nathanson 2003; *R. v. Rowbotham*). In Rowbotham Applications, the courts recognize that a trial is likely to be unfair if an accused person is not represented by competent legal counsel. The mega-trials of the Air India bombers and of serial killer Robert Pickton are examples of Rowbotham Applications that resulted in the government paying the legal expenses for the accused who were otherwise unable to secure legal aid representation.

Search and Seizure

Another fundamental power granted to police officers under the *Criminal Code* involves the ability to search and seize; however, given the intrusive nature of police powers to search and seize, police powers are carefully controlled and limited. Section 8 of the *Charter* stipulates that everyone has the right to be secure against unreasonable search or seizure.

Searching without a Warrant
There are two principal occasions on which police may conduct searches without a warrant. The first involves the search of a person subsequent to an arrest. The second involves the search of premises in exigent circumstances.

Search of a Person
The legal authority of police to search a person in the course of an arrest does not extend to persons who have been detained. However, in the course of making an arrest, police are legally authorized to search a suspect for the purpose of locating additional evidence related

to the crime for which they are being arrested. This is known as a "search incidental to a lawful arrest." During a search of an arrested suspect, if evidence is found of a crime unrelated to the offence for which the arrest was made, the suspect may face additional charges. For example, if a suspect is arrested for trafficking drugs and is discovered to have a handgun on his or her person, the suspect may face additional separate weapon charges. Thus, in the interest of their own safety, that of the public, and that of the suspect, police are authorized to search for any items such as possible weapons that may be used to escape, to harm the police or members of the public, or to harm the accused him- or herself. Police may also conduct a search of the immediate area in which the arrest was made when searching a person. However, this does not automatically justify an exhaustive search of a building or vehicles.

As McKenna (2002) has noted, police are under no requirement to conduct searches and therefore have some discretion in conducting a search of a person. Police may determine that it is unnecessary to undertake a search. If a search of a suspect is to be conducted, however, it is to be undertaken for a legitimate purpose such as those discussed above. A search cannot be conducted in a manner whereby the suspect is intimidated, humiliated, or pressured to confess and must not be conducted in an abusive manner (McKenna 2002, 46).

Varying with the circumstances of the arrest, three types of searches of a person may be permitted: (1) a relatively straightforward pat-down or frisk of outer clothing; (2) a body search, which may entail the removal of clothing; and (3) a body cavity search, which may involve X-rays or other significant intrusions that may require the assistance of medical personnel (McKenna 2002, 47). Of course, search techniques that entail greater degrees of intrusion require a correspondingly higher level of justification.

Search without a Warrant—Exigent Circumstances

In what are generally rare circumstances, emergency conditions may make it impracticable for police officers to obtain a warrant. In such **exigent circumstances**, police officers are authorized by section 529(3) of the *Code* to enter a house for the purpose of making an arrest without a warrant. In these circumstances police actions are justifiable on the grounds that police entry is necessary to prevent imminent bodily harm or death to occupants or to prevent the imminent loss or destruction of evidence.

The case of *R. v. Godoy* (1999), 131 CCC (3d) 129 (SCC) held that the police had a duty to investigate a 911 call and the authority to enter a home for the purpose of searching for the caller. In this case, police arrived at a home to investigate a disconnected 911 call. Godoy prevented the police from entering his home. It was subsequently determined that Godoy had assaulted his wife, who had initiated the emergency call for assistance. The Supreme Court of Canada held that when police respond to a 911 call they have a legal right to enter a home for the purpose of determining the well-being of occupants. While it may be an interference of privacy within the home, police entry in such circumstances falls within the scope of their duty to protect life and ensure safety and is therefore justifiable (see McKenna 2002, 64–5).

Search with Consent

In certain circumstances, police officers may simply ask for permission to conduct a search of a suspect, their belongings, their vehicle, or their homes. In these circumstances, if an individual grants permission for the search, the police are enabled to conduct a warrantless search and are thereby acting with legal authority. However, for the search to remain legal, the consent must be based on the "informed consent" of the individual. In other words, the consent must be informed, voluntary, and not extorted or coerced in any way. Police must therefore explicitly state both what they are looking for and what the ramifications will be should such things be located. As well, once an informed-consent search begins, the individual is entitled to ask that the police stop. That is, the individual may withdraw his/her consent at any time and the police are required to stop.

Closely related to the matter of searching with consent is the matter of "carding" or "street checks," which are practices that have been routinely used by police to query persons who come to their attention but who are not immediately or necessarily suspected of criminal activity. Criticized as constituting racial profiling for overly singling out minority group members, "carding" is considered in greater detail in Chapter 3.

Search with a Warrant

In most instances before police can search a place for evidence, a **search warrant** must be issued by a court official.[ii] A search warrant is simply a legal document issued by a court official that authorizes the police to search a specific location and to seize items that might be evidence of a crime. Failure of police to obtain a warrant may ultimately mean that the search is ruled unreasonable and any evidence obtained is deemed inadmissible. However, courts have considerable latitude in determining the admissibility of evidence that is obtained without a warrant. The criterion that is used to determine the reasonableness of the search and the admissibility of the evidence is whether or not the administration of justice is brought into disrepute.

According to section 487(1) of the *Criminal Code*, a justice can issue a search warrant for

- anything relating to an offence suspected against the *Criminal Code* or any other *Act* of Parliament;
- anything for which there are reasonable grounds to believe will be evidence of an offence or will disclose the whereabouts of a person who is believed to have committed an offence against the *Criminal Code* or other *Act* of Parliament;
- anything that is reasonably believed to be intended for use to commit any offence against a person for which a person may be arrested without a warrant; or
- any offence-related property.

Swearing an Information

In order to obtain judicial authorization for a warrant, police officers swear an oath before a court official affirming that they have reasonable grounds for believing that evidence exists in relationship to a criminal offence. In a document called an "Information to Obtain a Search Warrant" (sometimes called an ITO), the police must

- provide a full description of the items to be searched for. This includes declaring that the goods sought are in the possession of the accused and that they are related to a specific offence. The greater the detail that the information contains, the less

likely the JP will conclude that the police are on a fishing expedition and the more likely that the JP will grant the warrant (McKenna 2002, 70–1);
- state what offence is involved;
- swear that the officer has reasonable grounds for believing that specific items are in the premises to be searched, and the officer must articulate the grounds for that belief.

In other contexts and as necessary, police may also swear ITOs for the purpose of obtaining warrants that will enable them to conduct video surveillance, place tracking devices, and record telephone conversations. Police may also swear ITOs in order to seek court authorization to obtain body fluids for forensic DNA testing.

Case Study

Search and Seizure with a Warrant: The Pickton Investigation

a) On 5 February 2002, under s.487 of the *Criminal Code*, a search warrant was obtained to search the Pickton property and outbuildings for illegal guns. In part, the reasonable grounds to believe the guns were present on the property were derived from information provided by a confidential informer. During the execution of the warrant by members of the Coquitlam RCMP detachment, two members of the Missing Women Task Force were present.

b) In the search for guns, an asthma inhaler prescribed in the name of Serena Abotsway was found. Upon hearing this information over the police radio, one member of the Missing Women Task Force immediately recognized the name as one of the women missing from the Downtown Eastside of Vancouver who had last been seen in August 2001. Minutes later, another police officer reported over his radio that he had located photocopies of the personal identification of another of the women missing from the Downtown Eastside. Believing now that

there were reasonable grounds that the police were investigating murder(s), the search was stopped and the property secured.

c) The members of the Task Force returned to their office and one of the officers wrote and swore a new information to obtain (ITO) another warrant under s.487 of the Code to search for "physical things" related to the offence of murder. A Provincial Court Judge at the Port Coquitlam Courthouse granted this warrant on the evening of 6 February. It was to be the first of six search warrants that were granted to search the Pickton farm completely, including buildings and vehicles located there.

d) As the search proceeded it became apparent that evidence had been buried underground. As a result, the largest forensic crime scene search in Canadian history was undertaken. The entire site of 17 acres was searched by digging down to undisturbed ground and by sorting and sifting the soil using forensic and other experts. The search ended in November 2003.

Provincial Offences

The above considerations in regard to search and seizure are set out by the federal Parliament in the *Criminal Code* of Canada. The *Code*, however, does not authorize the issue of warrants in the course of investigations of breaches of provincial laws. Each province grants police the authority to conduct searches and seize evidence in the course of investigating violations of provincial laws; therefore, individual provincial laws must be examined carefully to determine if they authorize powers of search and seizure. In Ontario, for example, the *Ontario Provincial Offences Act* sets out procedures that must be followed in the investigation of violations of provincial laws and authorizes court-issued warrants for the search and seizure of evidence relevant to provincial offences.

Use of Force

A third fundamental police power authorized by the *Criminal Code* of Canada entails the legal use of both lethal and non-lethal force in the exercise of their duties. No other issue in policing is as potentially controversial as the police use of force, particularly when the use of force results in death.

In what is probably the highest-profile incident in Canadian police history, in October 2007 Robert Dziekański was subdued by four Royal Canadian Mounted Police officers at the Vancouver International Airport. In the course of subduing Dziekański, a conducted energy weapon (CEW; also known as a Taser) was discharged five times. Dziekański died within minutes after being Tasered, handcuffed, and left on the floor of the airport arrival area. Public reaction was immediate and intense, particularly when amateur video of the incident was posted to the internet. As Mr. Justice Thomas R. Braidwood commented in the final report of his Commission of Inquiry into the circumstances around Dziekański's death, "Mr. Dziekański's death appears to have galvanized public antipathy for the Force and its members. That is regrettable, because the most important weapon in the arsenal of the police is public support" (Braidwood 2010, 14).

A case in Toronto in 2013 similarly incited considerable public outrage toward the police. Eighteen-year-old Sammy Yatim was shot nine times and Tasered by police while standing alone in a streetcar that was surrounded by officers. Yatim was holding a knife. A Toronto police constable, James Forcillo, was convicted of second-degree murder and sentenced to a six-year jail sentence. The sentence was upheld by the Ontario Court of Appeal and the Supreme Court of Canada refused to hear any further appeal (Reddekop, April 30, 2018).

As Van Allen has noted, police powers of arrest and use of force are legally authorized in recognition of the reality that force—including deadly force—is sometimes necessary "to apprehend offenders, to compel their attendance in a court of law, to further investigations or to prevent or stop harmful acts" (Van Allen 2009, 83). In recognition that the use of force may sometimes be essential for effective law enforcement, use of force is sanctioned under section 25 of the *Criminal Code*.

> Everyone who is required or authorized by law to do anything in the administration or enforcement of the law

a) as a private person,
b) as a peace officer or public officer,
c) in aid of peace officer or public officer, or
d) by virtue of his/her office,

is, if she/he acts on reasonable grounds, justified in doing what she/he is required or authorized to do and in using as much force as is necessary for that purpose. [*Criminal Code* of Canada 1985]

Section 25 grants legal authority to use force not only to peace officers but to everyone. That is, read carefully, this section grants no more authority to police officers to use force than it does to ordinary citizens. Both citizens and the police are justified in using force as long as they are acting on reasonable grounds, justified in doing what is required, and using no more force than that which is necessary. What distinguishes the ordinary citizen from the police, however, is that in Canada and in many other jurisdictions, sworn police officers carry firearms and less lethal weapons as standard equipment and are trained in their use. Canadian police officers are therefore more likely than ordinary citizens to have the ability to deploy force, particularly deadly force. Nonetheless, in certain circumstances for the purpose of preventing loss of life or serious injury, ordinary citizens, just like the police, may justifiably resort to the use of force as long as it is reasonable and necessary in the circumstances.

Section 25, while authorizing police to use force, also constrains the use of force by the police to circumstances in which the police are acting lawfully. For example, if police were making an unlawful arrest, use of force would not be legal and indeed might constitute a criminal offence.

Police and others, including ordinary citizens, are also explicitly prohibited under section 26 of the *Criminal Code* from using excessive force and can be held criminally responsible.

Challenge Your Assumptions

Authorized Force

In 1986, after having been the victim of several armed robberies, pharmacist Steve Kesler began keeping a loaded shotgun under the counter at his drugstore in southwest Calgary.

In November of that year, Kesler was again robbed. On this occasion, he pursued the fleeing thief down the street with the shotgun in his hands. Subsequently he shot the thief in the back and killed him. Calgary police charged Kesler with second-degree murder. Kesler was found not guilty by a Calgary jury.

Given your understanding of sections 25 and 26 of the *Criminal Code*, do you think Kesler was justified in shooting the robber? If Kesler had been a police officer, rather than a private citizen, do you think the jury decision would have been different? Describe how you might feel and act had you been the victim of a series of armed robberies. Did Kesler take the law into his own hands? Should he have simply left the matter in the hands of the police?

Every one who is authorized by law to use force is criminally responsible for an excess thereof according to the nature and quality of the act that constitutes the excess. [*Criminal Code* of Canada 1985]

Use-of-Force Framework

As should be evident from the preceding discussion of Canadian criminal law, police are granted the authority to use force in the course of carrying out their lawful duties. Police, however, may be held criminally or civilly liable or both for the inappropriate use of force. Over approximately the last 40 years, law enforcement officials have sought to develop a conceptual tool that would aid in simplifying an understanding of the various dynamic contingencies that arise in the course of police encounters.

In 1999 a panel of 65 use-of-force experts and trainers from Canada and the United States were able to reach agreement on a single framework describing the use-of-force process utilized by police. This framework was endorsed by the Canadian Association of Chiefs of Police and was intended for use by police services and police officers across the country (Hoffman, Lawrence, and Brown 2004). This was an achievement of some significance since the agreement on the National Use-of-Force Framework represented "something no other country has yet been able to do" (Hoffman, Lawrence, and Brown 2004).

The illustration shown in Figure 8.1 is a visual conceptualization that seeks to convey the range of potential responses to police officer presence at a location of a call for service. The use-of-force framework represented in Figure 8.1 is a dynamic model subject to immediate change in a non-linear and non-sequential manner (Aveni 2003). That is, resistance to police (and police reactions to the resistance) do not proceed in a linear series of steps.

As Hoffman, Lawrence, and Brown have noted,

[i]mplementation of the national framework will ensure that police officers across the country receive consistent training in identifying, assessing and responding to use-of-force situations and that police officers, police organizations, the legal establishment, and the public across Canada have a common terminology and understanding [for] evaluating police use of force. [2004]

Embedded within the framework are key principles, including the following:

- The primary responsibility of a peace officer is to preserve and protect life.
- The primary objective of any use of force is to ensure public safety.
- Police officer safety is essential to public safety.
- The National Use-of-Force Framework does not replace or augment the law; the law speaks for itself.
- The National Use-of-Force Framework was constructed in consideration of (federal) statute law and current case law. [Hoffman, Lawrence, and Brown 2004]

Most importantly, the National Use-of-Force Framework is not a mechanism for justifying use of force by officers, nor does it stipulate specific response options in specific situations. Fundamentally, the framework was developed to assist in the training of police

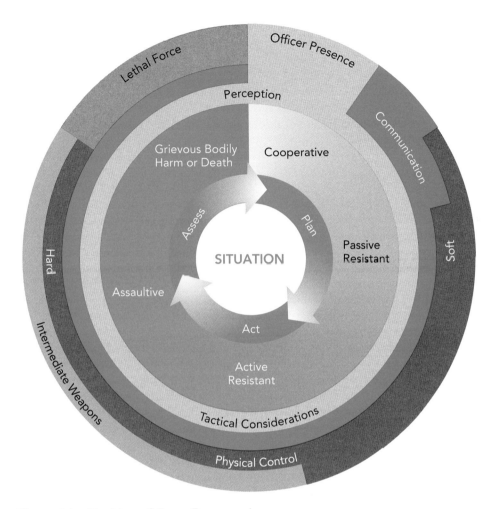

Figure 8.1   The Use-of-Force Framework

Source: The Canadian Association of Chiefs of Police, National Use-of-Force Model. Reprinted with permission.

officers and as a reference when making decisions. It is also intended as a common heuristic device for explaining police officer actions with respect to the use force, particularly in court hearings (Hoffman, Lawrence, and Brown 2004).

Priority Calls

General-duty patrol officers are routinely dispatched to calls for service. Calls that arrive at a 911 call centre are rated in priority sequence. Although the nomenclature of calls can vary from one police agency to another, the most urgent calls (involving potential loss of life or serious crime in progress) are classified as Priority 1 calls. Officers responding to Priority 1 calls are expected to give immediate attention to such calls. However, so said, responding officers have considerable discretion in deciding how to get there. Responding officers, depending on the priority given to the call, along with their distance from the destination, traffic, road and weather conditions, and time of day, may decide to activate their vehicle's emergency equipment (lights and siren) and drive as quickly and safely to the scene as possible. The exercise of discretion in how officers respond and the manner in which they operate their police vehicles was addressed in Chapter 5. Of course, activation of the emergency equipment does not absolve them from safety considerations. The same is true for police pursuits.

Police Pursuits

Two situations pose particular risks to patrol officers, both of which have received considerable attention in recent years and have resulted in a severe tightening of procedures. Both situations involve pursuits—either vehicle pursuits or foot pursuits (Dantzker and Mitchell 1998, 50). A pursuit occurs simply when a police officer attempts to detain or arrest a person of interest and the person fails to comply with the officer's request or command and endeavours to escape. The pursuit begins when the police give chase.

In relatively recent history, police in several Canadian jurisdictions have initiated vehicular high-speed pursuits that have led to the tragic deaths or serious injury of innocent bystanders when the suspect lost control of the vehicle or failed to stop for a traffic light. Invariably, the suspect was found not to be a violent offender fleeing a crime scene, but a youthful joyrider in a stolen vehicle who panicked at the sight of police lights behind him. Civil lawsuits in such cases have held police at least partially liable.

Of the two types of pursuits, vehicular pursuits are obviously the more dangerous, entailing high speeds and putting at considerable risk the pursuing officers, the suspects, and innocent bystanders. Recognizing the danger to all parties and cognizant of civil liability, police agencies in Canada have put very strict policies into place regarding vehicular pursuits. These policies stipulate the situations in which pursuits are permissible and specify procedures to be followed in the course of a pursuit. Unless the fleeing person is perceived on reasonable grounds to present an imminent and serious threat to others, vehicular pursuits are more than likely to be called off.

Police policies, particularly if patrol officers have identified the vehicle through the licence plate, require officers to abandon pursuits that have the potential to reach high speeds and endanger others. If a pursuit is warranted, pursuing officers, after engaging the emergency equipment (lights and sirens), are required immediately to alert the patrol supervisor via radio and provide the reason for the pursuit. They are also required to keep the supervisor immediately abreast of such factors as street location, road conditions, traffic congestion, nature of the neighbourhood, and the speeds being reached.

A major consideration underpinning these policies is that pursuing officers can get caught up in the heat of the chase and lose objectivity. Reporting the pursuit and its circumstances to the patrol supervisor is intended to shift responsibility for the pursuit from the pursuing officer to the supervisor, who has the authority to order the pursuit halted if he or she perceives that the circumstances (and evolving conditions) have grown dangerous. Patrol officers who ignore or neglect the supervisor's orders or who fail to adhere to departmental policies face departmental disciplinary measures.

While foot pursuits can be dangerous for patrol officers, they rarely hold the same potential for harming innocent bystanders. Empirical research on foot pursuits is lacking compared to the extensive studies conducted on vehicle pursuits. Nevertheless, many police agencies have implemented formal policies governing foot pursuits to ensure that officers, innocent bystanders, and suspects are not put at risk. The limited data compiled about police foot pursuits indicate that suspects intent on fleeing from the police are often impaired by drugs, alcohol, or mental illness and have prior criminal records, including convictions for violent behaviour (Kaminski and Alpert 2013).

Guidelines governing foot pursuits stipulate that, if two or more officers are in pursuit, they will not separate unless they remain in sight of each other. If a lone officer is engaged, he or she is expected to keep the suspect in sight from a safe distance. Restrictions prevent officers from following suspects into buildings, confined spaces, or wooded or isolated areas. Officers are also required to maintain radio contact (often difficult when running) and await support to facilitate the establishment of a containment area. As with vehicle pursuits, if a suspect's identity is established (or other information exists that allows for the suspect's later apprehension) and there is no immediate threat to the public or to police, pursuits are to be discontinued.

Active Shooter

Of significant importance to patrol officers is the recent development and implementation of **active shooter** response policies. While not a new phenomenon, police in Canada and elsewhere have been required to develop strategic responses to shooting incidents that occur in public places, schools, universities, or in work settings. Active shooter incidents present serious and complex challenges for first responders who are almost inevitably patrol officers.

As noted by the Conference Board of Canada (2015), these incidents are relatively rare in Canada compared to the United States. However, "[f]or law enforcement, whether they are dealing with a rapidly moving shooter or a barricaded suspect who might have taken hostages, makes a big difference in terms of how the situation is handled. It is the fluid, unpredictable environment that makes active shooter situations particularly dangerous to both law enforcement and civilians caught in the middle" (Conference Board Canada 2015, 3).

Particularly challenging for law enforcement generally is the lack of a clearly defined profile of an active shooter. Three very broad categories of active shooters have emerged:

- those who target their own school or workplace out of a perceived grievance against classmates, teachers, co-workers, or supervisors;
- those who suffer from psychological problems such that they act violently against a random target;
- those who are motivated by a terrorist ideology and who seek to cause mass casualties in order to create public fear and to draw attention to a political issue (Conference Board of Canada 2015, 6).

In the past, through the 1970s and 1980s, police officers were trained to set up a perimeter and contain an active shooter until Emergency Response Teams (ERTs) could deploy. However, by the 1990s, it had become apparent to law enforcement that delays in confronting the shooter could actually result in death or grievous harm to innocent persons. As a result, police agencies in Canada established and implemented Immediate Action Rapid Deployment (IARD) training programs. However, given the unpredictability of the virtually unlimited possible active shooter scenarios that could potentially play out, there is no one-size-fits-all training or response routine that can be mobilized. Just as the motivations of an active shooter are context-dependent, so are the optimal responses of law enforcement. Nonetheless, the decisive element in IARD training used by the RCMP and other Canadian police agencies is that police officers are now trained and expected to advance on the threat. The training thus puts emphasis on making contact, confronting the threat, and subduing it as quickly as possible. In other words, IARD allows trained police officers to engage an active shooter immediately, and to take whatever action they deem necessary, rather than attempting to contain the threat (Aulie 2017).

Active shooter incidents raise the threat potential for responding police officers. More specifically, events in Canada, such as the 2005 Mayerthorpe, Alberta, murder of four RCMP officers and the 2014 Moncton, New Brunswick, murder of two RCMP officers revealed that police officers were the intended target of active shooters. Alongside the IARD training programs, the RCMP has found that patrol officers armed only with handguns were underequipped and unable to respond adequately to the threats they faced. As a result, the RCMP has committed to acquiring and training all officers in the use of semi-automatic rifles (known as "patrol carbines"), which provide greater range and accuracy than the standard-issue handgun. Both IARD and the use of semi-automatic rifles are now incorporated in the curriculum taught new recruits at the RCMP training facility in Regina.

Complicating successful police intervention in active shooter scenarios is the resulting—and understandable—inevitable panic and chaos. For example, the 2014 Parliament Hill shooting death of Corporal Nathan Cirillo, a Canadian army reservist serving as a voluntary Honour Guard at the National War Memorial in Ottawa, triggered considerable concern and confusion since panicked members of the public found it hard to distinguish armed plainclothes

Ben Russell/EPA/Shutterstock

One strategy used in dangerous situations such as active shooter scenarios is the use of robots as a tool of reconnaissance. The robot pictured was used in Moncton to investigate a building in which an active shooter—who had shot three RCMP officers—was thought to have been hiding. The robot was used to determine whether the suspect was in the building and whether they had any hostages.

officers from potential active shooters. Furthermore, several off-duty officers in plain-clothes self-deployed as events unfolded, only adding to the confusion. Police themselves therefore had difficulty distinguishing other police officers from civilians and from potential active shooters (Conference Board of Canada 2015).

Additionally, as police responses become more sophisticated, so do active shooter strategies. For example, the 2020 Nova Scotia mass shooter dressed like an RCMP officer and drove a mock police cruiser, causing members of the public to be unable to distinguish the active shooter from the police, aiding in the shooter's ability to evade police for hours (Humphries, 2020).

With police agencies in Canada increasingly prepared to respond to critical incidents, it is perhaps fortunate that with regard to active shooters, Canadian numbers are low with no indications of an upward trend (Conference Board of Canada 2015, 5).

Conclusion

Chapter 8 began with a discussion of the essential component of modern policing: uniformed patrol work. Given the significance of patrol work to modern policing, attention was directed to several aspects of uniformed patrol work: patrol methods, patrol allocation, uniformed police relations with plainclothes detectives, and the three principal legal authorities granted to police officers by the *Criminal Code* of Canada. The chapter concluded with a review of high-speed pursuits and with a discussion of responses to active shooters.

Critical Thinking Questions

1. What do you think are the most important functions of uniformed patrol officers?
2. Does the *Charter* go too far in protecting the rights of persons suspected of committing crimes?
3. Describe the purpose and use of the National Use-of-Force Framework. Is such a framework necessary for Canadian police?
4. Of the three fundamental powers given to the police, which is the most important for police to be able to enforce the law effectively? Why?

Endnotes

i   In addition to an appearance notice or summons, accused persons may also be released on the basis of a signed promise to appear, a recognizance (a deposit of money or other valuable security, not exceeding $500), or an undertaking.

ii   Typically provinces appoint court officials other than provincial court judges to preside over such relatively routine matters as judicial interim release (bail hearings) and for determining arrest or search warrant applications. Often these officials are available to police officers at all hours of the day via telephone, facsimile, or video conferencing. In Ontario, for example, justices of the peace perform these functions. British Columbia utilizes officials designated as judicial justices.

9

Investigations

Learning Objectives

After reading and studying this chapter, students will be able to:

- Describe and discuss police investigations in Canada.
- Explain different police investigative techniques from patrol to complex major investigations.
- Describe and discuss the gathering of admissible evidence by applying investigative techniques and strategies within the boundaries of law and the *Charter*.
- Explain how disruption, mitigation, and proactive strategies work to prevent or reduce criminal activity.
- Describe and discuss investigations in the context of being successful or failed and how wrongful convictions may result.
- Describe and discuss how policing is a stressful occupation and can lead to detrimental health issues including post-traumatic stress disorder.

Introduction

There is no standard definition of what constitutes a police investigation; however, a typical one comprises a number of activities carried out by police. Fundamentally, an investigation is a form of inquiry undertaken by the police for the purpose of determining the truth of a matter. More specifically, a police investigation involves examining the facts of a specific situation, gathering information through appropriate legal means, and establishing whether there have been, or in some cases will be, any criminal offences committed. An investigation may involve conducting surveillance, debriefing confidential informers, interviewing witnesses, and having an analyst search the open internet for additional information. This chapter introduces the most common police investigative techniques and explains how they are used to gather admissible evidence for the court process and to assure public safety by disrupting criminal activity.

Investigation is what police work is really all about. Both uniformed and plainclothes police officers conduct investigations. The main difference between uniformed and plainclothes investigations rests in the complexity of the investigation and the specialized skill set required. As patrol officers are first responders and their time is limited, often it is not reasonable for them to carry out more time-consuming and complex investigations. Most plainclothes investigators have a breadth of patrol experience from which they learned how to multitask, protect crime scenes, work under pressure, and develop and refine investigative skill sets like interviewing. Most plainclothes investigators were competent patrol officers who have proven themselves and are ready to focus and add to their training and experience in more complex investigative strategies.

Uniformed patrol officers are generalists who, by virtue of being first responders, are exposed to virtually everything police officers must deal with. They are always first at a scene, have the most frequent contact with members of the public, and must deal with the challenge of never knowing what is coming next. As a result, uniformed patrol officers are often the first line of investigation.

For example, when a patrol officer is first at the scene at a homicide, most certainly the investigation will be passed on to plainclothes investigators who have the experience, training, time, and access to specialized resources to solve the homicide. It can take a sustained effort and multiple teams to deal with even a relatively straightforward homicide. Although, as discussed in Chapter 8, the rift between patrol and plainclothes is real, one should not believe that any given plainclothes investigator is necessarily a better investigator than one in patrol, but there is a difference in roles and responsibilities. Few complex investigations are initiated by plainclothes investigators. It is far more often patrol officers who deal with the situation in the first instance, secure evidence, and lay the groundwork for a successful investigation. Successful police work is about working as a team.

From a criminological perspective, much is known about uniformed patrol policing, community policing initiatives, and first-responder duties; however, there has not been much of a focus on plainclothes investigations. This chapter introduces the main plainclothes "detective" investigative strategies and how they may be used to solve crime.

Investigation is the process of identifying and lawfully acquiring pieces of a puzzle, determining how the pieces fit together, and learning what the puzzle itself looks like when complete. The scope of police investigations is vast, ranging from minor property offences to gathering evidence about organized crime or threats to national security. Depending on the size of a particular police agency, investigations as they become more complex and require certain expertise are typically broken down into specialized units. Larger police agencies will have plainclothes sections that are separated into such specialized units as drugs, fraud, robbery, arson, sex crimes, serious crime, and street crime. The street crime unit targets crimes committed by prolific offenders. Smaller police agencies, due to limited resources and budgets, tend to have more generalized investigative units that taken on a range of criminal investigations.

Attention to Detail

From the training academy through to recruit field training on the street, police officers are taught to pay attention to detail. Paying attention to detail may mean taking good notes, taking time to make relevant observations at a crime scene, or assessing a person by watching for **threat cues** in a potential use-of-force situation. It may also mean carefully observing body language and listening to voice tones and choice of words during an in-custody **warned interview**.

Attention to detail is particularly important when arriving at any crime scene, whether the crime scene is a fatal motor vehicle accident, an armed robbery, or a sexual assault. Indeed, there may be some truth in popular television "real crime" shows such as *The First 48*, which highlights that the first 48 hours after a crime are critical in identifying valuable evidence. However, since every case is different, criminal investigations may proceed in various ways.

Street Checks

Street checks by police officers can be an effective investigative tool. Police engage the public in a variety of situations, including questioning people at the location of a crime that has just occurred, conducting foot patrols in high-crime areas, or otherwise checking persons who appear to be suspicious. For example, if there has been a rash of car break-ins in a residential area, police may focus patrol efforts in the area during the times when these crimes have been committed. If a patrol officer observes an adult male wearing dark clothing, carrying a backpack and "actively checking" door handles on various parked cars at 2:00 a.m., the officer would have the legal authority to detain that person for the purpose of further investigation (*R. v. Mann* 2004 SCC; see also Chapter 2). Depending on how the police conduct themselves during street checks, including how the check itself is explained to the individuals checked, the results tend to be positive for both parties, more often than not. It is all about balance.

La Vigne, Lachman, Matthews, and Neusteter (2012, 5) stated that while pedestrian stops and searches may have a negative effect on police–community relations, they also present an opportunity to enhance interactions between law enforcement and the public. As long as police explain why they want to talk to any particular individual and maintain a professional, fair, polite, and respectful demeanour during street checks, the public will support this type of encounter. However, if police officers fail to take into account the potential for negative public perceptions of such encounters, police actions will not necessarily be viewed as legitimate or appropriate by the general public (Tyler and Fagan 2008, 6).

Canadian media outlets have sometimes referred to police street checks as "carding," a term that is often used to describe the manner in which some officers detain individuals and collect and document personal information about them. This characterization of street checks by the media as carding conveys the notion that such actions by the police fall outside the legal principles set out in *R v. Mann* 2004 SCC. So said, relative to certain interactions with the public, Ontario created "new rules" for Ontario police officers that took effect on January 1, 2017 (see https://www.ontario.ca/page/street-checks). Nova Scotia took the exceptional step of "banning" police street checks (Ray, 2019). While there may be subtleties in practice from region to region, "investigative detention" as defined within *R v. Mann* 2004 SCC remains the law in this country.

From the Patrol Officer to Specialized Units

Many calls for service attended by uniformed patrol officers require more time, effort, and resources than patrol officers have available. When that happens, other units, often specialized units of plainclothes officers or detectives, take over the investigation. Serious or child sexual assault, homicide, robberies, arson, and more complex drug investigations are among those that require time, resources, and at times, specialized expertise.

Assessing resources, time, and the type of investigative strategies needed is based on a number of factors, including the seriousness of the offence, what evidence is available in the first instance, and the strength of that evidence. For example, a shooting in a nightclub may have several independent witnesses and video evidence, both of which can be instrumental in identifying the shooter. Even with that type of evidence, there is a great deal of work to independently corroborate those accounts and observations of what transpired, along with establishing m.   e, identifying parties to the offence (i.e., a conspiracy; see *Criminal Code* section 21), and   rmining planning and intent.

A homicide related to drug or   activity can be even more difficult to solve. Issues such as witnesses being afraid to come to   d for fear of retaliation, being afraid of testifying, and many other issues complicate the   ring of evidence that can be presented in court. It is not uncommon for homicide, organi.   rime, and national security investigations to be forced to turn to the most complex, resou.   heavy, expensive investigative strategies to solve cases. Strategies requiring periods of pi.,   l and/or electronic surveillance (tracking devices) carried out by teams of police office.   cution of multiple judicial authorizations, and wiretap and undercover operations all .   ire substantial expertise and appropriate financial and human resources.

Linkage Blindness

Criminal offenders rarely pay attention to police geographic boundaries. Unfortunately, there is a well-documented history of Canadian police agencies in different jurisdictions failing to share information with each other. This has resulted in offenders continuing to commit crimes in two or more jurisdictions for prolonged periods. Examples of investigations in which police were subject to extended criticism include the Clifford Olson, Paul Bernardo, and Robert Pickton serial murder cases. In each of these cases, the offenders were committing their crimes in more than one police jurisdiction.

Steven Egger (1984) coined the phrase "linkage blindness" to describe the inability of police to connect crimes sharing a similar pattern due to a lack of effective police communication. Largely as a result of the above-mentioned cases, Canadian police have made significant efforts to address linkage blindness. For example, police agencies now maintain shared databases for searching, reporting, and managing ongoing investigations. Examples of shared databases include the Police Reporting and Occurrence System (PROS), Police Records Information Management Environment (PRIME), and the Automated

Criminal Intelligence Investigation System (ACIIS). (For more discussion about records management, see Chapter 10.)

Interagency collaboration and communication have also been fostered by the development of joint force operations (JFOs) in which two or more police agencies share human and financial resources. Cooperating agencies now routinely second specialized personnel to integrated policing units, such as the Combined Forces Special Enforcement Unit (CFSEU) whose mandate is to disrupt organized crime groups through comprehensive, sustained, focused investigations. CFSEU teams are present in Vancouver, Kelowna, Toronto, Montreal, Alberta, Nova Scotia, and Saskatchewan and are made up of RCMP and municipal and provincial police officers who are seconded or assigned to CFSEU. In recognition of the fact that crime, especially organized crime, has no borders, there are many other examples of police agencies working short- and long-term JFOs with agencies other than CFSEU. As well, agencies work together with the United States and other countries around the world every day. For example, the RCMP has regular member liaison officers who are posted for years at a time in Los Angeles; Bogota, Colombia; Pretoria, South Africa; Mexico City, Mexico; and many other locations.

Communication among Agencies

Effective policing entails effective communication at several different levels. Sharing information among police agencies is vital. For example, Mr. Justice Archibald Campbell conducted an inquiry into the criminal investigations of serial rapist and multiple murderer Paul Bernardo, who committed his crimes in southern Ontario in the early 1990s. Several police jurisdictions had been conducting ongoing simultaneous investigations before Bernardo was apprehended. Mr. Justice Campbell's examination of the simultaneous investigations concluded that had police worked together and shared information more openly, Bernardo would likely have been apprehended much sooner.

Among other conclusions, Justice Campbell identified the need for a system of case management for major inter-jurisdictional serial crime investigations. As Campbell noted in his final report, the shortcoming of police efforts to identify and apprehend Bernardo is "a story of systemic failure" (Campbell 1996, 1). Two years after the release of the Campbell report, the Kaufman Commission, also in Ontario, examined the wrongful conviction of Guy Paul Morin and found "systemic problems, as well as the failings of individuals." Justice Kaufman stated that "it is no coincidence that the same systemic problems are those identified in wrongful convictions in other jurisdictions worldwide" (Kaufman 1998, 1). In part, the findings of the Campbell and Kaufman inquiries fuelled the development of a robust accountability mechanism for police investigations in Canada.

Investigative Success, Failure, and Wrongful Convictions

Whether or not a police investigation is considered successful is a matter of context. Generally, a successful investigation is one in which the police are able to gather evidence that demonstrates whether or not the subject(s) in an investigation has (have) knowledge of or involvement in a criminal offence. An investigation that excludes a suspect from further consideration, and an investigation that supports criminal charges are both regarded as successes. At its most basic, the result of a successful investigation is the uncovering of truth.

The overwhelming majority of police investigations are successful. Routinely, police charge suspects with offences to which the vast majority of offenders plead guilty. While investigations may successfully identify the individual(s) responsible for an offence, police nonetheless may exercise discretion and decide not to pursue criminal charges. Examples of this may occur in cases where illicit drugs are seized but no charges are laid or, more simply, when warnings are given for traffic violations.

In the context of serious, complex investigations such as homicide, organized crime, and national security investigations, the ramifications of failures within the investigative process can have serious consequences. Unsolved crimes, unsuccessful prosecutions, unpunished offenders, and wrongful convictions bring the criminal justice system into disrepute (Rossmo 2008, 3).

Rossmo (2008) identifies police cognitive biases such as perception, intuition, tunnel vision, organizational traps, groupthink, rumour, ego, and probability errors as factors in failed investigations. Specialized investigative units within police agencies are now acutely aware of these potential pitfalls and address them through rigorous in-service training and by adhering to the principles of Major Case Management. However, every investigation has its own practical and legal hurdles and while many may be similar, none are ever the same. Critical thinking, objectivity, teamwork, information sharing, and close liaison with Crown counsel for legal advice on an ongoing basis are key to sound investigations.

Wrongful Convictions

Despite the many checks and balances throughout the criminal justice system, including the presumption of innocence and a range of due process safeguards—many of which were formalized in 1982 in the Canadian *Charter of Rights and Freedoms* (see Chapter 2)—Canada has nonetheless seen innocent people found guilty of crimes they did not commit. The reasons underpinning investigative failures may well be those that lead to wrongful convictions; however, there are always factors unique to each case. MacFarlane (2008, 6) identified two principal themes that were apparent in a review of wrongful conviction cases in Canada, other Commonwealth countries, and the United States. The first theme related to "public and media pressure on law enforcement agencies" and the second theme related to "the reaction of justice system participants to public and media perceptions of the case". Both themes are directly related to pressure to obtain results as quickly as possible, often setting the stage for an investigation or a prosecution to fail. The development and evolution of the principles of Major Case Management has been a key police response to investigative failures and a significant measure intended to avoid the previously listed investigative pitfalls.

Major Case Management is intended to control investigations of major criminal incidents by ensuring accountability; clear goals and objectives; planning; effective utilization of resources; and ongoing monitoring of the speed, flow, and direction of investigations. Major Case Management is a best-practices model or framework through which police manage investigations in order to ensure competent and successful results.

Challenge Your Assumptions

The Nine Elements of Major Case Management (MCM)

The following nine elements of Major Case Management (MCM) are relevant to understanding accountability in the course of investigation work:

1) the command triangle (team commander, primary investigator, file coordinator);
2) communication (briefings, media, collaborative police efforts/joint forces operations);
3) leadership and team building (accountability, work ethic, training);
4) management considerations (financial accountability and resourcing);
5) crime-solving strategies (investigative strategies appropriate to the circumstance to provide the best chance at gathering admissible evidence);

6) ethical considerations (in all aspects of the complete investigation, investigative strategy, and dealing with victims of crime and families);
7) accountability mechanisms (appropriate oversight of all functions);
8) legal considerations (search and seizure, legal applications, interview strategies); and
9) partnerships (within the lead police force and with other policing partners, solid working relationship with Crown counsel) (Royal Canadian Mounted Police 2012).

What parts of these did you expect to see as part of case management? Were there any you didn't expect?

Crime Scene

When any crime has occurred, an examination of the scene as quickly as possible is critically important. Evidence, particularly forensic evidence, can be lost, moved, or destroyed within a brief period of time. Microscopic DNA evidence is affected by weather and moisture at an outdoor crime scene, as well as by cold, heat, and other factors. Depending on the environment, DNA can degrade and be lost forever. Most often, police officers at a crime scene will make every effort to leave the scene *in situ* for photographs and measurements that record the crime. This may be critical to the rest of the investigation. For example, at a murder, cause of death, the way the body is positioned, the existence of blood spatter, and establishing how long the body has been there are all examples of how the police try to tell the story by working backwards to understand what happened, and ultimately to identify and charge the person or persons responsible. Maintaining the integrity of any crime scene and, from that, proper handling and further examination of any exhibits seized, are critical to investigations. The type of crime scene also dictates the need for other expertise.

Establishing the points of entry and exit at a residential break and enter assists in identifying how the offender entered the home and whether or not there may be forensic evidence, such as fingerprints or DNA. Examining the scene where a sexual assault took place is key to finding clues to establish what may have happened. At a murder scene,

Jack Dagley Photography/Shutterstock.com

Forensic evidence is easily lost, moved, destroyed, or missed without the help of experts to capture and preserve everything there is to find.

blood stain analysis, hair and fibre examination, and DNA swabbing are all methods of investigation that may locate key evidence that may be tied back to the person or persons who committed the murder.

A serious car accident may also be a crime scene. The photographs of the scene, assessment of skid marks, measurements of the distance from impact, and condition of the vehicles themselves are all evidence that piece back how the accident occurred. Such investigative efforts can establish the truth about the circumstances and identify who caused the accident.

Civilian Specialists

Police investigators regularly draw upon the skills of civilian scientists, doctors, and other highly specialized job functions to advance investigations. (For more discussion of forensic science and civilian specialists, see Chapter 10.) As dictated by the circumstances, an outdoor homicide scene in a forested area where the body appears to have been for some time may be subject to digital photography, physical measurements, fingerprints, hair and fibre examination, chemical analysis, and the use of experts in forensic odontology, anthropology, pathology, and entomology. For example, Dr. Gail Anderson, a forensic entomologist at Simon Fraser University, is often called upon to assist in determining how long the body has been dead and how long it has been in the forest by analyzing insect activity in and around the body. (Find out more at https://gsanderson0.wixsite.com/site). On human remains, forensic odontologists may assist with examination of teeth and may be called upon to prepare the tooth or teeth for a subsequent forensic process that will try to identify a DNA profile in the pulp of the tooth.

Police investigations in Canada do not unfold as shown on television shows such as the popular *CSI* series. While *CSI* will depict one police officer conducting his or her own crime scene analysis, performing some forensic lab work, conducting surveillance, and being the lead on the interview of the suspect, the reality is that most of these functions are specialized. It is generally not possible for one police officer to have skill sets required in all areas. For example, the patrol officer who shows up first at scene at a homicide in a house will first contain the scene and protect it without disturbing evidence. The next personnel at the scene may be forensic identification specialists who document the scene through photographs and measurements and then search for physical evidence including fingerprints and DNA.

Depending on the crime scene, blood spatter and other specialized examinations may take place. Any exhibits seized by the designated police officer will be carefully documented and any exhibit that may require forensic analysis by the laboratory will be assessed by a civilian scientist. DNA analysis will be carried out by a civilian scientist with appropriate expertise. From the investigative standpoint, a multitude of skill sets may be required.

Major Case Management

Any major investigation (homicide, international drug trafficking, gang, organized crime, or national security) in Canada is most commonly carried out by investigative teams who adhere to the principles of Major Case Management (MCM) as earlier described. Once the **MCM triangle** is in place, other expertise may be called upon, including legal application support and interview teams, criminal profilers, surveillance team members, and covert operations that may include undercover, wiretap, and other support services. While many police officers are cross-trained and very good at many things, the majority of serious investigations are dealt with by those with the highest skill sets in the area that is required. It is generally accepted that having many specialized units work in a team format brings about higher success rates. For example, on most occasions, a post-arrest, in-custody warned interview of a suspect in a murder is carefully planned weeks in advance by police officers who are highly trained for the purpose. The team members will analyze every piece of available evidence, consider all investigative theories, understand as much as they can about the person they will be interviewing, and develop strategies to help them seek the truth from the suspect. Often called fact-driven interviews, many hours of work go into preparation long before the suspect is even arrested.

DNA Evidence in Context

While forensic DNA evidence has revolutionized policing and been an incredible tool to help charge, convict, and exonerate suspects, it is important to understand that a DNA "hit," a crime scene match to an individual, may not in and of itself be sufficient to approve charges to engage the court process. For example, crime scene DNA on the body of a murder victim that is matched to a particular suspect is compelling and will direct the police to focus other investigative efforts on that suspect. Those investigative efforts will work on independently corroborating the DNA evidence. The complete investigation will focus on establishing motive, intent, and whether any planning was involved; identifying other persons who played a particular role and whether there was a conspiracy; confirming cause of death; and retrieving weapons or other physical evidence. In addition, while a DNA hit may seem like a sure thing, the danger of **tunnel vision** must always be mitigated through the active investigation of alternative theories and suspects who have been identified within the investigation.

Holdback Evidence

Holdback evidence is evidence that only the person or persons who committed the criminal offence would know about. (See also Chapter 14.) At a homicide scene where the cause of death was from the use of a firearm, holdback evidence might be the calibre of the bullet used, the number of times the victim was shot, and the locations of those shots. Another example of holdback could be the type and amount of accelerant used to commit an arson and the location where the fire ignited. Holdback evidence is carefully protected by police, even among the police officers involved in the investigation, in order to protect the integrity of the investigation for court purposes. Few investigators will be made aware of the holdback information. If information that only the suspect would know is obtained by police through the words of the suspect (using undercover operations, interview confession, wiretap) or can be corroborated from other investigative means, this evidence can be very compelling in court.

Neighbourhood Canvassing

Neighbourhood canvassing is a form of searching for witnesses and it often provides good results. For example, a drive-by shooting in a residential neighbourhood is a crime type where many relevant things could have been observed before, during, and after the shots were fired. When a drive-by shooting occurs, a statement from the person or persons who appear to be the intended victim(s) will be taken to determine why they may have been a target. Information from the victim(s) is complemented by police database checks and other investigative steps that are conducted contemporaneously. Officers canvassing a neighbourhood will ask people if they saw or heard anything at all, including the suspect vehicle itself or any suspicious vehicle in the area prior to the shooting. Often the path that the vehicle travelled can be ascertained by putting the puzzle pieces together from the individual pieces of information that a number of people give the police.

Inquiring about video surveillance in residential homes that look out onto the street can be very useful. Residents may have video and/or pictures of the actual vehicle. The canvass will often move out from the crime scene in concentric circles, putting all the information together. It is not uncommon for those involved in a drive-by shooting to have staged or planned their route and what they intend to do prior to carrying out

vmargineanu/iStockphoto

A group of officers canvass an area in Laval, Quebec. Canvassing is slow, tedious work, and it is often not known whether it will pay off with evidence until after it has been done. How can police services manage the time of their officers effectively to ensure time spent canvassing is time well spent?

the act. These actions may take place at a nearby school or gas station parking lot and, while apparently innocuous at the time, may become very important later to solving a serious crime.

Video Canvassing

Video canvassing of businesses and residences is an effective police investigative tool. For example, the collection and analysis of video evidence was critical to identifying those responsible for the damage done during the G8/G20 incidents in Toronto and the Vancouver riots of 2011. The tool has become a routine way to collect evidence of criminal acts and activity. Video canvassing entails police officers going door to door to businesses and residences and asking to view any video that may be available at the specific point in time that is relevant to the offence(s). Businesses and the public are not lawfully required to cooperate with police in such instances, but most do because the reduction of crime is in the broader public interest. However, if reasonable grounds exist to obtain a judicial authorization, police may also have the authority to search for and seize the required video, depending on the circumstances. As technology has evolved and vehicle dashboard video cameras are more common, police often solicit the public to submit "dash cam" video for a variety of investigations.

Interviews

Police interviewing is arguably the most fundamental aspect of any criminal investigation because it elicits the information from witnesses, victims, and suspects that is required to successfully resolve cases (Snook et al. 2010, 204). Witness testimony and suspect confessions are some of the most persuasive forms of evidence considered in a trial. There are many different kinds of interviews, including witness interviews, out-of-custody suspect interviews, post-arrest interviews, and in-custody warned interviews of suspects. The ability to talk to people and elicit information is a core investigative skill and significant training is invested by police agencies to develop this skill. Interviewing has evolved significantly over the years and it is common for police officers to carefully plan their interviews, setting out objectives, identifying themes, and knowing their investigation intimately. Knowing the right questions to ask, being an active listener, and assessing truthfulness are critically important to be a good interviewer. Truthfulness is measured in part by what is said in the interview, the choice of words used, and assessing the body language of the interviewee. As a best practice, all police interviews are audio and/or video recorded to secure the best evidence for the courts.

Confidential Informers

One important form of intelligence-led policing involves accepting information from individuals who wish to give information to the police in confidence. A confidential informer is a member of the public who provides information to the police about criminal activity on a voluntary and confidential basis. Police are duty and legally bound to protect the identity of confidential informers, for reasons including threats to the personal safety of those who report on criminal activity. Yet, not everyone who gives information to the police is a confidential informer. It is one thing to be an informer; it is another thing to be a confidential informer. One need not give information to the police (Alberta Justice and Solicitor General 2008). However, should the police agree to promise the individual confidentiality, this relationship is then considered a form of legal privilege. The privilege relates to the fact that the identity of the confidential informer will be protected in law, as will specific information provided by the informer that would tend to identify the informer. In law, informer privilege enjoys a protected legal status higher than that of doctor–client or even solicitor–client privilege. The rule of legal privilege related to confidential informers is summarized as follows:

> [I]nformer privilege is an ancient and hallowed protection which plays a vital role in law enforcement. It is premised on the duty of all citizens to aid in enforcing the law. The discharge of this duty carries with it the risk of retribution from those involved in crime. The rule of informer privilege was developed to protect citizens who assist in law enforcement and to encourage others to do the same. In summary, informer privilege is of such importance that it cannot be balanced against other interests. Once established, neither the police nor the court processes discretion to abridge it. [Public Prosecution Service of Canada 2014, 3]

Information from confidential informers requires ongoing reliability assessment by the police that should start with the police officer first asking the informer, "How do you know what you know?" (Is the information first-hand, second-hand, or the "word on the street"?) The police officer will also want to know the individual's motivation (for example, revenge, financial, or leading the police to take action on the competition) to come forward, why the person feels his or her identity must be kept confidential, how many other people know the same information, and what would happen if the police acted on the information provided.

For example, if the confidential informer tells the police officer that person A has two kilos of cocaine in an apartment, and that the informer saw it there one hour ago, it may be reasonable to believe that the cocaine will still be at the apartment; however, the question turns to who else may have seen the cocaine. If it is established that only one person would have known the cocaine was in the apartment and the police act on that knowledge by applying for and executing a search warrant based on the information from the informer, it is likely to "burn" the informer and so the police may choose not to proceed. Proceeding might not only affect the personal safety of the informer; it is likely that the Crown counsel would not be able to proceed with a prosecution because protecting informer privilege is a legal requirement (*R. v. Leipert* 1997, SCR). As Innes (2000, 381) noted, there are substantive practical concerns about secrecy and protecting the identity of confidential informers.

The credibility of a confidential informer is the most important factor to consider. For example, a Crime Stoppers' tip is from an anonymous source of unknown reliability. Therefore "on its face" a Crime Stoppers' tip may have little value; however, it may provide a starting point from which the police can take steps to independently corroborate the information given. On the other hand, should a Crime Stoppers' tip contain detailed specifics about a person or an event, it is possible that the police will not be able to use any of the information since any further investigation measures may result in the possible identification of the tipster, thereby putting him or her at considerable risk. For that reason, and depending on the circumstances, the content of certain Crime Stoppers' tips may never be relied upon as prosecutorial evidence.

Confidential informers whose identity is known to the police are assessed on the "three Cs" outlined by the Supreme Court of Canada (SCC) in *R. v. Debot* (1989): The information relied upon by police must be assessed as to whether it is compelling, whether the information is credible, and whether the information is independently corroborated. Debot (1989) confirms that "it is the totality of the circumstances that must meet the standard of reasonableness. Weaknesses in one area may, to some extent, be compensated by strengths in the other two."

The value of informers to the police is that informers possess insider knowledge. This knowledge is often acquired through the informer's own participation in crime or close affinity with those who engage in crime (Innes 2000, 358). Confidential informers can be extremely valuable to a police investigation because these individuals may be the only ones who have inside knowledge about the offences, the suspects, and key evidence. The police may not have been able to learn that information from any other source to that point. The police can then direct or re-direct their investigation accordingly. However, confidential informers are **not compellable** witnesses and therefore their overall value to the investigation is limited. For this reason and because the safety of confidential informers is a primary concern, dealing with informers is generally regarded as an area of high risk.

R. v. McKay 2016 BCCA presented a substantive change in law related to the handling of police information received from confidential informers. The decision revolved around the requirement of the Crown to disclose information from confidential informers. As discussed in Chapter 6, Stinchcombe disclosure requires the police to furnish all relevant "fruits of the investigation" evidence to the Crown in order to be reviewed and provided to defence counsel. Prior to McKay, police information related to confidential informers was rarely disclosed and essentially constituted a "blanket privilege." The McKay ruling set out specific circumstances where information received from confidential informers may be disclosed, with appropriate vetting applied to protect informer privilege (information that would identify, or tend to identify or "narrow the pool" of persons who could be the informer).

Judicial Authorizations

Section 8 of the *Charter* is the "right to be free from unreasonable search and seizure." As with all *Charter* rights, however, the Section 8 right is not absolute. As **agents of the state**, police have significant powers and among them is the ability to apply for judicial authorizations (for example, search warrants or production orders) to search for evidence. There are many different provisions in the *Criminal Code* (CC) and the *Controlled Drugs and Substances Act* (CDSA) that authorize the police to obtain judicial authorizations for specific purposes such as tracking (492.1 CC), production order (487.014 CC), general (487.01 CC), DNA (487.05 CC), search (487 CC), or search for controlled substances (11 CDSA) (*Criminal Code* 1985). To apply for any judicial authorization, the police officer must prepare an "information to obtain" or affidavit that lays out the facts and evidence about the case and states reasons why the police officer has reasonable grounds to suspect or to believe that the Justice should issue the warrant (or order) requested.

The essential test for the justice of the peace, Provincial Court judge, or Supreme Court judge reviewing an information to obtain or affidavit written by the police in support of warrant requests is to balance the societal interest in effective policing with individual privacy rights. In some way, each of these judicially authorized search tools allows the police to infringe on an innocent-until-proven-guilty person's Section 8 *Charter* right for the purpose of gathering evidence. Judicial authorizations of some kind are used in many police investigations and in all complex investigations.

Wiretap

Pursuant to Part VI (185, 186) of the *Criminal Code*, a police officer **affiant**, the police officer tasked with drafting the affidavit, will work together with a **designated Crown agent** and apply to the Supreme Court for an authorization to intercept private communications (a wiretap). This powerful tool constitutes a search; however, the search is for words and language, not for physical things. The test that the police must meet to obtain a full Part VI authorization is high, arising from the recognition of how intrusive this search tool is with regard to Section 8 of the *Charter*. While wiretaps can provide compelling evidence, this investigative strategy is very expensive and resource heavy, and is justified only in the most serious of matters. The checks and balances that the police must meet to be granted a full wiretap are significant.

Undercover Operations

Undercover operations have proven to be an effective tool to independently corroborate other evidence, to complement other investigative techniques such as wiretap investigations, and to obtain confessions. A great deal of planning and strategy is involved in determining the viability of a plan proposed by the investigative team wanting undercover operations. Short-term and longer-term undercover operations are carefully designed to help meet the objectives. In the short term, an undercover police officer may portray himself as a street-level drug dealer to do "buy and busts." Longer-term investigations can involve months of scenarios with the target(s), such as with the major crime technique.

The major crime technique (which has been referred to as Mr Big) is generally reserved for serious cases. Smith, Stinson, and Patry (2012, 319) note that this type of sting operation involves the use of undercover police officers to lure the suspect into becoming involved in a supposed criminal organization. Undercover officers befriend the suspect and involve him or her in a series of minor crimes and pay the suspect for these criminal activities. Once committed to the criminal organization, suspects are then interviewed for a higher-level job, but are told that they need to confess to some past crime as a form of insurance for the criminal gang. This confession serves as a pivotal piece of evidence against the defendant, often resulting in a conviction.

Criticism of the major crime technique has generally revolved around concern over false confessions. Information elicited from the suspect(s) through undercover operations must be independently corroborated by other evidence, and if statements made by the suspect match other evidence, especially holdback evidence (such as where the body of a homicide victim was hidden), this can be very compelling in court.

The Hart (SCC, 2014) decision is the law when it comes to police undercover operations. In Hart, the SCC highlighted the fact that the Mr Big technique is a Canadian invention and, as of 2008, it had been used more than 350 times. "The technique, used only in cases involving serious unsolved crimes, has secured confessions and convictions in hundreds of cases. The confessions wrought by the technique are often detailed and confirmed by other evidence." However, the SCC also said that "the suspects confess in the face of powerful inducements and sometimes veiled threats—and this raises the spectre of unreliable confessions." The SCC ultimately identified ten considerations as being relevant to Mr Big operations that the police must address in all future undercover operations.

Case Study

The Ten Considerations of R. v. Hart

Following the reasoning set out in the R. v. Mack (1988) decision, the 2014 Hart ruling by the SCC held that the following ten considerations are relevant to Mr. Big operations:

1) the type of crime being investigated and the availability of other techniques for the police detection of its commission;
2) the strength of the evidence causing the police to target the suspect;
3) the types and strength of inducements used by the police, including deceit, fraud, trickery, or reward;
4) the duration of the operation and the number of interactions between the police and the suspect;
5) whether the police conduct involved an exploitation of human characteristics such as the emotions of compassion, sympathy, and friendship;

6) whether the police appear to have exploited a particular vulnerability of the suspect such as mental, social, or economic vulnerabilities or substance addiction;
7) the degree of harm to the suspect that the police caused or risked;
8) the existence and severity of any threats, implied or express, made to the suspect by the police or their agents, including threats made to third parties where those threats carry an indirect threat to the accused;
9) whether an average person, with both strengths and weaknesses, in the position of the suspect would be induced to falsely confess;
10) the persistence and number of attempts made by the police before the suspect agreed to confess.

Police Agents

In another investigative strategy, police will recruit a civilian to act as a police agent. They enter into an agreement whereby the civilian will actively gather evidence on behalf of the police. This strategy may be for various serious investigations into organized crime, national security, homicides, and historical sexual assaults. Turcotte (2008) stated that law enforcement agencies feel that the "flipping" of criminal trade participants has become a necessary evil. The strategy may be considered high risk as the agent is most often infiltrating a target or group with the goal of gathering admissible evidence and then testifying against those whom the agent infiltrated. A police agent may be considered when no other viable investigative strategy is available to the police in the particular circumstance, or other investigative strategies have failed. For example, terrorism-related offences often involve individuals operating in close secrecy, a predicament that requires law enforcement officials to think creatively about how to extract information about a particular terrorist plot or group (Said 2010, 688).

There are a number of well-publicized cases where Canadian police have utilized police agents. *In R v. Vallee* (BCSC 2018), the police utilized several police agents, all of whom were former associates and friends of Cory Vallee, to gather evidence against him and others. Cory Vallee was a contract killer associated with the United Nations gang and later convicted for the first-degree murder of a rival gang member. In this case, two of the police agents were given the benefit of **immunity agreements** related to their own crimes and were paid $300,000 and 400,000 respectively, in exchange for gathering evidence against Vallee and for giving testimony about their actions. Witnesses who are accomplices of accused persons are often referred to as "Vetrovec witnesses," which is related to the Supreme Court of Canada case *Vetrovec v. The Queen* [1982]. The Vetrovec case examined how the courts should assess "unconfirmed testimony of accomplices." In the Vallee case, the judge noted that "extreme caution was required" relative to the credibility of the police agents.

In Canada, everything the agent does is guided by the *Charter* as if the agent were a police officer. Thus, pursuant to Section 25.1 of the Criminal Code, if the police direct the agent to break the law, the agent is subject to the same oversight as if he or she were a police officer.

E-Pandora

In 2004 and 2005, in Project E-Pandora, the RCMP utilized a police agent named Michael Plante to infiltrate the East End (Vancouver) chapter of the Hells Angels. He was paid a total of $1 million and is now in the witness protection program. As Bolan (2013) reported, Plante stated his reason for becoming a police agent was "to make a difference . . . and . . . to do something significant in [his] life" and not for a big payday. At the end of the investigation, twelve Hells Angels and associates were convicted for offences including trafficking cocaine and methamphetamine, extortion, conspiracy, possession of firearms and grenades, and contempt of court (Bolan 2013).

Behavioural Sciences

Behavioural sciences units are made up of highly specialized positions that are designed to support investigations in advancing serious crimes. Violent Crimes Linkage Analysis System (ViCLAS) personnel fall under the behavioural sciences umbrella in the RCMP, as do criminal profilers.

ViCLAS is a unit that analyzes information sent in from all police agencies who complete ViCLAS reports about serious crimes. The reports are comprehensive and cover information such as what the offender said to the victim, **modus operandi**, environment, time of day of the commission of the offence, and other factors. The information is designed to help identify unknown suspects by creating and analyzing links between case files.

Criminal profilers in Canada must meet internationally accepted standards as set by the US Federal Bureau of Investigation. The candidate must also complete studies at the FBI training academy in Quantico, Virginia.

Civilian Analysts

As will be covered in more detail in Chapter 13 in this textbook, civilian analysts are an excellent complement to the complete police investigation and are used by most Canadian police agencies. From analyzing crime trends and data from everyday occurrences, to analyzing phone records, to mining huge quantities of information from many databases, hard-working analysts provide critical support to police investigations. Intelligence-led policing relies heavily on the work of analysts and they are invaluable in helping uncover clues that are not easily found.

Mining Social Media to Support or Complement Other Investigative Strategies

The strategic challenges of monitoring social networks and transforming huge amounts of data into actionable intelligence can be a daunting task for police agencies (Community Oriented Policing Services and Police Executive Research Forum, 1). Police departments have recognized the value of using social media to obtain information, especially for tactical purposes such as gathering information about threats of mob violence, riots, or isolated criminal activity during otherwise lawful mass demonstrations. For example, at the 2010 G8/G20 summit held in Toronto, Ontario, documents obtained by the media showed that the RCMP and various Ontario police forces spent several months using undercover officers to infiltrate anti-war, anti-globalization, and anarchist groups before the summits in Huntsville and Toronto (Seglins 2011).

The Toronto Police Service collaborated with the RCMP, OPP, and other partners to form a Joint Intelligence Group (JIG) whose mandate was "to collect, collate, analyze and disseminate accurate information and intelligence in a timely manner to facilitate the decision-making process in both the planning and execution of securing the G8/G20 summits" (Toronto Police Service 2011). As part of that investigative strategy, the police and analysts within the JIG mined social media for information that could complement or independently corroborate other sources of information to support investigations into criminal activity and public safety issues. A similar JIG supported the 2010 Vancouver Winter Olympics. However, Davis III, Alves, and Sklansky (2014, 8) point out that the use of social media as an investigative tool is a practice that raises distinct issues pertaining to privacy and the risk of damaging public trust and willingness to engage with police.

The Report to Crown Counsel

The Report to Crown Counsel (RTCC) is a detailed, organized collection of information that tells a story about the offences alleged to have been committed by the suspects and provides all of the evidence gathered in support of charges to be considered for the court process. RTCCS vary in complexity and volume depending on the nature of the investigation. The evidence submitted for an impaired driving incident or a break and enter would be much less than the evidence collected from a massive joint forces organized crime file with multiple accused. The RTCC will include copies of any multimedia audio/video evidence, transcripts of statements from witnesses and accused, audio files, copies of warrants executed, and anything that the police have produced over the course of the investigation. The RTCC alerts the Crown to the nature and extent of the evidence to assist the Crown in considering charges and deciding what should be disclosed to defence counsel to meet Stinchcombe disclosure obligations (*R. v. Stinchcombe*, 1991, SCC). As highlighted in Chapter 6, the ruling in *R. v. Jordan*, 2016, SCC related to the right of the accused to a speedy trial is another important consideration for the Crown.

Disruption and Mitigation

Gang conflicts present themselves in any major city in North America and the threat to public safety is constant. Police work very hard to be proactive in disrupting gang activity and react quickly when violent acts are carried out, whether it be gang members shooting or killing rival gang members, or an incident where an innocent member of the public is harmed or killed. Many of these murders are retaliatory and situations present themselves where gang members are hunting other gang members in the streets. To stop these problems, the police engage multiple operations, some investigative to gather evidence of crimes, others to disrupt individual criminals and criminal groups. For example, the **Combined Forces Special Enforcement Unit** British Columbia (CFSEUBC) and the Vancouver Police Department created and engaged teams of specially trained uniformed police officers armed with intelligence-led strategies and sent them out in the field with specific instructions to target known criminal gang members and associates. These police officers are rigorous in checking these individuals on the street, in vehicles, and in businesses and restaurants. This creates the effect of the police taking back the streets, allows police to gather intelligence about criminal associates, and is a very effective enforcement tool that directly complements information and evidence gathered by other means.

Many business owners give the police the power to eject unsavoury customers such as known gang members from their establishments, simply by virtue of their presence. Police are aware that many of these gang members are at risk of being assaulted or shot by rival gang members, even in public settings. This reality presents an extreme risk to members of the public within the establishment and therefore the police remove the risk. An example of this was the 2012 murder of Vancouver gangster Sandip Duhre, who was publicly executed while sitting in a crowded restaurant at the Sheraton Wall Centre. The US women's national soccer team was nearby in the hotel lobby at the time (*CBC News*, 2012).

Disruption and mitigation strategies by police are often effective, and their effectiveness can be quantified by the reduction in violent crimes by the prolific offenders or targeted criminal group. Police are confident that homicides and other crimes of personal violence have been prevented through this sustained effort of acting on intelligence and information received and taking appropriate proactive steps to ensure the criminal acts are not carried out. Police can measure their efforts in a number of ways, including through wiretap investigations, undercover investigations, and information received from confidential informers. Unfortunately, the police are often not at liberty to publicly disclose how they know their disruption efforts have been successful and such efforts may very well not lead to a prosecution.

Police Officers and Mental Health

Policing is a distinctive occupation. According to G. Nemetz (personal communication, May 10, 2019), police patrol work is fraught with uncertainty and unpredictability. Patrol officers are routinely exposed to a variety of potentially traumatic events: violent deaths and injuries, serious motor vehicle accidents, occasional armed confrontations, and other potential physical threats to their well-being.

> Police officers are able to show greater strength than most others in dangerous situations. They are an elite group who are courageous enough to run towards danger to protect others. Yet despite their bravery, their mind and body absorb the hits from encountering a steady diet of critical incidents and other insidious stress events. Many officers will be heavily affected by the years of law enforcement stressors. Eventually, these officers will contend with personal emotional or physical fires. Although police officers will always remain an elite group, they are not invincible. Even model cops need career-long, proactive maintenance work to maintain psychological health. [Allen et al. 2014]

It is increasingly recognized that police officers, and especially first-responder patrol officers, are at risk for developing mental health problems such as post-traumatic stress disorder (PTSD) (McCarty and Skogan 2012). PTSD is an extreme form of critical-incident stress that includes nightmares, hypervigilance, intrusive thoughts, and other forms of psychological distress (Gilmartin 2002). Precise measures of the prevalence of PTSD among police officers in Canada are lacking. One study from the United States found the prevalence to be approximately 35 per cent in a cohort of officers (Austin-Ketch et al. 2012). A relatively recent survey of a large urban police force in Canada found similar levels of diagnosable PTSD (Griffiths, Pollard, and Kitt 2014).

Other relatively recent evidence suggests that the majority of police officers do not develop chronic PTSD (Yuan et al. 2011). Nevertheless, with greater awareness of post-traumatic stress disorders generally, police chiefs and senior administrators have taken progressive measures to respond to the consequences associated with work-related stress. Through employee assistance programs and extended health benefits, officers and their families are now routinely able to access professional counselling services. Many police agencies have implemented proactive stress management programs. Progressive departments have inaugurated orientation programs for new members and their families that facilitate the entire family's transition into the policing occupational culture (Torres, Maggard, and To 2003).

Many influences contribute to police officer stress. When an individual is continuously exposed to suffering and traumatization of others, they can develop secondary traumatic symptoms. Long hours, rotating shift work, irregular time with families, and on-the-job boredom contribute to the psychological stresses that are routinely part of police work. These and other features of the police occupation have an impact on officers' health and well-being (Duxbury and Higgins 2012). Other organizational stressors, only recently studied, derive from on-the-job interpersonal conflicts that result in strained relationships with both supervisors and peers. Additionally, the organizational climate, including lack of resources and ineffective management, may also impact stress in police officers (Shane 2010). It should be noted that stress is also common in the work of detectives and other plainclothes officers, such as undercover operators, many of whom are effectively on call all the time. These officers may work long hours and deal with challenging and often disturbing investigations that can take years to complete. Nemetz (2019) believes that cumulative stress should be recognized as a primary concern and that police supervisors should be held responsible for "setting the tone" by acknowledging the existence of psychological stressors, and for the willingness of their officers to seek professional assistance when required.

Negative portrayals in the media of police interactions with the public are not lost on police agencies or individual officers. Kirshman (2017) notes ". . . these are hard times to be a cop. There are days when it seems like the actions of a few have tainted the entire law enforcement profession. Policing is a complex profession, far more complex than most people understand."

In Canada, in recent years, post-traumatic stress disorder and other mental health concerns have become a significant public issue in regard to Canadian military personnel returning from combat missions in Afghanistan. A November 2014 Auditor General report severely criticized the federal government for its neglect of the psychological well-being of Canadian military veterans (Auditor General Canada 2014, Chapter 3). In the general context of a raised public awareness of the seriousness of mental illnesses including depression, it is not surprising that the mental health of Canadian military personnel has been placed in the spotlight. So it is with Canadian police personnel—many of whom experience on-the-job stressors not dissimilar to those experienced by Canadian soldiers. It can be anticipated that the mental well-being of Canadian policing personnel will continue to be a major human resource priority for officers and their families and a challenge for police administrators to provide sufficient resources.

The implementation of programs and services can also be a reactive response geared toward counselling assistance in the aftermath of a critical incident. Often, however, it is only after an officer and his or her family have come to realize that they are experiencing emotional or relationship difficulties, or both, that counselling services are sought. Compounding this issue is the recognition that officers may not seek or accept this professional assistance, even if offered. Typically, this is due to a traditional culture within the police department that may quietly stereotype those who have mental health issues as weak, thereby discouraging officers from getting the help they need (Armstrong 2014; Backteman-Erlanson 2013). A 2016 Public Safety report cited "significant stigma and in-organization culture" as barriers to public safety officers (such as firefighters, paramedics, and police) seeking assistance and contributed to an inability to accurately track and monitor the rates of PTSD within organizations (5). Nemetz (personal communication, May 10, 2019) believes that "police officers should be encouraged at the outset of their careers to figure out how to retire healthy." Police agencies must ensure that recruits are sufficiently educated during basic training to recognize and develop coping strategies for how police work may impact their lives.

Conclusion

Investigation is the foundational responsibility of the police. It is through the process of investigating that the police serve and protect, assure public safety, disrupt criminal activity, and gather admissible evidence to support charges to engage the court process. This chapter has introduced and highlighted many different investigative tools and strategies that are used in patrol and in major crime investigations. Each of the investigative strategies can be effective on its own, but each of them has limitations. When the tools are used collectively, the investigative process can generate powerful results through the gathering of admissible evidence to support successful prosecutions.

Critical Thinking Questions

1. How much of an impact does the *Charter* have on placing limits on various police investigative strategies?
2. Can the actions of the police be lawful, but later found to be contrary to the *Charter*?
3. At which stages of the criminal justice system will you find built-in checks and balances on police investigative strategies and actions?
4. Do you think the police in Canada have too many tools and too much power to investigate criminal activity?
5. Identify and discuss the types of events and experiences that may seriously impact mental health for police officers.

10

Operational Support

Learning Objectives

After reading and studying this chapter, students will be able to:

- Discuss and describe the nature and scope of support systems within the police department.
- Explain the differences between administrative and tactical support.
- Discuss and describe which roles are primarily sworn or civilian and why.
- Describe and explain the various units and roles that may be present in a police department.

Introduction

Operational support units may be integrated into a police department in many different ways, generally either as a distinct and separate group of units, on-call units, or integrated teams. However, what is important is to recognize the role that these units play in supporting the operations and investigations of other patrol and specialty units. Operational support units are unique in that their purpose is one of specialized support to enable investigators and general-duty officers to complete their tasks and investigate offences. These units generally do not lead investigations, nor do they recommend charges or clear cases. They may, however, provide key evidence to solve a case, or provide the administrative and tactical support to better allow sworn officers to complete their duties. Operational support units may be civilian or sworn member units, although certain specialty units, such as tactical support, are required to be sworn members.

It takes a large and complex team within the police department to solve cases and address crime issues. All members of the team, whether they are sworn investigators or civilian administrative support, provide crucial pieces of the coordinated effort.

This chapter will discuss some of the more prevalent support units that may exist in a police department. The reality of what support teams are in place in any department will depend on its unique needs and the needs of the community it serves. Other specialties may exist that are not discussed here, but that also serve a valuable role in the police service.

The discussion begins with surveillance and undercover teams, and discusses police resources such as scientific (forensic) and administrative support.

Covert Teams: Surveillance

Surveillance is a crucial and valuable tool in an investigator's tool belt when trying to solve a case. Surveillance may be used to follow a suspect who is of key interest in a crime, or a group of people involved in organized crime or gang activity. By utilizing surveillance, investigators can often acquire key evidence that links individuals to crimes, or pieces of evidence to individuals, or even individuals to other suspects.

Generally, investigations use covert surveillance, whereby persons of interest do not know they are being watched, nor have they consented to such deceptive tactics. The European Union has described three types of covert surveillance, which are helpful to classify the tactics used by Canadian officers as well. The first is **intrusive surveillance**, which involves monitoring of private premises or vehicles via hidden cameras or listening devices. This type of surveillance often requires specific court orders or warrants as it significantly infringes on an individual's privacy. The second category, **directed surveillance**, involves covert observation that is not deemed intrusive as it does not involve the use of hidden cameras or recording devices, and is generally directed at a specific individual. The last category is covert human intelligence sources, which involves situations whereby officers establish a personal relationship with an individual for the purpose of obtaining information (Lotus and Goold 2011). Often this type of covert surveillance makes use of undercover police officers or informers who deliver information about the person of interest to the police.

In addition to employing these intrusive, directed, or source-based surveillance measures, Marx (1988) described two broad types of covert investigations. The first involves setting a trap for an unknown offender, whereas the second involves gathering evidence on a known offender. In the first type of covert investigation, police are often involved in investigating a pattern or string of crimes. Without evidence that points to a suspect, they use covert tactics to try and encourage an offender to commit a crime, hoping to catch the offender responsible for the original string of crimes. A scenario such as the **bait car** program, whereby police plant specially equipped cars in strategic locations to encourage their theft, operates as a covert tactic aimed at encouraging the commission of an offence (stealing a car), ideally catching an offender who has committed other yet-unsolved car thefts. In the second type of investigation, police generally have a good idea of who may be committing a particular crime or series of offences. In this scenario, they may employ more covert and passive surveillance techniques in order to gather evidence that incriminates the individual. In cases such as this, audio recordings from phone conversations may provide the crucial evidence needed to charge an individual with a crime. This may occur if the suspect talks about the crime in a telephone conversation, unaware that the police are listening (Lotus and Goold 2011). Compared to undercover operations that may actively seek to provoke suspects into saying or doing something to incriminate themselves, audio and video surveillance have a more passive quality, whereby the police simply watch, look, and listen for incriminating evidence (Lotus and Goold 2011).

Some of the prevalent surveillance techniques are described further below.

Visual Surveillance

Visual surveillance requires that suspects are followed or surveilled in real time. Often this requires special teams working in undercover clothing and vehicles to physically follow the suspects and record their movements over a specified period. In that time, evidence regarding where they go, whom they interact with, and what property they are in possession of may all provide key evidence in investigations. For instance, surveillance operators may follow a suspect to observe his or her movements. During the course of their surveillance, the suspect attempts to dispose of a weapon that officers suspect was used in a crime. Officers may then be able to retrieve the weapon, link it to the crime, and link the weapon to the suspect. This information may provide some of the evidence against this individual in court.

This surveillance takes time, patience, and a great deal of training to ensure that the suspect or suspects do not know they are being followed and surveilled. They must blend

jtairat/Shutterstock.com

Video surveillance can make the work of police officers easier when it captures important evidence.

into and anticipate the suspects' movements through careful observation and background work on the suspects' daily routines (Lotus and Goold 2011). As this surveillance team needs to be highly specialized, where possible, departments may have sworn members operating as covert surveillance only, and assign them to various investigations in a support role. Smaller departments may require that their lead investigators conduct their own surveillance and act in a covert role if required for their investigation. Although not ideal, it is not always possible to have a dedicated specialty team in every department. Covert surveillance teams are trained in watching and gathering visual evidence from

Challenge Your Assumptions

Your Privacy—Video Surveillance in Public Places

Beyond the specific and directed surveillance efforts of law enforcement toward a specific target, general public video surveillance brings questions of privacy and security to the forefront of debate in Canada. Such public systems cast a wide net, subjecting everyone to scrutiny, even when they have done nothing to arouse suspicion or warrant a further look. Public surveillance essentially removes the expectation of privacy and anonymity that citizens may have as they move through their daily routines.

These recordings allow law enforcement to view individuals whom they may otherwise have no reasonable grounds or legitimate rationale to surveil. In addition, now with the advent and usage of automated recognition computer programs, the quantity of film and thus the scope of individuals under scrutiny has increased significantly. The number of cameras has also increased, which has further led to an increased amount of public scrutiny and data mining. Simply put, citizens are being watched a great deal every day in numerous locations, and are being subjected to scrutiny regardless of whether they should be the subject of any notice at all.

Not only does this raise privacy concerns, but it also causes apprehension that inferences may be drawn about people, or that the data captured may be used in discriminatory or inappropriate ways. Behaviour that would otherwise have gone unnoticed may be used to infer questionable activity by law enforcement. Not only does this present issues for rights and freedoms of law-abiding citizens, but may also have a "chilling effect" on behaviour as we become more accustomed to being watched throughout our day, regardless of whether there is any legitimate reason to do so (Office of the Privacy Commissioner of Canada 2006).

While our social contract requires citizens to give up a certain amount of personal freedom to ensure the safety and security of the group, we can debate whether the pendulum has swung too far toward encroaching on basic privacy rights in the name of public security. Should we be sacrificing our rights to exist without undue scrutiny simply to ease the ability to watch members of the public on the off chance they do something to sacrifice safety? Many would say absolutely not, while others point out, "What do you have to worry about if you've done nothing wrong?" While some may feel comfortable with limiting their personal privacy for greater security controls, others are seriously concerned about government and law enforcement overreach, and the possibility of unfairly and unjustly being caught in the surveillance net.

afar, recording images wherever possible or necessary, and importantly, in covert driving techniques to allow the surveillance team to follow suspects in a vehicle without being noticed. Covert surveillance teams are almost always sworn members, as the possibility of an encounter with a suspect necessitates powers of arrest and tactical defence training.

Audio Surveillance

If police have reasonable and probable grounds to believe that a target of an investigation will be in a particular place, and will communicate information that would provide evidence to support the investigation, they may make an application to obtain a **wiretap** to listen in on the target's conversations (*R. v. Thompson* 1990). As this type of surveillance utilizes listening devices, officers can listen away from the location of the suspect, generally within the police building or other secure location. This surveillance involves installing specialized technical equipment on a suspect's phone line to listen in on the suspect's conversations. The ability to install such listening devices is closely monitored by the courts, and is only available upon approval of a specialized warrant (see Chapter 9). The wiretap warrant, governed by Part VI of the *Criminal Code* of Canada, will outline what and whom may be listened to, how long their conversations may be taped and monitored, and what topics or information are to be gathered. These warrants are lengthy, detailed, and highly controlled to balance the public's right to privacy with the police's need to gather evidence. A judge must be satisfied that the applicant (the police) has "reasonable and probable grounds[i] to believe that a specific offence has been, is being, or is about to be committed" (*R. v. Madrid* 1994).

Once installed, special teams of wire operators record and listen to the conversations according to the warrant guidelines. Often these teams operate on a 24-hour-a-day basis until the warrant expires so as not to miss any crucial discussions. The relevant conversations are transcribed for the investigators to read and review for key pieces of evidence, although investigators may also listen in at various times during the surveillance. This type of work takes significant focus and stamina. Wire operators and transcribers may be sworn or civilian staff, or a mix of civilian operators and sworn supervisors. Again, the ability to operate this specialty squad is highly dependent upon the size and budget of a department. Not only is it costly to operate these types of teams 24 hours a day, but the infrastructure requirements are also significant. They require highly specialized recording and transcribing technology, as well as highly secure and impenetrable physical infrastructure to protect the information that is being recorded therein. The wire room is often one of the most secure places within a police department, with only approved personnel being allowed inside in order to protect the identity of the individuals who are being surveilled.

Other surveillance support units may operate on the technical support side, with the ability and expertise to install the wiretaps and other surveillance technology on the suspect's person, vehicle, or home. Installing wiretaps may involve gaining access to a suspect's home or property under false pretenses (such as staging a break-in or power outage) in order to install the equipment. Tracking devices on suspects' cars also require this highly technical skill, and gaining access to the vehicle can be difficult and risky. Rarely will investigators have the expertise or technical know-how to install these devices themselves, thus necessitating this specialized support unit. Again, as the ability to operate such a unit depends on the department size and budget, many smaller departments may hire or contract with larger departments to provide this service on an as-needed basis.

The proliferation of smartphones and text messaging present a new challenge to police departments with respect to surveillance monitoring. Conventional wiretapping may be less helpful in some situations and with groups who may operate exclusively via cell phones or texts, which may be more difficult to intercept. New legislation and changes to privacy laws are attempting to address this shortcoming and allow police greater powers of monitoring and surveillance while still balancing privacy concerns. New technology is also coming online in police departments, raising questions about scope and privacy. In particular, the police usage of the device called a Stingray has prompted numerous discussions about their legality under Canadian law, and how their use should be regulated. The Stingray is unlike a traditional wiretap, insofar as it focuses on capturing a wide net of cell phone signals. Acting as a faux cell tower, the Stingray attracts all cell phone signals within a particular radius, and thereby allows the police to record and monitor the cell phone usage of the individual they are surveilling. While a warrant is now required in order to direct a Stingray toward a target, it is the recognition that the device captures all nearby devices and users who are not covered by such a warrant, nor a part of the investigation, that is often felt to be problematic. Although assurances are always made that the police do not actively use this information without proper judicial authorization, there continues to be a lack of specific policy and limits on the usage of this device. The controversy surrounding this tool has also been confounded by many police agencies' denial of the use of this device, despite later acknowledgements that it was being used. Some speculated that the initial denial by police agencies was due to the existence of a non-disclosure agreement between the police services and the Stingray manufacturer. While undoubtedly non-malicious in intent, this cloud of dishonesty paired with a lack of proper guidance and agreement on the judicial authorization procedures early on have kept police on the defensive over the use of this tool. This is true as well in the United States, where the American Civil Liberties Union (ACLU) actively tracks police departments and other agencies who are known to use the Stingray, or have one in their possession.

Special Equipment and Tactics Teams

Emergency Response

Patrol officers all carry a variety of weapons and tactical devices on their duty belt to use as situations necessitate. However, some situations may escalate or become dangerous enough to require a more specialized response with a greater variety of weapons. In these instances, a specific team may be called in to respond to high-risk or dangerous situations. These may include serving high-risk warrants to individuals known to be violent or in the possession of weapons, or situations in which an individual has taken a hostage or is threatening the lives of others. The Tactical Support Team, also known as the Emergency Response Team, is specially trained and equipped to deal with these high-risk situations. (See Chapter 4 for more discussion on specialized training.) They carry numerous firearms and heavy-duty weapons, and have unique training in entry, exit, and combat tactics that go beyond the level of the patrol officer.

Emergency response teams spend a great deal of time physically training to deal with violent and high-risk individuals. They learn how to use multiple weapons, including automatic rifles and other high-powered devices. As high-risk offenders such as gang members or other organized crime figures may routinely be armed with dangerous weapons, it is crucial that the police response be similarly outfitted in order to protect themselves and others who may be involved or nearby. When deployed, the team not only carries numerous weapons, but also wears specialized body armour and shields in certain situations. Again, this is due to the risk associated with situations they are required to attend.

They are also trained in highly specialized procedures such as rappelling and other entry techniques should a situation necessitate it. For instance, if someone is holding a hostage in a building and has the entry doors barricaded, the tactical team is trained to rappel out of a helicopter and breach the roof to gain entry.

Flight Support

In addition to specialized tactical teams such as the emergency response teams discussed above, other special units may provide support by utilizing specialized vehicles, such as helicopters, to support front-line officers and investigations (see Chapter 8). Often these teams will be called out for situations that would benefit from a bird's-eye view of events, such as vehicle pursuits, traffic issues, fleeing suspects, or riot situations. As the helicopter can provide a visual perspective that is often not available to front-line officers, their support can be invaluable. Not all departments provide air-support services and, as with many specialized units, it is dependent upon necessity and availability. Edmonton Police Service is one of only a handful of police departments in Canada that maintain a flight unit made up of a helicopter pilot and a uniformed police officer. Officers must be with the service for at least eight years before applying, and those wishing to be pilots must hold a valid helicopter pilot's licence before applying to the unit. Some air units, such as the Saskatoon Police Service's Air Support Unit, are equipped with heat sensors and **infrared technology**. This further enables officers to track suspects and identify their location even while the suspect is fleeing on foot through buildings or other hidden areas. This technology may also be used to see within residences, although these types of scenarios may be deemed a legal search, and may necessitate obtaining a warrant to enter the home (even visually) (see *R. v. Tessling* [2004] 3 SCR 432).

Marine Units

For those areas with large bodies of water or that are located on a coastline, having a specialized policing unit able to patrol waterways and conduct search and rescue and other water-related duties is necessary for public safety (see Chapter 8). Police services such as the Vancouver Police Department and Toronto Police Service maintain marine units to support water patrol activities, as well as specialized search and dive operations. These units may also work with the Coast Guard or Canadian Border Services, depending on the location and boundaries they may be working within.

Police officers watch over the harbour district of Vancouver from the water. What unique elements of policing on bodies of water do you think might require special training?

Some marine units may also train officers in dive operations and SCUBA. Many specialized dive teams operate on an on-call basis, and do not form a full-time unit. Such is the case with the Saanich Police Department, whose dive team is called out when necessary, but whose members operate in a full-time capacity in different units within the department. This is similar to the RCMP Underwater Recovery Team, which is a volunteer unit whose members have full-time duties in various capacities throughout the region. All unit members must have SCUBA certification and have to undergo various training courses to prepare them for the duties of this specialized unit. This training includes not only dive manoeuvres, but also training in forensic recovery and other situation-specific needs.

Forensic Services

"Forensic" simply means "as applied to law." However, most people have come to closely associate the term in policing with **forensic science**, due in large part to such popular television programs such as *CSI: Crime Scene Investigation*. Although police departments do operate forensic science services, the reality is often far different from the television version. It is helpful to first think of forensics in the police department as falling into one of two broad categories: human forensics and digital forensics. The former involves studying **trace evidence**, which has had some sort of human contact or is biological in nature. Digital forensics, perhaps better thought of as "forensic computer science," involves a somewhat newer area of forensic sciences aimed primarily at computer and electronic devices.

Human Forensics—Biology, Chemistry, and Toxicology

Building on the discussion in Chapter 9, the study of trace evidence in relation to a criminal event is a painstaking and detailed process. Investigators may require hundreds of samples from a crime scene, as there is no way of knowing initially which one may provide the crucial evidence in the case. In general, investigators look for trace evidence that links the offender to the victim and/or the crime scene. This may be done in any number of ways; however, most often this link is established by lifting from the crime scene fingerprints matching the suspect, or from biological evidence such as blood, saliva, or semen that the suspect may have transferred to the crime scene or the victim. In police departments, these tasks often necessitate a two-stage process: the collection of the evidence and the analysis of that evidence. While some police forensic units may do both, others may require a secondary organization, such as an independent laboratory, to complete the analysis. This will often vary with the nature of the trace evidence being collected and analyzed, and whether the police service has laboratory analysis capabilities in-house.

Although there are numerous roles for forensic specialists within the department, when we discuss human forensics, we most often mean forensic biology, chemistry, or toxicology. Forensic biology most commonly is involved with the collection and analysis of biological samples to compare fingerprints or DNA profiles (Anderson 2010). These positions are most often filled with civilian scientists who operate in a lab outside of the police department (although the gathering of the biological evidence may be under the responsibility of the police forensic unit). As the DNA analysis is extremely specialized, those working in this area often have advanced science degrees in biology or a closely related field.

Forensic chemistry includes the analysis of fire debris (for ignitable liquids), gunshot residue (GSR), paint, glass, fibres, explosives, building materials, and soil (Anderson 2010). The forensic chemist will generally be responsible for analyzing any trace evidence that is not a bodily fluid. These positions follow **Locard's Exchange Principle**, stating that every contact leaves a trace. So while the actual evidence being analyzed may be rather common in nature, such as soil, it may contain evidence of contact between the suspect and the victim. For instance, in a hit-and-run accident, traces of paint and glass from the vehicle may be embedded in the victim. If the technician is able to pinpoint the type of paint used, this may help identify the class or type of vehicle that was involved, as most vehicles have unique colours assigned to different makes and models of cars in different production years (Anderson 2010). This information may help narrow down a suspect pool, or identify and locate a damaged car fitting that description, whereby further analysis may find linkage evidence on the suspect vehicle.

Forensic toxicology involves the analysis of bodily fluids to identify any toxic substances that may be present in the bloodstream or tissues of the individual. This most often includes screening for drugs and alcohol, but may also involve analysis of tools and equipment used in making drugs such as methamphetamine (Anderson 2010). Many forensic toxicologists have graduate-level degrees in toxicology, pharmacology, pharmacy, physiology, chemistry, or biochemistry.

Challenge Your Assumptions

Origins of DNA Analysis

The use of DNA evidence is often credited to a British geneticist, Alec Jeffreys, and his work in the 1980s in Britain on familial genetic markers. Jeffreys and his team had developed a technique whereby genetic material could be extracted from an individual's cellular material and "fingerprinted." Jeffreys's research forwarded the notion that DNA patterns were highly individual, and the chances of finding two people with the same genetic markers was extremely remote or nearly impossible. These findings paved the way for the first use of DNA analysis in a criminal investigation (Quinlan 2011).

In 1983, a woman in the United Kingdom was sexually assaulted and murdered. The police were unable to solve the case, and several years later another victim was murdered. The blood samples from both cases were sent to Alec Jeffreys for analysis. Using his "genetic fingerprinting" technique, he was able to conclude that the DNA left at both crime scenes was from the same individual. His technique also concluded that the genetic material found at each scene was different from that of the police's prime suspect, thereby exonerating him. A match to the DNA sample from the suspect was finally found following the testing of samples from 4500 men in the community and surrounding areas. This DNA match was used to convict the individual of sexual assault and murder, and thus became the first case that employed Jeffreys's technique in an investigation (Quinlan 2011). Since that time, DNA analysis has become a mainstay in criminal investigations whenever biological samples are found.

In Canada, the use of DNA analysis in criminal investigations dates back to 1989, when the RCMP used Jeffreys's technique in a sexual assault case that occurred in Ottawa. Originally, the samples in the case were going to be sent to a laboratory for analysis in the US; however, the RCMP made a proposal to establish the capacity to analyze samples locally, which ultimately saw the start of the RCMP forensic laboratories in Canada (Quinlan 2011).

Over the years, the use of DNA samples in criminal investigations grew, and ultimately led to the development of the National DNA Data Bank in 2000. The databank contains two sets of information: the first is DNA profiles of convicted offenders, and the second includes profiles from crime scenes where there is no suspect. These unidentified profiles are stored in the hope of eventually finding a match in the system.

The use of DNA, while now well accepted and entrenched within the criminal investigative system, is not without controversy and criticism. Early on, feminist groups opposed the use of DNA evidence in sexual assault cases as they felt it overshadowed the victim's testimony and undermined the value of witness evidence. Significant criticism was also launched against the math employed by the technique, specifically the use of population statistics, which critics attested were problematic and incomplete. The process by which samples were extracted and analyzed was also subject to scrutiny, leading to changes in the technique employed by the forensic laboratories (Quinlan 2011). Despite this, DNA evidence continues to be a mainstay in criminal investigations and often forms the cornerstone of the police's evidence.

Firearms, Bullets, and Toolmarks

This type of analysis involves the microscopic matching of the toolmarks made on bullets and cartridge cases upon firing (Anderson 2010). The specimens are therefore not biological pieces of evidence, but rather the weapons or other tools used in an offence. For instance, if a victim was shot, a crucial piece of evidence may be the comparison between a suspect's weapon and the bullet that was recovered from the scene. If the firearms examiner determines that the suspect's weapon was the one that fired the bullet that killed the victim, then this may form a key piece of the investigator's case. **Firearms examiners** may also determine how far away a weapon was fired from the target, the trajectory of that bullet, whether firearms or other weapons were in working order, or even the type of non-firearm weapon that was used in an offence by examining the toolmarks left on various materials at the crime scene.

Generally, this position requires a background in chemistry and/or physics; however, a great deal of additional training is required beyond the academic degrees in this area.

Training

The ability to provide forensic services of any kind within a police department will depend on the size of the department and the need for that type of operational support. Many small departments may contract with larger departments to provide this service. Those that do operate an in-house forensics unit are most often involved in the collection only of forensic samples at crime scenes, such as fingerprints, hair, fibre, blood, and other biological trace evidence. The collection of trace evidence is a complicated and very specific process, and is often handled by sworn police members, although some departments have begun utilizing civilians in these roles. Regardless of whether the department fills this role with sworn members or civilians, their training is extensive and ongoing. For many, the first steps are to be working within the police department and attending the Forensic Identification Course at the Canadian Police College in Ottawa. This 38-day course gives investigators all the basic knowledge of how to process a crime scene, including taking photographs, lifting and analyzing fingerprints, taking footwear and tire impressions, and processing a crime scene from start to finish. This will generally be followed by a period of practical learning at their home department, where the officers or civilians are mentored to fully develop their skills and ensure they are capable to collect and analyze evidence, and to testify as an expert witness.

In addition to having units for the collection of samples and identification of fingerprints, some departments, most notably the RCMP, also operate the laboratories that analyze samples and provide expert scientific testimony. The RCMP operates six labs nationwide, employing civilians in this highly specialized role. These civilian analysts must have a science-based educational background as described above, with most requiring a minimum of a Bachelor of Science, with a concentration in an applicable area.

In addition to these specialties, there are numerous other areas of forensic science that the police department may utilize in a particular case, although they rarely form a full-time position within the police department. These specialists may be forensic odontologists, who examine teeth and bite marks; forensic anthropologists, who examine skeletal remains; forensic artists, who may assist in identification by producing, manipulating, or constructing identities of victims or suspects from eyewitness testimony or human remains; and forensic entomologists, who use insects gathered from a decomposing body to determine the time of death (Anderson, 2010). These are just a few examples as, again, "forensic" means anything that is applied to law. The investigation of a crime may necessitate consulting with specialists from a wide range of disciplines to solve a case.

Digital Forensics

Digital forensics is a relatively new area, but has grown at an exponential rate in criminal investigations. With the proliferation of communication using computers and cell phones, investigators must extract and analyze large volumes of data from these devices. No longer limited to computer-crime–specific cases, digital evidence is a common element in almost all crimes. Most individuals in Canada now have a cell phone and many have a personal computer. These devices often contain emails that record important communication that may be relevant to a criminal investigation, as well as other personal information such as calendar entries and logs of activity that can provide valuable evidence to police agencies (Mouhtaropoulos, Li, and Grobler 2014).

The extraction of digital evidence often requires a specialist or technologist. A warrant may be required, particularly for "locked" cell phones or laptops; however, in some limited cases, some electronics may be searched at the time of arrest if the device is unlocked and accessible by the officer. The internal security structure of many devices, such as smartphones, necessitates specialized equipment to download the data contained in their memory. This may also be the case with laptops and other cell phones, particularly those that are password protected and must be "cracked." This requires specialized skill and the technology to access and download the information. This reality has led to one of the largest issues now with digital forensic examinations—that of demand for and availability of the technology and technologists. As with biological samples, investigators are often required to submit requests for analysis to specialized tech units within the police department or to an external laboratory. As staffing often lags behind demand, the backlog for analysis of electronic devices can be significant and may lead to delays in investigations. For instance, if an investigation results in the seizure of five cell phones and three laptops, each item will necessitate hours to download the information, and several more hours to pore over the information and pull out anything of value. If a department has 100 active cases under investigation, all which involve at least one cell phone for analysis, the workload and resulting backlog can understandably be enormous.

In addition to the enormous growth in digital evidence examination from cell phones and computers, the proliferation of cameras and digital video evidence has also necessitated a new area of investigative support. Larger police departments will often have an in-house video analysis unit that is responsible for the collection, authentication, and analysis of video images. Often these video images come from camera surveillance from streets or businesses, but may also be from videos taken on cell phones or personal video recording devices. Investigators may need analysts to enhance images from videos, determine whether any tampering or manipulation has occurred, or convert the image into a playable format for court. For those departments that may be considering police **body-worn cameras** (see Chapter 6 for further discussion), an entirely new unit may be needed to support the integration of this new technology.

All of these tasks require specialized skill sets, which has resulted in the expansion of this support role in recent years.

Administrative Support

Property Management

Police may seize, find, or gather property as part of an investigation, or during the course of their everyday duties if they observe abandoned or stolen items. The property may or may not be directly linked to a crime, but often it is all collected during the investigative process to ensure that a vital piece of evidence is not overlooked. This may include everyday household items if they contain forensic evidence, or property that is suspected of being stolen. For example, if police arrest an individual for shoplifting, and they find a large amount of property in that individual's possession and suspect it to be stolen, all those items are seized and logged by the department as possible evidence in an offence (and ideally are returned to their rightful owner following a resolution to the case). Physical property that does not require biological or chemical analysis is often logged into custody and held in a property office or secure property area. Before being stored, however, that piece of property must be entered into the database or police records system noting its description, the event that it is connected to, the officer who seized it, and other important information. The property must be easily searched, tracked, and retrieved for court if necessary. Many departments have civilian members to complete the database entries and log the property into evidence, while others have sworn members operating in that capacity. In either case, it can be a time-consuming process, particularly when a large volume of property is seized, as each item must be carefully entered into the database or records system, tagged, and filed. In 2013, the Edmonton Police Service was faced with the enormous task of seizing an extensive amount of property discovered after executing a search warrant on an individual's home. Inside, there were hundreds of items of stolen property, which filled four 5-tonne trucks. It took 28 officers and civilian EPS exhibit technicians just to complete the evidence seizure in this case (Mertz 2013).

Records Management

All police services maintain both electronic and physical records. While electronic police databases are steadily replacing paper reports, most police continue to use paper notebooks for their field notes and often amass a large amount of information during an investigation. These records must be entered into the database, maintained and updated, controlled for quality, and securely held. While front-line members and investigative officers spend a great deal of time writing notes and reports during the course of their duties, the support teams also have a large role to play in ensuring all the necessary information is entered, held, and communicated efficiently and according to Canadian legal requirements.

The input and maintenance of the records management system (RMS) can be one of the most time-consuming parts of an officer's day, and while the officer may be responsible for the initial entry of the event into the RMS, that file or record may go through several more quality control checks before the file is finalized and closed. Often this may include input from both civilian and sworn members to ensure the file is complete and contains all the necessary information, and that the investigation was detailed well within the officer's notes and is ready for court (if necessary).

Often, civilian members instead of sworn officers staff records units, although sworn members who are more familiar with police procedures often do investigative quality control. Having civilian members take on a certain amount of administrative duty allows sworn officers to maintain their street presence, while civilian members can apply their expertise to the maintenance of the records system. Within the records departments there may be clerks assigned to transcribing officers' notes or interview tapes; others to control the quality of file information; and still others to ensure all case documents are assembled, scanned, and logged for court. Other records units may be involved with providing criminal records searches to the general public, or providing other services to outside individuals or agencies.

The type of RMS varies among police departments, as there is not one nationally utilized database system. Many have developed their own systems, or have purchased management software that may "speak" to other databases with greater ease. Some departments, such as the Ontario Provincial Police, use a program called NICHE, originating from a company in Winnipeg, Manitoba. The RCMP in British Columbia utilize the **Police Records Information Management Environment (PRIME) RMS**, which is mandated for all police services in BC.[ii] However, the majority of RCMP detachments utilize the **Police Reporting and Occurrence System (PROS)**. Although all of these RMS systems are often capable of storing case notes, pictures, property descriptions, and numerous other pieces of information, they are not fully capable of making the police department paper free. A great deal of evidence continues to be transferred from digital to hard copy for court purposes, thereby increasing the administrative workload and decreasing the efficient harnessing of the RMS (see Chapter 9 as well).

Emergency Management Services: Communications/Dispatch

Emergency management services (EMS) can be defined as the response and organization of requests for emergency assistance during an incident (Clawson and Dernocoeur 1998 in Terrell 2006). The first step often comes when a member of the public calls 911 to initiate police action. The **communications centre**, or dispatch operations, performs one of the most vital and fast-paced roles in any police department. This unit may exist within the department and be staffed by civilian or police members, or it may operate outside the department and provide the service for a fee. For instance, the Toronto Police Service and Saskatoon Police Service hire and supervise their own dispatchers and call takers. They may be civilian operators who are specially trained and employed by the police department, or they may be sworn members who are assigned to the communications unit, possibly on light duties or while injured. Other departments may choose to contract out this responsibility to an external firm, as is the case with several police services in British Columbia who have agreements with E-Comm to provide all their call-taking and dispatching services. Regardless of which option a police department chooses, the communications centre becomes responsible for taking and directing all emergency calls that come into the department, and funnelling them through the service system. (See Chapter 7 for a discussion of the communications centre's role in police performance measurement.)

A dispatcher's top priority when an emergency call is received is to obtain a precise location and a description of the incident, which allows the dispatcher to know the type of response that is required. Dispatchers will attempt to ascertain the type of emergency, where the event took place, when it occurred, and who may have been involved (Terrell 2006). Once they have sufficient information, they will know what type of response is necessary (police, fire, ambulance), and how many units may be required. Procedures and protocols dictate what type of police response is required. Incidents are classified according to their priority, and whether they are happening at the moment (in progress) or happened in the past. Violent incidents that are occurring at that moment are given the highest priority response, typically recorded as Priority 1 by police agencies, and may result in the dispatcher sending numerous police units to the location as quickly as possible. Other events, such as a car break-in that occurred days or weeks ago, may not require such a quick response, and the operator may send one unit when it has time, which could be hours or even days later. In this way, dispatch operators control the availability and assignment of police resources to the community and make vital decisions concerning the speed and type of assistance that the public is given in any particular circumstance. All dispatch operations are guided by the particular police department's policy. Some departments, for instance, may require attendance at all motor vehicle accidents, while others will attend only when there are injuries. It is the dispatch operator's responsibility to determine the appropriate response based on each police department's unique policies.

Dispatchers are also a primary line of communication with the officers on the street and provide a vital link to safety, security information, and valuable intelligence from police databases. When officers are outside of their vehicles, they do not have ready access to their **mobile work station** (MWS) from which they can extract information about a person, vehicle, or specific address. This information may allow them to know whether they are about to engage a dangerous person or enter premises where guns are known to be present. Without access to this type of intelligence, officers may inadvertently place themselves at risk. However, by being able to request information from the communications centre, they can still benefit from all the intelligence contained in databases without having to be in their vehicle. This is particularly necessary for foot or bike patrol teams, as their only option for identifying a suspect or a vehicle will be through the dispatch operators.

The communications operators may also provide a valuable safety check for officers by maintaining a verbal connection to their whereabouts and their actions. This may be necessary for those who patrol alone or operate on transit vehicles or subway stations where they may be isolated from backup for a period of time.

Case Study

The New Era of Online Reporting

Police departments through the years have changed how the public can request assistance in many ways. Before the advent of police radios and dispatch systems, calls were often made directly to the officers or the Chief of Police (particularly in small towns). Once radio systems were incorporated, calls would be funnelled through one central number, often the police department's office. In 1959, Winnipeg followed the lead from the UK and instituted a single number, 999, for all emergency calls. However, in 1972, Canada recognized the advantage of having a single number for all emergencies that was easily remembered and would not overlap with any existing area codes or phone number prefixes, and all emergency numbers started moving over to the 911 number. Winnipeg officially changed over to the new number in 1972; London, Ontario, introduced its 911 system in 1974, and Toronto followed in 1982. Between 1977 and 1983, four cities in Quebec also introduced the 911 system. Prince Edward Island was the last province to roll out the 911 system, which was not introduced until 2000 (CBC Digital Archives, n.d.). During this time, many departments started to realize that many calls were not emergencies that required an immediate response, and thus set up non-emergency lines to complement the 911 system. The non-emergency number was intended to be used for situations that might require police follow up or guidance, but did not require that response to come quickly. This allowed the police agency to better triage their resource demands, while ensuring the public could report both emergencies and non-emergencies expediently.

What emerged next, perhaps not surprisingly, was the advent of online reporting. With the recognition that most of today's services are available online, it was only natural that the police departments would follow suit with an avenue for the public to report their victimization online as well. Although still in its infancy, online reporting has begun in several BC municipalities as well as most larger police agencies across Canada. Most share the same basis, which is that online reporting should only be used for non-emergency situations that do not have suspects and that do not require a police response. Should these conditions not apply, the public is still urged to contact either the non-emergency or 911 call centres as appropriate.

With the integration of this online reporting system, new questions emerge as to how it will function within the police agencies' service mandate, and how statistical reporting will be managed (see Chapter 7). Specifically, police agencies will undoubtedly require their communications or dispatch team to oversee the reports coming through the online reporting portal, to ensure they in fact do not require any follow up. Otherwise, true emergencies may be missed and lives may be in danger if someone did not understand the limitations or the intentions behind the online reporting.

In addition, the question of how to validate and confirm the existence of a criminal event must be considered for online reporting. Will these online reports form part of our official statistical reporting? Should they? If they will, how will the police agencies validate and score those events? If they will not, will our official statistics be missing a large proportion of non-emergency crimes due to the changes in reporting structures? All of these questions will need to be addressed as the online reporting system becomes more common. In the interim, however, it has become another tool for police agencies to better triage their service demands and work toward maintaining the 911 system only for emergencies.

Conclusion

Numerous units provide a supporting role to the investigative and operational side of policing, only a few of which are described in this chapter. Other support roles include units to assist with court procedures and document filing; auxiliary and/or traffic constables to assist with control of public movements or incidents; research and planning units that focus on internal tracking, planning, and reporting of efficiencies; media relations and public communications units (see Chapter 14); and crime prevention and community outreach units. All units within the police department, although varied in their roles and responsibilities, work together for the common goal of protecting persons and property, addressing crime in the community, and bringing offenders to justice. Without a coordinated response, police would not be able to function at the highest levels of efficiency. Regardless of whether a unit is sworn or civilian, each has a vital role to play in the overall resolution of a particular case or the effective response to a particular community concern. As police are also subject to very strict administrative and reporting rules, the administrative support is a large and vital aspect of the smooth functioning of the department.

Many roles require specialized training, either internally within the police department or before being hired. Some units, such as many forensic services, may operate independently of the police department, and some support services, such as communications and dispatch services in some jurisdictions, may be contracted out to external agencies.

Although persons in operational support roles may never arrest an individual or write a report to Crown counsel officially charging a suspect in a crime, the ability of front-line officers and investigators to do so is highly dependent on their backing and contribution.

Critical Thinking Questions

1. Why are support teams necessary? Shouldn't police have all the necessary skills to investigate a case from start to finish?
2. Should civilians be utilized within a police department, or should sworn officers be the only resource? What are the pros and cons of having a mixed department?
3. Should police conduct surveillance on suspects without their knowledge? Why or why not?
4. Why are forensic scientists and technologists employed within the police department? What are the benefits of having them embedded within the police service, or having police members act as forensic specialists?

Endnotes

i   Currently, the requirement is to satisfy reasonable grounds, with "probable" excluded.
ii This came about following the Robert Pickton investigation, because it was observed that having police services on separate (and inaccessible) databases hindered information and intelligence sharing.

PART IV

Current Trends and Challenges

11

Economics of Policing

Learning Objectives

After reading and studying this chapter, students will be able to:

- Describe and discuss the structure of policing in Canada.
- Describe and discuss how and why Canadian police structures evolved as they have.
- Describe and discuss the basic funding arrangements for policing in Canada.
- Identify and assess the basic cost drivers responsible for soaring costs of policing.
- Identify and assess the cost mitigation strategies under consideration.

Introduction

The spiralling costs of policing services in Canada have become a topic of considerable concern to elected and appointed officials at municipal, provincial/territorial, and federal levels of government; to police executives responsible for police budgets; and, increasingly, to Canadian taxpayers. In this regard, Canada is not alone. Other countries, including the United States and the United Kingdom, are experiencing significant cost increases with respect to the delivery of policing services (Gascon and Fogelsong 2010; Lunney 2012a). Of course, the irony is that alongside the rising cost of policing in Canada through the same period, crime rates have fallen dramatically. As pointed out in Chapter 1, even though crime rates increased for the fourth consecutive year in 2018, the crime rate was still 17 per cent lower than it had been a decade earlier (Moreau 2019).

The purpose of this chapter is to examine issues related to the basic economics of delivering policing services in Canada. The chapter presents an overview of the costs and expenditures associated with policing services, reviews the funding arrangements between the different levels of government, and describes the principal drivers that affect the cost of policing services in Canada. The chapter also considers the various innovations that are actively being considered as cost-mitigation measures not only by the various levels of government but also by police agencies themselves.

The Cost of Policing in Canada

Since 2002, overall spending on the criminal justice system has risen dramatically. Between 2002 and 2012, expenditures rose by some 23 per cent. In 2011–12, federal, provincial, and territorial governments together spent $20.3 billion on delivering criminal justice services. This includes expenditures on police, courts, and corrections (Office of the Parliamentary Budget Officer 2013, 1). However, of this $20.3 billion, $12 billion (or 59 per cent) was spent on policing (Leuprecht 2014, 2). In 2018, total expenditures on police services alone amounted to $15.1 billion dollars. Salaries, wages, and benefits accounted for 82 per cent or $12.5 billion of this total. In 2018, the average annual police salary was approximately $99,000. On a per capita basis, policing operating expenditures amounted to a cost of $318 per person (Conor et al. 2019). Not only is policing the highest-profile component of the overall criminal justice system, it is also the most expensive.

Police Structure in Canada

As reviewed in Chapter 1, in addition to First Nations policing services, there are three other principal levels of policing in Canada: national, provincial, and municipal. Canada's national police force is, of course, the Royal Canadian Mounted Police. Ontario and Quebec have their own provincial police: the Ontario Provincial Police (OPP) and the Sûreté du Québec (SQ). Newfoundland has its own provincial police, the Royal Newfoundland Constabulary, but also contracts the RCMP to deliver additional policing services. All other provinces and the territories contract with the RCMP for provincial policing services. Municipalities also provide policing services and either have their own stand-alone municipal police agency or subcontract the agency that serves as the provincial/territorial police agency (the RCMP, OPP, or the SQ, as the case may be) (see Office of the Parliamentary Budget Officer 2013, 4).

Police Funding in Canada

Funding arrangements for police services in Canada are complex due to the structure of policing in Canada.

In those provinces and territories that subcontract the RCMP to serve as provincial police (which is all but Ontario and Quebec), provincial/territorial governments contribute 70 per cent of the costs while the federal government contributes 30 per cent. The share of municipal expenditures in those communities in the

. . . provinces and territories relying on the RCMP depend on population levels. Municipalities with less than 5000 residents are not required to have a municipal police service and can continue to rely on provincial policing. Municipalities with more than 5000 residents are required to have a municipal police service. If the municipality has more than 5000 but less than 15,000 residents, it pays 70% of the expenditure for the police service and the federal government pays 30%. If the municipality has more than 15,000 residents, it pays 90% of the expenditure for the police service and the federal government pays the remaining 10%. [Office of the Parliamentary Budget Officer 2013, 4]

The cost-sharing formula is set out in **Police Services Agreements** that are negotiated among the federal government and provinces, territories, and municipalities. The RCMP is not a signatory to the agreements, which are negotiated by political leaders, not police.

Municipalities that opt to have their own stand-alone police agency pay 100 per cent of the costs.

Ontario and Quebec bear the responsibility for 100 per cent of the costs of their provincial police.

Ontario communities that subcontract the services of the OPP to serve as municipal police pay 100 per cent of the costs. Communities in Quebec that subcontract the SQ pay according to a system based both on population size and on the level of policing services they require (Securité publique Québec, n.d.).

Newfoundland pays 100 per cent for its provincial police force, the Royal Newfoundland Constabulary. As with the other provinces, for those parts of Newfoundland that rely on the RCMP, the province pays 70 per cent while the federal government pays 30 per cent (Office of the Parliamentary Budget Officer 2013, 5).

To understand properly the origin of current funding arrangements for Canadian policing and the mounting criticism of them, it is important also to understand the history of the structure of Canadian policing. A brief review of how the structure of Canadian policing has evolved over the years illustrates that current policing structures were largely driven by cost factors associated with the delivery of policing services.

The Evolution of the Structure and Delivery of Canadian Police Services

Robert Lunney, an experienced senior police officer and highly regarded commentator on Canadian policing matters, has documented the historical development of the structure of Canadian police services. As Lunney (2012b) points out, the *RCMP Act* authorizes the federal government to contract with provincial governments to allow the RCMP to serve as provincial police. Although the RCMP has had a presence on the Canadian prairies since the 1870s, contractual arrangements between federal and provincial governments date from 1905–6 when the Royal Northwest Mounted Police (RNWMP) were contracted to serve the newly created provinces of Alberta and Saskatchewan (Lunney 2012b, 434). However, when provincial governments passed laws in the early part of the twentieth century prohibiting the manufacture, distribution, and consumption of liquor, police were required to give priority to enforcing those laws. Subsequently, police resources dedicated to strict enforcement of prohibition laws conflicted with the federal government's priorities during World War 1, and provincial contracts with the RNWMP ended in 1916–17 (Lunney 2012b, 435).

The creation of the Alberta Provincial Police and the Saskatchewan Provincial Police subsequently allowed for the replacement of the RNWMP in Alberta and Saskatchewan

© Sir Alexander Galt Museum & Archives

Officers of the Writing-on-Stone (Alberta) detachment of the North-West Mounted Police, 1889.

respectively. The provinces of Manitoba and British Columbia had established their own provincial police agencies in the 1870s. The eastern provinces of New Brunswick, Nova Scotia, and Prince Edward Island operated their own relatively small provincial police forces during this time period as well.

In 1909, the province of Ontario created the Ontario Provincial Police and since 1944 has contracted policing services to communities throughout Ontario. In Quebec, the SQ, which had been established in 1870 as the provincial police, delivers policing services throughout the province.

In 1919, the federal government decided to merge the RNWMP with the Dominion Police Force, a federal agency that had been created in 1868 to enforce federal statutes, protect federal buildings, and enforce laws prohibiting counterfeiting of Canadian currency (Seagrave 1997, 23). Its jurisdiction, particularly after the creation of the North-West Mounted Police in 1873, had been primarily restricted to central Canada. In 1904, in recognition of the many members of the NWMP who volunteered to serve with Canadian mounted regiments that fought in the Boer War, King Edward VII honoured the NWMP by conferring the title Royal before its name and it became the Royal Northwest Mounted Police (RNWMP). With the merger of the RNWMP and the Dominion Police, the NWMP was renamed the Royal Canadian Mounted Police and its headquarters moved from Regina to Ottawa in 1920.

By 1928, the costs of policing were starting to concern Canadian provincial governments. Saskatchewan, in particular, sought a renewed provincial policing agreement with the RCMP. With the onset of the Great Depression in the 1930s, other provinces found it financially difficult to maintain the viability of their provincial police forces and the RCMP gradually assumed responsibility for provincial policing duties. In 1932, the RCMP took over the Alberta Provincial Police, the Manitoba Provincial Police, and the provincial police services in New Brunswick, Nova Scotia, and Prince Edward Island (Lunney 2012b, 435). When Newfoundland joined Confederation in 1949, agreements were negotiated with the RCMP to assume provincial policing responsibilities. Today the Royal Newfoundland Constabulary retains its status as a provincial policing agency but provides policing service only to a select number of communities. In 1950, the British Columbia Provincial Police was disbanded in favour of a contract with the RCMP and its members were absorbed into RCMP service.

Growing Municipal Resentment

In 2008, the Federation of Canadian Municipalities (FCM) released a report that revealed a simmering resentment regarding the burden placed on municipal governments across Canada by existing funding arrangements for policing services (see Federation of Canadian Municipalities 2008). Directed primarily at policing services contracted from the RCMP, the FCM report not only criticized the funding arrangements but also called into question both the lack of municipal control and the value received. The 2008 report noted that "between 1986 and 2006, municipal spending on police grew by 29 per cent (adjusted for inflation and population growth), nearly three times the spending growth experienced by the federal government and nearly twice that of provincial governments. In 2006, municipalities paid nearly 57 per cent of Canada's $9.9 billion policing costs" (FCM 2008, 11).

The report pointed out that the RCMP provides cost-shared services to nearly 200 communities across Canada, thus serving 15 per cent of the Canadian population; approximately 77 per cent of Canadians live in communities served by stand-alone municipal police departments; 6.5 per cent of Canadians live in communities served by provincial police agencies; and 0.51 per cent of Canadians are served by First Nations police (FCM 2008, 4).

Additionally, the FCM report noted that the federal share of provincial and municipal RCMP contract services dropped significantly from 50 per cent in 1976 to between 10 per cent and 30 per cent in 1990, and down to zero for all municipal contracts negotiated after 1990 (FCM 2008, 4). In short, as the president of the FCM declared in his introduction to the report, "Municipal property taxpayers across Canada are subsidizing the federal government's policing costs to the tune of over $500 million a year, and it has to stop. . . . Our report reveals a system that is badly broken and in urgent need of repair" (FCM 2008, 3).

Retrospectively, the 2008 FCM report appears to have been a catalyst for a serious reconsideration not only of the costs and funding arrangements for Canadian policing services but of the responsibilities, efficiencies, and resources of policing services across the country. Most certainly, within five years of the release of the FCM report, concerns about the funding and delivery of policing services had come to the attention of elected and appointed political leaders at all levels of government and to the attention of senior police officials. A series of reviews openly challenged the economic sustainability of modern policing and its priorities. For example, in January 2013, Public Safety Canada, the federal ministry responsible for public safety, initiated a two-day summit on the economics of Canadian policing. The summit brought together representatives of federal, provincial, municipal, and First Nations governments. Also in attendance were representatives of the Canadian Association of Police Boards, the Canadian Association of Chiefs of Police, and the Canadian Police Association, as well as other police leaders, frontline police officers, and academics. Speakers were invited from Canada, the United States, the United Kingdom, and New Zealand (Public Safety Canada 2013, 1).

In the wake of the 2013 summit, two independent Canadian research institutes, the Fraser Institute and the Macdonald-Laurier Institute, released research reports that sought to address policing costs, public expectations of police, and the sustainability of current police practices (see Di Matteo 2014; Leuprecht 2014). Also in 2014, the Institute for Canadian Urban Research Studies (ICURS), located at Simon Fraser University, released a report that examined the rising costs of policing alongside the corresponding increased public demand for police protection (see Institute for Canadian Urban Research Studies 2014). Finally, also in 2014, the federal government's Standing Committee on Public Safety and National Security released a report on the economics of policing in Canada. Clearly, by 2014 a serious debate had emerged in Canada regarding not only the increased costs that taxpayers were burdened with for police services but the long-term sustainability of Canadian policing in the future.

From the various reviews described above, it is apparent that considerable thought has been invested in trying to understand the nature of police budgets while continuing to meet police responsibilities regarding public safety. To understand the increasing costs of modern policing, it is necessary to consider the principal cost drivers or factors involved.

The Cost Drivers

Police Officer Strength and Compensation

As noted in Chapter 1, in 2018 Canada had a total of 68,562 police officers with a ratio of 185 officers per 100,000 population (Conor, Robson, and Marcellus 2019). However, compared to other countries in regard to police-officer-to-population ratios, Canada ranks comparatively low. Other countries such as the United States at 238, England and Wales at 244, Australia at 222, and Scotland at 337 per 100,000 have higher officer-to-population ratios (Standing Committee on Public Safety and National Security 2014, 6).

Even with Canada maintaining a comparatively lower officer–population ratio, the matter of police-sector compensation has been flagged as the principal driver behind costs that have increased by 40 per cent over the last decade (Standing Committee 2014, 10). As the Standing Committee noted, "Since 1999 police compensation has significantly outpaced inflation, and the costs of pensions, benefits and overtime have been major contributors to those costs" (Standing Committee 2014, 10). The Standing Committee also pointed out that police services have little room in their budgets for cost savings. That is, salary costs typically comprise between 80 and 90 per cent of budgets, leaving only somewhere between 10 and 20 per cent for other expenses such as service delivery and mandatory overheads associated with the acquisition and maintenance of infrastructure (such as buildings), technology, equipment including vehicles, and other overheads. In short, police executives have very little room for discretion in managing their budgets.

Leuprecht (2014, 9) has argued that the matter of police compensation has been complicated by the role that police unions have played in mobilizing political and public support to ensure that police wages and benefits remain competitive across the country. Often justifying demands for increased compensation by pointing to the inherently dangerous nature of police work, Leuprecht has suggested that police unions have leveraged public misperceptions to their advantage at the bargaining table. Leuprecht argues that policing is a relatively safe occupation and points out that waste collectors, certain hydro workers, and pilots face greater workplace hazards. He furthermore points out that police

... (u)nions are loath to relinquish pay and benefits—often extracted in return for salary concessions during difficult economic times—and justify their remuneration by the notion that they perform a popular, valuable, and sometimes dangerous service. [Leuprecht 2014, 9]

Additional complications driving police costs derive from the competitive arrangements that have evolved in terms of how police compensation packages are actually established. Most collective agreements between police unions and their employers establish a **comparative universe** of other Canadian police services (see RCMP 2015). In simple terms, the comparative universe is used as a benchmark for setting police salaries, pensions, group benefits, and working conditions. For example, the OPP collective agreement stipulates "an across the board wage increase ... equal to the percentage increase required to raise the salary rate of a first class constable to the highest first constable base rate in Ontario in effect on that date" (Leuprecht 2014, 10). Virtually all unionized police forces in Canada have similar provisions. As Leuprecht suggests, "This is a leapfrog method of increasing salaries: every time a police force in Canada gets an increase in salary, it raises all the boats in port" (Leuprecht 2014, 11).

RCMP pay scales are typically mandated to be within the top three police services in the country. However, this is not always adhered to and the RCMP is now believed to rank about thirty-fourth (Leuprecht 2014,11). This is in comparison to approximately 141 other non–First Nations policing agencies in Canada (Conor, Robson, and Marcellus 2019). A Supreme Court of Canada decision in early 2015 struck down the federal government's long-standing prohibition of the RCMP's right to form a union (Fitz-Morris 2015). It remains to be seen how the decision will affect future salary negotiations between members of the RCMP and the federal government.

The compensation package offered by a police service has a significant impact on the ability of a police service not only to recruit new officers but also to retain experienced ones. Thus, the competitiveness of compensation packages is another factor driving policing costs.

Another increasingly controversial matter driving policing costs is the number of sworn police officers who now who appear on various "Sunshine Lists" of government employees who earn in excess of $100,000 per year. Leuprecht has singled out the Toronto Police Service and notes that "almost 40 percent of the Toronto Police Services, 5400 sworn and 2500 civilian workforce (that is, 3181 employees)" make more than $100,000 per year (2014, 10). Police salaries are inflated principally due to the significant amount of earnings attributable to overtime. As with the matter of court waiting time, discussed below, the extent of overtime from a police managerial perspective is largely unpredictable and difficult to budget. For example, on any given day it is unpredictable just how many officers will call in "off-duty sick" (ODS). Combined with the difficulty of anticipating the number of officers who are on maternity or paternity leave, or who have simply taken holidays, it is often difficult to maintain adequate numbers of officers to patrol the streets. Other factors that influence overtime costs involve in-service training programs for regular members. Training courses often mean that a serving officer will be absent from his or her regular duties for a week or two. As a result, departments are forced to cover by bringing in officers who would otherwise be off duty or by extending overtime to those officers who are on duty.

Police overtime costs can also surge unexpectedly and uncontrollably as a result of sudden dramatic emergencies and/or potentially catastrophic events such as natural disasters including floods or major fires. Nowhere is this more evident than in the emergency police response to the shooting death of Corporal Nathan Cirillo at the National War Memorial in downtown Ottawa and the subsequent attack on Parliament Hill on 22 October 2014. In the hours and days following the shooting, the RCMP response entailed nearly $330,000 in overtime costs. The Ottawa Police Service incurred an even larger overtime bill of $375,000 (Burke and Beeby 2015).

While such costs may be an unavoidable overhead, there is widespread agreement about the need to develop the capacity of senior police administrators to monitor and control overtime costs (Griffiths and Pollard 2013).

The Changing Nature of Crime

In simple terms, modern crime has become more complex, technical, and mobile (Standing Committee 2014, 14). As result, as illustrated in Challenge Your Assumptions, police work has correspondingly become complex, technical, mobile, and expensive.

Increase in Calls for Service

It is now virtually a cliché to claim that law enforcement agencies have become the social and mental health services of first resort; that is, in the absence of alternatives, Canadian police have been forced to become the first responder to mental health–related calls. According to focus group discussions conducted by ICURS with police officers in British Columbia, many police officers reported they felt ill-prepared to deal with mentally ill patients despite having received additional training. The same focus group discussions revealed that approximately one-third of calls for service involve emotionally disturbed persons (ICURS 2014, 16). Compounding the problem is that calls for police to deal with mentally ill persons take time away from core policing functions. Inevitably, police who

---

Challenge Your Assumptions

Data Volume Growth

With respect to its complexity, Mike Cabana, RCMP Deputy Commissioner, Federal Policing, explained [to the Standing Committee on Public Safety and National Security] that the growth of data volume in any given investigation is staggering. He noted that investigations today can involve multiple telephone numbers and email accounts. One recent investigation included 350,000 telephone conversations and nearly one million text messages. Inevitably, the time devoted to analyze and compile such information is considerable.

Technology and globalization, which have empowered so many of us, have also empowered criminals. Financial and commercial crime, cyber-crime, the globalization of organized crime, and the heightened focus on national security and terrorism threats have expanded the focus of police work. As such, many criminal investigations are no longer confined to the territorial jurisdiction of specific police forces, provinces, or countries.

Source: Standing Committee on Public Safety and National Security. May 2014. *Economics of Policing*. 41st Parliament, Second Session. p. 15.

apprehend mentally ill persons spend hours simply waiting in emergency wards for those persons to be admitted by a doctor (Standing Committee 2014, 17). This was demonstrated in a 2008 Vancouver police study that documented a 16-day period (9 September to 24 September 2007) during which, of 1154 calls for service, 31 per cent (or 358 calls) were calls involving mentally ill persons (Wilson-Bates 2008). In the wake of **deinstitutionaliz-ation** (the closing of in-patient treatment facilities), a lack of mental health resources has meant a *de facto* downloading of responsibility to the police and correctional facilities.

Criminal Justice System Demands on Police Resources

Court Waiting Time

A series of inefficiencies within the routine operations of the criminal justice system have been identified as prime drivers of policing costs. For example, it was demonstrated by a study undertaken in Thunder Bay, Ontario, that 82 per cent of police officers who are subpoenaed to court never testify. Nevertheless, they are required to be there and the police service is left to absorb the cost of the officer's time (Standing Committee 2014, 18). As Edmonton Police Service Chief Rod Knecht testified before the Standing Committee on Public Safety and National Security,

> [i]t is different between police services and amongst collective agreements. For example, in the RCMP, if you go to court it's a four-hour callback, regardless of whether you testify or not. For other police services, it is eight hours. It can be time and a half; in some cases it's double time. It depends on whether it's right after a shift as opposed to a day off. It is different amongst jurisdictions and it depends on where it fits into your schedule. In most cases, that's all part of a collective agreement. [Standing Committee 2014, 18]

Additionally problematic in this regard is that such costs cannot often be predicted or budgeted in advance with any accuracy.

Changing Legal Environment

Since the enactment of the *Charter of Rights and Freedoms* in 1982, the Supreme Court of Canada (SCC) has rendered many decisions that have required significant changes to how modern police work is conducted. These decisions unintentionally and often unforesee-ably have added to the complexity and costs associated with police work. For example, the Standing Committee was told that, in the 1980s, processing an impaired driver would take two hours. Today, however, the same charges entail about eight or nine hours to process in order to comply with court stipulations regarding procedures police must follow to ensure the accused has been dealt with fairly and systematically (Standing Committee 2014, 19).

As Neil Robertson, legal counsel for the Regina Police Service, has pointed out, as a result of SCC decisions "policing is more procedurally complex, time consuming, and requires better record keeping" (Robertson 2012, 356). Given the obligations placed on the police by the SCC Stinchcombe decision in 1991 requiring the Crown to provide full disclosure of evidence to the defence, police have often been faced with an enormous task of cataloguing the fruits of their investigations. For example, at one point in the investigation of convicted serial killer Robert William Pickton, more than 20 police officers and support staff worked for more than two years on only disclosure obligations. The team eventually was reduced to six police officers but the entire process of disclosing evidence to the defence continued for five years. This, of course, did not include the active ongoing police criminal investigation—only the disclosure obligations mandated by the Stinchcombe decision (see *R. v. Stinchcombe* 1991).

Challenges of Policing Small, Rural, and Northern Communities

Isolation

As Conor, Robson, and Marcellus (2019) have shown, the average cost for policing in Canada in 2017 is approximately $318 per capita. According to the Standing Committee report (2014), the average cost of policing per capita in the territories leaps to $1000. Similarly, the average annual cost of an RCMP officer in southern Canada is $121,000 but in the territories it is $220,000.

Infrastructure costs for government-provided accommodation and for the maintenance of RCMP detachments in remote communities are also significantly higher. Transportation of prisoners from remote communities to other detachments that have holding cells adds significant costs. Likewise, facilitating the travel of RCMP members to and from remote communities for training and recertification purposes adds additional costs to policing in the north (Standing Committee 2014, 21).

Levels of Police Service Delivery

Not every community in the north is served by a police detachment. Policing is often provided only on a fly-in basis. With fewer detachments and greater geographic areas to be serviced, longer response times are a reality of northern policing.

Given the relative isolation of northern communities, not all police officers are suitable for remote postings and must be assessed medically and psychologically before being posted. According to the report of the Standing Committee, the Yukon Territory has come to insist that RCMP officers posted to the north not only want to live in the north but want to be actively involved in the community and are sincere in wanting to learn about Indigenous culture (Standing Committee 2014, 23).

In summary, given the various cost drivers and the challenges of delivering policing services in a country as geographically large and diverse as Canada, it is not surprising that a series of innovative measures have been considered in order to mitigate both costs and challenges.

Mitigation Strategies

Redefinition of Core Responsibilities of the Police

As noted earlier, Canada is not alone in having to confront spiralling costs associated with policing. One of the realizations that has dawned on politicians and senior police officials is the need to temper public expectations "about when, where, and how police services are delivered" (Standing Committee 2014, 28). This has entailed a reconsideration of core policing functions.

As Christian Leuprecht has suggested, one way to redefine core policing responsibilities is to separate out responsibilities that are genuinely dangerous and need to be addressed by trained, professional, armed police officers. This recognizes the fact that the vast majority of police work is not dangerous. Indeed, many of the duties performed by police can be as effectively and efficiently undertaken by non-sworn civilian members, special constables, community safety officers, or private security personnel. According to Leuprecht, reforms inaugurated in England and Wales allow local police to designate police community support officers and dispatch them to safe and "suspect-less" crime scenes as an investigating officer. Such alternate service delivery (ASD) has been success-fully implemented in Mesa, Arizona, where

> . . . a team of civilian investigators has been handling about 30 percent of all calls, including 50 percent of all calls for vehicle and residential burglary (provided they are no longer in progress), vehicle and copper theft, unsecured buildings, ac-cidents, traffic hazards and loose dogs (Gascon and Fogelsong 2010, 3–4,13). They also respond to "suspicious activity" (9 percent of calls) and "subjects disturbing" (15 percent). By and large, these do not require a sworn member to attend. Having a sworn member attend false alarms amounts to subsidizing cheap security and poor risk management. [Leuprecht 2014, 17]

Civilianization, or "the practice of assigning to non-sworn (civilian) employees police department work that does not require the authority, special training, or credibility of a police officer" holds the potential to be "a boundary changer" within policing (Griffiths and Pollard 2013, 109–10). Such alternate service delivery models also hold the potential to generate resentment and conflict within the established policing community. Police unions and senior police officers often demonstrate a reluctance to cooperate in any re-structuring that may lead to a reduction in the scope of traditional police responsibilities and subsequently jobs.

Yet another ground-breaking innovation that seriously challenges conventional police practice is that of **tiered policing**. Tiered policing, closely allied to the concept of civilian-ization, is being considered in many jurisdictions and is best described as policing services

---

Case Study

Medical Analogy

Chief Constable Bob Rich of the Abbotsford Police Department made the following analogy:

> The image I want to put before you is that of the 1950s: if you got sick, you phoned the doctor, and he actually came to your house with his little leather medical bag and checked you out. He made a house call. That's what police officers are doing for virtually every call, and it's an outdated and overly expensive way to respond to many calls for service.

Source: Standing Committee on Public Safety and National Security. May 2014. *Economics of Policing.* 41st Parliament, Second Session. p. 29.

Do you agree with Chief Constable Rich? What do you think could be done to change the situation he describes in his analogy?

structured in a pyramid. At the top of the pyramid are regular, uniformed, sworn police officers who possess full policing authority. Below this tier are community safety officers who are not trained to the level of the top tier and may not be armed with guns. Typically, community safety officers would engage with the community, solve local problems, and serve an intelligence-gathering function. The next tier, depending on a community's preference, might consist of private security personnel who are contracted to provide a range of minor enforcement functions such as parking and by-law violations and responding to minor disturbances of the peace and other nuisance calls. The bottom tier, now already evident in many jurisdictions, consists of volunteers and uniformed auxiliary officers with less training who would undertake routine functions such as directing traffic and crowd control at sporting events (Standing Committee 2014, 37–41).

The province of Alberta has sought to introduce tiered policing with the expansion of the duties of the Alberta Sheriffs Branch beyond merely providing courtroom security and transporting prisoners. These expanded duties include traffic violation enforcement, criminal investigation support, and provincial and national security functions.

In sum, alternate service delivery options such as those discussed above represent innovative ways to rethink and restructure core policing services.

Integrated Policing Resources

Already well established in British Columbia's Lower Mainland, integrated policing units combine policing resources from several different agencies to alleviate burdens on smaller departments. For example, the Integrated Homicide Investigation Team (IHIT), housed in the RCMP E Division headquarters in Surrey, British Columbia, combines the resources of the RCMP, Abbotsford, Port Moody, West Vancouver, and New Westminster police departments to investigate

> . . . homicides, suspicious deaths, and high-risk missing persons where foul play is suspected. IHIT covers the Lower Mainland District from Pemberton to Boston Bar, including Sechelt, and serves 28 RCMP communities and 4 municipal police communities. . . . IHIT is comprised of 109 employees including 80 police officers from the RCMP, New Westminster, Port Moody and Abbotsford and West Vancouver Police departments. [Integrated Homicide Investigation Team, home page]

Operational Reviews

As part of the recognized need to find cost-saving measures and to increase efficiencies with respect to service delivery, many police departments have engaged in operational reviews. For example, the Winnipeg Police Service (WPS) undertook an operational review of its core activities in 2013 (see Griffiths and Pollard 2013). As the Standing Committee reported, concrete findings suggested the need for more patrol officers on the street. However, given that the review also identified some 90 tasks currently done by police officers that could be performed by non-police personnel, there was no need to hire additional police officers (which would have increased the WPS budget). Instead, a relatively simple reallocation of human resources was sufficient (Standing Committee 2014, 32).

Carol Provins/Shutterstock

Alberta sheriff on duty during a protest at the Legislature in Edmonton. What are the consequences (positive and negative) for tiered policing?

While some police departments have sought the assistance of the academic community in undertaking extensive and detailed operational reviews, others have sought to contract major private sector corporations such as the chartered accountancy firm KPMG.

Eliminating Needless Duplication

It has become evident to political leaders and to senior police administrators that, across the country, there are efficiencies and cost savings to be obtained by ending administrative duplication. For example, until recently the RCMP maintained payroll and benefits in each region. There is now one payroll centre capable of serving the entire membership (Standing Committee 2014, 32).

The Standing Committee has also pointed to the police complaint processes that exist in all provinces. British Columbia, Alberta, Manitoba, Ontario, and Nova Scotia all have their own investigation agencies. Some provinces have two agencies with oversight responsibilities. For example, in British Columbia, the Police Complaints Commissioner oversees complaints made against the police, while the Independent Investigation Office investigates alleged criminal behaviour of police officers and incidents in which the use of force has resulted in serious injury or death. These oversight agencies, in addition to having their own investigators, also rely to some degree on the police who, in most instances, are either on site when an incident occurs or are the first responders. While the creation of such agencies has indubitably served to foster public confidence, there are opportunities for resource sharing. The recently created RCMP Civilian Review and

Complaints Commission will work with provincial oversight agencies to develop an integrated public complaints intake system (Standing Committee 2014, 33).

Efficiencies in Police Training

According to the report of the Standing Committee, it is estimated that the combined expenditure on police training in Canada is $1 billion annually. It is also noted that despite the significant costs associated with training new recruits and with re-qualifying serving members, little thought has been directed at how greater efficiencies might be achieved with respect to training. As the Standing Committee heard from training specialists, there is little agreement on the effectiveness of police training practices. Furthermore, it is not entirely clear that police training, particularly of recruits, adequately imparts the skills required to carry out modern policing. In this vein, Christian Leuprecht has raised the question as to whether modern police officers might be better prepared if less time were spent on emphasizing physical fitness and strength and more time spent on developing critical thinking and judgment skills. In an important sense this might serve to redirect the focus of future police officers from "law enforcement" to "peace officer" (Leuprecht 2014, 26).

With regard to ongoing training and re-qualifying of front-line officers, the Standing Committee pointed to the development and delivery of training through electronic learning platforms. Electronic learning formats are easily accessible and cost-effective. Not all essential police skills are best learned online. Nonetheless, the Canadian Police Knowledge Network (CPKN), a non-profit and financially self-sufficient organization, has partnered with the policing community to develop and deliver cost-effective training materials that

Jesse Winter/Toronto Star via Getty Images

York Regional Police give a tour of their training facility, including a 50-metre shooting range, pictured here. How are police training practices impacted by the economics of policing?

meet the needs of police agencies that have officers serving not only in urban areas but in remote and isolated areas as well (Standing Committee 2014, 36).

Shared Research Needed

Directly identified by Leuprecht (2014) and Robertson (2012) and by the report of the Standing Committee (2014), the greatest impediment to stimulating innovations in policing cost containment and to addressing the general challenges facing contemporary policing is the lack of publicly available research data. The United States and the United Kingdom are examples of countries in which coordinated research measured innovations in policing for their effectiveness. Scholars who gave evidence to the Standing Committee affirmed that independent police research capacity in Canada is lacking (Standing Committee 2014, 42–6). No independent agency or coordinating body exists to serve as a repository for research conducted on policing in Canada. Coordination and evidence-based policies could drive innovation to hold cost drivers in check and establish best practices for improving efficiencies within the criminal justice system.

Conclusion

This chapter examined issues related to the basic economics of delivering policing services in Canada. The chapter provides an overview of the costs and expenditures associated with policing services, reviews the funding arrangements between the different levels of government, and describes the principal drivers that affect the cost of policing to Canadian taxpayers. The chapter also briefly considered the various innovations that are actively being considered as cost-mitigation measures not only by the various levels of government but also by police agencies themselves. Of course, with innovative ideas to contain costs and to achieve greater efficiencies comes the need for sound research in order to evaluate success.

Critical Thinking Questions

1. What are the core responsibilities of the police? Should some of these responsibilities be downloaded to civilians or to a tiered system of policing?
2. Of the cost drivers discussed in this chapter, which is the most easily brought under control? Explain your answer.
3. Is independent research necessary to measure and understand the effectiveness of innovative police practices? Explain your answer.
4. Of the cost-mitigation strategies, which is the most likely to contribute to greater police efficiency? Explain your answer.

12

Policing and Crime Prevention

Learning Objectives

After reading and studying this chapter, students will be able to:

- Describe and discuss the police roles in crime prevention.
- Explain differences among community policing, evidence-based policing, problem-oriented policing, and intelligence-led policing.
- Describe CompStat, block watch, and broken windows approaches.
- Describe how hot spots policing can be effective to prevent and/or reduce crime.
- Explain how the professional (or traditional) model of policing originated, and how it was presumed to prevent crime.

Introduction

Sir Robert Peel advocated for the police role in crime prevention as early as 1829. Since that time, police departments' tactics for fulfilling this role have changed dramatically due to many different philosophical, technological, and legal shifts. Currently, police departments are realizing a return to community policing principles and a focus on Peel's primary principle, which is "The basic mission for which police exist is to prevent crime and disorder."

Most police action has historically been thought to be able to prevent crime. "Police strategists relied upon two ideas to prevent crimes: deterrence and incapacitation" (Braga 2008a, 5). This includes tenets of the professional (or traditional) model, which advocated for random patrols, rapid response, and reactive investigations. The justification for this model as a prevention or reduction model came from the intuitive belief that once offenders were caught, any future crime they might have committed would be prevented, and others would be similarly deterred by the example this provided. However, this was not often the reality of the outcome of confrontations between police and offenders. All too often the offender was not caught, or would be released following a very short time in prison. Having undergone little or no rehabilitation efforts, their situations were the same if not worse, and the conditions under which they were prompted to commit their first offence would surface again. This created the revolving-door phenomenon, primarily for low-level property offenders (Pollard 2008). Police were left to respond to the same offender over and over, preventing very little with each subsequent arrest. The futility of this approach began to be highlighted in the research literature, showing that responding quickly to crimes and arresting an offender did little to prevent or reduce crime rates in an area. Clearly, a different approach was necessary.

With the move toward a community policing approach, departments and the academic community began examining what worked in crime prevention and reduction, and started testing these strategies in real-world scenarios. The result was an impressive body of knowledge surrounding what impacts the police can and cannot have on crime, and the best way to utilize resources for certain issues. Interventions such as directed patrols, proactive arrests, and problem-oriented policing have shown to be effective at combatting areas of high crime activity (Braga 2005). With the increasing integration of computerized systems and analysis software into policing evaluations and departments, the knowledge about what works increases at a steady rate.

This chapter will orient the reader with the theoretical base for crime prevention in policing and discuss the guiding paradigms in policing and how the theories have informed these perspectives. The chapter will then discuss several newer movements in policing with respect to crime prevention, such as intelligence-led policing and hot spots policing. This chapter will integrate and refer to ideas and terms within Chapter 7 and Chapter 13 a great deal, so students should ensure they are read together.

Theoretical Base

Crime prevention overall cannot be seen or studied as one activity; rather, there is a spectrum of activities that may prevent crime at different times or places along the criminal continuum. Not all programs or initiatives may intervene at the same point; therefore, it is helpful when conceptualizing crime prevention efforts to consider their timing and the resultant expectations from an intervention aimed at a particular point in the criminal process. In 1976, Brantingham and Faust categorized crime prevention approaches into three main stages, much as in the medical model of disease prevention. These stages included (1) **primary prevention**, (2) **secondary prevention**, and (3) **tertiary prevention** (Brantingham and Faust 1976). Primary prevention described interventions or programs that sought to prevent the social or environmental conditions that made crime possible. In this way, primary prevention could theoretically prevent crime before it ever happened. Secondary prevention interventions hit a little further down the timeline of a criminal event, and were designed to intervene in emerging criminal situations or with potential offenders who were showing signs of criminal escalation. Secondary techniques would not necessarily prevent all crime before it occurred, but were aimed at preventing a problem from getting worse by early detection, identification, and intervention. Tertiary crime prevention occurred at the end of the criminal spectrum, after the crime had been committed. Although not classically thought of as prevention because the crime had already occurred, these interventions had the goal of preventing a criminal event from happening again. Generally, this came via incapacitation programs for known offenders.

In general, police have the most impact and opportunity within the secondary prevention realm. It is unrealistic to expect police to have influence over many broad social and environmental conditions that may foster crime, and as such, primary prevention programs tend to be more in the wheelhouse of governments and other social institutions. Similarly, tertiary programs most often focus on incarceration and/or rehabilitation programs for convicted offenders, neither of which involves the police to a great degree. While police certainly can be involved in either primary or tertiary prevention programs, their real impact tends to come from secondary intervention techniques and the identification of high-risk areas, targets, or offenders. This is primarily due to the wealth of knowledge and data collected by, and available for analysis by, the police. Police agencies are in a unique situation to be able to spot crime trends as they emerge, and can therefore plan intervention programs to stifle increasing activity, or target those individuals who are causing the majority of problems. Many of the programs or initiatives in this chapter can be classified as secondary crime prevention techniques, as they rely heavily on data collection and analysis to point to burgeoning problem places and offenders where the police should focus their efforts.

Much of the programs and/or guiding paradigms in this chapter share a theoretical body of knowledge stemming largely from **environmental criminology**. This area of criminology focuses on the distribution and interaction of targets, offenders, and criminal opportunities across time and space. The theories of environmental criminology place the focus and analysis on places, rather than personal motivation, which is the case with many classical theories of criminology. The three prominent environmental criminology theories are **rational choice**, **routine activities**, and **pattern theory**, which will be briefly summarized below.

Rational Choice, Routine Activities, and Pattern Theories

The premise of rational choice theory is that offenders will embark upon offending behaviour through a structured decision-making process that seeks the maximum benefit for the minimum amount of risk. Offenders are active in their decision-making process, and seek out and utilize social, environmental, and other cognitive schemas and cues to make their determination about whether to offend or not. The decision to offend is considered limited in its rationality, as it is constrained by the environment, social situations, circumstances, and an offender's time commitments. Concern must not be limited simply to the choice to offend or the target selection, as many other factors may be involved that will determine whether the offender continues the offence or desists following a change in the environment, situation, or determination of risk (Cornish and Clarke 1986).

The routine activity approach primarily focuses on the fundamentals of the criminal event and the chemistry of elements that are necessary for that event to occur. Criminal acts have three necessary features: the presence of a motivated offender, a suitable target, and the absence of capable guardians against the offence (Cohen and Felson 1979). Felson

AndreyPopov/iStockphoto

How does burglary encapsulate the three necessary features for crime? What are some of the strategies that people and police departments use to remove at least one of these features in order to prevent these kinds of crimes?

argues that anything that makes crime harder to commit also makes it less likely to occur (Felson 1986). In contrast to routine activity theory, rational choice theory asserts that these limits on opportunity are "costs" that reduce the "expected utility" of crime. From a self-control perspective, making crime harder to commit makes it less satisfying.

Pattern theory focuses on how crime happens in specific locations and at specific points in time. While focusing on the place of the criminal event, special attention is also paid to the offender's and victim's places in time, their travel to and from the event, and their awareness spaces that brought them into contact with each other. The criminal event can be understood in the context of people's normal movements through their everyday lives, which will vary depending on the time of day, day of week, month of year, or season. There is recognition that it is more often normal, legitimate activities of the victim and offender that shape crime patterns. Pattern theory can be seen to integrate new concepts with those forwarded by rational choice theory and routine activities theory (Brantingham and Brantingham 1978; Brantingham and Brantingham 1991).

Guiding Paradigms in Policing

Many paradigms have been utilized for policing strategies in general, and for crime reduction or other focused initiatives. Often these paradigms share similar interest in actions directed by research or evidence, and proactive rather than reactive actions.

Crime reduction programs may begin by selecting a particular paradigm on which to base initiatives, as this may aid members and policymakers in enacting goals and objectives that are both attainable and measurable. However, it may not be appropriate to limit the objective to one model or approach, as a more multifaceted archetype may be of greater use depending on the overall objectives and missions of the initiative. The overarching guiding paradigms of policing overall tend to follow one of two prevailing models: the professional (or traditional) model, or the community policing model. These models are discussed throughout this chapter. While no police department organizes its activities solely based on the tenets of one or the other, they are helpful as archetypes to see the progression of policing as both a profession and a science.

Professional Model or Traditional Policing

The **professional (or traditional) model** was largely a response to growing community unrest and concern over police corruption in the 1930s. During this time, departments were often known to lack professional standards, and scandals and abuse of authority were commonplace. In order to bring policing back from the brink of corruption, the new model emphasized discipline and structure, and relied heavily on a military backbone. Adding to the new reform were numerous technological innovations such as two-way radios and the incorporation of new scientific advances such as fingerprinting. Police departments also aimed to distance themselves from political influence, the source of much of the previous corruption. In practice, the day-to-day operations sought to focus on crime prevention. To accomplish this goal, the professional model advocated for three areas as the means to reach those ends: preventive patrol, rapid response to calls, and investigation and solving of more serious cases (Braga 2008a). The belief was that if these goals could be accomplished, crime would be deterred, the public would be assisted more rapidly, criminals would be caught in the act, and serious offenders would be incapacitated. The ends, however, were not realized through this approach.

During the 1970s, several of the assumptions of the professional model were tested to see if they actually accomplished the desired goals. One of the most cited studies was the Kansas City Patrol Experiment, which examined whether random patrols at varying levels would see an impact on crime levels in the same area (Kelling et al. 1974). Contrary to what was anticipated, crime rates appeared largely unaffected by any type of patrol, whether it was saturated or largely absent. Further studies showed some contradictory and some confirmatory results. Overall, the empirical support for random patrols' positive effect on crime rates did not materialize in the research literature. Put simply, police officers who spent time randomly driving around a city appeared to have little effect on crime at all.

Response times as well were held up as a viable crime prevention tool. The difficulty with this assumption is discussed further in this text (see Chapter 7); however, the overwhelming evidence pointed to the conclusion that responding rapidly to calls for service did little to nothing to help (a) solve crimes and (b) prevent crimes. In general, when a call is made, the crime has already occurred, thus thwarting the officer's ability to prevent that crime. In addition, rarely are crimes reported as they are occurring, so the chance of an officer arriving on scene in time to catch a perpetrator in the act is very rare. That is not to suggest that a fast police presence cannot stop the escalation or continuation of an offence, but as an overarching prevention strategy, it does not address the reality of most criminal offences.

The final means by which to prevent crime under the professional model, while intuitively attractive, was also largely unfounded. Although police departments should, for many good reasons, aim to find perpetrators and arrest them for their offences, this action does not in and of itself prevent crime. Most crimes are not serious enough to warrant decades behind bars, and as such, most (if not all) of the criminals found guilty at trial and sentenced to prison will eventually be released. Although some may not offend again, many find themselves in circumstances and situations similar to those that precipitated the offence in the first instance, and therefore may return to similar behaviour. Therefore, while the arrest may have stalled some of their offending behaviour, it rarely stops it altogether. This approach also ignores the issue of criminality that occurs behind bars, and while it may prevent an offender's victimization of the general public, it may not protect their fellow inmates.

Community Policing

Community policing (also referred to as **community-based policing**) is a philosophy and an organizational strategy that encourages partnerships between the police and the community, and advocates a collaborative response to prioritize and solve problems. Only by working together can the quality of life in a community improve. This is a move away from the traditional response that saw only police action as necessary in the fight against crime and disorder.

Often, however, community policing is identified by its activities in a department, rather than the organizational philosophy and strategy. This tends to see activities such as foot patrol or community storefront offices as evidence that a department is "community policing–based." Community policing is not in and of itself a set of activities, however, and despite some of these activities fitting well within the realm of community policing, their existence does not necessarily give credence to a department's ability to deploy according to community policing principles. Community policing can be better thought of as a process, rather than a product (Skogan 2006).

Many police departments report they adhere to community policing principles, although this usually comes by way of the incorporation of specific programs or initiatives within the police department, rather than a department-wide paradigm shift away from the traditional model. Many police departments incorporate storefronts, have limited foot patrols, may do some community outreach, and may place some emphasis on prevention activities; however, few departments can be said to embrace community policing as an overall philosophy within their organization. Some elements advocated by a community policing perspective seem to be particularly difficult for departments to incorporate, such as decentralized decision making and true community partnership (as opposed to information sources) (Braga and Weisburd 2007; Skogan 2006).

In terms of crime prevention, community policing holds a great deal of promise due to its commitment to create collaboration, interface with the community, and develop specific programs aimed at reducing fear and disorder in that community. When integrated as a guiding organizational philosophy, community policing can enable the local department to address crime issues at the ground level and provide responses specific to

Challenge Your Assumptions

Does Increasing Punishment Prevent Crime?

In 2009, the Conservative government was criticized by academics for being misguided and outdated (Galloway 2009), with even more criticism coming with the passing of Bill C-10 (*Safe Streets and Communities Act*), otherwise known as the Omnibus Crime Bill. With its focus on punishment, critics argued that government policies largely ignored the causes of violence and modern crime prevention methods. As a stark example, it was noted that at the time, the government spent $15 billion annually on police, courts, and correctional facilities, but only $70 million on crime prevention. With the passing of the Omnibus Crime Bill, Harper's Conservatives brought in a wave of new legislation that involved numerous mandatory minimum sentences aimed at keeping offenders in prison longer and promising to keep the public safer. The premise was that a clear statement of a minimum punishment level would satisfy primary prevention aims by deterring offenders who would fear the increasingly harsh sentences, and satisfy tertiary prevention efforts by keeping offenders in prison longer and, therefore, unable to commit crimes.

The issue is that research tells us this doesn't work in the broader sense of preventing or reducing crime. "The sole proponents of mandatory minimum sentencing in Canada appear to be politicians whose positions on the advantages of these laws are without a clear basis in either research or policy" (Sheehy 2001, 262).

More than three decades ago, the Canadian Sentencing Commission (1987) advocated the abolition of mandatory minimum sentences in favour of more presumptive sentencing guidelines that would allow the judiciary to depart from the guidelines if it was appropriate to do so. The Commission stated that mandatory minimums would effectively end the accused's incentives to plead guilty in return for a lesser sentence, which would have deleterious effects on case processing and court workloads. The Commission also advocated for abolishment as it felt mandatory minimum sentences would result in prosecutorial manipulation of charging systems, unduly harsh punishments, and negative infringement on judicial discretion (Gabor 2001). Despite this learned Commission's recommendation, by 1999 in Canada the *Criminal Code* had 29 offences that carried a mandatory minimum sentence, with 19 of those being created in 1995 with the passing of new firearms legislation in Bill C-68 (Mirza 2001). By 2007, this number had risen again to 40 (Fish 2008), and with the passing of Bill C-10 in 2012, Canada now sits with dozens of mandatory minimums for a wide array of offences from violent crimes to drug offences.

The Supreme Court dealt some blows to this legislation, however, when it upheld an Ontario Court of Appeal ruling that labelled a law requiring a mandatory minimum sentence for crimes involving prohibited guns unconstitutional. Before becoming prime minister, Liberal leader Justin Trudeau commented that the overuse of mandatory minimum sentences "isn't necessarily doing a service to Canadians, both by not necessarily keeping us that much safer and also wasting large amounts of taxpayers' dollars on unnecessary court challenges" (Canadian Press 2015).

The question is, therefore, should we continue to focus on punishment when we know it does little to deter or prevent crime? Are there other reasons why punishment is so popular? If we didn't punish offenders, what other options would we have? Should our justice policies be based on research or popular opinion?

and appropriate for the unique needs of the community. However, community policing as a philosophy is rarely touted as the only or best way to get the crime rate down. It is often difficult to evaluate this paradigm's effectiveness and some objectives (such as community cohesion, relationships with police, collaboration, and so forth) may reduce fear of crime, but may not immediately impact crime rates. In general, research tends to show that general tactics such as foot patrols or storefront officers not specifically deployed against a target population or area do little to reduce or prevent crime and disorder (Braga and Weisburd 2007). Some are more pessimistic about the promises of community policing, highlighting the relative lack of evidence regarding its overall ability to accomplish its goals beyond lowering the public's fear of crime (Mastrofski 2006).

Police-Centred Practices and Programs

Within the professional (or traditional) model, prevention practices were not emphasized explicitly, despite an underlying belief that the hallmark practices of this model could and would reduce and/or prevent crime. With a move toward the community policing approach, however, prevention became much more of a central focus in policing and related research, as practitioners and academics began to explore how the police could be most effective at not just fighting crime, but preventing it as well. This prevention movement saw a few primary programs or foci emerge out of the research, most notably problem-oriented policing, intelligence-led policing, hot spots policing, and CompStat approaches. These may be conceptualized in many ways, but are most appropriately thought of as guiding principles rather than specific programs. It may also be appropriate to consider them under the umbrella of evidence-based approaches, as all seek to find and assess programs or policies that "work" or show the most impact. They are intended to not only show police what courses of action are most appropriate and/or effective, but demonstrate a different way of thinking of the police role in modern crime prevention—from one of reactive crime fighter to one of strategic crime preventer.

Problem-Oriented Policing

In 1979, Herman Goldstein proposed a shift in policing away from the traditional call response focus to one that saw police as problem solvers aimed at examining the underlying conditions behind calls for service (Braga 2008a; see Figure 12.1). Goldstein's belief was that although answering the public's calls was an important activity, police should be focused as well on determining the underlying reasons behind the call and, in particular, why some problems seemed to recur. This shift in thinking acknowledged that responding to the same location, person, or similar call type over and over was doing little to stem any problems, and was using valuable resources in the police department with little effect on reducing or preventing crime. Alternatively, Goldstein proposed that by determining the underlying conditions and tailoring a response capable of reducing or eliminating those conditions, the police could be far more effective and efficient. In addition, emphasis was placed on collaboration between the police and other agencies when forming responses, and a particular emphasis was placed on the use of resources outside of the criminal justice system to increase the crime reduction potential of the response.

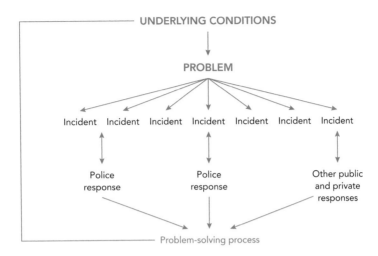

Figure 12.1 Underlying Conditions to Problem-Oriented Policing

Source: *Problem-Oriented Policing and Crime Prevention*, 2nd edition by Anthony A. Braga. Copyright © 2008 by Lynne Rienner Publishers, Inc. Used with permission of the publisher.

Goldstein's philosophy was given an operational structure termed the SARA model. Officers follow a process consisting of four stages:

1. *Scanning*—identifying the problem;
2. *Analysis*—analysis of the problem in depth to determine the underlying conditions;
3. *Response*—applying results from the analysis to form appropriate responses; and,
4. *Assessment*—evaluation of whether the response accomplished its objectives, or whether modification to the response is required (Braga 2008).

A problem, according to Goldstein, was defined as "a cluster of similar, related, or recurring incidents rather than a single incident; a substantive community concern; or a unit of police business" (Goldstein 1990, 66). This served to clarify the first step in the SARA process, as often problems would arise in the community or among the police community that did not fit within this guideline for a recurring incident, but that may have occupied a great deal of police resources with little or no impact on overall safety and disorder. By defining a problem in this way, **problem-oriented policing** first insists that one-off incidents not be classified as problems. One-off incidents, by their very nature, may never happen again and would thus be prevented regardless of any police action.

This definition also clarifies that the problem must be a substantive community concern, thereby requiring that there be some significant need or insistence by the community for the police to address the issue. This avoids the police focusing on issues that they may consider harmful but that are of little concern to the public. Likely this aspect of the definition aims to recognize that the police are there to care for and protect the public, and should be devoting much of their resources to doing so rather than furthering internal agendas. However, this does not mean that the police need to wait for the public to push for a particular problem to be solved—the scanning step can be done internally to highlight issues in the community, even without public input in the initial stages.

Problems may be identified by computer-assisted analysis or mapping to highlight hot spots (see Chapter 13 for more discussion) or areas of particularly high activity. This approach may differ from other tactics, such as empowering officers to solve problems they feel are most urgent or addressing citizen concerns about crime in their community voiced via public forums or community consultations. Each tactic holds its own merits in terms of identifying worthy problems. The officer may see and/or experience first-hand issues that have yet to come to the full attention of the public; the community, on the other hand, may be experiencing issues they have not fully let the police know about. Therefore, each forum may introduce different problems that may be worthy of solutions or attention by the police department. This all becomes part of the scanning process, which is aimed at identifying problems worth addressing.

> [P]roblem-oriented policing and data analysis are highly interdependent. A framework for problem-oriented policing is of little use if good data are not available and, similarly, complex data about crime problems require a meaningful framework for analysis. In fact, methods of capturing and analyzing data about crime problems have rapidly developed at the same time as advances have been made in the theory of problem-oriented policing agenda. [White 2008]

The second phase, analysis, begins the process of officers focusing their efforts on trying to analyze the possible cause(s) of the problem they have identified as worthy of attention in the scanning phase. There may be several precipitators to the problem, and each may suggest a relatively different course of action for the officers and/or others to take to solve the problem. What is crucial in this phase is for officers to go farther than simply focusing on the "who" of the problem and falling back on seeking to identify and arrest those responsible. Analysis of the problem and its underlying conditions may actually point to arrest as being the least effective response to a particular problem. Other approaches, such as situational crime prevention or other strategic responses, may see more gains than a traditional approach. Improving security, heightening awareness of an offender's tactics, or mobilizing community groups may show much more promise in solving the problem than putting all efforts toward numerous arrests.

Following these first two phases, the police department's response can be carefully put together to reach peak effectiveness in combatting the problem. Although problem-oriented policing advocates for a more strategic and targeted response than simply arrest and capture, this does not mean that arrest and capture are never appropriate responses. Rather, careful analysis may show that the problem is due to a small group of offenders, or perhaps even one or two offenders. In this scenario, it may be the most advantageous and effective response to put energy toward arrest and capture of that small group of offenders who are responsible for the most criminal activity. This, as well, is at the heart of intelligence-led policing, discussed below.

The last step in the problem-oriented policing approach is assessment, whereby the initiatives undertaken by the police (and partners) to combat a particular problem are evaluated as to whether they have had the desired effect. This is crucial for numerous reasons. The first and most important aspect of the assessment feedback loop is to ensure resources are not being spent in areas where they are not effective. If a police department is spending considerable time and energy combatting a problem in a specific way or using specific tactics, and those tactics are not seeing the desired results, then it is imperative for the department to adjust the strategy and re-assess. To not do so results in the perpetuation of the problem, as well as a misuse of public funds and resources via the police force. By consistently evaluating responses and adjusting accordingly, the police department remains effective, efficient, and accountable to the public.

To enhance this process and the use of SARA, Paul Ekblom (in Clarke and Eck 2003) has proposed the 5Is to capture, organize, and transfer the knowledge of good police practice. They are:

1. *Intelligence*—gathering and analyzing information on crime problems and their consequences, and diagnosing their causes;
2. *Intervention*—considering the full range of possible interventions that could be applied to block, disrupt, or weaken those causes and manipulate the risk and protective factors;
3. *Implementation*—converting potential interventions into practical methods, putting them into effect in ways that are appropriate for the local context, and monitoring;
4. *Involvement*—mobilizing other agencies, companies, and individuals to play their part in implementing the intervention; and
5. *Impact and process evaluation*—assessment, feedback, and adjustment (Clarke and Eck 2003).

Unfortunately, while impact and process evaluation is arguably one of the most crucial steps, it is generally the most overlooked. Evaluations tend to be the most difficult of the stages, and the most outside of the comfort zone of police departments. "[A]ssessment of responses is rare and, when undertaken, it is usually cursory and limited to anecdotal or impressionistic data" (Braga 2008a).

The effectiveness of problem-oriented policing in reducing crime and disorder was systematically studied in 2010. Overall, the researchers found a statistically significant, albeit modest, impact on crime and disorder of the problem-oriented policing approach. The researchers also found that many interventions that either failed or showed weaker results were a direct consequence of implementation failure or the inability to fully put the interventions into practice. Overall, the effects of a correctly implemented problem-oriented policing approach are overwhelmingly positive, although large crime benefits should not necessarily be anticipated in all instances (Weisburd et al. 2010).

Intelligence-Led Policing

Similarly to the problem-oriented policing and community policing movements, **intelligence-led policing** started to emerge in the 1990s in response to surging crime rates from the 1960s and 70s, and the failure of the traditional model of reactive policing to address these problems and get crime rates under control. Although often thought of as simply utilizing surveillance and information, intelligence-led policing is much more akin to a business practice than an intelligence-gathering technique (Ratcliffe 2011).

> Intelligence-led policing is a business model and managerial philosophy where data analysis and crime intelligence are pivotal to an objective, decision-making framework that facilitates crime and problem reduction, disruption and prevention through both strategic management and effective enforcement strategies that target prolific and serious offenders. [Ratcliffe 2008, 89]

The intelligence-led cycle is far more than simply gathering data or information. It builds on experience and knowledge of officers and analysts, who utilize the data and information to further their knowledge, and then turn that intelligence into action (see Figure 12.2).

Intelligence-led policing relies heavily on criminal intelligence analysis to inform these decisions, particularly when it comes to identifying the most prolific offenders. Often, offenders may be well-known to some front-line officers, but the true nature and extent of

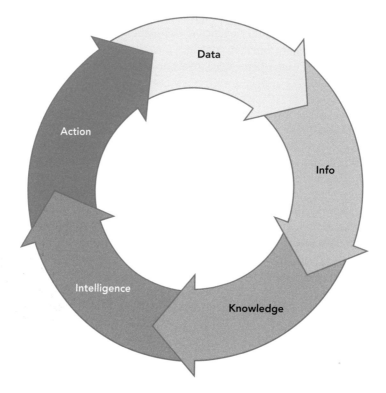

Figure 12.2   Intelligence-Led Policing Cycle

Source: Adapted from Ratcliffe J.H. 2011. Intelligence-led policing. In R. Wortley and L. Mazerolle, eds, *Environmental Criminology and Crime Analysis*. 267. New York: Routledge, Taylor & Francis.

their offending may not be fully realized without computerized analysis of their activity over time. Utilizing the objective analysis found in database searches can also highlight individuals who are extremely prolific, but who may have gone largely unnoticed due to a dispersed offending area or offence preference. However, recommendations for targets from criminal intelligence analysts must be utilized and actioned within the department for intelligence-led operations to be truly in effect. Intelligence without action holds little utility, as does action without intelligence.

As one of the more recent movements in policing, intelligence-led policing is still evolving and experiences differing levels of incorporation within police departments. While some departments have begun to set up units devoted to prolific offenders, the units are often small and ad hoc without significant institutional will behind them. However, the impact of these prolific or chronic offenders is beginning to be noticed and acted upon.

Although building a target list of prolific offenders is but one small element in intelligence-led policing, it is based on the observation that by focusing efforts on the few offenders who cause the most harm, the overall crime reduction and/or prevention effects will be far more impactful than spreading focus across all offenders.

This is a theoretical approach similar to hot spots policing, discussed next.

Hot Spots Policing

Research into the location of crime, emerging out of theories within environmental criminology (discussed earlier), found that crime is not spread evenly in space, but rather clusters in small areas. These areas of high crime concentrations have been termed

Case Study

Vancouver Police Department Chronic Offender Unit Quick Facts

In 2008, the Vancouver Police Department defined a chronic offender as a property criminal with 12 or more charges in the past 12 months, one who was identified as particularly problematic, or one who had a history of non-compliance with court orders.

At that time, approximately 380 offenders met these criteria, with 27 of those being considered "super chronics." These offenders averaged 71 police contacts each, for a total of over 26,000 police contacts since 2001 in PRIME. This group accounted for over 12,000 total charges overall, with an average of 33 each. The most prolific offenders had over 300 police contacts and over 150 charges

from 2001 to 2008. The top 10 per cent of offenders on this list had over 70 convictions each, while the top six offenders at the time had over 100 convictions each. As of 2008, the VPD Chronic Offender Unit was able to monitor about 50 of these offenders (Planning, Research & Audit 2008). Currently, the definition has been broadened to eliminate a requisite number of offences before an individual can be considered for inclusion on the "list"; however, this flexibility undoubtedly is in response to the intense demands of monitoring and handling these individuals, and the changing resources (or sworn officers) available to do so.

hot spots. (See Chapter 13 for a discussion of computerized mapping of hot spots.) Similarly to the intelligence-led policing approach of focusing efforts on the few prolific offenders for the most crime reduction/prevention impact, hot spots policing suggests that by focusing officer activity on those few areas where crime is highly concentrated—the hot spots—the positive impacts on crime and disorder will be far greater than a dispersed approach.

This approach to policing was first examined in the mid-1990s in Minneapolis. The argument was made that patrols could be far more effective if more tightly focused on those areas where crime was clustered, even if that meant little or no coverage in areas of little activity (Braga and Weisburd 2007). The proposal centred on the observation that, with limited resources, it made more sense to place those resources in areas requiring the most police response, and remove them from areas that did not demand police services. Although this meant differing levels of service to different areas of the city, in terms of the impact, the logic was sound.

This notion of focused police effort in small, identified areas runs somewhat counter to the traditional approach of random preventive patrols highlighted in the professional model. Indeed, research has shown the utility of focused effort over the more traditional approach of police patrol (Braga 2005). Similarly to the intelligence-led policing approach, hot spots policing utilizes the analysis capabilities and computerized knowledge of crime analysts to identify those areas that are either emerging or established hot spots, and that are appropriate for targeted intervention. Generally, these analysis products will be in the form of **crime maps** depicting those areas of highest concern (see Figure 12.3).

The Minneapolis Hot Spots Patrol experiment saw modest but statistically significant reductions in calls for service in hot spot areas that received approximately double the patrol attention (Sherman and Weisburd 1995 in Braga 2005). Many other examinations of hot spot policing and targeted patrol and area enforcement saw similar positive effects over control areas.

Despite many positive outcomes, criticisms have been levelled against hot spot approaches. Some come by way of conceptual critique, whereby the identification and definition of the hot spot may not be conducted in an objective or standardized way. This recognizes that a hot spot is a generalized concept and, as such, does not necessarily have clearly defined boundaries. Therefore, the identification of a hot spot may actually depend on who defines it and what parameters are used. Obviously, this may have implications for deployment decisions and resultant actions.

More tactical critiques recognize the danger that hot spot policing may encompass little more than saturation patrols over the short term in a particularly problematic area. This may impact crime and disorder in that area, but the effects generally dissipate once attention is pulled back. In addition, such emphasis may start to resemble a crackdown, which could see a greater propensity for aggressive policing that may in turn damage police–community relations and a return to the status quo once the treatment effect is removed. Rather than solving the problem, therefore, the increased patrol in hot spot areas may only serve to displace the problem or temporarily disrupt it at great cost to the department in terms of both operations and relationships.

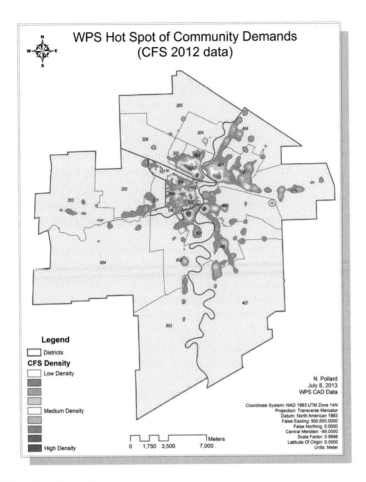

Figure 12.3   Hot Spot Map

Source: Griffiths, C.T. and Pollard, N. (2013). *Policing in Winnipeg: An Operational Review,* prepared for the Canadian Police Association. Vancouver, October. Reprinted with permission.

Despite reasonable criticisms, the theoretical underpinning of hot spot policing remains sound. To be effective, however, departments need to acknowledge the possible negative effects and work to establish lasting and long-term efforts directed at these hot spots to positively effect change.

CompStat

CompStat is best known as a program of accountability within police departments that utilizes up-to-date computerized statistics to deploy resources and reduce crime. Rolled out by the New York City Police Department (NYPD) in 1994, CompStat is now used in various forms by numerous agencies throughout North America and worldwide. (For the crime analyst's role in CompStat, see Chapter 13.) Although not classically thought of as a crime prevention tactic for police, CompStat can be shown to have a specific role to place in prevention efforts by providing the accountability and evaluation mechanisms so often missing from initiatives in this area.

The CompStat process is guided by four principles (Godown 2009):

1. *Accurate and timely intelligence*—Up-to-the-minute (or as current as possible) data is utilized to produce crime maps and other statistical products to assist in operational decisions about where to place resources and how to task them to address emerging issues.
2. *Effective tactics*—Command officers are responsible for deploying resources in ways that have been successful in the past, or are most appropriate for the issues that the intelligence has highlighted.
3. *Rapid deployment*—The use of and guidance from timely intelligence allows commanders to deploy resources quickly before crime problems escalate or get out of control. Responding days or weeks after a problem is identified is not sufficient—departments should be nimble and able to respond far more expeditiously.
4. *Relentless follow-up and assessment*—The CompStat meeting is one piece of the CompStat process; it provides the accountability mechanism for the tactics that were deployed to address issues highlighted by the intelligence. At the meeting, commanders are held to account for their decisions, and whether those tactics they chose to deploy were effective in addressing the crime problem. If they were shown to be effective, they likely continue as needed. If they do not, commanders are expected to rethink and redeploy.

In this way, CompStat is far more than the process of creating crime maps and statistical packages for commanders to use at a monthly meeting. It is a way of constantly adjusting and orienting strategies to be most effective, and remaining in tune with the ebb and flow of crime movements within a community. As such, CompStat can be seen as both a program and a way of doing business or an organizational philosophy. However, the face of CompStat tends to be the meeting in which commanders are held to task. This has often obscured the true nature of its aims.

> Too often, therefore, CompStat has been interpreted as primarily a meeting with a statistical computer program which, when it generates accurate and timely crime statistics, transforms a traditional bureaucracy into a flexible, adaptable police agency geared to effective crime control strategies. [Silverman 2006, 269]

CompStat also empowered police commanders to take control and do something about crime in their area. This fostered responsibility and creativity, and overcame some of the issues with the traditional model of reaction-based policing (Braga and Weisburd 2007). William Bratton, the New York City police chief who coined the term and developed the program, writes:

We created a system in which the police commissioner, with his executive core, first empowers and then interrogates the precinct commander, forcing him or her to come up with a plan to attack crime. But it should not stop there. At the next level down, it should be the precinct commander, taking the same role as the commissioner, empowering and interrogating the platoon commander. Then, at the third level, the platoon commander should be asking his sergeants . . . all the way down until everyone in the entire organization is empowered and motivated, active and assessed and successful. It works in all organizations, whether it's 38,000 cops or Mayberry, R.F.D. [Bratton 1998, 239 in Braga and Weisburd 2007, 7]

It is often difficult to assess the relative impact or success of CompStat, as more often than not it is instituted alongside other initiatives and, therefore, difficult to disentangle from those effects (Braga and Weisburd 2007). However, what CompStat can assist with is a greater emphasis on introspection on the part of the police department, and a greater focus on finding what works and addressing issues before they arise. Simply operating a monthly meeting where crime statistics are shown, however, should not be considered a crime-control strategy in and of itself, nor should that be considered the hallmark of the CompStat approach.

Broken Windows

The term **broken windows** is a metaphor developed by Wilson and Kelling in the early 1980s to describe their theory of police action in response to neighbourhood incivility. Put quite simply, the theory posits that if a broken window is left unattended and unmended, it will be a clear signal that the neighbourhood does not care about protecting its people or its property, thereby communicating to the would-be offender that the rules do not apply in the area (Sousa and Kelling 2006). In this way, the theory links minor instances of social disorder (such as the broken window) and more serious crimes. For police, this has translated into the necessity of not ignoring small instances of incivility and petty crimes, as these are the situations and circumstances that will lead directly to more serious crimes (Braga and Weisburd 2007). Putting an emphasis on controlling these minor offences will therefore have a corresponding positive effect on the level of serious offending. Research has shown that incivilities generate fear and tend to be associated with serious crime, and thus, effective police action at crime reduction and prevention should start with improving the general neighbourhood environment (Braga 2008b).

However, considerable criticism has been launched against both the theory and the implementation by police departments of the broken windows approach. For many, this perspective has led to an overemphasis on policing minor incivilities committed by the poor or homeless, or those most likely to be participating in loitering, panhandling, littering, or minor theft offences. What this therefore translated into is a sentiment that broken windows policing is in fact an attack on the poor in society, rather than a policy aimed at bettering life for everyone (Taylor 2006).

Another notable criticism of broken windows policing comes from the association with **zero-tolerance policing**, whereby police crack down on all minor disorders in an

Case Study

Does Graffiti Encourage Crime?

Graffiti and other signs of disorder make people feel uneasy, and may in fact have a psychological impact on people and their decisions to offend. Based on the broken windows approach developed by George Kelling at Rutgers University, researchers in the Netherlands sought to test this assumption with a serious of experiments. Their premise was that signs of disorder and law-breaking could influence the number of people who were prepared to litter and steal. This premise turned out to be correct.

The first study was conducted in an alley that was frequently used to park bicycles. Two conditions were created, wherein one displayed order and cleanliness, and the other showed signs of disorder using graffiti on the walls. A large sign in both conditions prohibiting graffiti was put up in clear view. All the bicycles that were placed in both conditions also were affixed with a flyer that needed to be taken off before the person could ride it. The idea was that the owners of the bicycles had the choice among taking the flyer with them, hanging it on another bicycle, or throwing it on the ground. In the disordered and graffiti-laden alley, 69 per cent of riders littered compared with only 33 per cent of those owners whose bicycles were held in the clean alley with no graffiti or signs of disorder.

In a similar experiment, researchers created two similar conditions, but with money visible in an envelope sticking out of a mailbox. In the "order" condition, the mailbox was clean and the area surrounding it had no litter or other signs of disorder. In the "disorder" condition, the mailbox was covered in graffiti, and in a sub-condition, the area was littered with paper, debris, and cigarette butts (sub-disorder condition). When the mailbox was clean and no debris littered the area, only 13 per cent of those passing by stole the envelope with the cash. However, when the mailbox was covered with graffiti, 27 per cent of those passing by stole the envelope. Even with no graffiti but with area debris (sub-disorder condition), 25 per cent still took the envelope.

effort to reclaim control. This often results in numerous arrests of marginalized individuals, often in a very public manner. However, the link between broken windows and zero-tolerance policing is one that was never made or advocated by the theory's originators (Taylor 2006). Rather, broken windows policing advocates a considerable amount of discretion and avoidance of heavy-handed police tactics. Although the broken windows approach appears to have support in the community as a crime reduction tactic, the devolution into zero tolerance has been shown to negatively affect police–community relations (Taylor 2006).

The available empirical evidence on the crime-control effectiveness of broken windows policing is mixed, and it is uncertain whether this type of strategy actually reduces crime (Braga and Weisburd 2007). Despite the continuing criticisms, there have been quasi-experimental studies that support the notion that people are more apt to commit crimes in areas that appear run-down, abandoned, or uncared for.

Do you think the graffiti in this alley affects the likelihood that this bicycle will be stolen?

These experiments supported Kelling's theory that disorder can breed more disorder, and indeed, even greater criminality. The message to take away was to encourage cleaner communities and attention to disorder as one tool to help curb criminality (Can the Can 2008).

Conclusion

The police role in crime prevention and reduction has evolved in recent decades to take on a far greater reliance on problem solving, analysis, and evidence-based approaches and evaluation. With advances in technology such as crime mapping and statistical analysis applied to police data, departments are in a far better position than ever before to both structure their responses to crime and disorder and measure those results for effectiveness and efficiency. With the incorporation of highly skilled and trained crime analysts, the profession has become far more strategic than in previous generations, particularly with pressures on budgets and resources.

Initiatives, paradigms, and programs such as problem-oriented policing, intelligence-led policing, hot spots policing, and broken windows share some underpinnings, and are best thought of as all parts of an evidence-based approach. All adhere to the notion of working smarter, not harder, and advocate for constant evaluation of whether initiatives are working to accomplish their goal. Problem-oriented policing advocates for a holistic approach to problem solving that first identifies a suitable problem and then devises strategies to solve that problem. Seemingly simple, the ability to both identify and respond to a problem may necessitate a very complex collaboration between police, community, and other partners. In addition, very often police are pulled by the public into situations that wouldn't necessarily meet the criteria for a problem, which drains resources and makes planning for longer-term initiatives more difficult. While a problem-oriented policing approach asserts that simply responding to calls for service is of little utility for crime prevention and reduction, police departments are certainly not in the position of simply refusing to participate in this traditional role.

Similarly, although an intelligence-led policing approach would advocate for resources to focus on prolific offenders, the department again is not able to simply ignore the non-prolific offenders. The community expectation of response, investigation, and arrest continues to pull focus and resources toward their traditionally reactive role. This is also the case with hot spots policing, insofar as police are not able to simply ignore calls for service in non–hot spot areas.

Of course, none of these approaches would suggest that police action only be centred on the most prolific offenders, the most prolific places, or the most pressing problems. Rather, there needs to be a balance between the requirement to respond to community requests for assistance and the requirement to focus on strategic initiatives to address crime problems. Ideally, by placing emphasis on both (and not simply responding), the offshoot will be a greater proportion of time for crime fighting, rather than simply crime responding.

Critical Thinking Questions

1. Which perspective, in your opinion, should police follow? Should they advocate approaches that have the most public appeal, or operate using only evidence-based approaches?
2. What are the differences between broken windows policing and zero-tolerance policing? Are they simply two different ways of referring to the same thing?
3. Why are all four steps of the SARA model important? During an enforcement initiative, which step do you think police (a) focus on most often, and (b) often neglect?
4. What are some of the downsides of moving away from the professional (traditional) model of policing? What would this change?

Intelligence-Led Policing and the Role of the Crime Analyst

Learning Objectives

After reading and studying this chapter, students will be able to:

- Describe the differences among information, intelligence, and data.
- Identify the intersection of intelligence-led policing, evidence-led policing, and crime analysis.
- Describe the history of crime analysis and its theoretical background.
- Identify the primary roles of different types of crime analysts.
- Identify the difference between standard and specialized analysis.
- Describe and explain crime mapping, geographic profiling, and social network analysis.

Introduction

Intelligence is the end product of an analytic process applied to data. [Prox 2014]

This chapter explores the emergence of intelligence-led policing as an overarching paradigm in police services, as well as the movement of many police departments toward an evidence-based or evidence-led approach to policy and strategy. These terms may be used in various ways to explain several approaches in how police perform their duties, but in the context of this chapter, these perspectives will be interwoven with the discussion surrounding the role of data, analysis, and the crime analysts who have become an integral part of the police services' strategy for working efficiently. Intelligence-led policing denotes an overall strategy whereby police services systematically collect, analyze, and share information to focus efforts on the most fruitful targets. Originally developed to respond to terrorist threats, this strategy has broadened to apply to the process of data-driven target selection (most often), insofar as it may relate to chronic or prolific offenders, or high-profile targets. The concept acknowledges that not all offenders have the same impact on public safety, nor on the criminal justice system. Therefore, by knowing the "best" targets in terms of positive impact on public safety, for example, police efforts may show more dramatic gains (Ratcliffe, 2012).

Speaking about a police service being evidence-led or evidence-driven refers to the guiding rationale for decision making with respect to larger operational strategies. What this term does not denote is a suggestion that police have not up to this point based their decisions on evidence. The "evidence" in this terminology refers not to evidence that is gathered in the process of a specific investigation, but the scientific or research evidence showing that various strategies, programs, or initiatives work to reduce crime, deter crime, enhance safety, and so forth. A growing body of research evaluates and tests various policing strategies, and can be used to make operational and large-scale strategic decisions (see Lum and Koper 2017). In this way, the police service that is informed by that body of research, and applies it to operational choices, can be thought of as being evidence-driven.

While intelligence- and evidence-led policing historically have been seen as adhering to slightly different strategies, most often now they are used interchangeably to indicate that a police service relies heavily on data and analytic support for deployment and activity decisions and evaluations. This has resulted in the emergence of a specialized civilian position within the police service, able to mine data and create intelligence to support the organization. How this emerged is discussed below.

Policing as a profession is unique in terms of how much information can be gathered from day-to-day interactions. In the early years of policing, officers would carry pieces of that information around in notebooks, gather it in paper-based case files, or commit much of it to memory. Documentation requirements for court proceedings were relatively simple compared to today's standards, and the volume of information was largely manageable and contained within a handful of file boxes. However, over the years, the amount of information, paperwork, and other data that is routinely gathered and stored during police operations has grown exponentially. Officers' interactions and the details they are required to record have also increased exponentially. Due to changes in technology, the law, and administrative procedure, basic notations in notebooks regarding an encounter are no longer sufficient. Now, the officer must record details of the event from start to finish, with rigour suitable to stand up in court. Today, police movements throughout their working day are recorded and time stamped, and the individuals whom they come across are logged along with the details of each encounter.

As these administrative duties and requirements have grown, so too has intelligence data and the ability to store and access information. This information age in policing has therefore given rise to the intelligence age and the move toward evidence-based policing. As most police departments now have sophisticated computerized records management software packages that interact with dispatch databases and communications centres, they are strategically placed to harness the power of that information by using it as intelligence. This has opened up a new realm of police information analysis; however, it is only recently that the focus has been on how to mine and utilize that information, and what skills and tools are necessary to turn it into actionable intelligence.

The move toward community policing and problem-oriented policing in recent decades, matched with the explosion of available information, has led to the development of strategies and philosophies within the police agency that focus on being intelligence led, and using evidence-based approaches to guide their policies and operational strategies instead of public pressure, intuition, or pure random chance. For instance, the public may feel that a particular neighbourhood is unsafe, and may demand increased patrols around that area to reduce the crime. However, based on analysis of the data, the police service discovers this area actually is no worse than any other neighbourhood and, thus, focuses its efforts on the areas with the highest statistical amount of crime rather than those with the most vocal citizens. In this way, police use intelligence to show the areas they should concentrate their efforts on to effect the most change, basing those operational decisions on the best available evidence (the statistics). This is separate from, but not unlike, the strategy of intelligence-led policing discussed in Chapter 12.

Being intelligence-led can permeate a department and influence decisions not only regarding who or where to target, but also when to deploy resources, where to deploy resources, what is attainable, what is successful, and what shows promise in various areas of crime prevention, crime reduction, and community policing. This focus on becoming intelligence-led has brought a surge in the specialized job of the crime analyst. Although many departments had sworn officers who would function as analysts at certain times in their careers (often when injured or on non-deployable duties), now police agencies rely on specialized and highly trained civilians to fulfill this role within the department. The role of crime analyst is no longer a place to "park" someone, but rather an integral part of the police service's strategic vision. The crime analyst may take on multiple duties and be involved in numerous responsibilities, including the collection, collation, interpretation, and presentation of data and information (White 2008), and has a crucial role to play in ensuring that a police service is intelligence-led.

The International Association of Crime Analysts (IACA) has defined a crime analyst as follows:

> Crime analysis is a profession and process in which a set of quantitative and qualitative techniques are used to analyze data valuable to police agencies and their communities. It includes the analysis of crime and criminals, crime victims, disorder, quality of life issues, traffic issues, and internal police operations, and its results support criminal investigation and prosecution, patrol activities, crime prevention and reduction strategies, problem solving, and the evaluation of police efforts. [International Association of Crime Analysts 2014]

As policing relies increasingly on intelligent information to guide interventions, the role of the analyst has become crucial to organizational and operational effectiveness (Cope 2004).

History and Theory

The work of analyzing crime patterns and utilizing information to aid the organization is not new. Before there were formal crime analysts, there were individuals identifying areas of high activity or places where the police should focus their efforts. This dates back as far as 1847 in London, where members of the London Metropolitan Police identified patterns of crime and assisted in collecting and analyzing crime statistics (Gwinn et al. 2008).

It was not until the mid-1950s that the term "crime analysis" made its way into the police culture and literature. The use of the term "crime analysis" in police culture and literature is primarily attributed to Orland Winfield Wilson (1900–72), who wrote numerous books on police administration and planning. He first used the term in the mid-1950s, as quoted here:

> The crime-analysis section studies daily reports of serious crimes in order to determine the location, time, special characteristics, similarities to other criminal attacks, and various significant facts that might help to identify either a criminal or the existence of a pattern of criminal activity. Such information is helpful in planning the operations of a division or district. [Gwinn et al. 2008, 10]

Although Wilson notes and discusses many modern functions of crime analysts, such as the interpretation and dissemination of crime statistics to aid in operations, there is little evidence that these products were being produced by police departments in the 1950s and 1960s (Boba-Santos 2013).

A new field of focus in criminology began emerging in the 1960s and 1970s that shifted focus from the "who" and "why" of the criminal event to "where" and "when." These theories, discussed elsewhere in this book, generally are part of environmental criminology and focus primarily on the criminal event and the physical and social environments necessary to foster that event and create opportunities for crime (Brantingham and Brantingham 1991; Cohen and Felson 1979; Cornish and Clarke 1986). This shift in focus brought an emphasis on analyzing where crime was happening and how the environment influenced criminal events (Boba-Santos 2013).

These theories provided a basis for the systematic analysis of strategic police actions and their impact on crime. Around the same time, the problem-oriented policing (POP) model of Herman Goldstein (discussed in Chapter 12) began to come into the mainstream, and crime prevention became much more of a focus. The theoretical development, alongside the practical applications of POP and emergence of analytic techniques, paved the way for modern crime analysis work and the development of methodologies to enable police to study their responses to problems (Boba-Santos 2013).

Although this movement began in the 1970s, it was not until the 1990s that crime analysis as a profession became prominent in police agencies (Gwinn et al. 2008). This was partly due to the availability and development of useful software applications, such as crime mapping, and the affordability and availability of powerful computers within police departments. Data, as well, became more plentiful only in the last several decades, partly from the utilization of computerized police databases, but also from the availability of data from government agencies and geographic and social data sources (Boba-Santos 2013). The analyst, armed with ability, theoretical background, practical construct, and technological tools, was now able to bring all these elements together to fully realize the potential in this role.

Today, crime analysts can be found in most medium and large police agencies, and specialized training and educational courses and programs have begun developing both in Canada and the United States. The crime analyst role ranges from short-term tactical analysis to longer-term strategic and administrative analysis, and the ability of the police agency to become (or remain) intelligence-led relies heavily on the placement and portfolio given to analysts throughout the department.

Types of Crime Analysts

The evidence-led police service relies on analysis to support numerous functions within the organization, from front-line operational deployment strategies to serious crime investigations to long-term administrative planning. What they all have in common, however, is the focus on finding the right information to maximize efficiency, effectiveness, and overall impact. Although in smaller organizations analysts may wear many hats and work with many different teams on very different assignments, larger organizations may support numerous specialized positions that are dedicated to a particular type of crime or to support specific units within the police department. While not all organizations have all the distinct positions discussed below, the distinctions are helpful in understanding how varied the job of an analyst may be. The most general distinction is often made between analysts dedicated to investigations and analysts dedicated to patrol or front-line operations.

Operations Support vs. Intelligence/Major Crime Analysis

Within many organizations, the majority of officers occupy either uniformed operational roles or plainclothes investigative roles. Each sworn role utilizes the experience and expertise of analysts in different ways, as reflected in two different crime analyst roles: operations support analyst and investigative analyst. Operations support analysts provide information to uniformed officers to support them being intelligence-led in the classic sense of resource prioritization, while investigative analysts most often provide case-specific analysis for plainclothes investigators.

Operations Support
The primary objective of the **operations support analyst** is to support patrol and front-line operations efforts by identifying trends, sprees, and constantly changing concentrations of crime throughout the city or region in which the police operate. These analysts provide intelligence to officers regarding where hot spots are emerging or continuing, when certain trends appear to be emerging, whether certain types of crimes or activities appear to be on the rise, or whether certain individuals are released or may be connected to recent activity. These analysis activities support the department in being **intelligence-led**. By using these products, commanders can focus resources toward the optimal locations, times, or individuals to have the most impact on disrupting or preventing criminal activity.

Investigative Analyst
The **investigative analyst** will generally provide a slightly different service to the department by actively participating in the investigation of specific cases. These analysts are most often utilized for gang, drug, or violent crime investigations, but can be assigned to any investigation within the organization. Their objective is to work alongside investigators and support their efforts to identify suspects and ultimately find the person or persons

responsible for specific offences. The analyst in these investigations may also take on the role of the "Red Team,"[i] a term used to describe the contrarian or those who provide alternate analysis. By focusing on objective data analysis, and remaining one step removed, the analysts in this capacity provide a counterbalance to investigators in order to assist their investigation conclusions and help avoid bias or blindness to alternate explanations.

While these two general distinctions based on function are helpful, Boba (2005) suggests there are three main categories of crime analysis: tactical crime analysis, strategic crime analysis, and administrative crime analysis (Boba-Santos 2013). These categorizations envision the focus of different types of analysts regardless of whether they support patrol or investigations.

Tactical Crime Analysts

The International Association of Crime Analysts (IACA) has existed since 1990, and was formed to develop and disseminate valuable standards of practice and techniques within the crime analysis profession. They have defined a **tactical crime analyst** in the following way:

> Tactical crime analysis is the analysis of police data directed towards the short-term development of patrol and investigative priorities and deployment of resources. Its subject areas include the analysis of space, time, offender, victim, and modus operandi for individual high-profile crimes, repeat incidents, and crime patterns, with a specific focus on crime series. . . . Most of the data used in tactical crime analysis comes from police databases, particularly police reports of crimes. [International Association of Crime Analysts 2014]

The processes and techniques of tactical crime analysts may include analyzing repeat incidents, finding patterns in the police data for officer action, and linking known offenders to unsolved offences (International Association of Crime Analysts 2014).

Tactical Analysts and CompStat

Many police services have integrated the accountability mechanism of CompStat into their evidence-led focus (see also Chapter 8). Often, this requires the assistance of tactical crime analysts who focus on preparing data and reports for the CompStat process for the organization (also see Chapter 7). CompStat stands for "computerized statistics" and was developed to keep police departments on track and provide a constant feedback loop about crime occurring in their areas and their response to it (for additional discussion, see Chapter 12). In CompStat meetings, an area's commanding officer reports to the chief or deputy about what has happened in the previous 28-day cycle, and what their response has been to any emerging trends. A 28-day cycle is typical as it allows for even comparison between time periods, rather than month to month, which would introduce errors as not all months have the same number of days.

CompStat involves analysis of crime occurrences and functions as an accountability mechanism for the head of a particular unit or geographic area. Should crime be trending upwards, the senior officer can develop a plan to deal with the emerging problem, and is accountable should efforts not be resulting in the anticipated outcomes.

CompStat entails a great deal of work by the analyst to update and validate the data, ascertain any emerging trends, and prepare numerous reports and items of analysis for commanders throughout the cycle. Analysts are responsible for creating all the charts, tables, and maps for the actual CompStat meetings when commanders present to the chief or deputy in charge. Some departments may have weekly target meetings at which the analyst is responsible for showing what crime trends have emerged in the previous week or where problems may be emerging that require attention. Commanders who have embraced the intelligence-led philosophy rely on the analysis to make their tactical and deployment decisions, and incorporate ongoing feedback into adjustments or changes in direction.

Strategic Crime Analysts

IACA defines a **strategic crime analyst** as follows:

> Strategic crime analysis is the analysis of data directed towards development and evaluation of long-term strategies, policies, and prevention techniques. Its subjects include long-term statistical trends, hot spots, and problems. Although it often starts with data from police records systems, strategic analysis usually includes the collection of primary data from a variety of other sources through both quantitative and qualitative methods. [International Association of Crime Analysts 2014]

This type of analyst may utilize techniques such as trend analysis, hot spot analysis, or problem analysis.

Some very basic examples of longer-term analysis of general crime trends can be seen in Table 13.1. The statistics in the table from the Vancouver Police Department help the organization track changes in violent crime over time and assist the analyst in spotting any anomalies or increases that the organization needs to be aware of.

Similarly to the VPD, Figure 13.1 shows that Calgary Police Service tracks both the quantity and average number of crimes year to year to better see not only whether the volume has increased, but also to compare to longer-term trends.

Table 13.1 Vancouver Police Department Yearly Stats Report—Violent Crime, 2017 and 2018

Criminal offences	Number of incidents 2017	Number of incidents 2018	2017 rate (per 1000)	2018 rate (per 1000)	% change (rate)
Violent crime	5268	5308	7.91	7.89	–0.2
Culpable homicide	19	15	0.03	0.02	–21.8
Attempted murder	16	18	0.02	0.03	11.4
Sexual offences	588	640	0.88	0.95	7.8
Assaults	4048	4042	6.08	6.01	–1.1
Robbery	597	593	0.90	0.88	–1.7

Source: Data: The Vancouver Police Department http://vancouver.ca/police/organization/planning-research-audit/stats-crime-rate.html

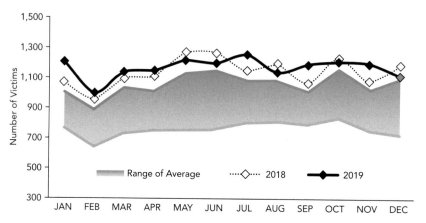

Figure 13.1   Calgary Police Service Statistics, Violent Crime, 2019

Source: Calgary Police Service, 4th Quarter 2019 Statistical Report. Compiled by: Centralized Analysis Unit, CIAS, Strategic Services Division © Calgary Police Service 2020.

Administrative Crime Analysts

IACA (2014) defines administrative crime analysis in the following way:

> Administrative crime analysis is analysis directed towards the administrative needs of the police agency, its government, and its community. As a broad category, it includes a variety of techniques and products, performed both regularly and on request, including statistics, data printouts, maps, and charts. Examples include workload calculations by area and shift, officer activity reports, responses to media requests, statistics provided for grant applications, reports to community groups, and cost–benefit analysis of police programs. In this category, we subsume the category described as "operations analysis" or "police operations analysis" by some texts. [International Association of Crime Analysts 2014]

Some of the functions of an administrative crime analyst may include patrol staffing analysis, resource deployment across the organization, and workload analysis. An example of crime analysis focused on administration can be seen in the recent Winnipeg Police Service Operational Review (Griffiths and Pollard 2013).

Figure 13.2 could help management see how workload demands have changed year over year. This may assist them in advocating for increases to staffing, strategies for re-deployment, or redistribution of resources throughout the department.

Similarly, the information from the example in Figure 13.3 may assist the department in knowing when to allocate more resources or how to modify shifting to ensure even coverage throughout the week.

To summarize, while there is often overlap among the three primary types of analysts as described by IACA, these distinctions help to illustrate the different roles and objectives an analyst may be a part of in the organization.

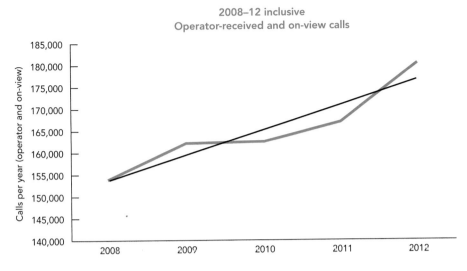

Figure 13.2   Patrol Workload Demands in Winnipeg

Source: Griffiths, C.T. and Pollard, N. (2013). *Policing in Winnipeg: An Operational Review*, prepared for the Canadian Police Association. Vancouver, October. Reprinted with permission.

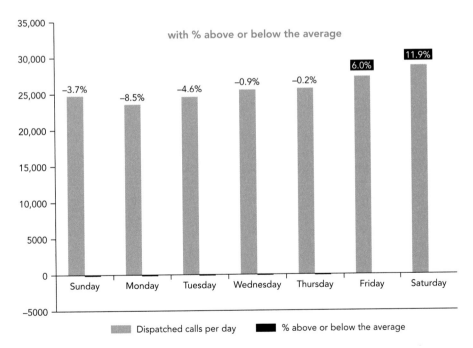

Figure 13.3   Dispatched Calls by Day of Week

Source: Griffiths, C.T. and Pollard, N. (2013). *Policing in Winnipeg: An Operational Review*, prepared for the Canadian Police Association. Vancouver, October. Reprinted with permission.

Table 13.2 Types of Analysts

	Tactical Crime Analysts	**Strategic Crime Analysis**	**Administrative Crime Analysts**
Objective*	Analysis of police data directed toward the short-term development of patrol and investigative priorities and deployment of resources	Development and evaluation of long-term strategies, policies, and prevention techniques	Analysis directed toward the administrative needs of the police agency, its government, and its community
Products	Short-term trend analysis, crime linkage analysis, offender profiling	Hot spot analysis, statistical trend analysis, program evaluation	Workload statistics, overtime statistics, community approval
Time Period of Analysis	Short Term: monthly or weekly trends	Long Term: yearly trends	Longer Term: quarterly or yearly trends
Data Sources	Police records	Police records as well as other internal and external databases, often limited to police databases	Police records and other internal and external databases, not limited to police data

*Objectives are from International Association of Crime Analysts. 2014. *Definition and types of crime analysis.* [White Paper 2014-02]. Overland Park, KS: Author. www.iaca.net/Publications/Whitepapers/iacawp_2014_02_definition_types_crime_analysis.pdf (accessed February 2016).

As noted, while the distinction among types of analysts is helpful to understand each role, rarely are the job descriptions so rigidly defined. More often, analysts are required to perform any or all of the functions of all three (see Table 13.2). Therefore, regardless of the job description, many analysts are required to have a similar skill set and knowledge of statistical and computer analytical packages. Some of the techniques will be described in the next section.

Standard Analysis

Analysts' toolkits contain many techniques they have developed over the years through their education and their practical training. Some are relatively general and non-specific to crime analysis, and others are highly specific and geared toward police and intelligence usage. Many of the methods used by analysts derive from the discipline of criminology, although these techniques often have their roots in other disciplines such as statistics, geography, and sociology. Some of the earliest usage of statistical analysis as applied to crime came in the 1800s by Quetelet and Poisson, who both focused on the study of crime (Brantingham and Brantingham 1997).

Counts, Rates, and Percentage Change

Counts, rates, and percentage change all have functions within the analyst's toolbox, and may need to be analyzed on an ongoing or sporadic basis. Counts are the most basic unit of measurement for police—they represent single occurrences of crimes, or more accurately, the tally of crimes that are of interest. In order to reach a count, the analyst simply has to tally the number of crime events that occurred over a specific time period, or in a specific geographic area, or that were a specific crime type. These counts then may form the basis for hot spot analysis, rates, and trend analysis (Brantingham and Brantingham

1997). However, simply counting the crimes that occurred is not always straightforward. The first issue concerns whether a crime occurred or not. Many events make their way into the police database when someone calls to report an activity or person they are concerned about. While the dispatch operator will enter the information into the database as it is relayed to them by the caller, the event the person has witnessed may or may not be a crime. Only upon further examination do the police know whether a crime has occurred. For example, suppose a person sees someone crawling through the side window of the neighbour's house. This conscientious person, suspecting someone is trying to break into the house, dutifully calls the police and reports the incident. The police respond to the address, and discover that the intruder is actually the homeowner, who lost his keys and was simply trying to gain access to his own house. The call that initially came in was "Break and Enter in progress," as that was what the caller believed he or she was witnessing, and what was therefore reported to the police dispatcher. However, no crime actually occurred (as it is not illegal to break into your own house). If the analyst were to simply query all the "Break and Enter" events in the database, this event would be included in the tally. The analyst, therefore, must be careful to exclude those instances where a crime has incorrectly been reported. This step is important, as the original call will remain in the police database, but will often have a follow-up code assigned to it such as **unfounded** or some other field that explains that no break and enter actually occurred.

The crime analyst must often be both a generalist and a specialist. Although crime analysts are expected to utilize the many tools, techniques, and technologies available to them, more often than not a major portion of their work involves very basic collation and dissemination of general crime trends. For instance, analysts may be involved in preparing for CompStat meetings with department heads, which will require basic statistical computations of the volume of crime in a past pre-defined period of time. Often, this will result in basic bar charts and graphs depicting the crime over the past week or month, for instance.

Analysts are also be expected to pull in regional, provincial, and/or national data to compare to the local trends, as is shown in Figure 13.4:

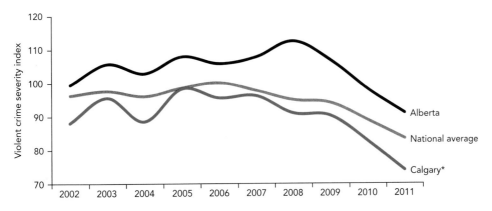

Figure 13.4   Calgary Police Service—Violent Crime Severity Index, 2002–11

Source: Annual Statistical Report 2007–2011. Compiled by: Centralized Analysis Section, Strategic Services Division. Copyright Calgary Police Service 2012. Reprinted with permission. www.calgary.ca/cps/Documents/-statistical-reports/2007-2011-annual-statistical-report.pdf?noredirect=1

Challenge Your Assumptions

When Rising Crime Rates Are a Good Thing

Another key responsibility of the analyst is to make sense of numbers. In addition to knowing the key metrics and methods to rely on, analysts must ensure they are mindful of the story behind these numbers. This is particularly important when assessing crime trends over time, or for particular offences. This is due to one crucial consideration when analyzing crime statistics—analysts are only *ever* analyzing a small percentage of the crimes that actually happened. Police can only count those crimes they are aware of, and therefore, if a crime occurs and is never reported or discovered, it will never make its way into the police database or the official statistics. For instance, victims of certain offences may be reluctant to come forward to police, leaving a particular offence vastly underreported in the official statistics. Such is the case for sexual assault. Statistics Canada estimates that underreporting rates may be as high as 90 per cent in some instances. For certain groups, such as sex workers, this reporting may be even lower due to the criminalization of the activity. However, police may be extremely influential when it comes to how many of these offences get reported.

When police agencies try and reach out to these marginalized groups and encourage them to come forward and report the sexual assault, this may result in a surge in reporting behaviour. The official statistics may show a sharp increase in sexual assault, even for previous years if historical crimes start to be reported. Without the proper context and discussion, this may cause fear and concern for many people who simply view the statistical increase in police-reported crimes when what these numbers really represent is a greater number of victims feeling comfortable coming forward and sharing their story with police. This, for many advocates and victims' groups, is viewed as a positive change and one worth celebrating, not fearing. For police, being aware of the influences behind the statistics will protect them from unfair criticism or motivation to change something that is actually producing a desired result.

In this way, rising crime rates should be celebrated, not criticized, and it is the analyst's responsibility to provide the proper context in which to interpret the story behind the numbers.

The question becomes, should police focus on getting reporting rates to increase? Should we rely on crime rates at all if underreporting is so common? How do we ever know what is truly happening if there are so many holes in the data? What can police do to encourage reporting of crimes?

The crime rate was described at length in Chapter 7, and analysts should be well versed in the strengths and limitations of this metric.

Percentage change is a third basic metric that police departments often rely on their analysts to produce. Many departments report on how they are doing on a monthly or yearly basis, and need to know in particular whether they are doing better or worse than last year or last month. To do this, the analyst must compute the percentage change of the current period from the previous period. Although the calculation for this metric is relatively simple (*[current period – previous period]/previous period*), the interpretation can be somewhat problematic due to the existence of small numbers. For instance, suppose a police department experienced two homicides in July and three in August. The analyst would calculate the percentage change, which would be as follows:

$$[3 - 2]/2 = 0.05 \text{ or } 50\%$$

While technically correct, simply reporting that homicides have increased by 50 per cent may result in panic and fear, as the number without any context sounds frighteningly high. Therefore, the analyst must consider not only how to calculate the numbers, but in what context they should be interpreted and shared.

Whatever metric is needed by the organization, the analyst's job is to ensure the collection, analysis, and interpretation of that metric is accurate and distributed correctly. As Gwinn et al. describe, "Two processes are at work:

1. Data becomes information when it is effectively analyzed.
2. Information becomes knowledge when it is effectively communicated." [Gwinn et al. 2008]

In addition to the general statistics described above, analysts may be required to develop and apply more specialized skills and techniques in their position. Some of these are described in the following section.

Specialized Analysis

Depending on their area of expertise and assignment, analysts may also utilize newer technologies that facilitate higher-level analysis of data. These may include geographic analysis and social network analysis. While software packages now allow the user to integrate many of these functions within one platform,[ii] many departments may not have fully implemented this functionality or integrated these new technologies.

Geographic Information Systems (GIS) and Crime Mapping

The **geographic analysis** of crime locations, focusing on where crimes happen, has become common in police departments, and is often now a skill required of crime analysts. Hot spot analysis involves the use of a geographic information system, or GIS. However, the integration and utilization of this type of analysis is relatively recent, with many departments gaining this capacity using **computerized mapping** only in the past 10 to 15 years. In the United States, as of 2001, nearly 70 per cent of large police departments (those with over 100 officers) utilized crime mapping in their department, while a similar study in the United Kingdom found that by 1999, only 44 per cent of police departments operated a crime-mapping facility (Leong and Chan 2013). Most large departments in Canada now have this capacity to differing degrees of utilization and integration within their agency.

The study of crime locations dates back centuries, however, to early European researchers who examined the levels of crime in different regional areas and whether the levels of crime were related to any social factors such as income (Boba-Santos 2013). Early geographic analysis in police departments was limited to **pin maps**, which often were made by sticking pushpins into a paper map placed on a wall. While these maps were useful for showing crime locations, they were onerous to update and did not show the detail that new software packages are able to show. Changing patterns were also difficult to capture, as were multiple crime locations, as only one pin could be placed on one location (although clusters of pins could indicate hot spots). Pin maps were also limited in size, and maps often had to be joined together to capture an entire area. Thus, while these types of maps could be used effectively for a short period of time, their value was extremely limited (Harries 1999).

Creating and analyzing crime locations involves more than simply placing addresses on a map. Skill is needed to effectively communicate the picture of the crime pattern, and the format and information may need to vary based on the audience. For example, maps for patrol officers need to contain information that is essential to them as they head out on their shift. This may entail showing maps of crimes that have occurred on the past shift, or perhaps overnight. Emerging hot spots that officers should be aware of in their area should be highlighted, or perhaps maps of smaller areas within an officer's jurisdiction should be shown (Harries 1999). For patrol officers, showing long-term trends or city-wide patterns may not be helpful to their immediate needs.

Conversely, creating a crime map for management may require a much longer view, as the senior executive may be interested in crime concentrations over the past quarter or year rather than simply the previous shift. Management may also need a more complete view of the entire city or jurisdiction, as often this audience may use maps to understand "where the action is" (Harries 1999) and to make decisions about where to allocate resources.

Another audience for whom crime maps are created is the general public. Many departments now put crime statistics online and may even have their websites set up to enable the public user to query and browse for certain crime types and/or time frames for events. For the analyst, preparing the data for the public will involve a process of **anonymizing** or vetting the data. As crime occurrences will involve a victim, care must be taken to ensure that personal information or identifying characteristics of the event could not point to the victim, their property, or the exact location of the incident. Therefore, addresses are often modified slightly to the closest intersection or middle of the block. Sensitive crimes or those of a sexual or violent nature may also be omitted from public disclosure to further protect victims or protect possible investigative leads. However, issues of data privacy may go further than simply protecting the victim, as this information may be used for purposes other than general public consumption. For instance, alarm companies may view these maps and target those homes that have seen a high number of burglaries (Leong and Chan 2013). Obviously, the objective is to inform the public, not to pave the way for unwanted business solicitations. Therefore, police departments should weigh the pros and cons of releasing all information, and consider the best way to inform the public while balancing privacy rights.

Social Network Analysis

Each individual may have numerous relationships with other people, and these relationships may be a crucial link to investigating and ultimately solving crimes. **Social network analysis** is the analytic process by which a person's relationships, instead of himself or herself particularly, are under scrutiny. This type of analysis may be of particular utility for investigations involving gangs or organized crime, although any type of offence may be suitable.

Police databases have a wealth of information related to individuals and their relationships to other individuals, places, vehicles, or things. For instance, if a group of offenders were arrested together, that association is a relationship and may provide valuable insight into a group's activities. If officers have a suspect in mind for a particular offence, but cannot locate that individual, then his or her relationships with other people become important pieces of information and may lead to the location of the suspect.

However, social network analysis goes further than simply exploring who may know whom, or who may be associated with a particular vehicle, house, location, and so forth. This type of analysis can use the intelligence about a person's social network to establish his or her placement in the network, that is, whether the person is a boss or a low-level associate, and how that person may be linked to other networks of individuals. For instance, an individual who knows many people within an organization may have a different value to police investigators than someone who only is loosely associated with a few people. Not only the number but the nature and type of these associations are of interest; social network analysis can assist in uncovering this knowledge.

In the past decade and a half, various software packages have made social network data analysis and presentation far more accessible. The major network software packages are UCINet, GraphPlot, Graphviz, Pajek, Multinet, and Krackplot, although there are others. UCINet was developed by three pioneers of computerized network analysis, Borgatti, Everett, and Freeman.

The software applies statistical techniques that can identify **centrality measures**, best understood as showing who may be at the centre of an organization and who is less important; **clique finders**, which may highlight sub-groups within a larger network; and **key players**, which may find individuals who are vital to disrupting the network in the most efficient way (Malm, Kinney, and Pollard 2008). For police departments with limited time and resources, it may be necessary to identify the individual who will cause the most disruption to the criminal network if arrested or put in jail, rather than trying to arrest everyone in the network. For example, if social network analysis can help identify the head of a particular crime group, and that person can be arrested, then the organization may crumble without that criminal leadership.

The software packages both analyze and visualize the social network. Figure 13.5 is an example of such a criminal network and shows how each in-dividual is related to each other. As can be seen, many people do not know each other directly, but are only connected through someone else. These are the types of relationships that can be analyzed and used in targeted police investigations.

Geographic Profiling

Another advanced technique that crime analysts may utilize to assist in investigations is **geographic profiling** (Rossmo 1999). Geographic profiling is essentially an information management system for serial crime investigation. It does not pinpoint an exact individual, but rather analyzes crime locations to determine the most probable area of the offender's residence. Criminal events, particularly criminal homicide, often have a multitude of geographic sites connected to the crime. These include the victim encounter, attack, murder, and body dump sites. By analyzing these sites from a geography-of-crime

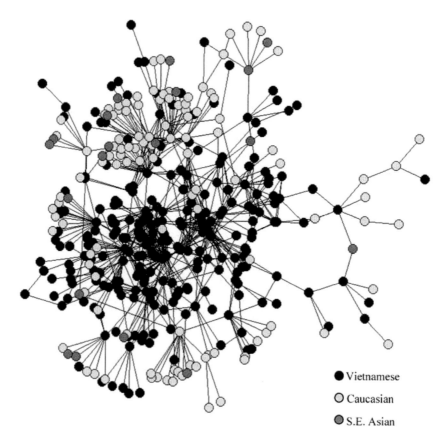

Figure 13.5   Social Network Relationships of Illicit Drug Producers

Source: Malm, A.E., J.B. Kinney, and N.R. Pollard, 2008. Social Network and Distance Correlates of Criminal Associates Involved in Illicit Drug Production. *Security Journal 21*, 77–94. Copyright © 2008, Macmillan Publishers Ltd. Reprinted with permission.

perspective, it is possible to outline the most probable area of the offender's residence. By using this technique, police investigations may narrow and refine their suspect search and streamline the investigative process. The computer system developed by Rossmo, called Rigel Analyst™, uses an algorithm to analyze the geographic sites of a serial crime. The results are then displayed as a three-dimensional probability surface that highlights the most likely area of the offender's residence (Rossmo 1995, 1999).

The Analyst within the Organization

The crime analyst may be a specific job within an organization, or may be part of a larger portfolio for one or more individuals. This may depend on the size of the organization and its internal capacity. Crime analysts may also be known by other titles such as intelligence analysts or research analysts. Although there are many types of analysts, all are involved with collecting, collating, distilling, interpreting, and disseminating data and

Case Study

Predictive Policing—Using Analysis to Predict the Future

Early in the origins of policing, Sir Robert Peel proposed that the primary function of the police should be the prevention of crime. However, a concentration on catching criminals and solving crimes took focus away from this goal, and prevention seemed to take a back seat to more visible and active pursuits such as crime control and public order maintenance. Despite this, it continued to be recognized that the most efficient way to deal with crime was to in fact prevent it. If police could "get in front of the train" and prevent crimes from happening, then the public would truly be safer. However, what was acknowledged was how difficult it was to prevent crimes in any large sense: efforts often were time-consuming and costly, and often were too quickly abandoned due to lack of results or dwindling interest or commitment. Despite this, academics and practitioners continued to explore ways to more efficiently predict when and where crimes might happen in an effort to focus on prevention and greater public safety.

Both groups turned to the wealth of data that is collected and maintained by police departments in an effort to find patterns within the criminal actions of individuals. Although people will often act randomly, and their decision-making process is immensely complex, at times patterns may emerge that point to a greater possibility of crimes happening at a particular time and at a particular location. It is these patterns that the Vancouver Police Department and a group of academic and practitioner partners began to explore to develop their ground-breaking system that proposes to stop crimes before they occur. The computer program analyzes numerous datasets using various logarithmic processes to evaluate the likelihood of a criminal event happening in the future. Using this technology, officers can then strategically place themselves so as to either dissuade the criminal action or prevent it from occurring altogether. "We will actually be deploying police units pre-emptively to where crime isn't happening, but where we're predicting it might," said Special Constable Ryan Prox, Analytics Services Coordinator with the Vancouver Police Department. Police cars are equipped with mobile terminals with touch screens for easy access to the data while on the go, so officers can make their own decisions on where they should be (CTV 2013). After extensive testing, the model showed promise in being able to positively identify areas where property crimes are most likely to occur.

Certainly, the ability to predict where crime will happen could herald a new frontier in policing and could change how departments respond to crime and criminals. However, when dealing with human motivation and movement, unpredictability reigns and the phenomenon of crime may adapt and change in response to these new systems. Critics also point to the possibility of bias within such algorithms, which could have an unintended result of over-policing an area that is predicted to be of higher criminal activity, and thus reinforcing the algorithm's bias in a feedback loop.

Such ethical questions have been raised extensively, and have impacted similar projects internationally, most notably with the announcement by the Los Angeles Police Department that they were ceasing to use the software PredPol (predictive policing) in their deployment systems. While the agency stated publicly that the decision was the result of the coronavirus's strains on resources, critics suggest it was actually due to the years of public pressure against the use of this type of tool.

information products throughout the police department (White 2008). With the proliferation of desktop analysis software, the ability to analyze data within the police department becomes both easier and more difficult at the same time: the powerful software packages will often do high-level analysis for the user quickly and easily; however, knowing how to wield and steer those software packages requires specialized skills and training (White 2008). Regardless of the title or tool, it is crucial to understand that crime analysis is essential for intelligence-led policing to work effectively because its purpose is to put the right information into the right hands at the right time.

> Policing is increasingly relying on intelligence to target, prioritize and focus interventions. . . . [T]he police can produce volumes of intelligence, which only becomes useful operationally after it has been interpreted, assessed and any potential patterns and linkages investigated. It is in the translation of raw information into operationally viable intelligence that analysis plays its crucial role. [Cope 2004]

Although the value of crime analysis, and the necessity for analysts, is more accepted than ever before, there are distinct challenges associated with this relatively new role within the police department. The first comes with the move toward a more civilian-led analyst structure, and the issues that arise with chain of command and tensions between sworn and civilian positions (see discussion of civilianization in Chapter 11). The second challenge comes with how the products or information are used or integrated into the department. As Cope (2004) observed, "A poor understanding of analysis amongst police officers, and a lack of understanding of policing amongst analysts, influenced the usefulness of analytical products for operational policing" (188). As this integration becomes more commonplace, both sides continue to learn from each other for the betterment of the evidence-based direction of the police service.

The issues surrounding civilian analysts arose in recent years as departments moved from having sworn officers perform these functions to hiring permanent civilian staff to operate in these roles. This change was made largely in recognition of the significant time and cost associated with training in analysis software and techniques. As officers tended to change positions every few years, departments were constantly losing their investment to other units in the department, and having to retrain each time someone new came into the analysis unit. By moving to a permanent civilian analyst role, not only were individuals coming into the position further along in their training, but they would also stay in the position for much longer than the police officers would. A drawback of this for the civilian analyst, however, is that movement or promotion within the department is relatively limited, and the individual is only able to function in that one particular role. This, of course, varies with the size of the department, but analysts will not have the same portability as sworn members within the police organization (Boba-Santos 2013).

This raises other issues with the civilianization of analysts in general. It has the end result of producing a new subgroup within the police department, one that may have a very different culture. In general, civilians in this role will be under the supervision of a sworn member; however, there may be instances whereby an analyst must make recommendations or even direct a sworn member to complete some action. This may create tension in the department, as the military structure of the police department often does not work well with non-police acting in a senior capacity (Cope 2004). Police departments may therefore need to evaluate their chain-of-command structures and assess whether the civilian analysts would function better in a centralized and independent chain of command, or dispersed and decentralized throughout the organization (O'Shea and Nicholls 2003).

Limitations in police officer knowledge of the capacities and possibilities associated with crime analysis also limit their utility within the department. As stated previously, officers may not realize the potential of the products analysts are able to produce, and may think of their products as poor or uninformative as a result (Cope 2004). The danger is that the analyst becomes a silent partner whose presence is overlooked and whose analysis products are ignored or passed over as unnecessary (Cope 2004).

Analysis may also serve to undermine some elements of core knowledge that sworn members have developed in their role. While the analytic products may allow for a rational view of a situation or event, it may at times contradict what an officer believes or has come to know about that situation or event. In this way, the objective analysis of the analyst may clash with the subjective and experience-based knowledge of the officer. For instance, officers may believe, through their direct experience, that a particular location within a neighbourhood is problematic and should be a priority for intervention; however, the analyst's data shows that the location is not significantly problematic and an alternate location should be the source of additional attention. This places officers in a dilemma—to go with their own instinct and experience, or to follow the data from an analyst who has no experience on the street (Cope 2004). This dilemma epitomizes one of the core challenges with integrating and utilizing crime analysis within a department; however, the more officers and analysts can work together and combine their disparate but complementary knowledge, the more successful initiatives and daily work will be. The observation that the interaction between analysts and front-line officers is limited and one-sided (with the analysts seeking to understand the front-line work) (Taylor, Kowalyk, and Boba 2007) is significant as it demonstrates that departments, even those with analysts, often do not integrate analysts into everyday work as much as they could.

This brings up the situation where crime analysis may be present within an organization, but is failing to live up to its potential within that organization. This, in turn, severely hinders the police service's ability to be intelligence- and evidence-led, as the analysts are most often the gatekeepers and translators of the intelligence.

The Analyst as the Bridge between Organizations

As information becomes more prominent in organizations and specialists are required more often to access and harness that information, many departments are now envisioning and setting up crime centres that bring all that data into one place, even from different departments and agencies. Often called Real Time Crime Centres, Real Time Operations Centres, or Real Time Information Centres, the goal is to establish a centralized computer facility that gives front-line officers and investigators access to essential information on demand, 24 hours a day. These data facilities may house all computerized police records, CAD records, GPS data, investigative case files, intelligence files on subjects

Courtesy of the Calgary Police Service

A day at the Calgary Police Service Real Time Operations Centre (RTOC).

of interest, satellite imagine data, closed-circuit television (CCTV) feeds, jail booking information, court records, probation/parole reports, and any other relevant electronic criminal justice database. The power of having all this information in one place is that officers and analysts can quickly access all there is to know about a particular person, place, or situation without any time or organizational delays. By bridging information silos, agency coordination is guaranteed rather than anticipated, and cross-communication and coordinated responses to crises or other situations can be streamlined and organized. For instance, in the Lower Mainland and other parts of the country, numerous police agencies may operate within a specific environment. By having information coordination ready and accessible to all, everyone can be better able to respond with complete, up-to-date information and the latest intelligence. The first Real Time Crime Centre was opened in New York by the New York Police Department in 2005. Since then, several larger departments in both the US and Canada have opened centres, including the Los Angeles Police Department, the Memphis Police Department, the Houston Police Department, and the Calgary Police Service.

When Crime Analysis Fails in an Organization

The success or failure of crime analysis relies first and foremost on the quality of the data that the analyst has to work with. Faulty information will produce flawed conclusions and ineffective tactical responses. As numerous individuals are involved with the data input system, that presents multiple pathways for error. If police or other individuals do not capture complete information, or if the information is incorrect and not controlled for quality, then intelligence will be extremely limited. In addition, many departments have information silos wherein they have multiple databases that do not "speak" to each other, and therefore important links are left to the individual analyst to make manually, allowing for greater human error and ignoring the pattern recognition capability of the computerized system. However, even with the best and most complete information, crime analysis may fail in an organization. There are three necessary components to ensure crime analysis efforts are well integrated into a department. When one or more of these components are missing, it is doubtful the analysis structure will function as anticipated or assist the organization to its fullest potential (Prox 2014).

1. **Limited Technological Capacity**—As analysis tools become more available and more powerful, the analyst must be able to harness this technology and utilize it to its fullest extent. Therefore, hardware that cannot support the latest software or the demands of the analytic power will ultimately limit what can be done. Additionally, not having access to the latest technology or objective-specific technology (such as mapping or social network analysis software) will limit the scope and effectiveness of the analysts' work.

2. **Limited Human Capacity**—Even with the latest in hardware and software, a department will not benefit from crime analysis without a qualified and highly trained analyst to harness the power of the technology to produce usable and actionable intelligence.

3. **Limited Organizational Process**—This third component involves management's willingness and ability to integrate the work and recommendations of the analysts into the department's procedures and strategies. This entails the department instituting formal mechanisms to actually utilize the intelligence products produced. These products must therefore drive the operations and become part of the decision management tree.

In addition, agencies may devalue the role of the crime analyst in various ways. This **hierarchy of value** may be evident in funding or staffing decisions whereby the analyst capacity may be reduced before the sworn member capacity is reduced. Analysts may also not be an integral part of management's team to work through problems, and may not be treated as professional equals within the organization (Lum 2013).

Organizations that are well equipped and positioned to integrate and capitalize on the skills and expertise of the trained crime analyst will see improvements in effectiveness and efficiency, and will be more intelligence-led than organizations that do not. However, the analysis will only be as good as the information going into the system, so data quality and organizational integration must go hand in hand. In this way, there continues to be an acknowledgement that despite the growing body of research that lauds the overall impact that intelligence-based approaches may have, without a department's commitment to following these paradigms and ensuring crime analysts are well incorporated and integrated into the department, the promises of these approaches may be overly optimistic (Lum and Koper 2017).

Conclusion

This chapter has focused the new era of the intelligence-led police agency and the pivotal role that crime analysts play in turning the plethora of information into actionable intelligence to drive evidence-based organizational decisions and strategies. This chapter has also explored the nature and type of analysis that can be done, and the role the crime analyst may hold within the police service. Although the term "crime analyst" can be an umbrella for all types of analysts, numerous functions and types of analysts may exist within an organization, and duties and specialties may be quite unique to each position. Some analysts may assist with gathering intelligence on specific suspects, while others may provide long-term trend analysis to help management better understand their staffing needs. All these roles supply a valuable service within the department, although their integration into police services is still limited in some areas. While most departments now have at least one analytic position within their service, often the capacity is underdeveloped or not well harnessed by the department. As the demand increases for police services to become more intelligence-led and evidence-driven, the role of the crime analyst will continue to expand.

Critical Thinking Questions

1. Should police departments focus more on intelligence-led approaches, which may result in a reduction in service to low-demand populations and/or places? Or should everyone expect the same level of attention regardless of the crime demands in their area?
2. Should analysts be generalists who are able to support all areas of the department, or specialists who have specific skill sets for a specific purpose? Compare the benefits and drawbacks of having multiple analysts for each unit within a department to having just one analyst to fulfill all roles.
3. Should police officers function as crime analysts? What are the benefits and drawbacks of having sworn members rather than civilian members do this analysis?
4. Should all departments invest heavily in the technological infrastructure needed to support high-level computerized analysis? What are the pros and cons of doing so? Is this necessary in all situations? How would a department know what it needs?

Endnotes

i   [Alternative Analysis], properly applied, serves as a hedge against the natural tendencies of analysts—like all human beings—to perceive information selectively through the lens of preconceptions, to search too narrowly for facts that would confirm rather than discredit existing hypotheses, and to be unduly influenced by premature consensus within analytic groups close at hand (Fishbein and Treverton 2004).

ii   Such as with IBM's i2 Analyst's Notebook.

14

Police and Media Relations

Learning Objectives

After reading and studying this chapter, students will be able to:

- Compare and contrast the two competing perspectives on the relationship between the police and the media.
- Describe the asymmetric relationship between the police and the media.
- Describe and discuss the role of police communications and media liaison units.
- Describe why media liaison units are essential features of modern policing.
- List and discuss the three logics underpinning police use of media.
- Describe how and why the police have adopted the use of social media.
- Identify and discuss the communications strategies that are used to balance the integrity of investigations, court processes, and the public's right to know.

Introduction

This chapter explores the evolving relationship between Canadian police agencies and the media. In order to discuss this relationship, it is first important to establish just what the term "media" refers to. For the purpose of this chapter, the term **media** is used to refer to any form of print or electronic communication that targets a mass audience (Bereska 2014, 93).

Traditionally, forms of media have primarily consisted of printed materials such as books, newspapers, magazines, and comics. Electronic formats that emerged in the twentieth century included a variety of communication modes that ranged from radio, movies, and television to recordings. More recently, mass media has entailed communication that depends on computer technology. These forms of media now include "websites, mobile computing, DVDs, CDs, blogs, smartphone apps, Twitter, and digitized forms of traditional media. These have been referred to as *new* or *emerging* media" (Bereska 2014, 93, italics in original). Additionally, a series of electronic, internet-based communication channels now facilitate relatively open, community-based input, interaction, collaboration, and information sharing. Websites and applications dedicated to open forums, blogging, social networking, and social curation comprise a series of computer-based communication channels generally known as **social media**. Examples of social media include Instagram, Facebook and Facebook Messenger, Twitter, YouTube, and WhatsApp among others.

Of particular relevance to a discussion of the relationship between police agencies and the media is the recognition of the media's ability to influence the dominant beliefs of a society. Indeed, many influential groups (for example, political parties, private corporations, government agencies) use the media as a vehicle by which they seek to shape society and its thinking (see Bereska 2014, 93). The most obvious example of this can be found in the success of commercial advertising.

Historically, early newspapers saw crime generally and the police specifically, as readily available and entertaining sources of newsworthy material that stimulated circulation. Early newspapers were also willing to cooperate with policing authorities by preparing the front page as a "wanted poster" to be circulated or publicly posted (Ericson, Baranek, and Chan 1989, 91).

It is also true that through the twentieth century and into the twenty-first, with the rising popularity of movies and, more recently, television and Netflix dramas (such as *Criminal Minds*, *Law and Order: Special Victims Unit*, *Blue Bloods*, and *The Blacklist*), particular images of police work, crime, and the justice system have been dominant. Indeed, crime dramas and police procedurals are consistently ranked among the most watched entertainment programs on TV (Donavan and Klahm IV 2015, 1262).

Thus, while television shows and Hollywood movies are fictitious, even when inspired by real events, entertainment media together with traditional news outlets nevertheless construct particular representations by which the broader community comes to view and understand crime, law and order, and social control (Lee and McGovern 2014, 10).

As others have observed (see Ericson, Baranek, and Chan 1989), there is a symbiotic but frequently conflicted relationship between the news media and the police. The relationship has also been described as asymmetric, with police agencies controlling much of the information that the media need in order to inform audiences about crime in their communities. As enforcers of the law, police are often in a position of power not only to define the nature of crime in the community, but also to frame crime as a problem to which they have the solution. While the media are autonomous and ultimately determine how and when particular crime issues are presented to the public, it is also true that "police organizations are unquestionably key primary providers and definers in the production of crime news" upon which the media depend (Lee and McGovern 2014, 10).

This chapter examines the nature of the relationship between police and the mass media and how it has evolved, particularly with the advent of social media. In democratic societies, it can be fairly argued that the police and the traditional media both have roles to play in ensuring that lawful and orderly conduct is promoted and maintained. While both institutions often require information from the public in order to carry out their respective mandates, they differ in orientation, operational techniques, platforms, and public perception (Pate, Abdullahi, and Abdullahi 2014, 97). As Christmas (2012, 43) has noted, law enforcement agencies have only recently recognized the importance of effective messaging to demonstrate transparency and to satisfy the public appetite for immediate and accurate information about crime, justice, and public safety. Traditional news reporters and their media outlets are also under constant pressure to produce stories in a demanding and competitive environment. In part, such competing pressures inevitably mean that an otherwise interdependent police–media relationship can sometimes be strained.

Competing Perspectives

In debates about the relationship of the traditional media and police in modern society, two prevailing opposite perspectives endure (see Reiner 2008). The conservative perspective tends to see media representations of the police and crime as undermining police by generally subverting their authority (for example, by overly focusing on such matters as police brutality) which, in turn, fosters disrespect not only for the police, but for law and order generally. On the other hand, the critical perspective sees both the news and entertainment media as grossly exaggerating the extent of crime. From the critical perspective, persistent media messaging in regard to violent crime (including the threat of terrorism) increases public fear and legitimates more intrusive, authoritarian criminal justice policies and policing practices (Reiner 2008, 316; see also Chapters 1 and 15 in this text).

The Media from the Police Perspective

News media report crime details to inform the public about what is happening in the community. However, for several reasons, the media may never know the full details of a criminal event. In the competitive rush to break a story, misinformation and speculative commentary may distort what transpired and, as a result, the public may be misinformed and consequently unreasonably panicked and sometimes angered. This sometimes occurs with print, radio, television, and internet-based news. Police officers are thus sometimes frustrated when information is not presented fairly or is framed in ways that misrepresent the situation.

On occasion, reporters, independently of the police, may identify a crime-related matter of some interest. Media inquiries can thus begin prior to police being aware of the crime. Possible witnesses may be located and interviewed by reporters who, in the process of gathering information, may influence the witnesses' recollection of what was seen or heard. Pictures and video recordings may be taken that compromise evidence that the police might otherwise choose not to disclose to the general public. Media reports can also release information that could unintentionally alert suspects and that the police would prefer to use as holdback evidence. That is, police may choose to withhold key details of a crime that would only be known by the offender (see **holdback evidence**, discussed in Chapter 9). Such details, in the course of later questioning by the police, may be described by a suspect thereby confirming his or her involvement in the crime. For example, if a weapon used in a particular crime was distinctive, only the person who used it would know what it was (see Ericson, Baranek, and Chan 1989, 128). In their haste to report crime details, media representatives may disclose critical pieces of evidence that inadvertently compromise police investigation strategies (see also Chapter 9).

In circumstances where police alert the media to an investigation already underway or provide information through press releases or controlled briefings, there are reporters who nonetheless will initiate their own inquiries by contacting victims, witnesses, and even suspects. Such initiatives rarely help the police as they proceed with their own investigations. Conflict may also sometimes arise out of the fact that the full scope of a criminal event is rarely immediately known. What may seem obvious to the public as reported by the media in the early stages of any investigation is often dramatically different once police investigators have completed detailed inquiries. Misinformation circulated to the public can be problematic and can jeopardize police investigations by generating false expectations, unnecessary fear, and even anger toward the police.

A New Relationship between Police and Media

The relationship between media and the police in Canada has evolved significantly in recent decades. Not long ago, police would provide very little information about crimes or suspects that were under active investigation (see McCormick 1995, 161). In fact, many police agencies simply refused to cooperate or share information with news media. By saying nothing, words and facts could not be twisted or misinterpreted and embarrassment of police officers and police agencies could simply be avoided.

It has been relatively easy for the police simply to cite privacy concerns or the risk of jeopardizing investigations or prosecutions as reasons for remaining silent. However, the police have not been able to prevent journalists or members of the public from disseminating and accessing information on the internet. With the internet facilitating the immediate transmission of vast amounts of sometimes false and misleading information, police have had to adapt in order to "get out in front" of information being made public. In short, police have learned that they have a stake in controlling information and how and when it is disclosed.

Pleas for Public Assistance

There are situations where police solicit the media's cooperation, for example, by releasing vehicle or suspect descriptions and asking for the public for assistance in locating them. This is common when the police believe that there may be an ongoing threat to the public and there is a pressing need to locate the person or vehicle. Other than public safety, the pressing need may be to locate, identify, and preserve evidence that may otherwise be lost, moved, or destroyed by offenders.

Police reaching out to the public through various media to help locate individuals who have outstanding arrest warrants is commonplace. In most daily newspapers, there is a small section on persons who are wanted for various offences including parole revocation. Warnings about high-risk sex offenders living in a particular jurisdiction are an increasingly regular feature in police news releases. In recent years, police agencies have provided information about serious public safety concerns such as the opioid crisis, particularly about the introduction and proliferation of fentanyl and other related dangerous synthetic drugs.

At times, police release information in what they perceive to be the public interest but also to illustrate that the police are sensitive to tragic events. For example, in early summer 2019, the Toronto Police Service released their report on the Danforth Shootings Investigation, a mass shooting event that took place on July 22, 2018. Two young girls died during this incident and others sustained serious injuries. The significance of releasing the report was highlighted by Toronto Police Chief Saunders, who said, "We took the unprecedented step of releasing our findings out of compassion for these families, and in recognition of the impact of this tragic and violent attack on our citizens and community" (Saunders 2019).

Case Study

Crowdsourcing and Investigations

Canadian police agencies have an increasing number of complex challenges to meet. Perhaps the most challenging concern is keeping up with evolving technology and using it to advantage. Technological innovations in wireless communications have facilitated new forms of criminal activity such as identity theft, fraud, sexual exploitation, and cyberbullying. These innovations have been used by criminals to exploit or harm others for personal gain. However, technology has also benefitted the police by increasing the scope and effectiveness of intelligence-led policing, thereby enhancing the ability of police to effectively disrupt criminal activity and to gather evidence. For example, a recent strategy facilitated by the seemingly limitless boundaries of the internet is commonly referred to as "crowdsourcing." Wilson (2016) has defined crowdsourcing as "engaging with the masses in order to get whatever it is you need." As Zercoe (2018) has noted, "the public has never been better positioned to aid police agencies (than) in the age of the smartphone; in no other time in history has our world been so heavily documented."

With varied success, police agencies around the world have employed the power of crowdsourcing information to advance investigations of all kinds. One example of a successful crowdsourcing strategy was demonstrated by the Toronto Police Service who credited their use of crowdsourcing through Twitter to solve the murder of Michael Pimental (*CBC News* 2015). However, as Nhan, Huey, and Broll (2015, 342) stated, "the internet has created an environment in which the public can and will choose to play a role in public criminal and other investigations that capture its interest." In other words, there are occasions where members of the public will take the initiative to "investigate" on their own and share their results online and/or send information to the proper authorities for consideration.

Nhan, Huey, and Broll (2015, 342) refer to these members of the public as "cyber vigilantes or digilantes." It can be argued that digilantes also hold the potential to do more harm than good in situations where "getting it right" is key. For example, public shaming and other forms of internet justice can easily lead to more serious ramifications, especially if the wrong person is identified and connected to the issue, event, or criminal act. Uncontrolled information can also jeopardize investigations (e.g., disclosing holdback evidence, or identifying or intimidating victims and witnesses) and otherwise interfering with prosecutions.

In one interesting approach, the Delta Police Department in Delta, BC, has integrated

continued

a form of crowdsourcing into their community policing strategy. In this approach, citizens can register that they have video capability (for example home security cameras) with the police. Should a criminal incident occur, police then have a potential source of video evidence (Delta Police Department, n.d.).

Private websites such as www.leedir.com or www.bellingcat.com also indicate an evolving hybrid relationship between the public and the police whereby police agencies appear to support public efforts by sharing pictures and video and soliciting additional identification or feedback.

The premise, however, that more investigative information is always better may not always be true. More specifically, a primary concern for police investigators is that information, pictures, video, or other electronic data must be able meet the "Debot test" (*R. v. Debot*, 1989) of being "compelling, credible and (independently) corroborated." Privacy issues inevitably arise regarding the need for police to protect images of those who are innocent or unconnected to the matter at hand. Challenges of sorting, analyzing, and managing volumes of electronic information also give rise to such matters as the legal requirements for police to adhere to Stinchcombe disclosure standards (*R. v. Stinchcombe* 1991; see also Chapter 6 and 9) and to Jordan timelines (*R. v. Jordan* 2016) regarding timely prosecutions (see also Chapter 9).

Looking ahead, it will be interesting to see how Canadian police agencies embrace technology and further develop strategies such as crowdsourcing as a viable investigative tool.

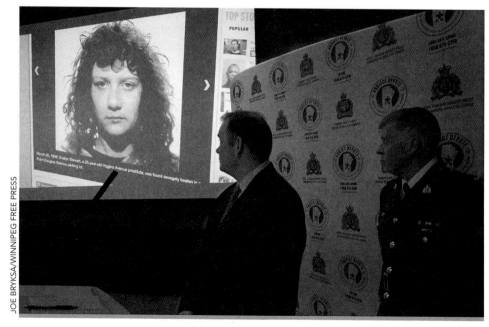

JOE BRYKSA/WINNIPEG FREE PRESS

In 2015, Winnipeg Police Detective Sergeant Randy Levasseur, left, and RCMP Inspector Dennis McGuffin asked the public to come forward with information on circumstances pertaining to the 1998 murder of Evelyn Stewart. What are the benefits of reaching out to the public for information, and what are the risks?

Cold Case Investigations

Police reach out to the public via various media to obtain information about current and historical unsolved cases as well. Cases that remain unsolved for years sometimes have stalled because there are no other known avenues of investigation for the police to follow up. All the leads have been exhausted. If that is the situation, police may take the relatively unusual step of releasing information about the crimes, evidence that had been carefully protected, in the hope that a member of the public may recognize the evidence or be aware of some piece of the puzzle that had been previously unknown to the police.

There are a number of examples where police have taken the approach that informing the public on exceptional, ongoing serious matters is the right thing to do. For example, in 2017, in the midst of increasing gang activity, the Surrey, BC RCMP took the unusual step of releasing the names and photographs of five young men to the media and advised the public to stay away from them due to the risk to public safety they presented. The reason justifying such a measure was that although the subjects were known to have been involved in the drug trade, police simply lacked sufficient legal grounds to arrest the suspects—the usual prerequisites for release and publication of names and photographs. The Officer in Charge of Surrey RCMP said: "We must assume that these men continue to be targets and, as such, we are advising the public to be cautious of any interaction with these five individuals." The officer added, "These investigations are particularly challenging for police with victims who do not want to cooperate even though they know the identity of the suspects" (Bolan, 2017).

Police Media Liaison Units

In Canada, and in most other western democratic countries, police agencies now have formal communications policies and strategies. Larger agencies have specialized communications or media relations units. Modern police agencies find that these units are essential for responding quickly and effectively to media needs. Police recognize that the media can provide essential support to police investigations by disseminating appropriate information. For example, matters dealing with public safety must be addressed promptly in order to reassure the public that they are safe and that the police are working to address the particular problem.

All Canadian police agencies have either at least one officer or a unit dedicated to communications or to a media liaison role. The number of personnel assigned to media liaison roles varies according to the size of the police agency. While there are different names for these units, their duties and responsibilities are similar. For example, the Peel Regional Police has a section referred to as the Corporate Communications Bureau—under which falls the Public and Media Relations Unit. The Calgary Police Service refers to their unit as the Public Affairs and Media Relations Unit. The Ontario Provincial Police and the Los Angeles Police Department have media relations units. The RCMP, depending on the province, most often refer to media units as Strategic Communications.

In Canadian police agencies, media liaison units not only engage with representatives of the traditional news media, they also field calls from within their own agencies and from other law enforcement agencies. The media liaison units have experience in addressing controversial issues in a way that is consistent with the police agency's media policy. The existence of such units illustrates that modern police agencies have become acutely aware of their need to manage and control the nature of information disclosed to the public. Such units are increasingly staffed by persons who are trained in such specializations as journalism, communication studies, and public relations (Lee and McGovern 2014, 15; Mawby 2010). Media liaison units also develop departmental policy guidelines and regulations governing media contact and often deliver in-house training and advice to operational police personnel (Lee and McGovern 2014, 28). For example, when individual police officers are contacted with respect to an investigation, the police officer may be required to contact the media liaison unit to obtain permission and/or advice on what they are able to disclose and how to articulate their responses.

Media liaison units also provide ongoing communications advice to major investigations by allowing the investigators to focus on the investigation without worrying about what can or cannot be said publicly. Decisions must be made on a case-by-case basis to balance the public's right to know against the integrity of an ongoing investigation. There are also privacy concerns to be considered and police may be civilly liable if persons whose involvement is uncertain are publicly identified.

On occasion, criminal events such as public shootings may generate considerable public outrage and fear. In order to allay public fear, police in Canada have taken the approach of confirming through the media, when appropriate, whether the incident was gang related or targeted as opposed to the action of a deranged individual. The public are then able to infer from such information that the incident was a relatively isolated event and that public risk is minimal.

Police media liaison units also undertake **media monitoring** and **content analysis** of media reports and serious crimes elsewhere. This helps police agencies stay abreast of what is being reported in the media about them. Media liaison units then work to control and counter misinformation that may be reported or that is felt by the police to be presented out of context. If coverage is deemed to be unfairly critical of the police, communications units will endeavour to see that a fairer balance ensues. In this regard, media liaison units furnish advice and guidance to senior police management on how to deal with emerging potential concerns both to the community and to the police agency itself. The reason for the consultation is to ensure that what is said is accurate and consistent with the agency's policies while protecting ongoing investigations and prospective prosecutions.

Media liaison units are increasingly involved in feature story writing by issuing periodic media releases that may highlight police actions in the community, identify emerging crime trends, or promote new crime-prevention initiatives. Such media releases are utilized by news reporters who, under time and resource constraints, often find it expedient to copy and paste the contents with only minor revisions into their news reports.

More recently, police agencies have recognized the benefits of providing information on police-maintained internet sites. Through such internet-based publications, police can regularly update and provide readily accessible information that can alert the public to such matters as trends in computer crime, internet security, or identity theft. Media liaison units thus maintain public websites and endeavour to provide timely updates (see, for example, the Halifax Regional Police and Halton Regional Police Service websites).

As do many other public and private institutions, police media liaison units have developed and maintain internal (intranet) websites with access restricted to employees of the police department. Intranet websites facilitate internal communication and information sharing in a timely yet relatively restricted manner. Increasingly, effective internal communication has been recognized as essential to building and sustaining employee morale and organizational pride. This is especially true in police agencies.

Social Media and the Police

The majority of Canadian police agencies routinely provide messages through social media sites (for example, Facebook and Twitter) to inform the public about crimes or incidents that may have just occurred. This may range from car thefts, robberies, and motor vehicle accidents to sexual assaults. Noteworthy in the growing use of social media by police agencies is the ability to simply bypass traditional news media (Mawby 2010, 125). Police media experts can frame messages about criminal events and about police strategies and responses and directly communicate them to the public. In this way, police can avoid the inevitable editorializing and spin that news reporters and editors inject into their coverage. Simply, with the advent of social media, police agencies now have direct control over information they wish to release to the public. While such control can prevent the spread of incorrect or misinterpreted information, it also has the potential for the police to simply skirt the prospect of news media holding them to account or otherwise directing criticism at them (see Mawby 2010, 131).

The Toronto Police Service was the first Canadian police department to integrate social media into their day-to-day operations arising from the belief that to engage the public more often and in more *meaningful* (emphasis in original) ways would lead to an improved level of trust between the police and the public (Meijer and Thaens 2013). Goldsmith (2015) takes the position that social networking technologies have a greater potential than previous technologies to rapidly change police practices. One positive aspect of the police use of social media is the ability to humanize police officers in order to break down barriers to communication. For example, the use of humour is often an effective icebreaker. In 2019, in the midst of a heatwave, the Braintree Police Department in Massachusetts, USA, created a Facebook post which said "Folks—due to the extreme heat, we are asking anyone thinking of doing criminal activity to hold off until Monday" (CBS Boston 2019). Over the same weekend, New York Police Department tweeted "Sunday has been cancelled. Stay indoors, nothing to see here" (Marcelo 2019).

One example that illustrates how social media can negatively impact a police investigation is related to the intensive hunt for Kam McLeod and Bryer Schmegelsky, suspects in the murders of three individuals in northern British Columbia in the summer of 2019. As Hristova (2019) reported, the "speculative nature of social media allows for misinformation to be forwarded," which increases and complicates the police investigation, as they must critically assess each piece of information to assess validity.

Police use of social media as an investigative tool is of growing importance to most police departments in Canada. Most police agencies have analytical support staff who mine open social media sites to acquire information about persons or groups of interest to the police. It is remarkable how careless individuals involved in criminal activity can be in posting photographs, or in identifying their location, vehicle, associates, and family members. This information may not be "evidence" on its own but, when collated with evidence from other investigative means, may provide relevant independent corroborative evidence. Police agencies may also use social media as a primary investigative tool in covert operations. For example, in January 2019, the Vancouver Police Department deployed an online strategy in order to arrange hotel meetings with men who were seeking sex with underage girls. The "sting" resulted in the arrest of 47 men from various social backgrounds and stature (Canadian Press 2019).

As noted earlier, there is often a tension or strain between the police and traditional news media. Often this is due to the control that the traditional media outlets have over the reporting and editorial process. What the police see as key aspects of a story may simply be cut. Similarly, journalists and editors make decisions about just what details are to be reported and may put an editorial spin on a particular issue that presents information in a light not necessarily to police liking.

Bystander Media

For a majority of Canadians, owning a smartphone has evolved from a luxury to a necessity. Anyone with a smartphone can now snap a picture or capture video of unfolding events and upload it to a social media platform. Generally, anything involving alleged police misconduct has the potential "to go viral." Such is the emergence of the phenomenon now known as **bystander media**.

From a policing perspective, the advent of bystander media presents the possibility of diminishing public trust in the police. Simply put, "in an age where any citizen can capture officer misconduct on their smartphone, a single video upload can serve to erode the trust of millions of Canadians overnight." Notwithstanding some research (Maxson, Hennigan, and Sloan 2003, for example) that suggests that traditional news media are NOT the strongest influence on public perceptions of the police, in reality most Canadians do not have regular direct contact with the police and therefore their perceptions about crime and the police are largely shaped by a variety of media sources. More recent research by Miethe, Venger, and Lieberman (2019) on the impact of social media appears to affirm this. Indeed, Newell (2019) has stated that visual-media–based citizen journalism is often framed as a form of "witnessing" and the citizens' cameras as "technologies of truthtelling" (63). Video images of police use of physical force in various situations are not uncommon on television, in online news accounts, and on social media platforms.

To be certain, in a number of incidents in recent years, video of police actions captured by members of the public has provided an account of events dramatically different from that provided by the police. Media dissemination of video footage of lethal and non-lethal police encounters has thus contributed to greater public scrutiny of police practices and in some cases were the impetus for change to policy and training (Miethe, Venger, and Lieberman 2019, 35). For example, the use of conducted energy weapons (Tasers) was reassessed and training updated by Canadian police agencies following the 2007 Tasering death of Robert Dziekański at the Vancouver International Airport, and the public release of video footage recorded by a civilian witness. Likewise, the shooting of 18-year-old Sammy Yatim by Toronto Police Constable James Forcillo on a Toronto streetcar in July of 2013 was recorded on video, not only by civilian witnesses but by Toronto Transit Commission video recorders located on the streetcar. Public outcry provoked by the incident subsequently culminated in the 2019 launch of an inquest by the coroner's office of Ontario which, while not legally binding, can offer recommendations for policy and procedural changes to police practices.

According to Brown (2016, 294), use of force by police is the greatest source of citizens' complaints and has caused more controversy and public concern than any other issue. This would appear to be borne out in the Dziekański and Yatim cases. Visual accounts of police–citizen interactions have and continue to shape public perceptions of the appropriateness, fairness, and acceptability of police behaviour (Parry, Moule, and Dario 2019, 413).

Boivin, Gendron, Faubert, and Poulin (2019) found that media exposure (i.e. from television shows) appears to inflate positive opinions about the police but that repeated media exposure to images of police abuse led respondents to overestimate the level of misconduct and, presumably, the use of force (367). Newell (2019) found that the primary concerns of police officers regarding bystander video arise out of their fears about visibility and exposure, the potential for misrepresentation or misinterpretation of their conduct, and physical interference with their daily work (71)

In considering the wide-ranging consequences of bystander media capturing a violent arrest or a use-of-force altercation involving the police, fundamental questions arise. Do the prospects of being "caught on video" change police behaviour or impact their decisions in resolving a situation? Does such exposure undermine public confidence and trust in the police?

Whatever the answers, it is clear that the effect of bystander media on police conduct and public perception of police actions will remain a focal point for ongoing research.

Toronto Police have been recognized for their effective use of social media. Do you follow your local police service's Twitter account?

Media Influence on Public Perceptions of Crime

As has been duly noted by several commentators, "the construction and public consumption of crime stories is complex, bi-directional, and multidimensional" (Mawby 2007; Reiner 2002 in Lee and McGovern 2014, 11). It is readily apparent that the power of mass media can quickly and effectively influence public opinion and political sentiments. For example, in the United States in 2014 and early 2015, there were a number of high-profile incidents (for example, Michael Brown in Ferguson, Missouri; Eric Garner in Staten Island, New York; and Trayvon Martin in Florida) where trust in the police with respect to race relations and the use of force captivated the public. Sadly, similar incidents (for example, the brutal in-custody death of George Floyd filmed in its entirety on a public street (Hill et al. 2020) , the fatal shooting of Breonna Taylor during a drug raid (Glover et al. 2020) and the tragic circumstances of the murder of Ahmaud Arbery (Thomson Reuters 2020) have led to significant public protests and demands for police reform in 2020 (*CBC News* 2020).

Each of these incidents was also extensively reported in Canada. Such media attention served to shift attitudes toward the police in dramatic ways (Baker, Goodman, and Miller 2015; Blow 2012; Chuck 2014).

All forms of media are powerful and public sentiment about police can quickly change. In an era in which claims about "fake news" and "alternative facts" are increasingly common, a growing number of people doubt the veracity of anything they hear, read, or view from mainstream news or social media sources. Canadian police agencies are not immune to this aura of doubt and mistrust.

It is true that media can influence public opinion in both positive and negative ways. A 2018 Angus Reid Institute survey focused on "levels of confidence" in components of the justice system (police, criminal courts, Supreme Court of Canada). The results showed Canadians were slightly less confident in these components compared to 2016, yet confidence levels were still significantly higher than in 2012. One negative result of the survey was the finding that the levels of confidence in the police and the courts had declined among "visible minorities" (Angus Reid 2018).

On the other hand, significant numbers of Americans report using the mass media as their primary source of information about crime, and these stories are the context for most mass-media accounts of police work. The recent trend toward tabloid-style journalism—even in mainstream media—appears to reduce public confidence and trust in the police (IACP 2001).

Yet other studies show that the media are not the strongest influence on public opinion of the police. According to Maxson, Hennigan, and Sloan (2003), the media did not appear to be a source of negative opinion of the Los Angeles Police Department. Instead of relying on the media for their opinions, respondents appeared to react primarily to their own experiences and expectations in forming opinions of their local police. A report from the National Institute of Justice (2014) found that media accounts of police misconduct do influence perceptions of the police, but less so than personal interactions. The findings of a small study sample of people from Los Angeles, California, found that race and ethnicity affected assessment of police demeanour.

Logic of Police–Media Engagement

As much of the foregoing discussion has illustrated, police agencies in modern democracies have come to realize the importance of cultivating a positive working relationship with the media. As Lee and McGovern (2014) have argued, three key and overlapping logics (purposes) underpin contemporary relationships between the police and the media:

- the management of public *risks* and the *responsibilization* of the public;
- the management of police *image*—or "image work";
- attempts to increase confidence or *trust* in policing, and in the *legitimacy* of police organizations (Lee and McGovern 2014, 40, italics in original; see also Chapter 1 in this text).

As will be discussed in Chapter 15, preoccupation with risk has become a dominant concern throughout society in the early twenty-first century. As many criminologists have noted, police have become principal actors both in defining risks and in advising how these risks should be mitigated. As such, police media strategies have emerged in order to manage "what, when, by whom, and to what ends information can be released to the media and public" (Lee and McGovern 2014, 43). In simple terms, police share information in ways that not only alert and educate members of the public about risks that may put in them in danger, but do so in ways that encourage responsible behaviour in order to minimize risks generally (note Chapter 1).

Police are concerned about their public image and want to ensure that media representations of the police are presented in a fair and positive light. Persistent negative views of the police lead to a lack of trust and confidence, and, inevitably, to a lack of public cooperation. The police are not alone in the concern to sustain a positive public image. Throughout the late twentieth century, many private corporations and public institutions engaged in public relations to ensure that their organizational images were positively portrayed.

The matters of trust, public confidence, and cooperation relate directly to the legitimacy of the police. Police agencies have become cognizant of the importance of trust and, indeed, have embraced such related measures as "citizen satisfaction" and "public trust" as useful and quantifiable measures of their overall performance (see Chapter 7). As illustrated below, police have become alert to public opinion polls as indicators of the job they are doing in the community (Lee and McGovern 2014, 51–2).

Public opinion of the police is directly related to the legitimacy that police possess. That is, how the public perceive the police affects the public willingness to accept and/or respect police authority specifically and, more generally, the law. Such matters are related to the public's willingness to approach police, to report crime, and to otherwise cooperate with police investigations—all of which are essential to effective policing (Lee and McGovern 2014, 53, 57).

Over and above their reliance on media liaison officers and police-issued press releases, regular crime reporters often nurture professional and personal relationships with police personnel in order to establish and maintain trust (Mawby 2010, 134). As noted

Challenge Your Assumptions

Claims-Making: Cops and Killer Weed

As various criminologists have noted, police often work in conjunction with the media to promote particular images and claims about crime and criminals that support the goals of police work. News media are the principal means by which police communicate with the public. A symbiotic relationship has thus emerged between the police and the media—the police depend on the media to transmit police perspectives, and the media depend on the police for information about criminal activity that most reporters will not observe first-hand.

In a compelling 2014 study, *Killer Weed: Marijuana Grow Ops, Media and Justice*,[i] scholars Susan Boyd and Connie Carter provide a comprehensive content analysis of over 2500 news articles published between 1995 and 2009 to show how major newspapers in Canada "framed" marijuana grow operations in British Columbia. As Boyd and Carter demonstrate, the media uncritically accepted a series of RCMP-funded studies that propagated the belief (1) that marijuana was a threat to public safety, and (2) that its production and distribution was dominated by violent, ethnically based, organized criminal gangs.

The authors carefully examined the studies, noting that they were undertaken by a principal researcher who was employed as an RCMP research chair at a college in British Columbia. As is the academic convention at colleges and universities, the studies were not peer reviewed, nor were they published in academic journals— typically the "gold standard" for judging *bona fide* research findings. Furthermore, as Boyd and Carter reveal, the studies used a faulty research methodology, lacked scientific rigour, and reached conclusions that were not supported by evidence. Nonetheless, the reports were enthusiastically endorsed by the RCMP, released to the public, and uncritically embraced and cited

by a zealous media only too happy to report "the facts" about the dangers of marijuana production. In this way, the images of marijuana and its production and distribution were demonized. The imagery served to communicate and justify to the public what the police were doing in their aggressive stance against marijuana and marijuana grow operations.

Using a 2011 report by the Canadian Centre for Justice Studies (CCJS) that they obtained through a freedom of information request, Boyd and Carter refute RCMP claims that grow operations are dominated by organized crime. According to the CCJS report, only five per cent of offenders taken to court were affiliated with organized crime. Furthermore, despite the imagery that the grow operations were principally controlled by ethnic minorities, the CCJS report shows that over 90 per cent of convicted operators were not only Caucasian but Canadian citizens. The authors do not deny that ethnic, organized criminal gangs are involved in grow operations or that violence is used for criminal purposes. What they do contend, based on their review of all the evidence, is that claims about the extent and nature of organized crime involvement are grossly exaggerated.

The propagation of misleading images thus fuelled public fear and escalated the perception of risk. In turn, this justified a series of intrusive responses that extended beyond the criminal law. Partnerships among police, fire departments, electrical inspectors, municipal bylaw enforcement personnel, and BC Hydro (the major public hydro-electric provider in British Columbia) personnel combined their efforts to monitor and police grow operations using punitive civil laws and procedures (such as property seizures) in ways that bypass the criminal law and traditional protections afforded under the *Charter*.

earlier, these relationships are inevitably asymmetrical to the extent that journalists depend on such police contacts for insider information to augment their news reports. As a result, news reporters may succumb to accepting information at face value without subjecting it to rigorous and independent verification.

Conclusion

This chapter has reviewed a series of considerations regarding the relationship between the police and the mass media, including a brief discussion of two competing perspectives by which the relationship between the police and the media can be considered.

The chapter also noted that the relationship between the police and the media in Canadian society has evolved. Initially, police agencies were guarded and defensive with respect to providing information regarding crime and criminals to the news media. However, through the twentieth century, police agencies came to realize that it was in their best interests to cultivate a closer working relationship with news media. Thus, the police came to recognize that the media constituted "a resource to be harnessed, not a threat to be shunned" (Ericson, Baranek, and Chan 1989, 93). In order to engage traditional news media on terms that better suited police agencies, many modern police agencies have allocated considerable budgets and human resources to the establishment of media liaison units to coordinate public communications. As well, with the wide availability of internet access and with a phenomenal growth in mobile communications, police have cultivated the capacity to communicate directly and proactively with the public through the development of sophisticated information-sharing websites and through the strategic use of social media, often aimed at specific populations such as youth and seniors. Thus, to some extent police can now bypass traditional media outlets. This independent capacity enhances the police ability to (a) project and protect their public image, (b) control and apprehend criminality, and (c) promote the aims, ideologies, and interest of the police (Chibnall 1977 in Mawby 2010, 136). It was also suggested that this independence may allow the police to avert the prospect of traditional news media holding them to account or otherwise directing criticism at them.

Critical Thinking Questions

1. Is there a symbiotic but asymmetric relationship between the police and the media? Discuss.
2. Describe and discuss the two competing perspectives on the relationship between the police and the media.
3. What benefits might the police receive by releasing information to the public through the traditional media? What problems might arise when the police release information through the traditional media?
4. Can members of the public be confident that what they read in the media about crime is true and accurate? Explain your answer.

5. Is the police ability to bypass traditional media by relying on social media a positive development? Explain your answer.
6. Would the police ever be justified in releasing information that would deliberately misinform the public? Explain your answer.

Endnote

i   For a synopsis and commentary on *Killer Weed*, see the review by C. Reasons (2014) in the *Canadian Journal of Criminology and Criminal Justice*, available at /www .ccja-acjp.ca/pub/en/review-killer-weed-marijuana-grow-ops-media-and-justice-based-policymaking/ (accessed 9 November 2015). In September 2020, this article was available at https://www.ccja-acjp.ca/pub/en/reviews/game-day-gangsters-crime-and-deviance-in-canadian-football/.

National Security Policing in the Twenty-First Century

Introduction

On 11 September 2001, 19 militants associated with Al-Qaeda, an Islamic extremist group, hijacked four passenger aircraft and crashed them in suicide attacks against several targets in the United States, including the twin towers of the World Trade Center in New York and the Pentagon near Washington, DC. The fourth plane crashed in a field in Pennsylvania. Millions of horrified viewers around the world watched the attacks on the World Trade

Center on both live television and subsequent rebroadcasts. Indeed, as former Minister of Public Safety Vic Toews stated, "The events of September 11, 2001 changed the way the world viewed terrorism" (Toews 2013, 1).

Since these dramatic events in 2001, the United States, Canada, the United Kingdom and, indeed, most western democratic countries have maintained a **hypervigilance** (a state of extreme watchfulness motivated by collective fear and foreboding) against similar repeat attacks. The hypervigilance appears to be singularly focused on the perceived threat of violent Islamic zealotry waged both by international extremist groups and by homegrown domestic extremists.

Before reviewing and assessing Canada's responses and strategies to deal with perceived terrorist threats in the twenty-first century, it is important to recognize that throughout the twentieth century Canada was not immune to violence perpetrated by domestic extremists seeking to further political or religious aims. Although the "Sons of Freedom" Doukhobors and the FLQ terrorists are virtually forgotten in the modern era of widespread fear and anxiety over radical fundamentalist groups such as Al-Qaeda and more recent movements variously known as ISIS (Islamic State of Iraq and Syria), ISIL (Islamic State of Iraq and the Levant) or Daesh, Canada through much of the twentieth century wrestled with its own brands of domestic terrorism and other perceived threats to domestic security. To be certain, fears and anxiety surrounding "terrorist" threats to Canadian national security are not new. A cursory review reveals that such concerns characterize much of Canadian history,

This chapter provides an overview of the circumstances that have shaped Canadian policing and security agencies charged with the responsibilities of national security.

The Origins of Canadian Security Services

To understand properly the structure and responsibilities of national security in Canada in the early twenty-first century, it is important first to have an awareness of the history of Canada's security services.

Canada's security services developed "gradually and incrementally" since John A. Macdonald first assigned such duties to an embryonic collection of secret police agents in 1864. In 1868 Macdonald formalized these arrangements by creating the Dominion Police Force (Rosen 2000, 2; see also Chapter 11). These duties entailed providing security for federal government buildings and providing information and intelligence on possible threats to Canada's security. Use of undercover agents and paid informers was common (Whitaker, Kealey, and Parnaby 2012). The North-West Mounted Police were later tasked with performing similar intelligence activities in western Canada (Rosen 2000, 2).

From the late 1860s through the First World War (1914–18) the security functions of the Dominion Police grew, largely in response to fears about labour unrest, anarchism, and, particularly, the threat of communism.

The Fenians

Of particular concern at the time was the threat posed by a group of influential North American Irish patriots who had formed a secret society, the Fenian Brotherhood, dedicated to gaining Ireland's independence from Great Britain. In the late 1860s the **Fenians** orchestrated a series of attacks from the United States on Canadian military facilities in the hope of bringing pressure to bear on Great Britain. The need for greater security and intelligence became apparent following the 1868 assassination in Ottawa of Thomas D'Arcy McGee, a Father of Confederation and an outspoken critic of the Fenians (see Whitaker, Kealey, and Parnaby 2012).

South Asian Radicals

Independently but coinciding with the security functions assumed by the Dominion Police, the federal department of immigration also initiated security policing measures to track and thwart the politicization of immigrant South Asians on Canada's west coast. Canadian immigration personnel surreptitiously worked to recruit paid informers to report on the activities of leading members of the South Asian community not just in British Columbia but throughout the west coast of the United States. South Asian leaders also sought to resist the racial inequality embedded in Canada's immigration policies.

As British subjects legally entitled to settle freely within the British Empire, about 5200 South Asians, most of whom were Sikhs from the Punjab, were becoming increasingly strident in their opposition to revisions to the Canadian *Immigration Act* that sought to curtail Asian immigration (Whitaker, Kealey, and Parnaby 2012, 39). The resistance to restrictive immigration came to a head in May 1914 with the arrival of the *Komagata Maru* carrying 376 Indian immigrants who were refused entry. From May to late July, when the *Komagata Maru* and its passengers returned to India, major confrontations erupted over Canada's refusal to allow the immigrants to land. The confrontations occasionally became violent, particularly when immigration officers tried to take the ship by force (Whitaker, Kealey, and Parnaby 2012, 53).

The Doukhobors

In the late nineteenth century a Christian religious sect known as Doukhobors, seeking to escape perceived persecution in Tsarist Russia, began a mass immigration to Canada in the hope of finding religious and political freedom. Under provisions of the *Dominion Land Act*, Canadian federal legislation enacted to encourage settlement of the Canadian west, large tracts of land were made available to immigrants on condition that the lands be settled and made agriculturally productive. The Doukhobors were quick to take advantage of the opportunity.

During the period leading to and following World War I (1914–18), there was a growing intolerance toward Doukhobors, who had been granted exemption from military service on the grounds of conscientious objection. As the Doukhobor colony prospered in British Columbia, public resentment grew stronger. In 1922 the government seized Doukhobor property as a punitive measure for their failure to ensure their children attended school. In protest, an ultra-conservative faction of the Doukhobors retaliated with mass demonstrations of public nudity and by burning public schools to the ground. This marked the first of many incidents of violence. In 1924, the ultra-conservative faction assassinated the Doukhobors' primary leader by exploding a bomb on a railcar that killed the leader and eight others, including a member of the BC legislature.

In response, the federal government toughened the *Criminal Code* with measures specifically addressing Doukhobor conduct, including the imposition of a three-year sentence for any public nudity intended as a form of protest. Indeed, in 1932, 745 men, women, and children were detained for public nudity. More than 600 adults were sentenced to three years' incarceration and 365 children were placed in orphanages or juvenile detention facilities. These children grew up to become extremists and activists in the Sons of Freedom who, after World War II (1939–45), actively and violently resisted further government intrusions (Yerbury and Griffiths 1991, 338). The Sons of Freedom are discussed below.

Labour Activism and the Winnipeg General Strike (1919)

Prior to and during the years of the First World War, the national government had become concerned about militant activism and a radicalized union movement. In the aftermath of the Bolshevik Revolution in Russia in 1917, the Canadian federal government harboured fears of European immigrants who had become radicalized and sympathetic to communist ideals. With the end of World War I, massive unemployment, inflation, and unionism contributed to a growing unease in Canada. This unease manifested in the federal government's increased surveillance of radical union members and Bolshevik sympathizers. The Royal Northwest Mounted Police were encouraged to infiltrate the major unions in an effort to keep abreast of activities judged to be subversive and a threat to Canada's economic well-being.

Undercover Mounted Police members, under the direction of the Criminal Investigations Branch located in Northwest Mounted Police headquarters in Regina, were directed to investigate and infiltrate "individuals and organizations that espouse the pernicious doctrines of Bolshevism" in the main centres of radical activity: Winnipeg, Calgary, and Vancouver (Horrall 1980, 173). Investigators were to gather intelligence about plans and communicate it sufficiently in advance of any action so that intended disturbances would be prevented. Indeed, such prevention is the fundamental objective of any intelligence service (Horrall 1980, 174).

On the basis of reports from undercover operators, Royal Northwest Mounted Police senior officers were not alarmed at the activities of the union organizers. In reports to Ottawa, senior officers made it clear that union organizers shared the goal of uniting workers in order to bring about changes in social and economic conditions but were averse to the use of force or violence. Primarily, activists wanted to improve working conditions and to secure the right to collective bargaining. In his communication with his political masters in Ottawa, the commissioner of the RNWMP, A.B. Perry, "did not identify the existence of any sinister plot to overthrow the government by force, either by western radicals or foreign agents" (Horrall 1980, 182).

Senior bureaucrats in Ottawa, for reasons that remain both unknown and unclear, chose to interpret the intelligence reports in a way that portrayed union activism as an effort to subvert existing social and political conditions in order to establish a "'Soviet Government' based upon the 'Dictatorship of the proletariat'" (Horrall 1980, 183).

In May 1919 Winnipeg unions called for a general strike that was to last from 15 May to 25 June. It was the most famous strike in Canadian history. Over 30,000 workers walked off their jobs. Fears in Ottawa escalated that the strike was the start of a revolutionary conspiracy. Ottawa acted decisively and moved to have union leaders arrested and charged with sedition. On 21 June, the uniformed members of the RNWMP, on horseback, charged the crowd of strikers. Known as "Bloody Saturday," the police action resulted in many injuries and one death. The strike quickly ended, leaving a legacy of resentment and hostility toward the federal government and the RNWMP.

In the months leading up to the Winnipeg General Strike, the RNWMP had succeeded in building an effective intelligence-gathering network. Undercover detectives and paid informers had successfully penetrated the suspect unions and gathered important information that had been dutifully conveyed to superior officers. However, what had become apparent was that even though timely reports had been communicated to Ottawa, the interpretation and meaning attributed to them was problematic. Reports prepared by the commissioner had contained graphic accounts from field agents who often made inferences and drew conclusions that differed markedly from those of their superiors. In Ottawa, there was no coordinating body able to analyze the forwarded material. No capacity existed to determine the accuracy of the accounts or to draw meaningful conclusions about the information conveyed up the chain of command. This led to inconsistency, confusion, and misinterpretation (Horrall 1980, 185).

In the wake of the Winnipeg General Strike, Prime Minister Sir Robert Borden realized that the national intelligence service was inadequate and moved to bring about significant changes to the federal system of security and policing (Horrall 1980, 186–7). Commissioner Perry was tasked with offering recommendations for the reorganization of federal policing and national security functions.

Perry, alert to the fact that many municipal police departments were unionized and were sympathetic to the goals of the Winnipeg General Strike, recommended a consolidation and expansion of the RNWMP, who were by law prohibited from unionization. In

A photo of the Winnipeg General Strike riots, 10 June 1919. Imagine the chaos and damage done by horses charging through crowds this thick 11 days later.

University of Manitoba Archives & Special Collections, Winnipeg Tribune fonds, PC 18 (A.81-12), Box 70, Folder 7188, Item 2.

November 1919, Perry's recommendation led to the amendment of the *Royal Northwest Mounted Police Act* to create a new policing body. The Dominion Police were absorbed into the Mounted Police, headquarters were relocated from Regina to Ottawa, and the RNWMP was renamed the Royal Canadian Mounted Police. As historian S.W. Horrall observed, "it is no exaggeration to say that the Royal Canadian Mounted Police is but one more offspring of the Winnipeg General Strike" (Horral 1980, 190).

National Security through World War II and the Cold War

From 1920 to 1946, national security activities were the responsibility of the RCMP's Criminal Investigations Branch (CIB). In 1936, a specialized Intelligence Section with a mandate to collect and analyze national intelligence data was established within the CIB. During this time, national security concerns stemmed from threats lingering from the early twentieth century, so much intelligence work was directed at the communist movement (O'Connor 2006a, 26). With the outbreak of World War II, national security work took on a greater emphasis and RCMP resources grew. Not surprisingly, at this time attention was directed at fascist and Nazi organizations in Canada. RCMP policies restricted covert intelligence gathering to domestic Canada and, as a result, the RCMP developed trusting liaisons with both British and American security services for international intelligence data. Through the Second World War, RCMP activities, particularly in western Canada, were also directed at monitoring enemy aliens—immigrants and Canadian citizens who were perceived as constituting a threat to national security given their family ties to Germany, Italy, or Japan. The RCMP played a significant role throughout World War II in registering and overseeing the apprehension and internment of such enemy aliens (O'Connor 2006a, 26). On Canada's west coast, this ultimately led to the internment and relocation of some 23,000 Japanese Canadians.

Sons of Freedom

In 1943, in an effort to increase productivity and efficiency on behalf of the war effort, the government compelled Doukhobor men to contribute their labour to specific work projects. This initiative provoked nude protests by some 3500 Doukhobors in Nelson, British Columbia, and in Vancouver. The provincial government responded by passing a law making public nudity an offence punishable by whipping (Yerbury and Griffiths 1991, 338).

As conflict with both the provincial and federal levels of government intensified, disagreements and infighting within the sect spread. Even these internal disputes led to nude protests and to the burning of the members' own homes and vehicles as public displays of their commitment to their faith. Impromptu acts of violence such as bombings and arson of electrical transmission lines, bridges, government buildings, and schools were undertaken by the radicalized group now calling themselves the Sons of Freedom. In 1953, 170 Doukhobor children who were not attending school were apprehended and made wards of the province. They were housed and schooled in internment camp–like settings until 1959.

By the late 1950s the Sons of Freedom had aggressively increased their attacks on railway lines, power transmission lines, government buildings, and public ferries. In 1960 more than 106 bombings and arsons were carried out (Yerbury and Griffiths 1991, 341).

According to Yerbury and Griffiths (1991), the violent actions of the Sons of Freedom compelled the Royal Canadian Mounted Police to form a specialized investigation unit. The Special D unit (D for "depredations") of the RCMP was formed in August 1962 in response to approximately 259 bombing incidents and other "acts of depredation" perpetrated by the Sons of Freedom that year (Holt 1964).

The Special D unit consisted of a select force of ten officers, most of whom spoke Russian. It was their task to assemble evidence against the Sons of Freedom. The RCMP in the Kootenays consisted of 200 men; additional emergency squads were formed from detachment members flown into the area from throughout Canada to make mass arrests of the defiant Doukhobors (Holt 1964, 8; Yerbury and Griffiths 1991, 341).

The Gouzenko Spy Affair

After World War II, the Gouzenko spy affair stimulated changes to RCMP national security priorities. Igor Gouzenko was a clerk employed at the Soviet embassy in Ottawa in 1945 who in the course of his employment discovered the existence of several Russian spy networks operating covertly in Canada. Gouzenko took classified Soviet documents proving the existence of the spy networks and sought permanent residence and protection in Canada for himself and his family. The reverberations of his defection and the subsequent arrest of 12 suspects were especially felt in Great Britain and the United States. Gouzenko's disclosures were solid evidence that the threat posed by communism was real. Some observers have suggested that the Gouzenko spy affair marked the beginning of the Cold War (Whitaker, Kealey, and Parnaby 2012, 179).

For the RCMP, the Gouzenko spy affair was an embarrassment. The very threat that they had long been clamouring about had materialized right under their noses. In 1946 the Special Branch, reporting directly to the RCMP commissioner, was created to engage in counter-espionage and counter-intelligence activities. It was also expected to ensure the federal government employees were loyal and trustworthy (Rosen 2000, 2).

By 1956, the Special Branch had been elevated in stature to a directorate—the Directorate of Security and Intelligence or I Directorate—under the control of an assistant commissioner (O'Connor 2006a, 27). In 1969, the branch was renamed the Security Service and placed under the control of a civilian director who reported jointly to the RCMP commissioner and to the federal Solicitor General (O'Connor 2006a, 27; Rosen 2000, 2).

The Mackenzie Commission of Inquiry (1969)

Other scandals led to the creation of the Mackenzie Royal Commission, which in 1969 recommended that the Security Service be severed from the RCMP and be constituted as "a new civilian non-police agency . . . quite separate from the RCMP . . . without law enforcement powers" (Mackenzie in O'Connor 2006a, 28). More specifically, the Mackenzie report expressed reservations about a single agency having joint responsibility for security intelligence and the coercive powers of a police force. It also concluded that the RCMP lacked the sophistication and ability to analyze intelligence data competently.

According to John Sawatsky (1980), the RCMP was not pleased with the prospects of seeing the security functions severed and given to a civilian service.

The FLQ and the October Crisis, 1970

The **October Crisis** in 1970 was precipitated by actions taken by radicals who sought the political and economic independence of the province of Quebec from Canada. Through the 1960s, the **Front de Liberation du Québec (FLQ)**, a group of loosely organized separatists inspired by Marxist-Leninist ideology, resorted to the use of violence as a means of achieving their political goal of an independent Quebec (Pelletier 1971, 55). From 1963 to 1970, the FLQ were responsible for over 200 violent actions, including bombings, bank robberies, and kidnappings. At least five persons died as a result of FLQ actions. Most of the bombings were directed at federal government facilities including Canada Post letterboxes, post offices, and railroads. The FLQ also bombed the Montreal Stock Exchange (Corrado 1981, 459).

In the fall of 1970, British trade commissioner James Cross was kidnapped from his residence by four men posing as deliverymen (Canadian Broadcasting Corporation, n.d.). The kidnappers, members of the FLQ, threatened to kill Cross unless the Canadian government released 23 members of their organization jailed for their involvement in various crimes committed by the Front. The kidnappers insisted that the jailed members were political prisoners and demanded that their political manifesto be read on national television (CBC, n.d.). According to the Canadian Broadcasting Corporation, the FLQ manifesto on Radio-Canada stated in part,

> We have had enough of promises of work and prosperity. When in fact we will always be the diligent servants and bootlickers of the big shots . . . we will be slaves until Quebecers, all of us, have used every means, including dynamite and guns, to drive out these big bosses of the economy and of politics who will stoop to any action however based, the better to screw us. . . . [CBC, n.d.]

Initially, both the federal government headed by Prime Minister Pierre Trudeau and the Quebec provincial government headed by Premier Robert Bourassa downplayed the kidnapping. However, the crisis escalated five days after Cross's abduction when another group of FLQ extremists then kidnapped a senior member of the provincial Cabinet, Quebec Minister of Labour Pierre Laporte.

On 16 October 1970, in response to the premier of Quebec's request for help, Prime Minister Trudeau invoked the *War Measures Act*. Soon the Canadian army was dispatched to protect politicians and government buildings. The *War Measures Act* gave the army and police across the country extraordinary legal powers to apprehend what was now perceived to be a widespread insurrection. The *Act* suspended basic civil rights and liberties and allowed police to conduct searches and to make arrests without warrants. Those arrested could be held for prolonged periods without charges and without the legal right to consult a lawyer. It was the first time in Canadian history that the *War Measures Act* had been invoked without the country actually being at war. Police soon arrested some 405 suspects, some of whom were detained for 21 days. Most were released without being charged.

On 17 October an FLQ communiqué led authorities to a parked car. In the trunk of the car was the body of Pierre Laporte. He had been strangled to death. This marked the first political assassination in Canada in 102 years since the murder of Thomas d'Arcy McGee. Public sentiments that had initially sympathized with the FLQ quickly turned.

After two months of being held in captivity, James Cross was released as part of a negotiated deal that allowed his kidnappers to leave Canada for Cuba. Years later, all of Cross's kidnappers returned to Canada to face charges. Laporte's killers were captured and sentenced either to life sentences for murder or 20 years for kidnapping.

In the aftermath of the October Crisis it became evident that the FLQ was not the sophisticated major paramilitary organization that many had believed. Rather, it was an informal group organized into small, independent cells whose members shared the dream of an independent and socialist Quebec. At most, the group consisted of 35 members (CBC, n.d.). Serious questions were raised about the competence and effectiveness of the RCMP's domestic security and intelligence capabilities. Their inability to have detected and prevented the various actions undertaken by the FLQ was seen by the federal government as a major problem. Allegations were later to emerge that seriously challenged not only the RCMP's organizational capabilities in regard to domestic security but its overall integrity. The allegations were significant enough to warrant the appointment of a judicial inquiry to examine the RCMP's abilities and its involvement in illegal activity.

The Keable and McDonald Public Inquiries

In the immediate aftermath of the FLQ crisis, the federal government was stunned by the incompetence of the RCMP security services (Rosen 2000, 4). The RCMP had been unable to recruit informers and had not been able to infiltrate the FLQ (Sawatsky 1980, 261). The RCMP had also become reliant on the Quebec and Montreal police agencies. As Sawatsky has suggested, the RCMP consisted mostly of white Anglo-Saxon Protestant (WASP) officers who were unfamiliar with and unsympathetic to Québécois nationalism. Anglophone members of the RCMP undertook the analysis of intelligence provided by the provincial and Montreal police, and failed to comprehend the political significance of the data being provided.

Beyond the 1970 crisis, the prospect of Quebec independence had become a legitimate political aspiration of many Québécois. The government asked the RCMP to become more proactive in assessing the extent of the separatist movement (O'Connor 2006a, 30). In response, an overzealous RCMP embarked on intelligence gathering, infiltration, harassment, and disruption of organizations seeking Quebec independence. The tactics, many not authorized by law, included illegal opening of mail; arson of a building in order to prevent a meeting of separatists with radical Americans; breaking into the offices of a French news agency, the Agence de Presse Libre du Québec (APLQ) (CBC, n.d.), and carting away half a ton of paper files; breaking into the offices of the Parti Québécois (PQ) and stealing membership files; and theft of dynamite for the purpose of blaming a suspect group (O'Connor 2006a; Sawatsky 1980). It would subsequently become known that such dirty tricks were directed not just at Quebec separatists but at a range of politically active groups deemed to be left-wing radicals. Public disclosure of these activities of the RCMP Security Service occurred when RCMP, Quebec, and Montreal police officers pleaded guilty to criminal charges related to planting explosive devices in the province of Quebec.

By 1976, the PQ had been democratically elected and formed the government in Quebec. When revelations regarding the RCMP activities in Quebec became public, the PQ launched a provincial inquiry. In 1977, Mr. Jean Keable was appointed to chair a provincial Commission of Inquiry into police operations on Quebec territory. His appointment generated considerable concern in Ottawa within both the federal government and the RCMP (Whitaker, Kealey, and Parnaby 2012, 306).

Further disclosure from the convicted police officers revealed that the RCMP had also misled the Solicitor General, the Cabinet minister responsible for the RCMP, about its activities. At this point, the commissioner of the RCMP requested a federal public inquiry to clear the air. In 1977, Donald McDonald, an Alberta judge, was appointed to chair a federal public inquiry (Whitaker, Kealey, and Parnaby 2012, 306).

With two inquiries underway—one provincial and one federal—the federal government soon became anxious about the terms of reference of the Keable inquiry. Specifically, the federal government and the RCMP objected to the Keable inquiry's intent to examine the day-to-day activities of the federal police. Initially, the federal government sought to have the Keable inquiry declared unconstitutional. Subsequently, the matter was heard by the Supreme Court of Canada, which restricted the terms of the Keable inquiry to investigating only the actions of specific individuals in specific cases within Quebec. To the relief of the federal government and the RCMP, the provincial inquiry was not to be allowed to review the internal operations of the RCMP (Belanger 2000)

With the Keable inquiry in Quebec and the McDonald inquiry in Ottawa, the doors were wide open for public revelation of the unlawful security measures that had occurred not exclusively, but primarily, in Quebec (Whitaker, Kealey, and Parnaby 2012, 308).

The McDonald Commission was to affirm the many transgressions committed by the RCMP in the name of national security. Of particular concern in the findings was the inability of the RCMP to distinguish between subversion and legitimate political dissent. Reservation was also expressed in regard to the obvious anti–left-wing bias. Nowhere was this more evident than in the Commission's discovery that the RCMP Security Service maintained a name index containing 1.3 million entries representing 800,000 files on individuals (Whitaker, Kealey, and Parnaby 2012, 9).

The McDonald Commission offered a number of significant recommendations, none more profound than that the Security Service be removed from the RCMP. Indeed, this had been voiced—but ignored—previously in the recommendations tendered by the Mackenzie Commission of Inquiry in 1969. The McDonald Commission felt strongly that the coercive power of a police force was inconsistent with effective security intelligence gathering (O'Connor 2006a, 32). In simple terms, the Commission believed that law enforcement should be separate and distinct from collecting security intelligence.

As with the Mackenzie Commission, the McDonald Commission recommended that a "a more mature, more experienced, better-educated personnel, . . . and a more participatory, less authoritarian style of management" be implemented (O'Connor 2006a, 33). Additionally, the McDonald Commission recommended that greater political scrutiny and oversight be exercised over the security intelligence function.

The McDonald Commission also recommended that the security intelligence agency not have police powers such as arrest and search and seizure. It recommended that police officers accompany security agents making surreptitious entries under judicially approved warrants. The McDonald Commission did not advocate that the RCMP should be removed entirely from national security matters. Rather, the Commission envisioned that a collaborative arrangement would be developed in which an independent security agency would have the primary role of gathering intelligence, while the RCMP would assist in executing various judicially approved warrants. The RCMP would continue to fulfill its primary responsibilities of preventing crime and arresting criminals (O'Connor 2006a, 30–36).

Canadian Security Intelligence Service (CSIS)

Following the public release of the McDonald Commission report, the government acknowledged acceptance of its primary recommendation: the establishment of a civilian security intelligence agency. In 1984, Bill C-9 was passed into law to establish the Canadian Security Intelligence Service (CSIS). Also established were two agencies to provide oversight to CSIS and its activities: the Security Intelligence Review Committee (SIRC) and an Inspector General (IG) for CSIS to review the activities of CSIS and report to Parliament.

The mandate of CSIS is to "collect, analyze and retain information and intelligence regarding activities that, on reasonable grounds, may be suspected of posing a threat to the security of Canada. CSIS [through the Minister of Public Safety] reports to and advises the federal government on these threats" (O'Connor 2006a, 129). The *Canadian Security Intelligence Service Act* defines a variety of "threats to the security of Canada": espionage and sabotage detrimental to the interests of Canada; threats or the use of violence for the purpose of achieving a political, religious or ideological objective; covert unlawful acts intended to lead to the destruction or overthrow by violence of the constitutional established system of government in Canada. As noted by O'Connor (2006a, 129), lawful advocacy, protest, and dissent are not included in the definition of a threat.

The primary role of CSIS is to advise the federal government. It may also liaise with and offer advice to provincial ministers responsible for policing. CSIS personnel are thus engaged in the collection, collation, evaluation, and analysis of information with respect to issues covered under the CSIS mandate. Taken together, these activities culminate in the production of what is referred to as intelligence.

In order for CSIS to intercept communications, obtain documents or other information, or enter premises covertly, it must obtain judicial authorization in the form of warrants. To even apply to the court for a warrant, CSIS must have the approval of the Minister of Public Safety.

A significant part of the CSIS mandate entails its liaisons with other government agencies in order to disseminate intelligence data. With the permission of the federal Minister of Public Safety, CSIS can cooperate with international organizations, foreign governments, and other appropriate institutions. Any written agreements that CSIS makes with provincial governments or foreign bodies must be approved by the Security and Intelligence Review Committee—the CSIS oversight body.

CSIS may disclose information it obtains to Canadian police agencies if that information will assist in law enforcement. It may also provide information to officials in International Affairs or National Defence, or to any federal minister if the Minister of Public Safety believes it to be in the public interest (O'Connor 2006a, 138). CSIS also shares responsibilities with a range of other agencies that have an involvement in national security:

- Communications Security Establishment (CSE);
- Citizenship and Immigration Canada;
- Canada Border Services;
- Transport Canada;

- Canadian Air Transport Security Authority;
- Canadian Coast Guard;
- Financial Transactions and Reports Analysis Centre (FINTRAC);
- Canada Revenue Agency;
- other agencies that play a role in national security such as Health Canada, Environment Canada, Canadian Nuclear Safety Commission, etc.

In 1984, when CSIS was established, the future of intelligence services in Canada looked promising, albeit not without some problems. Most importantly, the RCMP felt that it had been chastised by the removal of its security responsibilities. In reality, though, while the *CSIS Act* created a new civilian agency, the passage of the *Security Offences Act* at the same time gave the RCMP clear responsibility for the investigation of criminal offences arising out of threats to Canada's security as specified in the *CSIS Act* (Whitaker, Kealey, and Parnaby 2012, 367). In other words, security responsibilities never left the RCMP. Tensions and a lack of cooperation soon became apparent. This became abundantly clear in regard to the Air India disaster.

Sikh Extremists and the 1985 Bombing of Air India Flight 182

On 23 June 1985, Air India Flight 182, off the coast of Ireland and en route to New Delhi, was ripped apart by an explosion killing all 329 people on board. Most of the occupants were Canadians of Indian origin. The bomb that destroyed the aircraft had been hidden in luggage that had been placed on a plane in Vancouver before being transferred to Air India Flight 182 in Toronto. It was the largest mass murder in Canadian history (Major 2010).

Police authorities came to believe that Sikh extremists fighting for an independent homeland had sabotaged the Boeing 747. The prime suspect, Talwinder Singh Parmar, died in 1992 in India at the hands of Indian police authorities. In 2003, Inderjit Singh Reyat pleaded guilty to manslaughter, and two other suspects were found not guilty (Bronskill 2015).

A federal Commission of Inquiry headed by former Supreme Court Justice John Major concluded, "A cascading series of errors contributed to the failure of our police and security forces to prevent this atrocity" (Major 2010).

The subsequent investigation by the RCMP and the then newly created Canadian Security and Intelligence Service (CSIS) became the longest and most complex domestic terrorism investigation in Canadian history. It was marred by error, incompetence, and inattention by the RCMP, CSIS, and other authorities (Major 2010). As noted by Whitaker, Kealey, and Parnaby (2006, 375), the bombing of Air India Flight 182—with CSIS less than a year old—was the worst intelligence failure in Canadian history.

The Air India Failure

The intelligence process used by CSIS was seriously deficient in coordination, organization, and communication. Poor relations existed between CSIS and the RCMP.

Intelligence warnings about possible threats to Air India flights had been given to CSIS by the government of India. CSIS, however, failed to appreciate the full extent of the threats. Surveillance conducted by CSIS on known Sikh activists in British Columbia was weak and amateurish. Electronic intercepts (wiretaps) were approved but, due to a lack of adequate resources, translation and transcription of tape recordings were inadequate. In turn, this meant that a proper analysis of the intelligence data was virtually non-existent. When the tapes were processed, they were erased. Erasure of the tapes was to be problematic and embarrassing for CSIS when the criminal charges went to trial.

Intelligence that was developed by CSIS was provided to the RCMP. However, the RCMP ignored it (Whitaker, Kealey, and Parnaby 2006). The RCMP also failed to share its own intelligence with CSIS and, as a result, CSIS was unable to see the reality of the Sikh terrorist threat.

Perhaps one of the biggest obstacles to cooperation and coordination between CSIS and the RCMP lay in in the fact that when the decision was made to create a new civilian intelligence agency, members of the RCMP who had been working on national security were given the option of joining the civilian agency. Many members chose to make the transition to the new agency, bringing with them experience, contacts, know-how, and pre-established mindsets. As Whitaker, Kealey, and Parnaby have noted, these officers, based on decades of Cold War perceptions, tended to see threats to Canadian security arising primarily from communists.

The failures in coordination, organization, and communication between the two agencies not only meant an inability to prevent the Air India bombing but led to serious problems with the evidence that was later introduced in the criminal trials of those who were subsequently charged. The problems in Canada's national security agencies in regard to the disastrous handling of Air India became the subject of the Royal Commission of Inquiry by Mr. John Major, who submitted his final report, *Air India Flight 182: A Canadian Tragedy*, in 2010, 25 years after the bombing. His report identified shortcomings with intelligence gathering and investigative procedures both prior to the bombing and after.

Policing after 9/11

After 9/11, the Canadian public was shocked and terrified that Canada might experience a similar calamity. Fear of a similar strike on Canadian soil was real both for the Canadian public and Canadian security agencies. Almost immediately, pressure from the Bush administration in the United States forced CSIS and the RCMP to give attention to Islamic jihadist movements. For Canadian security personnel, the perceived potential threat was as real as it had been in the earlier eras of Fenian, Doukhobor, and Sikh extremism (Whitaker, Kealey, and Parnaby 2012). The Canadian government responded quickly. Budget allotments for national security and law enforcement increased dramatically, particularly in regard to immigrant screening. As well, the CSIS workforce was increased by almost 25 per cent (Whitaker, Kealey, and Parnaby 2012).

Embracing the fervour of the Bush administration, Canadian security agencies committed themselves to greater cooperation with a set of strategies based on the integration of international and domestic security measures.

Federally, the government moved quickly to toughen laws. In October 2001 the government introduced the *Anti-Terrorism Act* (Bill C-36), which created measures that allowed for the identification, prosecution, conviction, and punishment of terrorists and terrorist organizations. It also gave enhanced investigative powers to law enforcement and security agencies (Goff 2014, 27). The bill became law in December 2001.

The move to integrate intelligence functions on an international basis proved to be controversial. As Whitaker, Kealey, and Parnaby (2012, 440) have claimed, "For the RCMP and later CSIS, closer cooperation with a reckless US administration and with new and uncertain allies with dubious human-rights records would turn out to be a mine-field." This was to be proven in what has become known as the "Maher Arar affair"—another disaster for RCMP and CSIS security operations resulting in yet another Royal Commission of Inquiry.

The Maher Arar Affair

Maher Arar, a Canadian citizen of Syrian heritage and a computer engineer, was detained in September 2002 during a stopover on a return flight to Canada from the North African country of Tunisia. While changing planes at New York City's JFK airport, he was detained by US authorities and then subjected to **extraordinary rendition** (transferred secretly) to Syria, where he was imprisoned for a year in a notorious jail and tortured. Finally, released without charges and allowed to return to Canada, Maher Arar received an apology and compensation from the Canadian government for its role in his treatment (Amnesty International, n.d.).

Arar's incarceration and torture had serious consequences in Ottawa. The O'Connor Inquiry was established to inquire into the actions of Canadian officials that had led to his arrest, incarceration, and torture. The Commission determined that Arar's torture came as the direct result of the abuse of intelligence-sharing agreements with US authorities (Whitaker, Kealey, and Parnaby 2012, 481). Commissioner O'Connor found that Arar had become a **person of interest** in Project A-O Canada, a joint intelligence operation between the RCMP, CSIS, and the Americans. Project A-O Canada was an integrated investigation team operated primarily by A Division of the RCMP in Toronto and O Division in Ottawa. It also included members of the Ontario Provincial Police and the Toronto Police Service.

One of the **targets** of Project A-O Canada had a casual acquaintance with Maher Arar. As a result of surveillance that monitored a coffee meeting between a target and Arar, Project A-O Canada began to build a profile of Arar and put him under surveillance. Soon Arar's wife was also under scrutiny (O'Connor 2006b, 53–6).

Project A-O Canada also sought information about Arar from US Customs, US Immigration and Naturalization Service (INS), and the FBI. In various communications with American authorities, Arar and his wife were incorrectly described as being associated with a "group of Islamic Extremist individuals suspected of being linked to the Al-Qaeda terrorist movement" (O'Connor 2006b, 62).

As the O'Connor Commission subsequently revealed, at some time in early 2002 Project A-O Canada had provided the FBI with a wholly unauthorized "data dump" (digital files stored on compact disks) of all the material compiled in the course of its investigations. While perceived by Canadian security officials as only a person of interest, Arar nevertheless came to the attention of the Americans under a false and completely erroneous characterization. Given the close relationship that had evolved between the FBI and the CIA following 9/11, all information given to the FBI by Project A-O Canada could have been provided to the CIA. It was on the basis of this information that American authorities seized him. Once again, Canadian security officials were complicit in a mistake of major proportion (Whitaker, Kealey, and Parnaby 2012, 482). The mistake grew bigger yet when it came to light that CSIS and the RCMP knew that Arar was being detained by Syrian military intelligence and was being subjected to torture.

In the aftershocks of the Maher Arar affair, the RCMP took the brunt of the criticisms for allowing an innocent man to be arrested, detained, and tortured. The affair forced the resignation of RCMP Commissioner Guiliano Zaccardelli and, as a gesture by the federal government signalling the need for systemic changes to the RCMP, led to the unprecedented appointment of a civilian commissioner (Whitaker, Kealey, and Parnaby 2012, 482).

The New Urgency

At the time of the attacks on the World Trade Center and the Pentagon, principal responsibility for terrorist surveillance and national security fell within the purview of the Canadian Security Intelligence Service (CSIS) and the Communications Security Establishment (CSE—see Challenge Your Assumptions, below). Since the 11 September attacks, Canadians have seen significant revisions to laws and policies as security services restructured themselves to effectively respond to threats to national security.

As noted above, the RCMP is the police agency designated to have principal responsibility for investigating criminal acts of terrorism. While the RCMP has principal responsibility, other major police forces work together with the RCMP in a joint forces capacity (Royal Canadian Mounted Police, 2020). The RCMP leads and maintains oversight of **Integrated National Security Enforcement Teams (INSETs)** across the country, with teams based in Vancouver, Calgary, Edmonton, Toronto, Ottawa, and Montreal. The nature of the integrated teams means that RCMP officers work alongside municipal or provincial counterparts to share intelligence and resources to deal with information related to national security.

INSETs have a broad mandate to detect and disrupt any actual or intended terrorist acts. The mandate of INSETs includes the collection, analysis, and sharing of intelligence about individuals, groups, or events that are a threat to national security. By capitalizing on the joint forces model and working together with partners in law enforcement and with other agencies, they provide an enhanced capacity to make sure that all information is fully investigated.

High-Risk Travellers (HRT)

The Government of Canada has acknowledged that radicalized individuals have travelled abroad to other countries to join terrorist groups and participate in warfare. It has also acknowledged this phenomenon is not new (Public Safety Canada 2014, 3). As far back at the Spanish Civil War (1936–9), Canadians, sympathetic to the democratically elected Republicans, travelled to Spain to fight the fascist dictatorship of General Francisco Franco who had gained the support of Hitler and Mussolini. Labelled as communist sympathizers by the RCMP, Canadians who volunteered to fight on behalf of the Republicans were feared to be going to gain experience in revolutionary work in order to overthrow the Canadian government (Whitaker, Kealey, and Parnaby 2012, 140).

In the current climate of hypervigilance, individuals suspected of travelling abroad to engage in extremist activities have recently been referred to as Canadian Extremist Travellers (CETs). Public Safety Canada has confirmed that CETs have been trained in combat warfare and that some actually have combat experience. Recent amendments to the *Criminal Code* address CETs. For example, sections of the *Criminal Code* prohibit individuals from leaving or attempting to leave Canada for the purpose of facilitating terrorism in another country. Additionally, terrorist acts committed outside of Canada can now be prosecuted in Canada. However, as reports from Public Safety Canada have indicated, there has not been an influx in the number of CETs who have returned to Canada. Their numbers remain stable. Nonetheless, Canadian police are increasingly tasked with monitoring suspected CETs (Public Safety Canada, 2019a).

Terrorist Risks

Given the perception that radical Islamic jihadists are in our midst, it appears that threats to the safety and security of Canadians will remain a high priority for law enforcement and national security agencies. As noted below, the police have been compelled to embrace a new policing paradigm that represents a hybrid of both security and crime-control policing. For some observers this is worrisome. Crime-control policing has historically meant reactive responses to crimes that have already been committed. However, security policing, if it is to be effective, requires an emphasis on "anticipatory, proactive, and preventative strategies" (Murphy 2007, 459). Police are thus in the process of reorienting themselves from responding to crime to predicting it (see Chapter 12).

Risk Society

The Emergence of Risk Society

As the twentieth century came to a close, criminologists and sociologists became intrigued with the concept of risk. Leading scholars began analyzing society in general and responses to crime specifically in terms of the concept of risk. For these scholars, the study of risk is as much about how society operates as it is a study of how new techniques and interventions, including and beyond the public police and the criminal law, have emerged to control our behaviour (Rigakos 1999a). For many academics in sociology and criminology, the study of the police, the law, the criminal justice system, and other social institutions reveals much about the nature of the society in which we live. For these academics, the principal interest is not so much to improve the police or to solve problems of crime. Rather, the nature and operation of police and the type and extent of crime are windows through which academics look in order to see how society operates.

Influenced by the work of Michel Foucault (1975; 1978) and Ulrich Beck (1992), risk society theory has now become a major perspective within critical criminology. However, discussions about risk society are often ponderous and difficult to understand. What follows provides a simplified overview of risk society theory, how it has influenced criminological thinking, and how it helps to understand the current fears and responses to perceived dangers with regard to terrorism following the 11 September 2001 attacks in the United States.

Challenge Your Assumptions

CSIS and the RCMP: A Complicated Relationship

The primary mandate of CSIS is to investigate threats, analyze information, and produce intelligence to advise the Government of Canada in order to allow it to protect the country and its citizens (CSIS, n.d.). The role of the police in Canada is to gather admissible evidence to support a successful prosecution. Unfortunately, these roles clash in the criminal justice system. CSIS's primary purpose is the gathering of intelligence data that is routinely dependent on confidential informers; enforcement is not a principal concern. With the disclosure requirements of criminal proceedings that have been set out by the Supreme Court of Canada in the **Stinchcombe decision**, the RCMP work under the premise that all relevant evidence and its sources will be given over to defence counsel. This very practice endangers the security of CSIS sources, operational methods, and protected information shared by foreign agents (Whitaker, Kealey, and Parnaby 2012, 444). Thus, there is a systemic reluctance on the part of CSIS to share intelligence for fear of putting sources in jeopardy. As you continue to read below about some of the further difficulties with interagency relations, think about your assumptions before reading this chapter, and to this point, around how the police and intelligence agencies may have worked together. What are some things to keep in mind when working, as a police officer, with another intelligence agency?

Information from Foreign Sources

National security investigations are inextricably tied to working together with foreign countries and sharing information. The majority of those countries have different laws, with national security a principal concern of most governments. In liberal democracies, like Canada, the federal government's responsibility is to counter threats and challenges within a national security framework that guarantees accountability and the protection of civil liberties. However, in the interests of sustaining Canadian security, intelligence agencies may on occasion have to cooperate with countries that are less obligated to respect the rule of law and human rights. International collaboration, including the exchange of information, is often critical to Canada's national security. Obviously, this causes significant problems for Canadian intelligence and law enforcement agencies and our criminal justice system. The exchange of information with foreign partners raises unique legal, policy, and operational challenges.

Communications Security Establishment (CSE)

The Communications Security Establishment (CSE) is another civilian agency that, similar to CSIS, has difficulty in working together with the police due to how they carry out their work. CSE had its origins in the in the Second World War when a special Canadian civilian agency was created to assist the military in encrypting military messages and in decrypting enemy signals that had been intercepted. Through the war, Signals Intelligence (SIGINT) provided intelligence analysis and dissemination of vital information to the Canadian military, Canadian Foreign Affairs, and the Allies. As communications technology became increasingly sophisticated through the twentieth century, the role and mission of SIGINT evolved. Today the mission of CSE is "To provide and protect information of national interest through leading-edge technology, in synergy with our partners." Their vision includes "Safeguarding Canada's

continued

security through information superiority." CSE, which receives its mandate from Canada's *National Defence Act*, has three primary functions:

- to acquire and use information from the global information infrastructure for the purpose of providing foreign intelligence, in accordance with Government of Canada intelligence priorities;
- to provide advice, guidance, and services to help ensure the protection of electronic information and of information infrastructures of importance to the Government of Canada; and
- to provide technical and operational assistance to federal law enforcement and

security agencies in the performance of their lawful duties (CSE n.d.).

CSE—like all other Canadian security agencies—is required to conduct its activities in accordance with all Canadian laws, including the *Privacy Act*, the *Criminal Code* of Canada, and the Canadian *Charter of Rights and Freedoms*. However, for reasons similar to those that limit the utility of CSIS intelligence in criminal investigations, Canadian law enforcement cannot often rely on the methods and technology utilized by CSE and its partners because serious problems arise with regard to Stinchcombe requirements when evidence is disclosed.

What Is Risk Society?

According to risk society theory, the twentieth century witnessed significant transformations in the way society was structured. For example, observers point to the significant changes to traditional social institutions that once bonded people together: church, school, work, and family. Changes in these institutions were related to accelerating changes in technology and the globalization of economic, political, and social relationships (Beck 1992 in White, Haines, and Eisler 2013, 223). Taken together these transformations have contributed to the rise of **individualization**—the process whereby individuals become less connected to community norms and values. As a result, there is a weakening of collective identities and a decrease in the sense of belonging. Individuals come to believe that they alone must shape their own lives by taking greater control over and responsibility for their well-being. Correspondingly, this also means that individuals become less reliant on government-provided services such as public health care, welfare, and public education and on the criminal justice system to protect them (White, Haines, and Eisler 2013, 223). These developments also serve to inform the neo-liberal perspective and the processes of **responsibilization** addressed by David Garland (2001) and discussed earlier in Chapter 1.

Together these changes have contributed to the growth of widespread perceptions within society that people are increasingly at risk physically and psychologically in a world that is unstable and rapidly changing (Giddens 1990 in White, Haines, and Eisler 2013, 223). Risk society is thus characterized by a pervasive awareness of human-made risks that come from the existence of such threats as weapons of mass destruction, global warming, environmental devastation, economic uncertainty, pandemics, massive displacement of refugee populations, crime, and, of course, terrorism. Equally as important, risk society is seen as organized around the management of these risks (Hogeveen and Woolford 2012, 387). More specifically, the management of risk has given rise to the proliferation in many social organizations of measures and practices routinely used in the insurance, banking, credit, health care, and pension management industries. These industries compile and store reams of personal information and use statistical sciences to calculate probabilities as a basis for profiling clients, customers, applicants, and patients (Rigakos 1999b, 139). These profiles are then used as a basis for determining the degree of risk within particular groups over time. For example, the insurance industry compiles significant quantities of personal information (age, gender, place of residence, occupation, level of education, income, health, distances travelled to/from work/school, etc.) in order to assess the likelihood of some future event occurring (such as a car accident or fire damage). This assessment constitutes a risk score used to determine the probability of having to pay a claim on an insurance policy. The information compiled on individuals is aggregated or totalled such that the information then becomes the basis for determining not only the risk levels, but also the insurance premiums. **Actuarialism** is the term that refers to the scientific methods used by the insurance industry to make such calculations.

Western democratic societies have now become so preoccupied with managing risks that police, other criminal justice agencies, and many other social institutions have come to adopt actuarial practices similar to those of the insurance industry to predict and minimize future offending (Hogeveen and Woolford 2012, 387). These practices have become sufficiently common in the twenty-first century that criminologists have now begun to speak of "actuarial criminology."

Actuarial Criminology?

Actuarial criminology uses risk-prediction tools to inform strategies to govern crime through the management of risks. That is, rather than trying to address the causes of crime or seeing crime as a social problem to be solved, actuarial criminology takes crime to be inevitable and seeks to develop risk-reduction strategies to lessen crime's social costs (Hogeveen and Woolford 2012, 389). Law-abiding citizens are encouraged to become responsible for protecting themselves. As well, relatively new strategies about how to best manage the risks associated with crime have been fostered. For example, routine activities theory, rational choice theory, situational crime prevention, and environmental criminology, including Crime Prevention Through Environmental Design (CPTED), have been embraced by criminologists, the police, and other crime prevention specialists as strategies to reduce opportunities to commit crime (O'Grady 2014, 140; Rigakos 1999b, 142; see also Chapters 1 and 12).

In risk society, jurisdiction for managing the risks associated with crime and other threats to public safety has diffused from the state. As described below, many institutions beyond the criminal justice system and other agencies of government now rely on risk prediction and risk management. New forms of decentralized control have emerged in which the state no longer exercises power and control over the population (O'Grady 2014, 137).

Policing in a Risk Society

In their distinctive study of police work, *Policing the Risk Society*, Richard Ericson and Kevin Haggerty (1997) have argued that police work has been transformed by the emergence of the risk society. Given the never-ending need for information and knowledge by the growing array of institutions engaged in risk management, police have become the principal generators and brokers of knowledge regarding risk. The major consumers of police-generated risk knowledge—beyond the other components of the criminal justice system—now include such institutions as welfare and social security agencies, educational institutions, the retail industry, employers, credit and banking institutions, regulatory agencies, motor vehicle agencies, and, of course, insurance companies. In the search for security in the age of risk and uncertainty, knowledge is essential for successful risk management. Furthermore, the demand for knowledge is insatiable (Ericson and Haggerty 1997; O'Malley 1999, 139). It is Ericson and Haggerty's contention that police work has been transformed not only by risk society but also by the knowledge demands of risk-management institutions. By way of example, Ericson and Haggerty note the myriad interests who demand, judge, and process the knowledge generated in the course of a traffic accident investigation that may take one hour to investigate but three hours to write up:

> [T]he provincial motor vehicles registry requires knowledge concerning the place of the accident, the vehicles involved, and the persons involved. This is needed for risk profiling that can be used in accident prevention, traffic management, resource allocation, and automobile industry compliance. The automobile industry requires knowledge concerning the safety of its vehicles, for two reasons: first, so that vehicular safety can be improved, and second, to address the concerns of regulatory agencies and consumer groups. Insurance companies require knowledge that enables them to allocate responsibility in the particular case and to create statistical profiles for the determination of risk, premium levels, and compensation levels. The public health system requires knowledge concerning how the injuries in the accident occurred, as well as knowledge for statistical profiles that can be applied to the provision of emergency services personnel in the future. The criminal courts require knowledge that will provide adequate evidence for prosecution and demonstrate proper procedure in generating the evidence. The police administration requires knowledge that can be used to account for property seized and persons processed, knowledge for the national computerized records system and its own record system, and knowledge for scientific "human resources" management of police officer activity. [1997, 24]

The primary thesis of Ericson and Haggerty is that while police are indeed still involved in traditional criminal law enforcement, order maintenance, and service provision, public police work has shifted dramatically. In risk society, police work principally entails the provision of security through surveillance and information gathering designed to identify, predict, and manage risk.

Case Study

Anti-Terrorism Legislation: Why the Controversy?

On 21 June 2019, an Act respecting national security matters (known as the *National Security Act*, 2017) was passed into law. According to an official press release issued jointly by the federal Minister of Public Safety and Emergency Preparedness, Minister of Justice and Attorney General, and the Minister of National Defence, this legislation was intended to modernize and enhance Canada's national security laws (Public Safety Canada, 2019b).

To a large extent, the *National Security Act* 2017 sought to rectify controversial provisions that were contained in the *Anti-Terrorism Act* that had been enacted in 2015 by the Conservative government under Prime Minister Stephen Harper. Provisions in the 2015 legislation had been roundly criticized for giving CSIS, the RCMP, and other security agencies unprecedented new powers without appropriate oversight mechanisms. More specifically, organizations concerned about civil liberties had argued that

- in the unprecedented expansion of CSIS powers to disrupt and reduce threats to security, a wide range of legitimate protest activities would be susceptible to interference and disruption;
- the measures offered no description of the types of tactics that would be available to CSIS, only that CSIS would be prohibited from acting in ways that caused death, bodily harm, or perversion of justice or violated sexual integrity. The measures made no mention of the deprivation of liberty, right to privacy, or freedom of expression;
- CSIS, with formal authorization, would be empowered to violate the *Charter of Rights and Freedoms*;

- the amendments expanded the powers to detain persons on the basis of lowered levels of suspicion;
- government agencies would be empowered to share information across a wide range of agencies in the interests of national security; and
- robust oversight and effective reviews of national security agencies were conspicuously unaddressed.

The *National Security Act*, passed by the Liberal government of Prime Minister Justin Trudeau in 2019 following widespread public consultation, sought to remedy these concerns by enhancing accountability and transparency with regard to anti-terrorist measures. To this end, the legislation established a National Security and Intelligence Review Agency (NSIRA) and an Intelligence Commissioner to ensure that activities of Canadian security agencies were reasonable, necessary, and in compliance with Canadian laws and values. NSIRA has authority to review the actions of CSIS, the Communications Security Establishment (CSE) and the ability to scrutinize the actions of any federal agency involving national security and intelligence, including the RCMP.

As noted above, the 2015 *Anti-Terrorism Act* expanded the role of CSIS such that it could engage in proactive actions intended to disrupt or otherwise thwart threats to Canadian security. This was of particular concern given that CSIS had been originally created in order to formally separate intelligence-gathering functions from policing functions after the widespread abuse of police powers by the RCMP during the 1960s and 1970s (Seal 2019). As well, the 2015 legislation empowered both CSIS and CSE to gather, compile and retain "datasets" or electronic

continued

archives of intelligence information pertaining to Canadian citizens (Tunney 2019).

The 2019 Liberal legislation also created the *Communications Security Establishment Act* and for the first time formalized the CSE and its responsibilities into public law (Seal 2019). This legislation also permitted CSE to engage in "cyber operations" such as hacking against entities or foreign agents outside of Canada (Seal 2019). Canadian citizens and residents, however, are not to be subjects of such operations unless they are known to have associations with persons of interest. Concerns have thus been raised with regard to infringements on journalists who, in the course of their reporting duties, conduct interviews or compile information on persons under surveillance by Canadian security agencies.

Among other considerations, the Liberal legislation revises provisions regarding "No Fly" lists created and maintained by the Minister of Transport. Intended to prevent persons who are suspected on reasonable grounds of engaging in activity that would threaten transportation or who are travelling for the purpose of committing a terrorist act, "No Fly" lists have been controversial; no more so than when misidentification errors have resulted in preschool children being forbidden from flying with their parents. Also problematic is that persons are not notified of being added to the list and there is no way for individuals to learn if they have been placed on it.

To the dismay of civil rights groups, the 2019 Liberal legislation leaves many of the 2015 provisions intact.

THE CANADIAN PRESS/Justin Tang

Some Canadians (such as those pictured here) protested Bill C-51, the 2015 *Anti-Terrorism Act*, which, among other things, expanded surveillance powers of CSIS. What historical events in Canada do you think justify the passing of Canadian anti-terrorism legislation? Based on historical developments reviewed in this chapter, is increased authority for Canadian security agencies reasonable and justified? Is increased oversight of Canadian security agencies reasonable and necessary?

Canadian criminologist Christopher Murphy (2007) has noted that toward the end of the twentieth century, political theorists believed that public policing was being transformed by a host of non-governmental agencies that were assuming greater responsibility for the protection of people and their property. This view is consistent with the development of risk society theory and actuarial criminology discussed in this chapter and with the views of David Garland about the "crime complex" discussed in Chapter 1. As Ericson and Haggerty (1997) argued—before the events of 9/11—police and police work have been transformed by the fact that police have become the principal definers of risk knowledge.

Murphy, however, holds the view that the events of 9/11 have led to the **securitization** of Canadian policing. As he notes, "Securitization describes a politically and socially constructed process by which governments and the media present threats to national or state security in a highly dramatized and persuasive form of public discourse" (Buzan, Waever, and de Wilde 1998 cited in Murphy 2007, 451). In other words, the threats generated by 9/11 have given national governments and the police a new justification for reclaiming their central role in ensuring domestic security (Murphy 2007, 450). Instead of a contraction of police services, the new security paradigm has given police and government a powerful and expanded role in providing security.

Securitization of Canadian policing has occurred alongside the proliferation of messaging from politicians, police authorities, and a range of "security experts" about Canadians having a "smug complacency, naïve liberalism, a false sense of security." Experts warned that Canada has become a hiding place for terrorist sleeper cells, a haven for illegal immigrants and refugees, a safe haven for money laundering and terrorist fund-raising, and that Canada has a weak border security system (Murphy 2007, 452).

In this context of anxiety and apprehension, it is not surprising that Canadians have been willing to accept a range of measures to increase the powers and abilities of Canada's security services. As Murphy has shown, these measures have included

- dramatic increases in special budgets allocated toward national security (RCMP, CSIS, Communication Security Establishment, and Military Intelligence); and
- expansion of police powers making it easier for police to get search warrants, detain without charges, compel testimony, expand legal surveillance, use "reasonable suspicion" rather than "reasonable belief" as a justification for police action, and create in-camera hearings (2007, 457).

Conclusion

This chapter began with the assertion that to properly understand modern national security policing it was necessary first to understand how national security policing has evolved since its inception. For that reason, the chapter traced key incidents over the history of Canadian police efforts to maintain national security. The circumstances surrounding perceived threats to Canadian domestic peace and security in the years 1867 to 2001 involving the Doukhobors, the FLQ, and Sikh extremists were reviewed. The responses of the authorities responsible for policing these threats were also examined.

Subsequently, the chapter examined the origins and evolution of Canadian security services and their role in ensuring domestic security through the twentieth century. Several significant failures, most notably the inability to have prevented both the FLQ October

Crisis of 1970 and the Air India bombing in 1982, led to a series of Royal Commissions that offered recommendations for improving Canadian security. These reports were briefly reviewed and considered for their impact on Canadian security agencies.

In turn, the chapter also considered how the events of 9/11 have impacted not only Canadian society in general, but its laws and security services. To make sense of developments with regard to the perception of risks associated with terrorism, the concepts of risk society and actuarial criminology were reviewed.

Finally, the chapter examined very recent measures that the Canadian government has resorted to in its efforts to further reduce the risks associated with modern terrorist threats. Measures to toughen the laws and to give greater powers to security forces provide empirical affirmation to the principal ideas of risk society theory and actuarial criminology. That is, as the Canadian government reacts to the perceived threats posed by potential radicals with extraordinary policing measures, the need for greater vigilance becomes self-evident. With increasingly strident intelligence gathering and information sharing by a myriad of Canadian security agencies comes a greater awareness of risk; and the greater the awareness of risk, the greater the need for vigilance by gathering even more knowledge. Ultimately, this has resulted in a paradoxical cycle of fear and self-perpetuating uncertainty—consistent with the risk society in which we now live.

Critical Thinking Questions

1. Compare the security concerns about Fenians, Dukhobors, and the FLQ to current concerns about the perceived threat of radical Islamic terrorism.
2. What is dissent? What is subversion? What is terrorism? Who decides which should be subject to surveillance and law enforcement?
3. Why have Canadian security agencies been primarily concerned with persons holding left-wing or communist political beliefs?
4. Is it more important to ensure individual liberties or to protect society? Justify your answer.
5. Do we currently live in a risk society? Is risk society an accurate way to describe Canadian society in the twenty-first century?
6. Is a paradoxical circle of fear evident in modern Canadian society with regard to alleged threats to national security?

Glossary

accountability The fact or condition of being accountable; responsibility (*Oxford English Dictionary*).

acquitted The outcome of a criminal trial in which the accused is found not guilty.

active shooter An individual actively engaged in killing or attempting to kill people in a populated area.

actuarialism A term used by insurance companies to refer to the calculation of risks of future possible events such as accidents or fires.

adjudication phase The phase of a trial in which evidence is introduced in court to a judge or jury in order for a decision to be made.

administrative accountability Administrative accountability is related to the management of running the police agency. This includes support of operations from a financial perspective, budget management, and forecasting.

administrative crime analysis Analysis directed toward the administrative needs of the police agency, its government, and its community. As a broad category, it includes a variety of techniques and products, performed both regularly and on request, including statistics, data printouts, maps, and charts. Examples include workload calculations by area and shift, officer activity reports, responses to media requests, statistics provided for grant applications, reports to community groups, and cost–benefit analysis of police programs.

affiant The police officer who is tasked with drafting legal applications.

agents of the state Individuals who perform duties on behalf of the government. The police enforce the laws of the state.

anonymizing A process whereby data is modified to remove private and/or specific information about a crime location or incident. This may involve replacing a specific address with an address that corresponds to the closest intersection to protect privacy.

appearance notice An official notice compelling a person to appear in court to face charges.

arrest rates The number of arrests made in a particular time frame or geographic area or for a particular reason or incident. May be a function of the total number of suspects, or may simply be a tally of the number of individuals arrested.

arrest warrant A court document issued when there are reasonable grounds to believe someone has committed a criminal offence. An arrest warrant authorizes the police to arrest a person.

attrition An inevitable circumstance in which police agencies lose police officers who leave policing, join another police agency, or, most commonly, retire after completing their service.

bail A conditional release of an accused person who is awaiting trial, formally referred to as "judicial interim release."

bait car A car that has been specially equipped with cameras, locks, and engine kill switches, allowing police officers to trap and capture individuals who steal these cars.

balance of probabilities In civil cases a judge or jury considers the evidence on a balance of probabilities and determines which side's case is more probable. A balance of probabilities is a lower standard of proof than that of reasonable doubt in criminal cases.

balanced scorecard A measurement-based strategic management system, originated by Robert Kaplan and David Norton, that provides a method of aligning business activities to the strategy and monitoring performance of strategic goals over time.

body-worn cameras (BWCs) Small recording devices worn by police officers that record audio and visual data during police encounters with the public.

broken windows policing A perspective that advocates addressing lower-level or minor crimes before they escalate into larger problems or more serious criminal activity.

burden of proof In criminal cases, the onus to prove guilt beyond a reasonable doubt rests entirely on the prosecution. The accused person does not have to prove his or her innocence. In civil cases, the onus is on a plaintiff to prove the case on a balance of probabilities.

bystander media A phenomenon related to the fact that a majority of people have the immediate ability to record video, document, and share anything they choose over the internet. As it relates to police, there are potential impacts on decision making and investigations, in addition to the effect on public perception of police.

call stacking Stacking allows dispatchers to assign or *stack* multiple calls to a single unit, where they wait in the queue until an officer is able to respond to them.

Canadian Police Information Centre (CPIC) A closed police database system that is maintained by the RCMP and contains information including criminal records, warrants, stolen property, and alerts for police. It interfaces with provincial and territorial motor vehicle branch records and limited aspects of the United States National Crime Information Center (NCIC).

case law The law as established by the outcome of earlier cases; precedent law.

centrality measures A statistical measure within social network analysis that is best understood as showing who may be at the centre of a criminal organization and who may be less important.

civilian observation A civilian observer is assigned to a police investigation to ensure that the investigation is conducted with impartiality.

civilianization The increasing trend in which civilian staff in police departments take over responsibilities once undertaken only by sworn police officers.

clearance rates Clearance rates represent the ratio of solved crimes to the total number of crimes. It is generally expressed as a percentage, such as "50 per cent of all homicides are solved (cleared)." It is often thought of as a success rate within police departments. The higher the clearance rate, the more successful the police are thought to be at solving crimes.

clique finders A statistical measure within social network analysis that may highlight sub-groups within a larger criminal network.

code 2 Operating a police vehicle with emergency lights only, driving as safely as possible, yet often outside of the guidelines of the respective *Motor Vehicle Act*, such as exceeding posted speed limits or stopping and clearing an intersection, then continuing on through the red light.

code 3 Operating a police vehicle with full emergency lights and siren, driving as safely as possible, yet often outside of the guidelines of the respective *Motor Vehicle Act*, such as exceeding speed limits or stopping and clearing an intersection, then continuing on through the red light.

code driving A common police term for driving outside of the guidelines set out within the provincial or territorial *Motor Vehicle Act*.

code of silence A condition in effect where a person either voluntarily or involuntarily withholds information that is important to a situation or circumstance.

colonialism The practice of taking control over another country by occupying it with settlers and exploiting it economically.

Combined Forces Special Enforcement Unit Provincial joint forces units that have a presence in different cities and provinces across Canada.

common law Law that has evolved through custom or through other judicial decisions rather than being established by statutory laws. Sometimes referred to as case law. See also precedent and *stare decisis*.

communications centre The part of the police service or external agency that acts as the first point of contact for phone calls to the police department, generally through a 911 service. The communications centre is responsible for taking and directing the calls to the police department according to individualized terms of service.

community policing (also **community-based policing**) The system of allocating police officers to particular areas so that they become familiar with the local inhabitants, with a focus on proactive crime prevention (as opposed to crime solving).

comparative universe A benchmark used for setting police salaries, pensions, benefits and working conditions.

CompStat (short for Computer Statistics) A combination of management philosophy and organizational management tools for police departments.

computer-aided dispatch (CAD) Law enforcement agencies use CAD to facilitate incident response and communication in the field. CAD systems, in many cases, are the first point of entry for information coming into the law enforcement system. Typical CAD system functions include resource management, call taking, location verification, dispatching, unit status management, and call disposition. Additionally, mapping functionality, interface with mobile data computers (MDC), and interfaces with other external local, territorial or provincial, and federal information systems may be included. Call takers, dispatchers, and their supervisors are primary users of CAD. Units in the field may interact via mobile data computers (Law Enforcement Information Technology Standards Council [LEITSC] 2003).

computerized mapping Geographic analysis that utilizes commercial-grade geographic software, such as ArcGIS or MapInfo, to digitally project and visualize crime locations on a computerized map for analysis. This is in contrast to traditional pin maps, which consider crime locations, but do not use a computer to do so.

consensus perspective The view that the law and government actions (including those of the police) reflect a society's widely shared values, beliefs, and sentiments.

constitutional obligations The government and agents of the government such as the police must carry out their work within the spirit and intent of the Canadian *Charter of Rights and Freedoms.*

content analysis An assessment of any written, oral, visual, or electronic communication to determine the meaning, purpose, or effect of that communication.

core competencies Defined knowledge, skill set, and abilities of a particular area of expertise in policing.

core values All police forces have similar core values that they believe are representative of their police force and its officers. Common core values include honesty, respect, integrity, and accountability.

crime complex A term coined by David Garland to refer to the cluster of public concerns about perceived high crime rates, high levels of fear, and the emotive politicization of punitive criminal justice polices.

crime maps The computerized visualization of crime activity within an area to highlight hot spots or other geographic distributions of crime for police action.

crime rate The ratio of crimes in an area to the population of that area, usually expressed per 100,000 population per year.

Crime Severity Index Developed by Statistics Canada, the Crime Severity Index is a complementary tool to traditional crime rates and allows for comparison not only of volumes of crime, but of their relative severity or seriousness.

critical perspective A view that the law and government actions (including those of the police) are shaped and used in ways that reflect the long-term interests of powerful groups in society.

decolonization Undoing the harms of colonialism, including unlearning the beliefs embedded within colonialism.

deinstitutionalization In the interest of cost saving, beginning in the 1950s with the advent of psychoactive drug therapies, inpatient mental health institutions were closed and patients reassigned to community-based facilities such as group homes.

dependent model The situation of the police investigating themselves. A police force may investigate one of their own internally or the police force may engage another police force to carry out an investigation into the actions of one of their officers or units.

designated Crown agent In Part VI CC wiretap investigations, the Crown agent brings the application to Supreme Court. The Crown agent is specially designated in writing by the Attorney General of the respective province.

detention Police may temporarily detain someone on the grounds of reasonable suspicion for the purpose of gathering information. For example, police have legal authority to detain someone suspected of impaired driving for the purpose of conducting a breathalyzer test.

digital forensics A new area of forensic examination involving digital or computer devices. This may involve the forensic extraction and analysis of digital information such as call logs, text messages, website history, email, etc.

directed surveillance Surveillance that involves covert observation of an individual, but not with the use of hidden microphones or cameras.

discretion The freedom to decide what should be done in a particular situation.

dispatch (see **communications centre**)

displacement The relocation in time or space of crime or criminals, usually as a result of police crime-prevention or crime-attack strategies.

disposition phase The phase of a trial following the adjudication phase in which the judge makes a determination as to an appropriate outcome. In criminal cases, the outcome is referred to as a sentence. In a civil case, the outcome is referred to as a remedy.

DNA Deoxyribonucleic acid, a self-replicating material present in nearly all living organisms as the main constituent of chromosomes. It is the carrier of genetic information and unchangeable.

due process Fair treatment through the normal judicial system.

electronic metadata trawling The retention and surveillance of massive caches of telephone and internet communications, including those of ordinary citizens, for the alleged purpose of national security.

environmental criminology Theoretical perspectives that consider the time, place, and circumstances of an event, and not just the motivation of the offender.

ethics Moral principles that govern a person's or group's behaviours.

executive branch The branch of government responsible for implementing, supporting, and enforcing the laws. Federally in Canada this consists of the prime minister and his or her cabinet of appointed ministers. Provincially, it consists of the premier and his or her cabinet.

exigent circumstances Emergency situations requiring immediate intervention or aid.

extrajudicial measures Police taking steps other than officially engaging the court process; for example, a no-case seizure of a small quantity of an illicit substance, established as being for personal consumption.

extraordinary rendition The covert transfer of political or military prisoners to secret prison locations in foreign countries, often for the purpose of interrogation under torture.

Fenians A group of North American Irish patriots in the nineteenth century dedicated to Irish independence from Great Britain.

field trainer A more senior police officer who is tasked with training a new recruit in the field (on the road). The recruit will already have been successful in basic training at the academy.

firearms examiner A forensic scientist who is an expert in evidence regarding firearms, toolmarks, and ballistics. Firearms examiners may also perform serial number restoration and analyze how close a gun may have been to a target in a crime.

First Nations Policing Policy Introduced in 1991 by the federal government, First Nations Policing Policy sought to provide First Nations across Canada with police services that are professional, effective, culturally appropriate, and accountable to the communities they serve. (See www.firstnationspolicing.ca)

First Nations Policing Program A tri-partite initiative among federal, provincial or territorial, and First Nations or Inuit communities to support professional and responsive policing services to First Nations and Inuit communities.

five Cs A reference that defines desirable qualities of a police recruit. The five Cs are courage, character, commitment, compassion, and communication.

forensic chemistry The application of chemistry in a legal setting.

forensic science Any scientific field that is applied to the field of law.

forensic toxicology The application of toxicology in a legal setting.

Front de Libération du Québec (FLQ) In English, Quebec Liberation Front; a radical group dedicated to Quebec's independence from Canada.

full answer and defence A constitutionally protected right based upon the premise of innocent until proven guilty. In order to be able to make full answer and defence in a court proceeding, the accused must be provided with the evidentiary "fruits of the investigation" that the police have gathered.

generalizability The ability to state the results from an analysis as true to a larger or broader population. For instance, a survey of 100 people from Toronto may not be generalizable or represent the views of all Canadians.

genocide The deliberate and systemic extermination of national, racial, political or cultural groups.

geographic analysis Analysis that considers crime locations and looks for patterns with respect to where crimes are happening in the jurisdiction.

geographic profiling An information management system for serial crime investigation. It does not pinpoint an exact individual, but rather analyzes crime locations to determine the most probable area of the offender's residence.

Globe and Mail **test** For Canadian police, it is a reminder that one day any given investigation, interview, or action of the police could end up on the front page of *The Globe and Mail* national newspaper and therefore police should keep in mind what the public would think.

guilty beyond a reasonable doubt In criminal cases, the prosecution must prove the guilt of the accused person to a standard at which a judge or jury is satisfied that, based on the evidence, there is no reasonable doubt as to guilt. If there is a reasonable doubt, the accused person must be acquitted.

habeas corpus (Latin) The legal right to challenge being held in custody; for example, the legal right to a hearing to determine appropriateness of bail release.

hierarchy of value When resources become limited, police departments may have to prioritize certain functions over others. This often means filling some positions while keeping others vacant, or dissolving certain units considered lower priority and putting those resources into higher-priority units.

high policing Policing related to maintaining the political status quo that is frequently reliant on confidential informers. National security policing would be considered high policing.

high-risk policing Examples include patrol policing, emergency response teams, dealing with confidential informers, legal applications.

holdback evidence Crime scene evidence that police investigators intentionally do not make public and that may only be known by the offender; for example, the type of weapon used. It is intended that corroborative evidence will be gathered independent of the holdback. This evidence often comes from the suspect him- or herself, as learned through interviews, or undercover or wiretap operations.

hot spot A location with a high concentration of offences, offenders, or targets.

hot spot policing Focusing law enforcement efforts at locations of high crime concentrations. A hot spot may be a general area of high crime activity or a particular address. This is advocated as a more effective approach than random patrolling and enforcement.

hybrid investigation An investigation comprising a civilian oversight body whose involvement in the investigation goes beyond the role of mere overseer.

hypervigilance A state of extreme watchfulness motivated by collective fear and foreboding.

immunity agreement A formal deal in which the Crown counsel agrees to refrain from all forms of prosecutorial consideration (including the reduction or staying of charges; an agreement by Crown counsel to a less severe sentence; or an agreement concerning judicial interim release) that can be granted in return for information or testimony. The granting of immunity from prosecution is an extraordinary exercise of prosecutorial discretion by Crown counsel.

in situ (Latin) Literally to remain in place, undisturbed.

individualization The processes by which individuals become less connected to community norms and values.

information A document submitted under oath by police to a court official containing allegations that the police have reasonable grounds to believe that particular person has committed a specific offence and should be arrested. An information to obtain (ITO) may also be sworn before a court official in order to obtain a search warrant.

infrared technology Infrared is electromagnetic energy at a wavelength or wavelengths somewhat longer than those of red light. An infrared camera detects infrared energy (heat) and converts it into an electronic signal, which is then processed to produce a thermal image on a video monitor.

input measures The amount of financial and nonfinancial resources (in terms of money, material, and so forth) that are applied to producing a product or providing a service (output). Effort is also referred to as inputs (www.seagov .org/resources/).

Integrated National Security Enforcement Teams (INSETS) Teams made up of officers from police agencies across Canada working with the RCMP in a joint force capacity.

intelligence-led policing A business model and philosophy where data analysis and intelligence inform strategic enforcement actions that target prolific and serious offenders.

interdependent model Civilian oversight of the conduct of the police.

intrusive surveillance Surveillance that utilizes hidden cameras or microphones to conduct covert monitoring of private premises.

investigative analyst A crime analyst who is focused on providing analytic support for investigators, often in relation to a particular case or series of cases. This analysis tends to include intelligence profiles of suspects, linkage analysis of similar crimes, and other in-depth products aimed at assisting investigators with solving a crime.

judicial interim release A conditional release from custody granted to an accused person awaiting trial. Often referred to as "bail."

judiciary The judiciary is independent of the other two branches of government and is responsible for interpreting and applying the law.

key players A statistical measure within social network analysis, which may find individuals who are vital to disrupting the network in the most efficient way.

Komagata Maru The name of the ship carrying 376 Indian immigrants that was refused permission in 1914 to land in Vancouver.

lateral transfer The transfer of a police officer to another police force.

legislative branch The branch of government responsible for the creation of law. Federally, in Canada, this is known as Parliament, which consists of the House of Commons and the Senate. Provincially, in Canada, it is known as the Legislature, except in Quebec, where it is called the National Assembly.

Locard's Exchange Principle When any person comes into contact with another object or person, a cross-transfer of physical evidence (or trace evidence) occurs.

master status The tendency of others to view a person in terms of a key attribute such as that person's authoritative role in society. A police officer has master status.

MCM triangle The roles of team commander, primary investigator, and file coordinator as the foundation of any MCM structure.

media Any form of print or electronic communication that targets a mass audience.

media monitoring Ongoing review of all forms of media that relate to the police force, their police officers, and individual investigations or situations. Police media liaison units routinely track and assess media coverage of both crime and police actions.

mobile work stations (MWS) Laptops, generally mounted in police vehicles, that are securely connected to police databases and allow officers to conduct mobile entering, querying, and communicating.

modus operandi A particular way of doing something, especially one that is characteristic or well established.

morals Concerned with the principles of right and wrong behaviour and the goodness or badness of human character.

multicultural mosaic The mix of ethnic groups, languages, and cultures that co-exist.

not compellable A legal status referring to a person who may not be called upon to testify by either Crown or defence counsel, for example, where the person is protected by "informer privilege"; i.e., a confidential informer for the police.

occupational culture A distinctive pattern of thought and behaviours shared by members of the same occupation that is reflected in language, values, attitudes and beliefs.

October Crisis A political crisis in Canada in 1970 precipitated by the kidnapping of British diplomat James Cross and the assassination of Pierre Laporte, a minister in the Quebec provincial government. The crisis led former Prime Minister Pierre Trudeau to invoke the *War Measures Act*, giving the police and military extraordinary authority.

operations support analyst A crime analyst who is focused on providing analytic support for front-line operations, such as patrol and traffic units. This analysis tends to include hot spot maps and other products that examine the distribution of crime across time and space to assist with deployment decisions.

outcome measures The basic unit of measurement of progress toward achieving desired results. An outcome may be initial, intermediate, or long term (www.seagov.org/resources/).

output measures A measure of the quantity of a service or product provided (may include a quality component) (www.seagov.org/resources/).

over-policing When police are overly attentive to particular communities, for example, racialized communities in which laws are strictly applied.

paramilitary model An organizational structure that is similar to the military command and control hierarchy.

parole A conditional release from incarceration.

pattern theory A theory within the environmental criminology paradigm that focuses on how crime happens in specific locations and at specific points by paying particular attention to victim and offender travel patterns and awareness spaces.

penitentiary In Canada, penitentiaries are operated under the jurisdiction of the federal government and are used for the incarceration of anyone who has been sentenced to a term of confinement longer than two years.

performance measure or indicator A quantifiable indicator of progress, achievement, and efficiency that includes outcome, output, input, cost-output, cost-outcome, and factors that influence results (www.seagov.org/resources/).

person of interest Someone whose involvement in possible criminal activity is unclear and about whom more information is needed.

pin maps Traditionally, a pin map involved placing push pins on a paper map, generally hung on a police department wall, to show crime locations. A pin map, however, can also be done digitally, using computerized mapping software to digitally project "pins" (crime locations) onto a computerized map.

plaintiff The party in a civil case who initiates a legal action.

police defensive techniques A subset of basic police training that teaches skills such as hand-to-hand combat, ground fighting, methods to gain physical control of individuals, use-of-force tools, and handcuffing techniques.

police investigating another police force When a police force engages another force to investigate one of its officers or units on more serious or high-profile matters. This is done in the spirit of objectivity and independence.

police investigating police When a police force investigates one of its own officers or units internally. Most often, this approach is taken on minor misconduct allegations.

Police Records Information Management Environment (PRIME) The database program mandated for all police services within British Columbia. PRIME contains information related to every event that occurs within a police department and contains details about the persons, property, and vehicles involved in each event.

Police Reporting and Occurrence System (PROS) The occurrence management software utilized by many police agencies, including several of the RCMP detachments, to enter, access, and exchange case file information.

Police Services Agreements Agreements negotiated between the federal government and provinces, territories, and municipalities. Such agreements are often referred to as "contract policing" under which the RCMP provide policing services to provinces, territories, and municipalities.

policy-based inquiries Mandated to examine a particular area or issue of public policy and to make recommendations for future policy direction.

Precedent A decision or interpretation of law established by a judge or judges in a previous legal case that may become binding in other similar cases. See *stare decisis*.

preferred qualifications Assets to enhance the chance of being successful in the selection process to become a police officer recruit; for example, life experience and maturity, higher education, ability to speak multiple languages, being identified as a visible minority or female.

prejudicial Actions or evidence that may bias the accused person's right to a fair trial.

primary prevention Interventions or programs aimed at stopping criminal behaviour before it starts.

prison In Canada, prisons are operated under the jurisdiction of provincial and territorial governments. They are used for the incarceration of anyone who has been sentenced to a term of confinement less than two years.

probation A court-ordered sentence to be served in the community under supervision.

problem-oriented policing A paradigm of policing that advocated that police should determine the underlying causes of calls for assistance in order to solve the problem rather than respond over and over with no effect. This perspective gave rise to the SARA model.

professional (traditional) model of policing A policing paradigm emerging from corruption in the 1930s. This model advocated for rapid response, reactive investigations, and random patrols as a way to prevent and curb criminal activity. Subsequent research generally has refuted the prevention capability of this approach.

promise to appear Release given to an offender under a promise to attend court on a specific date.

public confidence A measure of public sentiment with regard to trust in a person or institution.

public policing Police services that are provided by the state and have the principal mandate of enforcing state laws.

qualitative measures Measures that are generally not based on counting or numerical representations of performance. These may include open-ended questions from user satisfaction surveys, or other verbal or written responses.

quasi-criminal laws Laws that are not formally criminal laws but that bear a resemblance to criminal laws in that they often carry penalties upon conviction for violation. For example, *Motor Vehicle Acts* and *Liquor Control and Licensing Acts* passed by provincial governments are not formally criminal law. Quasi-criminal law are regarded as "regulatory laws" and carry a range of (relatively minor) penalties such as fines and/or the suspension of licences. Rarely do these laws allow for incarceration.

racial profiling Use of racial stereotypes to single out individuals and groups as being more deserving of police attention.

racialization The process by which race is constructed as a category that is real, different, and unequal and in ways that have consequence for economic, political, and social life.

racialized policing Policing that reflects the broader society's construction of racial differences and that leads to differentiation among people on the basis of racial features.

rational choice theory A theory within the environmental criminology paradigm that assumes that offenders will embark upon offending behaviour through a structured decision-making process that seeks out the maximum benefit for the minimum amount of risk.

reasonable grounds A principle of law that is read and defined in the *Criminal Code* of Canada and in case law. Reasonable grounds are essentially an assessment of available information or of a situation, in the totality of the circumstances. The premise of what constitutes reasonable grounds is that the assessment is made by a "reasonable person" dispassionate of the situation or circumstance. In criminal law, a police officer may have "reasonable grounds to suspect" or the stronger position of "reasonable grounds to believe."

reasonable grounds to believe A higher standard than reasonable grounds to suspect. Reasonable grounds to believe that a person has committed, was found committing a criminal offence or (based upon the evidence known at the time) is about to commit an indictable offence is guided by Sec 495 CC and generally triggers an arrest. The reasonable grounds to believe standard is also the foundational requirement for the majority of judicial authorizations that may be sought by police officers to search and seize evidence.

reasonable grounds to suspect Generally, when a police officer learns of information, makes an observation or otherwise suspects that a person has committed or is about to commit an indictable offence, s/he may detain that person for the purpose of further investigation. In line with Section 495 C.C., "found committing an offence" rises to the reasonable grounds to believe standard, which is the foundational requirement for an arrest.

recruitment A structured process designed to identify potential candidates who would be successful police officers.

recruitment standards The basic requirements to become a police officer in Canada.

recruits Candidates who have been screened through the selection process to start basic training.

redaction The censoring or obscuring of part of a text for legal or security purposes (*Oxford English Dictionary*).

respondent The party in a civil case who must answer or respond to the claims made by the party initiating the legal action.

response times The time between when a call (usually from 911) is assigned to an officer and the time that officer arrives on scene.

responsibilization A partnership of citizens, community groups, and private interests that are encouraged by the police to take responsibility for ensuring the safety and security of their communities.

resurgence The effort to see life outside colonial practices, reconnecting to homelands, communities, and traditional cultural activities such as dancing, singing and drumming.

routine activities theory A theory within the environmental criminology paradigm that outlines a criminal event is the result of the interaction between a motivated offender, suitable target, and lack of capable guardianship.

Rupert's Land The name given to the vast territory which encompassed the Hudson Bay watershed—about 3.9 million square kilometres. With regard to modern boundaries, it included northern Ontario, northern Quebec, much of the three Prairie provinces, and most of southern Nunavut.

SARA model The problem-oriented policing perspective gave rise to the SARA model for responding to problems. This model has four stages: scanning, analysis, response, and assessment.

scenario-based training An aspect of training that mimics real-life situations. Scenario-based training can be carried out in various forms including online courses, at the training academy, or as questions on promotional exams. It may be used to have police officers maintain their competency in certain skill sets or specific areas of knowledge (e.g., first aid, use of force, violence in relationships, dealing with individuals in mental-health situations, harassment, and others).

SCUBA Self-contained underwater breathing apparatus.

search warrant A court order issued to police authorizing them to conduct a search of a person, location, or vehicle for evidence of a crime. A search warrant will also authorize seizure of the evidence.

secondary prevention Interventions or programs aimed at people or places identified as at risk of increasing levels of criminal activity.

securitization Process by which threats to national or state security are presented in a dramatized and persuasive manner.

self-accountability In the context of being a police officer, self-accountability means taking full responsibility for one's actions on and off duty.

social media Websites and applications that enable users to create and share content or to participate in social networking

social network analysis The analytic process by which a person's relationships, instead of himself or herself specifically, is under scrutiny. It is the number of associations as well as the nature and type of these associations that is of interest and that social network analysis can assist in uncovering. This type of analysis may be of particular utility for investigations involving gangs or organized crime, although any type of offence may be suitable.

stare decisis (Latin) The legal principle that means "to stand by decided matters" and that ensures consistency in the interpretation and application of the law by the courts.

statute A written law enacted by a legislature; sometimes referred to as an *Act*.

Stinchcombe decision A unanimous decision by the Supreme Court of Canada in 1991 requiring that Crown counsel disclose all evidence, including evidence favourable to an accused person, to the defence.

strategic crime analysis The analysis of data directed toward development and evaluation of long-term strategies, policies, and prevention techniques. Its subjects include long-term statistical trends, hot spots, and problems. Although it often starts with data from police records systems, strategic analysis usually includes the collection of primary data from a variety of other sources through both quantitative and qualitative methods.

supervisory accountability In the context of police work, a supervisor is responsible for his or her actions and decision making as well as the actions and decision making of the police officers reporting to the supervisor. The higher the rank, the greater the level of accountability. For example, a chief constable is accountable for the actions of every employee in that police force.

surveillance Continuous observation of a place, person, group, or ongoing activity in order to gather information.

tactical crime analysis The analysis of police data directed toward the short-term development of patrol and investigative priorities and deployment of resources. Its subject areas include the analysis of space, time, offender, victim, and modus operandi for individual high-profile crimes, repeat incidents, and crime patterns, with a specific focus on crime series. Most of the data used in tactical crime analysis comes from police databases, particularly police reports of crimes.

targets Person who are subjects of ongoing criminal investigations.

telescoping People's tendency to recall events as occurring either more recently than they actually did, or farther back in time than they actually did. This may threaten the reliability and validity of survey responses.

tertiary prevention Interventions or programs aimed at curbing repeat criminal behaviour or activity.

threat cues Verbal or physical cues that may signal the intentions of the individual. For example, an individual reaching into his or her pockets may signal an intent to harm a police officer.

tiered policing Involvement of a range of organizations and individuals in delivering multilevel policing services and functions, for example, civilian volunteers, private security, community agencies, and regular police.

trace evidence Small particles that are transferred when two objects touch or are dispersed by an action or movement.

tunnel vision A tendency to focus on a single or limited goal or point of view.

ultra vires (Latin) An action that does not have legal authority.

under-policing A lack of police attentiveness toward certain communities. For example, police tend to be less concerned with domestic violence if they believe it is accepted in some ethnic communities.

unfounded Suspected crimes that may be reported to the police, but that upon further investigation turn out not to be a crime at all. This may occur when witnesses think they are seeing an offence in progress but have misunderstood the circumstances.

vetting Text in documents that is, on specific legal principles, made unavailable for review by defence counsel; for example, information from confidential informers that would identify or tend to identify the informer.

victimization survey A survey that asks respondents directly whether they have been a victim of crime in a particular period of time, generally in the past year.

warned interview An interview undertaken by police with an individual under arrest or detention, following the individual having been advised on the record of his or her Section 10(a) and (b) *Charter* rights and his or her constitutional right to silence.

wiretap Device that is installed or has the ability to intercept private communications.

zero-tolerance policing An approach that advocates that police enforce all laws, no matter how minor, as a way to curb criminal activity and control offending.

References

Chapter 1

Auditor General Canada. 2014. *First Nations Policing Program—Public Safety Canada*, Chapter 5. Ottawa: Office of the Auditor General of Canada.

Bayley, D.H. and C.D. Shearing. 1996. The future of policing. *Law and Society Review* 30 (3): 585–606.

Brodeur, J.P. 2010. *The Policing Web*. New York: Oxford University Press.

Canadian Pacific Police Service. CP Police Service. http://cpr.ca/en/safety/cp-police-service (accessed March 2016).

Conor, P., J. Robson, and S. Marcellus. 3 October 2019. Police resources in Canada, 2018. *The Juristat*. Catalogue no. 85-002-X. Ottawa: Canadian Centre for Justice Statistics, Statistics Canada.

Ericson, R.V. and K.D. Haggerty. 1997. *Policing the Risk Society*. Toronto: University of Toronto Press.

Garland, D. 2001. *The Culture of Control: Crime and Social Order in Contemporary Society*. Chicago, IL: University of Chicago Press.

Garland, D. and R. Sparks. 2000. Criminology, social theory and the challenge of our times. *British Journal of Criminology* 40: 189–204.

Kiedrowski, J., N.A. Jones, & R. Ruddell. 2017. Set up to fail? An analysis of self-administered Indigenous police services in Canada. *Police Practice and Research* 16 (6): 584–98. doi: 10.1080/15614263.2017/1363973.

Law Commission Canada. 2002. In search of security: The roles of public police and private security. Discussion paper. Ottawa: Law Commission of Canada.

Li, G. 2008. Private security and public policing. *The Juristat*. Ottawa: Canadian Centre for Justice Statistics, Statistics Canada.

Loader, I. 2000. Plural policing and democratic governance. *Social and Legal Studies* 9 (3): 323–45.

Mawby, R.I. 2008. Models of policing. In T. Newburn, ed. *Handbook of Policing*. 2nd edn. 17–46. London: Routledge.

Moreau, G. 22 July 2019. Police-reported crime statistics in Canada, 2018. *The Juristat*. Ottawa: Canadian Centre for Justice Statistics, Statistics Canada.

Ontario Provincial Police. 2017. *Annual Report*. https://collections.ola.org/ser/226827/2017.pdf (accessed August 2020).

Phyne, J. Fall 1992. Prohibition's legacy: The emergence of provincial policing in Nova Scotia, 1921–1932. *Canadian Journal of Law and Society* 7 (2): 157–84.

Public Safety Canada. 2018. Policing in Indigenous communities. https://www.publicsafety.gc.ca/cnt/cntrng-crm/plcng/brgnl-plcng/index-en.aspx (accessed 19 September 2020).

———. First Nations Policing Program. https://www.publicsafety.gc.ca/cnt/cntrng-crm/plcng/brgnl-plcng/index-eng.aspx (accessed March 2016).

Ray, Arthur, J. 2009. "Hudson's Bay Company" in *The Canadian Encyclopedia*. https://www.thecanadianencyclopedia.ca/en/article/hudsons-bay-company (accessed 14 September 2020).

Rigakos G. and C. Leung. 2006. Canada. In T. Jones and T. Newburn, eds., *Plural Policing: A Comparative Perspective*. 126–38. New York: Routledge.

Royal Newfoundland Constabulary Activity Report. 2018. https://www.rnc.gov.nl.ca/wp-content/uploads/2019/05/Activity-Report-2018.pdf (accessed August 2020).

Royal Newfoundland Constabulary Corporate Plan 2018–2021. https://www.rnc.gov.nl.ca/corporate-plans/rnc-corporate-plan-2018-2021-printable/ (accessed August 2020).

Seagrave, J. 1997. *Introduction to Policing in Canada*. Scarborough, ON: Prentice Hall.

Shearing, C. and P. Stenning. 1987. Say "cheese": The Disney order that is not so Mickey Mouse. In C. Shearing and P. Stenning, eds., *Private Policing*, 317–23. Newbury Park, CA: Sage.

Statistics Canada. Police resources in Canada, 2017. *The Daily*. Ottawa: Statistics Canada, 2018.

Sûreté du Québec. The Sûreté du Québec. https://www.sq.gouv.qc.ca/en/the-surete-du-quebec (accessed 23 May 2019).

Zytaruk, T. 24 March 2020. Fight to keep Surrey RCMP "not over," campaign vows. Surrey Now-Leader. https://www.surreynowleader.com/news/fight-to-keep-surrey-rcmp-not-over-campaign-vows/ (accessed 21 April 2020).

Chapter 2

Boyd, N. 2002. *Canadian Law: An Introduction*. 3rd edn. Toronto: Nelson.

Brodeur, J.P. 2010. *The Policing Web*. New York: Oxford University Press.

Burstein, P. 2004. The importance of being an earnest criminal defence lawyer. In J.V. Roberts and M.G. Grossman, eds. *Criminal Justice in Canada: A Reader*. 158–68. Scarborough: Thomson Nelson.

Criminal Code of Canada. 1985. http://laws-lois.justice.gc.ca/eng/acts/C-46 (accessed November 2015).

Department of Justice. 2005. *Canada's System of Justice*, Ottawa: Communications Branch, Catalogue No. J2-23/2005.

Forcese, D. 1999. *Policing Canadian Society*. Scarborough, ON: Prentice Hall.

Hogg, P. 1985. *Constitutional Law of Canada*. Toronto: Carswell.

Ibrahim v. R. [1914] AC 599.

Ismaili, K., J.B. Sprott, and K. Varma, eds. 2012. *Canadian Criminal Justice Policy: Contemporary Perspectives*. Don Mills, ON: Oxford University Press.

Jones, C. 2015. Criminal law in Canada. In N. Boyd, ed., *Understanding Crime in Canada: An Introduction to Criminology*. 51–68. Toronto: Edmond Montgomery.

Major, J.C. 2010. *Air India Flight 182: A Canadian Tragedy. Final Report of the Commission of Inquiry into the Investigation of the Bombing of Air India Flight 182.* Ottawa: Government of Canada. http://epe.lac-bac.gc.ca/100/206/301/pco-bcp/commissions/air_india/2010-07-23/www.majorcomm.ca/en/reports/finalreport/default.htm (accessed 24 June 2015).

Manarin, B. 2004. Prosecution and the exercise of discretion in everyday practice. In J.B. Roberts and M.G. Grossman, eds. *Criminal Justice in Canada: A Reader.* 146–57. Scarborough: Thomson Nelson.

McKenna, P.F. 2002. *Police Powers I*. Toronto: Prentice Hall.

Osborne, J.A. 1995. The Canadian criminal law. In M.A. Jackson and C.T. Griffith, eds, *Canadian Criminology: Perspectives on Crime and Criminality*. Toronto: Harcourt Brace.

R. v. Feeney [1997] 2 S.C.R. 13

R. v Golden, [2001] 3 S.C.R. 679

R. v Le, [2019] SCC 34

R. v Stillman, [1997] 1 S.C.R. 607

R. v. Mann. 2004. 3 SCR 59, 2004 SCC 52 (CanLII) https://www.canlii.org/en/ca/scc/doc/2004/2004scc52/2004scc52.html (accessed November 2015).

R.v Saeed, [2016] 1 SCR 518

Seagrave, J. 1997. *Introduction to Policing in Canada*. Scarborough, ON: Prentice Hall.

Seguin, R. and K. Mackrael. 22 November 2011. Quebec angered by Ottawa's refusal to budge on crime bill. *The Globe and Mail.* https://www.theglobeandmail.com/news/politics/quebec-angered-by-ottawas-refusal-to-budge-on-crime-bill/article554586/ (accessed August 2020).

Chapter 3

Alfred, G.T. 2009. Colonialism and state dependency. *International Journal of Indigenous Health* 5 (2): 42–60.

Beedie, N., D. Macdonald, and D. Wilson. 19 July 2019. *Towards Justice: Tacking Indigenous Poverty in Canada*. Saskatoon: Upstream.

Ben-Porat, G. 2008. Policing multicultural states: Lessons from the Canadian model. *Policing and Society* 18 (4): 411–25.

Brannigan, A. 1984. *Crimes, Courts and Corrections: An Introduction to Crime and Social Control in Canada.* Toronto: Holt, Rinehart, Winston.

Canadian Multiculturalism Act (R.S.C., 1985, c. 24 (4th Supp.))

CBC News. 22 March 2016. Ontario regulation bans random carding by police. www.cbc.ca/news/canada/toronto/yasir-naqvi-carding-1.3501913 (accessed 17 July 2016).

Chan, J. 1997. *Changing Police Culture: Policing in a Multicultural Society.* Cambridge. Cambridge University Press.

Citizenship and Immigration Canada. www.cic.gc.ca/english/department/index.asp (accessed 5 August 2015).

Cole, D.P. and M. Gittens. (Co-chairs). 1995. *Report of the Commission on Systemic Racism in the Ontario Criminal Justice System.* Toronto: Province of Ontario.

Comack, E. 2012. *Racialized Policing: Aboriginal People's Encounters with the Police.* Halifax & Winnipeg: Fernwood Publishing.

Conor, P., J. Robson, and S. Marcellus. 3 October 2019. Police resources in Canada, 2018. *The Juristat.* Catalogue no. 85-002-X. Ottawa: Canadian Centre for Justice Statistics, Statistics Canada.

Couto, J.L. 2018. Hearing their voices and counting them in: The place of Canadian LGBTQ+ police officers in police culture. *Journal of Community Safety and Well-Being* 3 (3): 84–7.

———. 2014. Covered in blue: Police culture and LGBT police officers in the province of Ontario. Unpublished M.A. thesis, School of Communications and Culture, Royal Roads University, Victoria, BC.

Evans, P. 24 September 2005. Diversity, freedoms make us unique. *National Post.*

FemNetNorth. 2016. *Colonialism and Its Impacts. Resource Development in Northern Communities: Local Women Matter #3.* Ottawa: Canadian Research Institute for the Advancement of Women.

Fitzgerald, R.T. and P.J. Carrington. 2008. The neighborhood context of Aboriginal urban crime. *Canadian Journal of Criminology and Criminal Justice* 5 (3): 523–57.

Gillis, W., J. Rankin, and P. Winsa. 28 October 2015. Ontario sets strict new limits on police street checks. theStar.com. www.thestar.com/news/crime/2015/10/28/province-to-unveil-limits-on-carding.html (accessed 28 November 2015).

Goff, C. 2017. *Criminal Justice in Canada.* 7th edn. Toronto. Nelson Education.

Government of Canada. 2019. Ending long-term drinking water advisories. https://www.sac-isc.gc.ca/eng/1506514143353/1533317130660 (accessed 19 April 2020).

Graham, K.A.H and S.D. Phillips. 2007. Another fine balance: Managing diversity in Canadian cities. In Keith Banting, Thomas Courchene, and Leslie Seidle, eds, *Diversity and Canada's Future: Recognition, Accommodation and Shared Citizenship.* Montreal: Institute for Research on Public Policy.

Hamilton, A.C., and C.M. Sinclair. 1991. *Report of the Aboriginal Justice Inquiry of Manitoba: The Justice System and Aboriginal People.* Winnipeg: Province of Manitoba.

Hassell, K.D. and S.G. Brandl. 2009. An examination of the workplace experiences of police patrol officers: The role of race, sex, and sexual orientation. *Police Quarterly* 12 (4): 408–30.

Hunter, J. 24 October 2019. BC introduces legislation to align its laws, policies with United Nations' Indigenous rights declaration. *The Globe and Mail.* https://www .theglobeandmail.com/canada/british-columbia/ article-bc-introduces-legislation-to-align-its-laws-policies-with-united/ (accessed 19 April 2020).

Kennedy, G. 31 January 2019. Harrison author shares Halq'emeylem family in graphic novels. *The Chilliwack Progress.* https://theprogress.com/community/ harrison-author-shares-halqemeylem-family-in-graphic-novels/ (accessed 19 April 2020).

La Prairie, C. and Stenning, P. 2003. Exile on Main Street: Some thoughts on Aboriginal over-representation in the criminal justice system. In D. Newhouse and E. Peters, eds., *Not Strangers in These Parts: Urban Aboriginal Peoples* 179–93. Ottawa: Policy Research Initiative.

Leadership Conference of Civil and Human Rights. Stonewall Riots: The Beginning of the LGBT Movement. www.civilrights.org/archives/2009/06/449-stonewall .html (accessed 8 August 2015).

Macdonald, N. and C. Gillis. 27 February 2015. Inside the RCMP's biggest crisis. *Maclean's.*

Marcoux, J. and K. Nicholson. 2017. Deadly force: Fatal encounters with police in Canada: 2000–2017. CBC. https://newsinteractives.cbc.ca/longform-custom/ deadly-force (accessed 19 April 2020).

Martin, A. 9 October 2019. Jeremy Dutcher sees symphony tour as "critical turning point." *Regina Leader-Post.* https://leaderpost.com/entertainment/local-arts/ jeremy-dutcher-sees-symphony-tour-as-critical-turning-point (accessed 19 April 2020).

Monchalin, Lisa. 2016. *The Colonial Problem: An Indigenous Perspective on Crime & Injustice in Canada.* Toronto: University of Toronto Press.

National Inquiry into Missing and Murdered Indigenous Women and Girls (MMIWG). 2019. *Reclaiming Power and Place: The Final Report of the National Inquiry into Missing and Murdered Indigenous Women and Girls.* Ottawa: Government of Canada. https://www .mmiwg-ffada.ca/final-report/ (accessed 19 April 2020).

O'Neill, M. 2016. Revisiting the classics: Janet Chan and the legacy of "Changing Police Culture." *Policing and Society* 26 (4): 475–80.

Ponting, J.R. 1998. Racism and stereotyping of First Nations. In V. Satzewich, ed., *Racism and Social Inequality in Canada: Concepts, Controversies and Strategies of Resistance.* Toronto: Thompson.

Province of Manitoba. September 2014. Women and policing in Canada: A status brief and discussion paper. www

.gov.mb.ca/msw/publications/women_in_policing.pdf (accessed 10 August 2015).

R. v. Gladue. 1999. 1 SCR 688, [1999] 1 RCS 688, [1999] SCJ No 19, [1999] ACS no 19, 23 CR(5th) 197, 133 CCC (3d) 385.

R. v. Ipeelee. 2012. 1 SCR. 433

RCMP. Historical events in RCMP–Indigenous relations. http://www.rcmp-grc.gc.ca/en/historical-events-rcmp-indigenous-relations (accessed 19 April 2020).

Reasons, C., S. Hassan, M. Ma, L. Monchalin, M. Bige, C. Paras, and S. Arora. 2016, July–December. Race and criminal justice in Canada. *International Journal of Criminal Justice Sciences* 11 (2).

Roberg, R., K. Novak, and G. Cordner. 2005. *Police and Society.* 3rd edn. Los Angeles: Roxbury Publishing.

Sklanksy, D.A. 2006. Not your father's police department: Making sense of the new demographics of law enforcement. *Journal of Criminal Law and Criminology* 96 (3): 1209–43.

Statistics Canada. 2017(a). Immigration and ethnocultural diversity: Key results from the 2016 Census. *The Daily.* October 25.

———. 2017(b). Aboriginal Peoples in Canada: Key results from the 2016 Census. *The Daily.* October 25.

———. 2017(c). *Census Profile, 2016 Census.* https://www12 .statcan.gc.ca/census-recensement/2016/dp-pd/prof/ details/page.cfm?Lang=E&Geo1=PR&Code1=01&G eo2=&Code2=&SearchText=Canada&SearchType= Begins&SearchPR=01&B1=All&TABID=1&type=0 (accessed 19 April 2020).

———. 2 August 2017(d). *Same-Sex Couples in Canada in 2016.* August 2. Available at: https://www12 .statcan.gc.ca/census-recensement/2016/as-sa/98-200-x/2016007/98-200-x2016007-eng.cfm (accessed 19 April 2020).

———. 20 March 2018. *First Nations People, Métis and Inuit in Canada: Diverse and Growing Populations.* https://www150.statcan.gc.ca/n1/pub/89-659-x/89-659-x2018001-eng.htm (accessed 19 April 2020).

Stenning, P. 2003. Policing the cultural kaleidoscope: Recent Canadian experience. *Police and Society* 7: 13–77.

Szeto, J.K. 2014. *Policing Diversity with Diversity: Exploring Organizational Rhetoric, Myth, and Minority Police Officers' Perceptions and Experiences.* Theses and dissertations (comprehensive). Paper 1674.

Truth and Reconciliation Commission of Canada. (2015). *Truth and Reconciliation Commission of Canada: Calls to Action.* Winnipeg: Truth and Reconciliation Commission of Canada.

United Nations. 2008. United Nations Declaration on the Rights of Indigenous Peoples.

Whitaker, R., G.S. Kealey, and A. Parnaby. 2012. *Secret Service: Political Policing in Canada from the Fenians to Fortress America.* Toronto: University of Toronto Press.

Younging. G. 21 March 2013. The Rhetoric and the Reality. Aboriginal Gathering Place Lecture Series. Surrey, BC: Kwantlen Polytechnic University.

Zinger, I. 2018. *Annual Report to the Minister of Public Safety, 2017–2018*. Ottawa: Office of the Correctional Investigator, Government of Canada.

Chapter 4

Aiello, R. 9 March 2018. Trudeau names Brenda Lucki new commissioner of the RCMP. *CTV News*. https://www.ctvnews.ca/politics/trudeau-names-brenda-lucki-new-commissioner-of-the-rcmp-1.3836040 (accessed 9 March 2019).

Alpert, G.P., R. Dunham, and M. Stroshine. 2006. *Policing Continuity and Change*. Long Grove, IL: Waveland Press.

Arnold, J. November 2013. "The five Cs of law enforcement leadership." *The Police Chief* 80: 22–7.

Baker, T.E. 2011. *Effective Police Leadership: Moving beyond Management*. Flushing, NY: Looseleaf Law Publications, Inc.

Bordeleau, C. 2015. *Summit on the Economics of Policing and Community Safety—Innovation and Partnerships*. Ottawa: Public Safety Canada. https://www.publicsafety.gc.ca/cnt/rsrcs/pblctns/smmt-cnmcs-plcng-2015/index-en.aspx (accessed August 2020).

Cao, L. 2011. Visible minorities and confidence in the police. *Canadian Journal of Criminology and Criminal Justice* 53: 1–26.

Christmas, R. 2013. *Canadian Policing in the 21st Century: A Frontline Officer on Challenges and Changes*. McGill-Queen's University Press.

Civilian Review and Complaints Commission for the RCMP (CRCC). 2017. *Report into Workplace Harassment in the RCMP*. https://www.publicsafety.gc.ca/cnt/rsrcs/pblctns/smmt-cnmcs-plcng-2015/index-en.aspx (accessed August 2020).

Cohen McCullough, Debra R. and Deborah L. Spence. 2014. Recruiting today for tomorrow's agency. *The Police Chief* 8 (March): 24–9.

Conor, P. 28 March 2018. Police resources in Canada, 2017. *The Juristat*. Ottawa: Canadian Centre for Justice Statistics, Statistics Canada.

——, J. Robson, and S. Marcellus. 3 October 2019. Police resources in Canada, 2018. *The Juristat*. Catalogue no. 85-002-X. Ottawa: Canadian Centre for Justice Statistics, Statistics Canada.

DeClerq, K. 18 September 2018.Ontario Police College no longer testing new recruits in physical fitness: memo. *CTV News*. https://toronto.ctvnews.ca/ontario-police-college-no-longer-testing-new-recruits-in-physical-fitness-memo-1.4099292 (accessed August 2020).

Discover Policing. What Does It Take? http://discoverpolicing.org/what_does_take/?fa=skills_abilities (accessed November 2015).

Dunham, R. 2010. *Critical Issues in Policing, Contemporary Readings*. 6th edn. Long Grove, IL: Waveland Press, Inc.

Duxbury, L. 2015. *Summit on the Economics of Policing and Community Safety—Innovation and Partnerships*. Ottawa: Public Safety Canada. https://www.publicsafety.gc.ca/cnt/rsrcs/pblctns/smmt-cnmcs-plcng-2015/index-en.aspx (accessed August 2020).

Edmonton Police Service. Join EPS. http://www.joineps.ca/ (accessed 3 March 2019).

Gaines, L. and Miller, R. 2013. *Criminal Justice in Action: The Core*. 7th edn. Nelson Education.

Government of Canada. 2016. Employment equity. https://www.canada.ca/en/public-service-commission/jobs/services/gc-jobs/employment-equity.html (accessed August 2020).

Harris, K. 6 October 2016. Mounties offer apology and $100M compensation for harassment, sexual abuse against female members. *CBC News*. https://www.cbc.ca/news/politics/rcmp-paulson-compensation-harassment-1.3793785 (accessed 3 March 2019).

Iacobucci, F. July 2014. *Police Encounters with People in Crisis*. An independent review conducted by the Honourable Frank Iacobucci for Chief of Police William Blair, Toronto Police Service.

International Association of Chiefs of Police (IACP). Discover Policing. Skills and Abilities. https://www.discoverpolicing.org/about-policing/skills-and-abilities/ (accessed 3 March 2019).

LePard, Doug, and Michelle Davey. May 2014. Managing change: A success story in a culture resistant to change. *The Police Chief*, 81: 50–3.

Merlo Davidson. Merlo Davidson Settlement. https://merlodavidson.ca/en/ (accessed 3 March 2019).

Nemetz, G. 4 March 2019. Criminology 4440 Police and Community. Guest speaker. Douglas College.

Niagara Regional Police Service. Information Sessions. https://www.niagarapolice.ca/en/careersopportunities/informationsessions.asp (accessed 3 March 2019).

Ontario Association of Chiefs of Police (OACP). Latest News. http://www.oacp.on.ca/programs-courses/constable-selection-system (accessed 3 March 2019).

Ontario Ministry of Labour. Lie Detector Tests. www.labour.gov.on.ca/english/es/pubs/guide/liedetectors.php (accessed November 2015).

Palmer, A. (2015). *Summit on the Economics of Policing and Community Safety—Innovation and Partnerships*. Ottawa: Public Safety Canada. https://www.publicsafety.gc.ca/cnt/rsrcs/pblctns/smmt-cnmcs-plcng-2015/index-en.aspx (accessed August 2020).

Public Safety Canada. 2013. *2013 Summit on the Economics of Policing: Strengthening Canada's Policing Advantage*. Summit Report, 16–17 January. Ottawa.

Regina Police Service. Selection Process. http://reginapolice.ca/recruit/officer-recruitment/selection-proces/ (accessed 3 March 2019).

Royal Canadian Mounted Police (RCMP). no date a. Cadet Training. http://www.rcmp-grc.gc.ca/en/cadet-training (accessed 3 March 2019).

———. no date b. Physical Standards to Become an RCMP Officer. http://www.rcmp-grc.gc.ca/en/physical-standards (accessed 3 March 2019).

———. no date c. Women in Policing. https://www.rcmp-grc.gc.ca/en/women-in-policing (accessed 21 September 2020).

———. no date c. https://www.rcmp-grc.gc.ca/ab/community-communaute/reserve-eng.htm (accessed 3 March 2019).

Saint John Police Force. Core Values. http://www.saintjohn.ca/en/home/cityhall/protectiveservices/police/about/policeadministration/CoreValues.aspx (accessed March 3, 2019).

Statistics Canada. 2017a. *Census Profile.* 2016 Census. https://www12.statcan.gc.ca/census-recensement/2016/dp-pd/prof/index.cfm?Lang=E&HPA=1 (accessed 25 February 2019).

———. 2017b. *Visible Minority and Population Group Reference Guide.* Census of Population, 2016.

———. No date. *Visible minority of person.* https://www23.statcan.gc.ca/imdb/p3Var.pl?Function=DEC&Id=45152 (accessed 21 September 2020).

Toronto Police Service. no date (b). Frequently Asked Questions. http://www.torontopolice.on.ca/careers/uni_faq.php#q04 (retrieved 3 March 2019)

———. no date (c). How Do I Become a Toronto Police Officer? http://www.torontopolice.on.ca/careers/uni_become_officer.php (accessed 3 March 2019).

———. no date (a). Toronto Police Service Develops. http://www.torontopolice.on.ca/cdrg/resources/Core_Values.pdf (accessed 3 March 2019).

Victoria Police Department. Candidate Selection Process. https://vicpd.ca/candidate-selection-process (accessed 3 March 2019).

York Regional Police. What It Takes—Women's Recruiting. https://www.yrp.ca/en/careers/What-It-Takes---Women-s-Recruiting.asp (accessed 3 March 2019).

Chapter 5

Alain, M. and M. Gregoire. 2008. Can ethics survive the shock of the job? Quebec's police recruits confront reality. *Policing and Society: An International Journal of Research and Policy* 18 (2): 169–89.

Albrecht, J. 2011. Examining police discretion and the use of firearms involving the New York City police department. *Pakistan Journal of Criminology* 3 (2 and 3): 1–10.

Allen, M. and T. Superle, T. 2014. Youth Crime in Canada, 2014. Ottawa: Statistics Canada. https://www150.statcan.gc.ca/n1/pub/85-002-x/2016001/article/14309-eng.htm (retrieved March 9, 2019).

Angus Reid Global. 2014. Confidence in police, courts, sees significant rebound over 2012 sentiment. pp. 1–8. http://angusreid.org/canadian-confidence-in-police-courts-sees-significant-rebound-over-2012-sentiment (accessed November 2015).

Broadwell, M., B.R. McCarthy, and B.J. McCarthy. 2002. *Justice, Crime and Ethics.* Cincinnati, OH: Anderson Publishing Co.

Bronitt, S. and P. Stenning. 2011. Understanding discretion in modern policing. *Criminal Law Journal* 35 (6): 319–32.

Carrington, P. and J. Schulenberg. September 2008. Structuring police discretion: The effect on referrals to youth court. *Criminal Justice Policy Review* 19 (3): 349–67.

Criminal Code of Canada. 1985. http://laws-lois.justice.gc.ca/eng/acts/C-46 (accessed November 2015).

Department of Justice. 2015. *Public Perception of Crime and Justice in Canada: A Review of Opinion Polls.* http://justice.gc.ca/eng/rp-pr/csj-sjc/crime/rr01_1/index.html (accessed 22 February 2015).

Fraehlich, C. and J. Ursel. 2014. Arresting women: Pro-arrest policies, debates, and developments. *Journal of Family Violence.* 29: 507–18.

Gleason, T. 2006. Ethics training for police. *The Police Chief* 73 (11). www.policechiefmagazine.org

———. 2007. Ethics training for police. *The Police Chief* 74 (6). www.policechiefmagazine.org

Goldstein, H. 1977. *Policing a Free Society.* 95–100. Cambridge, MA: Ballinger Publishing Company.

Hughes, E.C. 1945. Dilemmas and contradictions of status. *American Journal of Sociology* 50 (March): 353–9.

Linden, R. 2012. *Criminology A Canadian Perspective.* 7th edn. Toronto: Nelson Education.

Lundman, R. 1980. *Police and Policing: An Introduction.* New York: Holt, Rinehart, and Winston.

O'Donnell, E. April 2011. Fostering ethical and humane policing. *e-Journal USA* 15 (10).

Oxford English Dictionary. www.oxforddictionaries.com (accessed May 2015).

Papenfuhs, S. 6 April 2011. Ethical dilemmas cops face daily. www.policeone.com

R. v. Beare; R. v. Higgins. 1988. 2 SCR 387, 1988 CanLII 126 (SCC) https://www.canlii.org/en/ca/scc/doc/1988/1988canlii126/1988canlii126.html (accessed November 2015).

R. v. Beaudry. 2007. 1 SCR 190, 2007 SCC 5 (CanLII) https://www.canlii.org/en/ca/scc/doc/2007/2007scc5/2007scc5.html (accessed November 2015).

R. v. Mann. 2004. 3 SCR 59, 2004 SCC 52 (CanLII) https://www.canlii.org/en/ca/scc/doc/2004/2004scc52/2004scc52.html (accessed November 2015).

Rowe, M. September 2007. Rendering visible the invisible: Police discretion, professionalism and decision-making. *Policing and Society* 17 (3): 279–94.

Seglins, D. 21 December 2010. Public faith in local police still high: EKOS. *CBC News.* www.cbc.ca/news/canada/public-faith-in-local-police-still-high-ekos-1.931664 (accessed November 2015).

Stephens, J. and P. Sinden. 2000. Victims' voices: Domestic assault victims' perceptions of police demeanor. *Journal of Interpersonal Violence* 15: 534.

Stinson, P., J. Liederbach, and T. Freiburger. 2012. Off-duty and under arrest: A study of crimes perpetuated by off-duty police. *Criminal Justice Policy Review.* 23 (2): 139–163.

Sunahara, D. 2004. A model of unethical and unprofessional police behaviour. *The Canadian Review of Policing Research.* Vol. 1.

UNICEF Canada. 25 October 2011. *Bill C-10: A Rush to a Stricter Youth Criminal Justice System.* Brief submitted by UNICEF Canada to the House of Commons Standing Committee on Justice and Human Rights. www.parl.gc.ca/Content/SEN/Committee/411/lcjc/PDF/Briefs/C10/UNICEF-EN.pdf (accessed February 2016).

Ursel, J., and D. Farough. 1986. The legal and public response to the new wife abuse directive in Manitoba. *Canadian Journal of Criminology* 28: 171–83.

Wilson, J.Q. April 2011. Police ethics. *e-Journal USA* 15 (10). http://photos.state.gov/libraries/amgov/133183/publications/Ethical%20Policing_041311.pdf (accessed November 2015).

Youth Criminal Justice Act. 2002. http://laws-lois.justice.gc.ca/PDF/Y-1.5.pdf (accessed November 2015).

Chapter 6

Azpiri, J. and S. Little. 2019, January 31. RCMP investigator in Surrey Six case admits to sexual affair with witness. *Global News.* https://globalnews.ca/news/4912767/surrey-six-witness-sex-brassington/ (accessed August 2020).

Behn, R.D. 2001. *Rethinking Democratic Accountability.* Washington, DC: Brookings Institution Press.

Canadian Civil Liberties Association. Policing Powers, Use of Force, and Police Accountability. https://ccla.org/policing-powers/ (retrieved 29 August 2020).

Civilian Review and Complaints Commission for the RCMP. https://www.crcc-ccetp.gc.ca/ (accessed 15 April 2020).

———. *Police Investigating Police–Final Public Report.* https://www.crcc-ccetp.gc.ca/en/police-investigating-police-final-public-report (modified 31 December 2014; accessed 29 August 2020).

Clark, M., R. Davidson, V. Hanrahan, and N. Taylor. 2017. Public trust in policing: A global search for the genetic code to inform policy and practice in Canada. *Journal of Community Safety & Well-Being* 2 (3): 101–11.

Cory, J. 2001. *The Inquiry Regarding Thomas Sophonow.* Manitoba Justice. Province of Manitoba. http://digitalcollection.gov.mb.ca/awweb/pdfopener?smd=1&did=12713&md=1 (accessed November 2015).

Cotter, A. 2015. Spotlight on Canadians: Results from the General Social Survey Public Confidence in Canadian Institutions. Statistics Canada.

Criminal Code of Canada. 1985. http://laws-lois.justice.gc.ca/eng/acts/C-46 (accessed November 2015).

Ferguson, G. January 2003. *Review and Recommendations Concerning Various Aspects of Police Misconduct.* Volume I. Commissioned by Julian Fantino, Chief of Police, Toronto Police Service.

Fridell, L., R. Lunney, D. Diamond, and B. Kubu with M. Scott and C. Laing. 2001. *Racially Biased Policing: A Principled Response.* Washington, DC: Police Executive Research Forum.

Friedman, M. 2014. What happens when we don't trust law enforcement? The importance of law enforcement's role in our society's well being. *Psychology Today* September 9.

Goff, C. 2014. *Criminal Justice in Canada.* 6th edn. Toronto: Nelson Education.

Gouvernement du Québec. *Police Act.* https://www.securitepublique.gouv.qc.ca/en/police-prevention/laws-and-regulations/police-act.html (accessed August 2020).

Independent Investigations Office of British Columbia (IIOBC). Home page. http://iiobc.ca, home page (accessed August 2020).

Kaufman, Fred, QC. 1998. *The Commission on Proceedings Involving Guy Paul Morin.* (The Kaufman Commission). https://www.attorneygeneral.jus.gov.on.ca/english/about/pubs/morin/morin_esumm.pdf (accessed November 2015).

Klockars, C., S. Ivkovich, W. Harver, and M. Haberfeld. May 2000. *The Measurement of Police Integrity.* National Institute of Justice. Research in Brief. US Department of Justice.

Lamboo, T. 2010. Police misconduct: Accountability of internal investigations. *International Journal of Public Sector Management* 23 (7): 613–31.

Malm, A. 2019. Promise of police body-worn cameras. *Criminology & Public Policy.* 1–12. wileyonlinelibrary.com/journal/capp © 2019 American Society of Criminology

McDevitt, J., C. Posick, R. Zschoche, D. P. Rosenbaum, M. Buslik, and L. Fridell. February 2011. *Police Integrity, Responsibility, and Discipline.* National Police Research Platform. National Institute of Justice.

Murphy, C. and P. McKenna. 2007. *Rethinking Police Governance, Culture and Management: A Summary Review of the Literature.* Prepared for the Task Force on Governance and Cultural Change in the RCMP, Public Safety Canada. Halifax, NS: Dalhousie University.

New York City Police Department (NYPD). About. Body-Worn Cameras. https://www1.nyc.gov/site/nypd/about/about-nypd/equipment-tech/body-worn-cameras.page (accessed August 2020).

O'Connor, Christopher D. 2008. Citizen attitudes toward the police in Canada. *Policing: An International Journal of Police Strategies & Management* 31 (4): 578–95.

O'Connor, D. R., F. Kristjanson, and B.L. Gervais. 2007. *Some Observations on Public Inquiries.* Canadian Institute for the Administration of Justice, Annual Conference, 10 October 2007, Halifax, Nova Scotia.

Office of the Privacy Commissioner February 2015 https://www.priv.gc.ca/en/privacy-topics/public-safety-and-law-enforcement/gd_bwc_201502/

Ontario Special Investigations Unit. www.siu.on.ca (accessed May 2015).

Oppal, W.T. 19 November 2012. *Forsaken: The Report of the Missing Women Commission of Inquiry.* British Columbia.

Oxford English Dictionary. www.oxforddictionaries.com (accessed May 2015).

Province of Nova Scotia. Mission. https://www.novascotia.ca/opcc/ (accessed August 2020).

Province of Saskatchewan. Saskatchewan Public Complaints Commission. https://www.saskatchewan.ca/government/government-structure/boards-commissions-and-agencies/saskatchewan-public-complaints-commission (accessed August 2020).

R. v. Beaudry. [2007] scc 5, [2007] 1 SCR 190, 276 DLR (4th) 1; 216 CCC (3d) 353; 44 CR (6th) 57 at para 48

R. v. Brassington. [2019] BCSC 265

R. v. Dixon. [1998]. 1 S.C.R. 244 https://scc-csc.lexum.com/scc-csc/scc-csc/en/item/1595/index.do

R. v. Haevischer. [2014] BCSC 1863. Date: 20141002 Docket: X072945-B Registry: New Westminster.

R. v. Jordan. [2016] 1 SCR 631, SCC 27 (CanLII)

R. v. McNeil. 2009. 1 SCR 66, 2009 SCC 3. https://www.canlii.org/en/ca/scc/doc/2009/2009scc3/2009scc3.html (accessed November 2015).

R. v. O'Connor. 1995. 4 SCR 411, 1995 CanLII 51 (SCC). https://www.canlii.org/en/ca/scc/doc/1995/1995canlii51/1995canlii51.html (accessed November 2015).

R. v. Stinchcombe. 1991. 3 SCR 326, 1991CanLII 45 (SCC) www.canlii.org/en/ca/scc/doc/1991/1991canlii45/1991canlii45.html (accessed November 2015).

Randall, S. and J. Ramirez. October 2011. *Policing the Police: Formal and Informal Police Oversight Mechanisms in the Americas.* University of Calgary. Prepared for the Canadian Defence and Foreign Affairs Institute.

Roberts, J. April 2007. Public confidence in criminal justice in Canada: A comparative and contextual analysis. *Canadian Journal of Criminology and Criminal Justice.* 153–84.

RCMP External Review Committee. https://www.erc-cee.gc.ca/index-en.aspx (accessed August 2020).

Royal Canadian Mounted Police (RCMP). 2016, December 7. RCMP to postpone use of body worn cameras. News release. http://www.rcmp-grc.gc.ca/en/news/2016/6/rcmp-postpone-use-body-worn-cameras (accessed August 2020).

Royal Canadian Mounted Police Act. 1985. https://laws-lois.justice.gc.ca/PDF/R-10.pdf

Schillemans, T., M. Van Twist, and I. Vanhommerig. March 2013. Innovations in accountability: Learning through interactive, dynamic, and citizen-initiated forms of accountability. *Public Performance & Management Review* 36 (3): 407–35.

Sherman, L.W. 1974. Introduction: Towards a sociological theory of police corruption. In L.W. Sherman, ed., *Police Corruption: A Sociological Perspective* 1–39. New York: Anchor Books/Doubleday.

Special Investigations Unit (SIU). Home page. www.siu.on.ca, home page (accessed August 2020).

Sutton, R. 28 December 2009. Policing with honor: The three levels of accountability. Police1. www.policeone.com/patrol-issues/articles/1983356-Policing-with-honor-The-three-levels-of-accountability (accessed November 2015).

The Province. 9 October 2014. Wearable cameras coming for police? A10. www.theprovince.com

The Queen v. Mercer. 2006. OJ 5522 in *R v. Heffernan*, 2014 SKQB 345 (CanLII), http://canlii.ca/t/gfghh (accessed March 2016).

Tinsley, P. 2009. The Canadian Experience in Oversight. A presentation for the UNDP-sponsored Basra Justice Workshop, 8–9 August 2009.

Transparency International. Corruption Perceptions Index. https://www.transparency.org/cpi2018 (accessed August 2020).

Valiante, F. 2019, February 10. Montreal rules out body cameras for police, saying cost not worth results. *CTV News.* https://www.ctvnews.ca/canada/montreal-rules-out-body-cameras-for-police-saying-cost-not-worth-results-1.4290330 (accessed August 2020).

Van Allen, B. 2009. *Police Powers: Law, Order and Accountability.* Toronto: Pearson.

Wain, N., and B. Ariel. 2014. Tracking of Police Patrol. *Policing* 8 (3): 274–83.

Chapter 7

Blumstein, Alfred. 1999. Measuring what matters in policing. In Robert H. Langworthy, ed., *Measuring What Matters: Proceedings from the Policing Research Institute Meetings.* Washington: National Institute of Justice, Office of Community Oriented Policing Services.

Bratton, William J. 1999. Great expectations: How higher expectations for police departments can lead to a decrease in crime. In Robert H. Langworthy, ed., *Measuring What Matters: Proceedings from the Policing Research Institute Meetings.* Washington: National Institute of Justice, Office of Community Oriented Policing Services.

Carmona, Salvador and Anders Gronlund. 2003. Measures vs actions: The balanced scorecard in Swedish law enforcement. *International Journal of Operations & Production Management* 23 (12): 1475–96.

Carter, Peter and Ann McGoldrick. 1994. Delayering in the police force: A structural response to cost, quality and public accountability. *Management Research News* 17 (7/8/9): 63–7.

Cockcroft, Tom and Iain Beattie. 2009. Shifting cultures: Managerialism and the rise of "performance." *Policing: An International Journal of Police Strategies & Management* 32 (3): 526–40.

Garland, D. 2001. *The Culture of Control: Crime and Social Order in Contemporary Society.* Chicago, IL: University of Chicago Press.

Geerken, Michael. *Performance Measurement for Justice Information System Projects.* Center for Society, Law and Justice, Texas State University. Washington: Office of Justice Programs; Bureau of Justice Assistance, 2008.

Greasley, Andrew. 2004. Process improvement within a HR division at a UK police force. *International Journal of Operations & Production Management* 24 (3): 230–40.

Illumina Research Partners. 2013. *Calgary Police Service 2013 Citizen Survey.* Calgary: Illumina Research Partners for Calgary Police Commission.

Integrated Riot Investigation Team. 23 July 2013. *Fact Sheet.* Vancouver: Vancouver Police Department.

Johnson, J., R. Berry, J. Eaton, R. Ford, and D.E. Nowicki. 1999. To whom do we answer? In Robert H. Langworthy, ed., *Measuring What Matters: Proceedings from the Policing Research Institute Meetings.* Washington: National Institute of Justice, Office of Community Oriented Policing Services.

Kelling, George. 1999. Measuring what matters: A new way of thinking about crime and public order. In Robert H. Langworthy, ed., *Measuring What Matters: Proceedings from the Policing Research Institute Meetings.* Washington: National Institute of Justice, Office of Community Oriented Policing Services.

Kiedrowski, J., M. Petrunik, T. Macdonald, and R. Melchers. 2013. *Canadian Police Board Views on the Use of Police Performance Metrics.* Compliance Strategy Group prepared for Law Enforcement and Policing Branch Public Safety Canada. Report No. 31, 2013.

Klockars, Carl B. 1999. Some really cheap ways of measuring what really matters. In Robert H. Langworthy, ed., *Measuring What Matters: Proceedings from the Policing Research Institute Meetings.* Washington: National Institute of Justice, Office of Community Oriented Policing Services.

Maguire, Edward R. 2003. Measuring the performance of law enforcement agencies. *CALEA Online Newsletter* (CALEA Online) 83–4.

Mazerolle, Lorraine, Sacha Rombouts, and James McBroom. 2007. The impact of COMPSTAT on reported crime in Queensland. *Policing: An International Journal of Police Strategies & Management* 30 (2): 237–56.

Mazowita, Benjamin and Cristine Rotenberg. 2019. The Canadian Police Performance Metrics Framework: Standardized indicators for police services in Canada. *The Juristat.* Catalogue no. 85-002-X. Ottawa: Canadian Centre for Justice Statistics, Statistics Canada.

Milligan, Stacy Osnick, Lorie Fridell, and Bruce Taylor. 2006. *Implementing an Agency-Level Performance Measurement System: A Guide for Law Enforcement Executives.* Washington: National Institute of Justice, Police Executive Research Forum.

Moore, Mark H. and Anthony A. Braga. 2003a. Measuring and improving police performance: The lessons of CompStat and its progeny. *Policing: An International Journal of Police Strategies & Management* 26 (3): 439–53.

———. 2003b. *The "Bottom Line" of Policing: What Citizens Should Value (and Measure!) in Police Performance.* Washington: National Institute of Justice, Office of Justice Programs, Police Executive Research Forum.

Moore, Mark H. and Margaret Poethig. 1999. The police as an agency of municipal government: Implications for measuring police effectiveness. In Robert H. Langworthy, ed., *Measuring What Matters: Proceedings from the Policing Research Institute Meetings.* Washington: National Institute of Justice, Office of Community Oriented Policing Services.

Municipal Research and Services Center. 1994. *Level of Service Standards—Measures for Maintaining the Quality of Community Life.*

Pare, Paul-Philippe and Marc Ouimet. 2003. A measure of police performance: Analyzing police clearance and charge statistics. *The Canadian Review of Policing Research* 1: 23–42.

Perreault, Samuel and Shannon Brennan. 2010. *Criminal Victimization in Canada, 2009.* Ottawa: Statistics Canada.

Plant, Joel B. and Michael S. Scott. 2009. *Effective Policing and Crime Prevention: A Problem-Oriented Guide for Mayors, City Managers, and County Executives.* Washington: US Department of Justice, Office of Community Oriented Policing Services.

Roberts, David J. 2006. *Law Enforcement Tech Guide for Creating Performance Measures That Work: A Guide for Executives and Managers.* Washington: US Department of Justice, Office of Community Oriented Policing Services.

Shane, J.M. 2010a. Organizational stressors and police performance. *Journal of Criminal Justice.* 38: 807–18. DOI: 10.1016/j.jcrimjus.2010.05.008.

Skogan, Wesley G. 1999. Measuring what matters: Crime, disorder, and fear. In Robert H. Langworthy, ed.,

Measuring What Matters: Proceedings from the Policing Research Institute Meetings. Washington: National Institute of Justice, Office of Community Oriented Policing Service.

Stephens, Darrel W. 1999. Measuring what matters. In Robert H. Langworthy, ed., *Measuring What Matters: Proceedings from the Policing Research Institute Meetings*. Washington: National Institute of Justice, Office of Community Oriented Policing Services.

Verma, Arvind and Srinagesh Gavirneni. 2006. Measuring police efficiency in India: An application of data envelopment analysis. *Policing: An International Journal of Police Strategies & Management* 29 (1): 125–45.

Chapter 8

Anlie, T, 2017. Stopping an active shooter: Training prepares officers to confront threat, *RCMP Gazette* 79 (2). http://www.rcmp-grc.gc.ca/en/gazette/stopping-an-active-shooter (accessed 19 April 2020).

Aveni, T.J. 2003. The force continuum conundrum. *Law and Order* 51 (12): 74–7.

Bayley, D. 1994. Police for the future. In T. Newburn, ed. (2009), *Key Readings in Criminology*, 574–9. Portland, OR: Willan Publishing.

Boydstun, J.E., M.E. Sherry, and N.P. Moelter. 1977. *Patrol Staffing in San Diego*. Washington, DC: Department of Justice.

Braidwood, T.R. 2010. *Why? The Robert Dziekanski Tragedy*. Braidwood Commission of Inquiry on the Death of Robert Dziekanski. British Columbia.

Conference Board of Canada. 2015. Active Shooter Incidents, Six Key Insights. Briefing. December. https://conferenceboard.ca/temp/a60bc9ae-7012-4b44-bbcb-0ac5401346b9/7595_Active_Shooter_BR_.pdf (accessed 21 October 2019).

Criminal Code of Canada. 1985. http://laws-lois.justice.gc.ca/eng/acts/C-46 (accessed November 2015).

Dantzker, M.L. and M.P. Mitchell. 1998. *Understanding Today's Police*. Canadian edn. Scarborough, ON: Prentice-Hall.

Ericson, R.V. 1981. *Making Crime: A Study of Detective Work*. Toronto: Butterworths.

———. 1982. *Reproducing Order: A Study of Police Patrol Work*. Toronto: University of Toronto Press.

Forcese, D. 1999. *Policing Canadian Society*. Scarborough, ON: Prentice Hall

Frontier Centre for Public Policy. February 2001. *One-Officer versus Two-Officer Police Cars in Winnipeg*. Winnipeg: Frontier Centre for Public Policy.

Hoffman, R., C. Lawrence, and G. Brown. 2004. Canada's National Use-of-Force Framework. *The Police Chief* 71 (10). www.policechiefmagazine.org/magazine/index.cfm?fuseaction=display_arch&article_id=1397&issue_id=102004 (accessed February 2016).

Humphries, A 18 May 2020. Nova Scotia mass shooting: New information about murder delayed by government lawyers. *National Post*. https://nationalpost.com/news/nova-scotia-mass-shooting-new-information-about-murder-rampage-delayed-by-government-lawyers (accessed September 2020).

Kaminski, R.J. and G.P. Alpert. January 2013. Recent findings on police foot pursuit. Research in Brief, *The Police Chief* 80: 14.

Kessler, D.A. 1985. One- or two-officer cars? A perspective from Kansas City." *Journal of Criminal Justice* 13: 49–64.

Ladouceur. 1990. 56 C.C.C. (3d) 22 (S.C.C.)

McKenna, P.F. 2002. *Police Powers I*. Toronto: Prentice Hall.

Menton, C. 2008. Bicycle patrols: An underutilized resource. *Policing: An International Journal of Police Strategies & Management* 31 (1): 93–8.

Nathanson, A.I. 2007. Rowbotham applications: Levelling the playing field. Paper presented to The Advocates' Club, 17 November.

R. v. Godoy. 1999. 131 CCC (3d) 129 (SCC)

R. v. Rowbotham. 1988. 41 CCC (3s) 1 (Ont. C.A.).

R. v. Schmautz. 1990. 2 SCR 398.

Reddekop, L. (20 April 2018). Court dismisses Cst. James Forcillo's appeal in Sammy Yatim case. *CBC News*. https://www.cbc.ca/news/canada/toronto/court-dismisses-const-james-forcillo-s-appeal-in-sammy-yatim-case-1.4639411 (accessed September 2020).

Roberg, R., K. Novak, and G. Cordner. 2005. *Police and Society*. 3rd edn. Los Angeles: Roxbury Publishing.

Van Allen, B. 2009. Police Powers: Law, Order and Accountability. Toronto: Pearson.

Chapter 9

Alberta Justice and Solicitor General. May 2008. *Confidential Police Informants (Privilege)*. https://justice.alberta.ca/programs_services/criminal_pros/crown_prosecutor/Pages/confidential_police_informants.aspx (accessed November 2015).

Allen, S., C. Jones, F. Douglas, and D. Clark. (May 2014). Keeping our heroes safe: A comprehensive approach to destigmatizing mental health issues in law enforcement. *The Police Chief*.

Armstrong, J. 18 July 2014. "I was scared of appearing weak": First responders speak out on PTSD. *Global News*. http://globalnews.ca/news/1460326/i-was-scared-of-appearing-weak-first-responders-speak-out-on-ptsd/ (accessed September 2020).

Auditor General Canada. Fall 2014. *Mental Health Services for Veterans*, Chapter 3. Ottawa: Office of the Auditor General of Canada. https://www.oag-bvg.gc.ca/internet/English/osh_20141127_e_40003.html (accessed September 2020).

Austin-Ketch, T.L., J. Violanti, D. Fekedulegn, M.E. Andrew, C.M. Burchfield, and T.A. Hartley. 2012. Addictions and the criminal justice system: What happens on the other side? Post-traumatic stress symptoms and cortisol measures in a police cohort. *Journal of Addictions Nursing* 23 (1): 22–9.

Backteman-Erlanson, S. 2013. Burnout, work, stress of conscience and coping among female and male patrolling police officers. Unpublished doctoral thesis. Umea, Sweden: Faculty of Medicine, Department of Nursing.

Bolan, K. 28 January 2013. Inside the Angels, Part 1: The man who broke the East End biker gang. *Vancouver Sun.* www.vancouversun.com/news/inside+angels+part+infiltrated+angels/7876815/story.html (accessed November 2015).

Campbell, A. 1996. *Bernardo Investigation Review. Summary: The Report of Mr Justice Archie Campbell.* https://www.attorneygeneral.jus.gov.on.ca/.../10_Campbell_Summary.pdf

CBC News. 18 January 2012. Gangster shot dead at Vancouver's Wall Centre. www.cbc.ca/news/canada/british-columbia/gangster-shot-dead-at-vancouver-s-wall-centre-1.1223071 (accessed March 2016).

Community Oriented Policing Services and Police Executive Research Forum. 2013. Social Media and Tactical Considerations tor Law Enforcement. Washington: US Department of Justice.

Criminal Code of Canada. 1985. http://laws-lois.justice.gc.ca/eng/acts/C-46 (accessed November 2015).

Davis III, E., A. Alves, and D. Sklansky. 2014. Social media and police leadership: Lessons from Boston. *New Perspectives in Policing Bulletin.* Washington, DC: US Department of Justice, National Institute of Justice.

Duxbury, L. and C. Higgins. 2012. Summary of key findings: Caring for and about those who serve: Work-life and employee well-being within Canada's police departments. http://sprott.carleton.co/wp-content/files/Duxbury-Higgins-Police2012_keyfindings.pdf.

Egger, S. 1984. The killers among us: An examination of serial murder and its investigation. PhD dissertation. Sam Houston State University

Gilmartin, K. 2002. *Ethics-Based Policing . . . Undoing Entitlement.* http://emotionalsurvival.com/ethics_based_policing.htm (accessed November 2015).

Griffiths, C.T., N. Pollard, and L. Kitt. 2014. Police officer health and wellness. Presentation at the American Society of Criminology Annual Conference. San Francisco, 19–22 November 2014.

Innes, M. 2000. Professionalizing the role of the police informant: The British experience. *Policing and Society* 9: 357–83.

Kaufman, Fred. 1998. *The Commission on Proceedings Involving Guy Paul Morin.* (The Kaufman Commission). https://www.attorneygeneral.jus.gov.on.ca/english/about/pubs/morin/morin_esumm.pdf (accessed November 2015).

Kirshman, E. 26 June 2017. Cops and PTSD: Why you should care, what you can do. *Psychology Today.* https://www.psychologytoday.com/ca/blog/cop-doc/201706/cops-and-ptsd-0 (accessed September 2020).

La Vigne, N., P. Lachman, A. Matthews, and S.R. Neusteter. August 2012. *Key Issues in the Police Use of Pedestrian Stops and Searches.* Research Papers. Justice Institute Policy Center.

MacFarlane, B. 2008. Wrongful convictions: The effect of tunnel vision and predisposing circumstances in the criminal justice system. Prepared for the Inquiry into Pediatric Forensic Pathology in Ontario, The Honourable Stephen T. Goudge, Commissioner. Online at https://www.attorneygeneral.jus.gov.on.ca/.../pdf/Macfarlane_Wrongful-Convictions.pdf.

McCarty, W.P. and W.G. Skogan. 2012. Job-related burnout among civilian and sworn police personnel. *Police Quarterly,* 16 (1): 66–84.

Nemetz, G. 2019. Registered clinical psychologist. Vancouver, BC. Personal communication. May 10.

Police Services Act Ontario. Regulation 58/16. Collection of Identifying Information in Certain Circumstances—Prohibition and Duties. https://www.ontario.ca/laws/regulation/160058 (accessed September 2020).

Public Prosecution Service of Canada Deskbook. 3.11 Informer Privilege (1 March 2014).

Public Safety Canada. 2016. Ministerial Roundtable on Post-Traumatic Stress Disorder in Public Safety Officers. Regina, Saskatchewan.

R. v. Debot. 1989. 2 SCR 1140, 1989 CanLII 13 (SCC). www.canlii.org/en/ca/scc/doc/1989/1989canlii13/1989canlii13.html (accessed November 2015).

R. v. Hart. 2014. SCC 52. www.canlii.org/en/ca/scc/doc/2014/2014scc52/2014scc52.html (accessed November 2015).

R. v. Jordan. 2016. 1 SCR 631, SCC 27 (CanLII).

R. v. Leipert. 1997. 1 SCR 281. www.canlii.org/en/ca/scc/doc/1997/1997canlii367/1997canlii367.html (accessed November 2015).

R. v. Mack. 1988. 2 SCR 903, 1988 CanLII 24 (SCC). www.canlii.org/en/ca/scc/doc/1988/1988canlii24/1988canlii24.html (accessed November 2015).

R. v. Mann. 2004. 3 SCR 59, 2004 SCC 52 (CanLII). https://www.canlii.org/en/ca/scc/doc/2004/2004scc52/2004scc52.html (accessed November 2015).

R. v. McKay. 2016. BCCA 391.

R. v. Stinchcombe. 1991. 3 SCR 326, 1991 CanLII 45 (SCC) www.canlii.org/en/ca/scc/doc/1991/1991canlii45/1991canlii45.html (accessed November 2015).

R. v. Vallee. 2018 BCSC 892 (CanLII).

Ray, C. 18 October 2019. Street checks permanently banned in N.S. after review calls them illegal. *CBC News.* https://www.cbc.ca/news/canada/nova-scotia/halifax-street-checks-illegal-1.5326217 (accessed September 2020).

Rossmo, K. 2008. *Criminal Investigative Failures*. CRC Press. Taylor and Francis Group.

Royal Canadian Mounted Police. 2012. *Major Case Management Guide*. Canadian Police College.

Said, W. 2010. The terrorist informant. *Washington Law Review*. 85: 687.

Seglins, D. 24 June 2011. G8/G20 summit opponents infiltrated by police. *CBC News*. www.cbc.ca/news/canada/g20-g8-summit-opponents-infiltrated-by-police-1.1059275 (accessed November 2015).

Shane, J.M. 2010. Organizational stressors and police performance. *Journal of Criminal Justice*. 38: 807–18. DOI: 10.1016/j.jcrimjus.2010.05.008.

Smith, S., V. Stinson, and M. Patry. 2012. Confession evidence in Canada: Psychological issues and legal landscapes. *Psychology, Crime and Law* 18 (3): 317–33.

Snook, B., J. Eastwood, M. Stinson, J. Tedeschini, and J. House. April 2010. Reforming investigative interviewing in Canada. *Canadian Journal of Criminology and Criminal Justice*. 203–18.

Toronto Police Service. June 2011. G20 Summit Toronto Ontario June 2010. Toronto Police Service After-Action Review.

Torres, S., D. Maggard Jr., and C. To. October 2003. Preparing families for the hazards of police work. *The Police Chief* 70 (10).

Turcotte, M. 11 December 2008. Shifts in police-informant negotiations. *Global Crime* 9 (4): 291–305.

Tyler T. and J. Fagan. 2008. Legitimacy and cooperation: Why do people help the police fight crime in their communities? *Ohio State Journal of Criminal Law* 6: 231–75.

Vetrovec v. The Queen. 1982. 1 SCR 811, 1982 CanLII 20 (SCC).

White, P. 15 November 2019. Toronto Police report shows one instance of carding in 2018. *Globe and Mail*. https://www.theglobeandmail.com/canada/toronto/article-toronto-police-have-discontinued-carding-report-indicates/ (accessed September 2020).

Yuan, C., Z. Wang, S.S. Inslicht, S.E. McCaslin, T.J. Metzler, C. Henn-Haase, B.A. Apfel, H. Tong, T.C. Neylan, Y. Fang, and C.R. Marmar. 2011. Protective factors for posttraumatic stress disorder symptoms in a prospective study of police officers. *Psychiatry Research* 188: 45–50. DOI:10.1016/j.psychres.2010.10.034.

Chapter 10

Anderson, G.S. 2010. *All You Ever Wanted to Know about Forensic Science in Canada but Didn't Know Who to Ask!* British Columbia Institute of Technology. Burnaby: BCIT.

CBC Digital Archives. Call 999 emergency line for help in Winnipeg. https://www.cbc.ca/archives/entry/winnipeggers-call-999-for-help (accessed September 2020).

Lotus, B., and B. Goold. 2011. Covert surveillance and the invisibilities of policing. *Criminology & Criminal Justice* 12 (3): 275–88.

Marx, G.T. 1988. *Undercover: Police Surveillance in America*. Berkeley: University of California Press.

Mertz, E. 12 September 2013. Officers conduct largest stolen property seizure in EPS history. *Global News*. http://globalnews.ca/news/837500/officers-conduct-largest-stolen-property-seizure-in-eps-history/ (accessed 6 February 2015).

Mouhtaropoulos, A., C. Li, and M. Grobler. 2014. Digital forensic readiness: Are we there yet? *Journal of International Commercial Law and Technology* 9 (3): 173–79.

Office of the Privacy Commissioner of Canada. 2006. https://www.priv.gc.ca/information/guide/vs_060301_e.asp (accessed May 2015).

Quinlan, A. 2011. Tracing the "messy" history of forensic DNA analysis in Canada. *Studies in Sociology of Science*, 2 (2): 11–18.

R. v. Madrid. 1994. BCJA 1786, at 82 (BCCA 1994).

R. v. Tessling. 2004. 3 SCR 432

R. v. Thompson. 1990. 2 SCR 1111 (SCC 1990).

Terrell, I.S. May 2006. Understanding 911 dispatch teams across context: Implications for theory, information technology, and practice. PhD thesis in Information Sciences and Technology. Pennsylvania: Pennsylvania State University.

Chapter 11

Burke, A. and D. Beeby. 5 March 2015. RCMP overtime costs for Ottawa shooting nearly $330K. *CBC News*. www.cbc.ca/news/canada/ottawa/rcmp-overtime-costs-for-ottawa-shooting-nearly-330k-1.2983330 (accessed February 2016).

Conor, P., J. Robson, and S. Marcellus. 3 October 2019. Police resources in Canada, 2018. *The Juristat*. Catalogue no. 85-002-X. Ottawa: Canadian Centre for Justice Statistics, Statistics Canada.

Di Matteo, L. September 2014. *Police and Crime Rates in Canada: A Comparison of Resources and Outcomes*. Vancouver: Fraser Institute.

Federation of Canadian Municipalities. 2008. Towards Equity and Efficiency in Policing: A Report on Policing Roles, Responsibilities, and Resources in Canada. Ottawa.

Fitz-Morris, J. 16 January 2015. RCMP officers have right to collective bargaining, Supreme Court rules. *CBC News*. www.cbc.ca/news/politics/rcmp-officers-have-right-to-collective-bargaining-supreme-court-rules-1.2912340 (accessed 30 November 2015).

Gascon, G. and T. Fogelsong. December 2010. Making police more affordable: Managing costs and measuring value in policing. *New Perspectives in Policing*. Harvard Kennedy School, National Institute of Justice.

Griffiths, C.T. and N. Pollard. October 2013. *Policing in Winnipeg: An Operational Review*. Prepared for the Canadian Police Association. Vancouver.

Integrated Homicide Investigation Team. http://bc.rcmp-grc.gc.ca/ViewPage.action?siteNodeId=2142&languageId=1&contentId=-1 (accessed February 2016).

Institute for Canadian Urban Research Studies (ICURS). 2014. *Economics of Policing: Complexity and Costs in Canada, 2014.*

Leuprecht, C. 2014. The Blue Line or the Bottom Line of Police Services in Canada? Arresting Runaway Growth in Costs. Ottawa: Macdonald-Laurier Institute.

Lunney, R. 2012a. Hearing footsteps: The economics of policing. *Blue Line Magazine*, Aug./Sept. 12–13.

———. 2012b. Galloping off in all directions: An analysis of the new federal–provincial agreement for RCMP contract police services and some implications for the future of Canadian policing. *Canadian Public Administration*, 55 (2): 433–50.

Moreau, G. 22 July 2019. Police-reported crime statistics in Canada, 2018. *The Juristat*. Ottawa: Canadian Centre for Justice Statistics, Statistics Canada.

Office of the Parliamentary Budget Officer. 20 March 2013. *Expenditure Analysis of Criminal Justice in Canada.* Ottawa.

Public Safety Canada. 2013. 2013 Summit on the Economics of Policing: Strengthening Canada's Policing Advantage. Summit Report, 16–17 January. Ottawa.

R. v. Stinchcombe. 1991. 3 SCR 326, 1991CanLII 45 (SCC) www.canlii.org/en/ca/scc/doc/1991/1991canlii45/1991canlii45.html (accessed November 2015).

Robertson, N. September 2012. Policing: Fundamental principles in Canadian context. *Canadian Public Administration* 55 (2): 343–63.

RCMP. 2015. *Fair Compensation for the RCMP*. RCMP Pay Council, Ottawa.

Seagrave, J. 1997. *Introduction to Policing in Canada.* Scarborough, ON: Prentice Hall.

Sécurité publique Québec. The six levels of police service according to population size. www.securitepublique.gouv.qc.ca/en/police-prevention/police-service-levels.html (accessed 11 April 2015).

Standing Committee on Public Safety and National Security. May 2014. *Economics of Policing.* 41st Parliament, Second Session.

Wilson-Bates, F. January 2008. *Lost in Transition: How a Lack of Capacity in the Mental Health System Is Failing Vancouver's Mentally Ill and Draining Police Resources.* Vancouver Police Board.

Chapter 12

Braga, A.A. 2005. Hot spots policing and crime prevention: A systematic review of randomized controlled trials. *Journal of Experimental Criminology* 1: 317–42.

———. 2008a. *Problem-Oriented Policing and Crime Prevention.* 2nd edn. New York: Criminal Justice Press.

———. 2008b. *Crime Prevention Research Review No. 2: Enforcement Strategies to Prevent Crime in Hot Spot Areas.* Washington, DC: Department of Justice Office of Community Oriented Policing Services.

———, and D.L. Weisburd. 2007. Police innovation and crime prevention: Lessons learned from police research over the past 20 years. *National Institute of Justice (NIJ) Policing Research Workshop: Planning for the Future.* p. 33. Washington, DC: US Department of Justice.

Brantingham, P.J. and P.L. Brantingham. 1978. A theoretical model of crime site selection. In M.D. Krohn and R.L. Akers, eds, *Crime, Law and Sanctions.* Beverly Hills, CA: SAGE Publications, Inc.

——— and F.L. Faust. 1976. A conceptual model of crime prevention. *Crime & Delinquency* 22 (3): 284–96.

Brantingham, P.L. and P.J. Brantingham. 1991. Notes on the geometry of crime. In P.J. Brantingham and P.L. Brantingham, eds, *Environmental Criminology.* 2nd edn. 27–54. Prospect Heights, Illinois: Waveland Press, Inc.

Can the can. 20 November 2008. *The Economist.*

Canadian Press, The. 14 April 2015. The Supreme Court quashes mandatory minimum sentence for gun crimes.

Canadian Sentencing Commission. 1987. *Sentencing reform: A Canadian approach: Report of the Canadian Sentencing Commission.* Ottawa: Minister of Supply and Services Canada.

Clarke, R., and J. Eck. 2003. *Become a Problem-Solving Crime Analyst in 55 Small Steps.* Jill Dando Institute of Crime Science, University College, London.

Cohen, L.E., and Felson, M. August 1979. Social change and crime rate trends: A routine activity approach. *American Sociological Review,* 44: 588–608.

Cornish, D. and R.V. Clarke. 1986. *The Reasoning Criminal: Rational Choice Perspectives on Offending.* New York: Springer-Verlag.

Criminal Code of Canada. 1985. http://laws-lois.justice.gc.ca/eng/acts/C-46 (accessed November 2015).

Felson, M. 1986. Linking criminal choices, routine activities, informal control and criminal outcomes. In D. Cornish and R. Clarke, eds, *The Reasoning Criminal: Rational Choice Perspectives on Offending,* 119–28. New York, NY: Springer-Verlag.

Fish, M.J. 2008. An eye for an eye: Proportionality as a moral principle of punishment. *Oxford Journal of Legal Studies* 28 (1): 57–71.

Gabor, T. 2001. Mandatory minimum sentences: A utilitarian perspective. *Canadian Journal of Criminology* 43: 385–405.

Godown, J. August 2009. The CompStat process: Four principles for managing crime reduction. *The Police Chief* 76 (8).

Goldstein, H. 1990. *Problem-Oriented Policing.* New York, NY: McGraw-Hill, Inc.

Kelling, G.L., T. Pate, D. Dieckman, and C.E. Brown. 1974. *The Kansas City Preventive Patrol Experiment: A Summary Report.* Washington, DC: Police Foundation.

Mastrofski, S. 2006. Community policing: A skeptical view. In D. Weisburd and A.A. Braga, eds, *Police Innovation:*

Contrasting Perspectives. 44–76. Cambridge: Cambridge University Press.

Mirza, F.R. 2001. Mandatory minimum prison sentencing and systemic racism. *Osgoode Hall Law Journal* 39 (2): 491–515.

Planning, Research & Audit. 2008. Assessing Sentencing Across Criminal Careers: An Examination of VPD's Chronic Offenders (Quick Facts). Vancouver, BC: Vancouver Police Department.

Pollard, N. 2008. Assessing Sentencing across Criminal Careers: An Examination of VPD's Chronic Offenders. Vancouver: Vancouver Police Department.

Ratcliffe, J.H. 2008. *Intelligence-Led Policing.* Cullompton, UK: Willan Publishing.

———. 2011. Intelligence-led policing. In R. Wortley and L. Mazerolle, eds, *Environmental Criminology and Crime Analysis.* 263–82. New York: Routledge, Taylor & Francis.

Sheehy, E. 2001. Mandatory minimum sentences: Law and policy. *Osgoode Hall Law Journal* 39.

Silverman, E.B. 2006. CompStat's innovation. In D. Weisburd and A.A. Braga, eds, *Police Innovation: Contrasting Perspectives.* 267–83. Cambridge: Cambridge University Press.

Skogan, W.G. 2006. The promise of community policing. In D. Weisburd and A.A. Braga, eds, *Police Innovation: Contrasting Perspectives.* 27–43. Cambridge: Cambridge University Press.

Sousa, W.H., and G.L. Kelling. 2006. Of "broken windows," criminology, and criminal justice. In D. Weisburd and A.A. Braga, eds, *Police Innovation: Contrasting Perspectives.* 77–97. Cambridge: Cambridge University Press.

Taylor, R.B. 2006. Incivilities reduction policing, zero tolerance, and the retreat from coproduction: Weak foundations and strong pressures. In D. Weisburd and A.A. Braga, eds, *Police Innovation: Contrasting Perspectives.* 98–116. Cambridge: Cambridge University Press.

Weisburd, D., C.W. Telep, J.C. Hinkle, and J.E. Eck. 2010. Is problem-oriented policing effective in reducing crime and disorder? Findings from a Campbell systematic review. *Criminology & Public Policy* 9 (1): 139–72.

White, M.B. 2008. *Enhancing the Problem-Solving Capacity of Crime Analysis Units.* Washington, DC: US Department of Justice, Centre for Problem-Oriented Policing, Office of Community Oriented Policing Services.

Chapter 13

Boba, R. 2005. *Crime Analysis and Crime Mapping.* Thousand Oaks, CA: Sage.

Boba-Santos, R. 2013. *Crime Analysis with Crime Mapping.* 3rd edn. Thousand Oaks, CA: SAGE Publications, Inc.

Brantingham, P.L. and P.J. Brantingham. 1991. Notes on the geometry of crime. In P.J. Brantingham and P.L. Brantingham, eds, *Environmental Criminology.* 2nd edn. 27–54. Prospect Heights, Illinois: Waveland Press, Inc.

———. 1997. Mapping crime for analytic purposes: Location quotients, counts, and rates. In D. Weisburd and J. T. McEwen, eds, *Crime Mapping and Crime Prevention.* 263–88.

Cohen, L.E., and Felson, M. August 1979. Social change and crime rate trends: A routine activity approach. *American Sociological Review,* 44: 588–608.

Cope, N. 2004. Intelligence-led policing or policing-led intelligence? Integrating volume crime analysis into policing. *British Journal of Criminology* 44: 188–203.

Cornish, D. and R.V. Clarke. 1986. *The Reasoning Criminal: Rational Choice Perspectives on Offending.* New York: Springer-Verlag.

Fishbein, W. and G. Treverton. 2004. *Rethinking "Alternative Analysis" to Address Transnational Threats.* Washington, DC: CIA: The Sherman Kent Center for Intelligence Analysis.

Griffiths, C.T. and N. Pollard. October 2013. *Policing in Winnipeg: An Operational Review.* Prepared for the Canadian Police Association. Vancouver.

Gwinn, S. L., C. Bruce, J.P. Cooper, and S. Hick. 2008. *Exploring Crime Analysis: Readings on Essential Skills.* 2nd edn. North Charleston, SC: International Association of Crime Analysts.

Harries, K. 1999. *Mapping Crime: Principle and Practice.* Washington, DC: US Department of Justice, Office of Justice Programs.

International Association of Crime Analysts. *Definition and Types of Crime Analysis.* [White Paper 2014-02]. Overland Park, KS.

Leong, K. and S.C. Chan. 2013. A content analysis of web-based crime mapping in the world's top 100 highest GDP cities. *Crime Prevention and Community Safety* 15 (1): 1–22.

Lum, C. Fall 2013. *Is Crime Analysis "Evidence-Based"?* Translational Criminology: Center for Evidence-Based Crime Policy, George Mason University.

——— and C.S. Koper. 2017. *Evidence-Based Policing: Translating Research into Practice.* New York: Oxford Univ. Press.

Malm, A.E., J.B. Kinney, and N.R. Pollard. 2008. Social network and distance correlates of criminal associates involved in illicit drug production. *Security Journal* 21: 77–94.

O'Shea, T.C. and K. Nicholls, K. 2003. *Crime Analysis in America: Findings and Recommendations.* Washington, DC: US Department of Justice, Office of Community Oriented Policing Services.

Prox, R. 25 September 2014. Special Constable, Vancouver Police Department. (N. Pollard, Interviewer).

Ratcliffe, Jerry. 2012. *Intelligence-Led Policing.* London: Willian. DOI: 10.4324/9780203118245.

Rossmo, D.K. 1995. Place, space, and police investigations: Hunting serial violent criminals. In J.E. Eck and D.A.

Weisburd, eds, *Crime and Place: Crime Prevention Studies, Vol. 4.* 217–35. Monsey, NY: Criminal Justice Press.

——. March 1999. Geographic profiling system helps catch criminals. *GeoWorld*: 41.

Taylor, B., A. Kowalyk, and R. Boba. 2007. The integration of crime analysis into law enforcement agencies: An exploratory study into the perceptions of crime analysts. *Police Quarterly, 10* (2): 154–69.

White, M.B. 2008. *Enhancing the Problem-Solving Capacity of Crime Analysis Units.* Washington, DC: US Department of Justice, Centre for Problem-Oriented Policing, Office of Community Oriented Policing Services.

Chapter 14

Angus Reid. 20 February 2018. Confidence in the justice system: Visible minorities have less faith in courts than other Canadians. http://angusreid.org/justice-system-confidence/ (accessed 23 July 2019).

Baker, A., J. Goodman, and B. Miller. 13 June 2015. Beyond the chokehold: The path to Eric Garner's death. Nytimes.com.

Bereska, T.M. 2014. *Deviance, Conformity and Social Control in Canada.* 4th edn. Toronto: Pearson.

Blow, C. 16 March 2012. The curious case of Trayvon Martin. Nytimes.com.

Boivin, R., A. Gendron, C. Faubert, and B. Poulin. 2017. The malleability of attitudes toward the police: Immediate effects of the viewing of police use of force videos. *Police Practice and Research* 18 (4): 366–75.

Bolan, K. 31 July 2017. Surrey RCMP issue warning over suspected gangsters targeted in recent shootings. *Vancouver Sun.* https://vancouversun.com/news/crime/surrey-mounties-issue-public-warning-over-five-suspected-gangsters-involved-in-recent-shootings (accessed September 2020).

Boyd, S.C. and C.I. Carter. 2014. *Killer Weed: Marijuana Grow Ops, Media and Justice.* University of Toronto Press. Toronto.

Brown, G. (2016). The blue line on thin ice: Police use of force modifications in the era of cameraphones and YouTube. *British Journal of Criminology* 56: 293–312.

Canadian Press. 24 January 2019. Vancouver police arrest 47 men in sting targeting alleged predators looking for sex with teens. *Globe and Mail.* https://www.theglobeandmail.com/canada/article-vancouver-police-arrest-47-men-in-sting-targeting-alleged-predators/.

CBC News. 10 December 2015. Social media clues lead to arrest of man in 2012 Toronto killing. https://www.cbc.ca/news/canada/toronto/mike-pimentel-killing-serial-1.3358573 (accessed September 2020).

——. 5 June 2020. Canadians hold protests, vigils for Black lives lost at the hands of police. https://www.cbc.ca/news/canada/canadian-floyd-anti-racism-rallies-1.5599792 (accessed September 2020).

CBS Boston. Braintree Police: "Hold Off" on crime this weekend due to "extreme heat." https://boston.cbslocal.com/2019/07/20/braintree-police-hold-off-on-crime-this-weekend-due-to-extreme-heat/ (accessed 23 July 2019).

Chibnall, S. 1977. *Law-and-Order News: An Analysis of Crime Reporting in the British Press.* London: Tavistock Publications.

Christmas, R. Summer 2012. An arranged marriage: Police–media conflict and collaboration. *Canadian Graduate Journal of Sociology and Criminology* 1 (1).

Chuck, E. 13 August 2014. The killing of an unarmed teen: What we know about Brown's death. www.nbcnews.com

Delta Police. Community Watch Program (CWP). https://deltapolice.ca/cwp/

Donovan, K. and C.F. Klahm IV. 2015. The role of entertainment media in perceptions of police use of force. *Criminal Justice and Behavior* 42 (12): 1261–81.

Ericson, R.V., P.M. Baranek, and J.B.L. Chan. 1989. *Negotiating Control: A Study of News Sources.* Toronto: University of Toronto Press.

Glover, S., C. Richards, C. Devine, and D. Griffin. 23 July 2020. A key miscalculation by officers contributed to the tragic death of Breonna Taylor. *CNN Investigates.* https://www.cnn.com/2020/07/23/us/breonna-taylor-police-shooting-invs/index.html (accessed September 2020). Goldsmith, A. 2015. Disgracebook policing: Social media and the rise of police indiscretion. *Policing and Society* 25 (3): 249–67.

Halifax Regional Police. 2015. Police News. https://apps.halifax.ca/news (accessed November 2015).

Halton Regional Police. 2015. Newsroom. www.haltonpolice.ca/PublicAffairs/Newsroom/Pages/default.aspx (accessed November 2015).

Hill, E., A. Tiefenthäler, C. Triebert, D. Jordan, H. Willis and R. Stein. 31 May 2020. How George Floyd was killed in police custody. *The New York Times.* https://www.nytimes.com/2020/05/31/us/george-floyd-investigation.html?auth=login-email&login=email (accessed September 2020).

Hristova, B. 2 August 2019. Social media bedevils hunt for BC murder suspects. *Vancouver Sun.* http://epaper.vancouversun.com/@Colin_Campbell.4/csb_j0fmTulB_BEjwF4KhJYe8XnnkznjP9lzoWQs5G_t5GlkvuB0mzIJx8ch6AnphXop (accessed September 2020).

IACP. 2001. The general image of police. In *The public image of police: Final report to the IACP by the George Mason University Administration of Justice Program.* https://www.theiacp.org/resources/the-public-image-of-police (accessed September 2020).

Lee, M. and A. McGovern. 2014. *Policing and Media: Public Relations, Simulations and Communications.* Routledge, London.

Los Angeles Police Department. Newsroom. www.lapdonline.org/newsroom (accessed November 2015).

Marcelo, P. 21 July 2019. "Sunday has been cancelled": Heat and humidity grip U.S. East Coast. *Globe and Mail.* https://www.theglobeandmail.com/world/article-sunday-has-been-cancelled-heat-and-humidity-grip-us-east-coast/ (accessed 21 July 2019).

Mawby, R.C. 2007. Criminal investigation and the media. In T. Newburn, T. Williamson, and A. Wright, eds. *Handbook of Criminal Investigation.* Cullompton: Willan.

Mawby, R.C. 2010. Police corporate communications, crime reporting and the shaping of policing news. *Policing and Society* 20 (1): 124–39.

Maxson, C., K. Hennigan, and D. Sloan. 2003. *Factors That Affect Public Opinion of the Police.* National Institute of Justice. Office of Justice Programs. US Department of Justice.

McCormick, C. 1995. *Constructing Danger: The Misrepresentation of Crime in the News.* Fernwood, Halifax.

Meijer, A. and M. Thaens. 2013. Social media strategies: Understanding the differences between North American police departments. *Government Information Quarterly,* 30: 343–50.

Miethe, T., O. Venger, and J. Lieberman. 2019. Police use of force and its video coverage: An experimental study of the impact of media source and content on public perceptions. *Journal of Criminal Justice* 60: 35–46.

National Institute of Justice. 2014. *Perceptions of Treatment by Police.* www.nij.gov/topics/law-enforcement/legitimacy/pages/perceptions.aspx (accessed March 2016).

Newell, B. 2019. Context, visibility, and control: Police work and the contested objectivity of bystander video. *New Media and Society* 21 (1): 60–76.

Nhan, J., L. Huey, and R. Broll. 2017. Digilantism: An analysis of crowdsourcing and the Boston marathon bombings. *British Journal of Criminology* 57: 341–61.

Parry, M., R. Moule Jr., and L. Dario. 2019. Technology-mediated exposure to police-citizen encounters: A quasi-experimental assessment of consequences for citizen perceptions. *Justice Quarterly* 36 (3): 412–36.

Pate, U., M. Abdullahi, and U. Abdullahi. 2014. Police–public media relations: Issues and challenges. *Research on Humanities and Social Sciences.* 4 (26).

Peel Police. Media Contacts. https://www.peelpolice.ca/en/who-we-are/media-contacts.aspx (accessed 21 July 2019).

R. v. Debot. 1989. 2 SCR 1140, 1989 CanLII 13 (SCC). www.canlii.org/en/ca/scc/doc/1989/1989canlii13/1989canlii13.html (accessed November 2015).

R. v. Jordan. 2016. 1 SCR 631, SCC 27 (CanLII).

R. v. Stinchcombe. 1991. 3 SCR 326, 1991CanLII 45 (SCC) www.canlii.org/en/ca/scc/doc/1991/1991canlii45/1991canlii45.html (accessed November 2015).

Reasons, C. 2014. Review—Killer weed: Marijuana grow ops, media and justice-based policy making. *Canadian Journal of Criminology and Criminal Justice.* www.ccja-acjp.ca/pub/en/review-killer-weed-marijuana-grow-ops-media-and-justice-based-policymaking/ (accessed 9 November 2015).

Reiner, R. 2008. Policing and the media. In T. Newburn, ed, *Handbook of Policing.* 2nd edn. 313–335. London; Routledge.

Saunders, M. 21 June 2019. Chief Mark Saunders releases findings of Danforth Shootings Investigation. Toronto Police Service News Release.

Thomson Reuters. 17 July 2020. Georgia men charged with killing Ahmaud Arbery plead not guilty to murder charges. *CBC News.* https://www.cbc.ca/news/world/georgia-arbery-murder-pleas-1.5653390 (accessed September 2020).

Wilson, J. 2016. Crowdsourcing and criminal investigations: Evidence management in the digital world. Nice. https://www.nice.com/protecting/blog/Crowdsourcing-and-Criminal-Investigations-Evidence-Management in-the-Digital-World-595 (accessed September 2020).

Zercoe, C. 1 February 2018. Policing in the 21st century: 5 key considerations for crowdsourcing evidence. PoliceOne.com. https://www.policeone.com/police-products/investigation/evidence-management/articles/5-key-considerations-for-crowdsourcing-evidence-HVjxlxnkcGtGerqH/ (accessed September 2020).

Chapter 15

Amnesty International. no date. Maher Arar. www.amnestyusa.org/our-work/cases/usa-maher-arar (accessed 1 August 2015).

Beck, U. 1992. Risk Society: Toward a New Modernity. London: Sage.

Belanger, C. 2000. Chronology of the October Crisis, 1970, and its aftermath. Marianapolis College, Montreal. http://faculty.marianopolis.edu/c.belanger/quebechistory/chronos/october.htm (accessed 20 July 2015).

Bronskill, J. 23 June 2015. RCMP say 1985 Air India bombing investigation "active and ongoing." *The Globe and Mail.*

Canadian Broadcasting Corporation. no date. *The October Crisis.* CBC Learning website. www.cbc.ca/history/EPISCONTENTSE1EP16CH1PA4LE.html (accessed 20 June 2015).

Canadian Intelligence Service Canada. https://www.csis-scrs.gc.ca/index-en.php (accessed February 2016).

Communications Security Establishment. https://www.cse-cst.gc.ca/en (accessed February 2016).

Corrado, R.R. 1981. Contemporary political crime: National and international terrorism. In M.A. Jackson and C.T. Griffiths, eds, *Canadian Criminology: Perspectives on Crime and Criminality.* 451–69. Toronto: Harcourt Brace Jovanovich.

Criminal Code of Canada. 1985. http://laws-lois.justice.gc.ca/eng/acts/C-46 (accessed November 2015).

Ericson, R.V. and K.D. Haggerty. 1997. *Policing the Risk Society*. Toronto: University of Toronto Press.

Foucault, M. 1975. *Discipline and Punish: The Birth of the Prison*. London: Penguin.

———. 1978. *The History of Sexuality, Vol. 1. An Introduction*. New York: NY: Random House.

Garland, D. 2001. *The Culture of Control: Crime and Social Order in Contemporary Society*. Chicago, IL: University of Chicago Press.

Goff, C. 2014. *Criminal Justice in Canada*. 6th edn. Toronto: Nelson Education.

Hogeveen, B. and A. Wolford. 2012. Contemporary critical criminology. In R. Linden, ed, *Criminology: A Canadian Perspective*. 7th edn. 377–407. Toronto: Nelson.

Holt, S. 1964. *Terror in the Name of God: The Story of the Sons of Freedom Doukhobors*. Toronto/Montreal: McClelland and Stewart.

Horrall, S.W. 1980. The Royal North-West Mounted Police and labour unrests in western Canada, 1919. *Canadian Historical Review* LXI (2): 169–90.

Keable, J.F. 1981. *Report of the Commission of Inquiry into Police Operations on Quebec Territory*. Quebec: Department of Justice.

McDonald, D.C. August 1981. *Freedom and Security under the Law*. Vol. 1. Commission of Inquiry Concerning Certain Activities of the Royal Canadian Mounted Police. Ottawa.

Mackenzie, M. 1969. *Report of the Royal Commission on Security*. Ottawa.

Major, J.C. 2010. *Air India Flight 182: A Canadian Tragedy. Final Report of the Commission of Inquiry into the Investigation of the Bombing of Air India Flight 182*. Ottawa: Government of Canada. http://epe.lac-bac.gc.ca/100/206/301/pco-bcp/commissions/air_india/2010-07-23/www.majorcomm.ca/en/reports/finalreport/default.htm (accessed 24 June 2015).

Murphy, C. 2007. "Securitizing" Canadian policing: A new policing paradigm for the post 9/11 security state? *Canadian Journal of Sociology* 32 (4): 449–75.

O'Connor, D. 2006a. *A New Review Mechanism for the RCMP's National Security Activities*. Report of the Commission of Inquiry into the Actions of Canadian Officials in Relation to Maher Arar. Public Works and Government Services, Ottawa. December.

———. 2006b. *Report of the Events Relating to Maher Arar*. Report of the Commission of Inquiry into the Actions of Canadian Officials in Relation to Maher Arar. Public Works and Government Services, Ottawa. September.

O'Grady, W. 2014. *Crime in Canadian Context*. 3rd edn. Toronto: Oxford University Press.

O'Malley, P. February 1999. Governmentality and the risk society. *Economy and Society* 28 (1): 138–48.

Pelletier, G. 1971. *The October Crisis*. Translated by Joyce Marshal. Toronto: McClelland & Stewart.

Public Safety Canada. 2014. *2014 Public Report on the Terrorist Threat to Canada, Ottawa*. www.publicsafety.gc.ca/cnt/rsrcs/pblctns/2014-pblc-rpr-trrrst-thrt/index-eng.aspx (accessed 1 August 2015).

———. 2019a. *2019 Public Report on the Terrorism Threat to Canada*. April 2019 update. Ottawa: Government of Canada.

———. 19 June 2019b. Statement from Ministers Goodale, Lametti, and Sajjan on the passage of Bill C-59 in Parliament.

Rigakos, G.S. 1999a. Hyperpanoptics as commodity: The case of the parapolice. *Canadian Journal of Sociology*. 24 (1): 381–409.

Rigakos, G.S. 1999b. Risk society and actuarial criminology: Prospects for a critical discourse. *Canadian Journal of Criminology* (April): 137–50.

Rosen, P. 2000. *The Canadian Security Intelligence Service*. Parliamentary Research Branch. Ottawa.

Royal Canadian Mounted Police (RCMP). *National Security Criminal Investigations*. https://www.rcmp-grc.gc.ca/nsci-ecsn/index-eng.htm (accessed September 20, 2020).

Sawatsky, J. 1980. *Men in the Shadows: The RCMP Security Service*. Toronto: Totem Books.

Seal, A. 2019. A new national security act for Canada. OPENCANADA.ORG, April 11.

Toews, V. 2013. Ministerial Foreword. *Building Resilience against Terrorism: Canada's Counter-Terrorism Strategy*. Ottawa: Government of Canada.

Tunney, C. 23 June 2019. Canada's national security landscape will get a major overhaul this summer. *CBC News*. https://www.cbc.ca/news/politics/bill-c59-national-security-passed-1.5182948 (accessed September 2020).

Union of Spiritual Communities of Christ Doukhobors. www.usccdoukhobors.org/information.htm# (accessed 30 June 2015).

Whitaker, R., G.S. Kealey, and A. Parnaby. 2012. *Secret Service: Political Policing in Canada from the Fenians to Fortress America*. Toronto: University of Toronto Press.

White, R., F. Haines, and L. Eisler. 2013. *Crime and Criminology: An Introduction*. 2nd edn. Don Mills, ON: Oxford University Press.

Yerbury, J.C. and C.T. Griffiths. 1991. Minorities, crime and the law. In M.A. Jackson and C.T. Griffiths, eds, *Canadian Criminology: Perspectives on Crime and Criminality*. 315–46. Toronto: Harcourt Brace Jovanovich.

Index